THE AMERICAN COLONIES

IN THE

EIGHTEENTH CENTURY

THE AMERICAN COLONIES

IN THE

EIGHTEENTH CENTURY

BY

HERBERT L. OSGOOD, Ph.D., LL.D.

PROFESSOR OF HISTORY IN COLUMBIA UNIVERSITY

VOLUME IV

Gloucester, Mass.

PETER SMITH

1958

CONTENTS

VOLUME IV

PART III (CONTINUED)

CHAPTER V

NEW JERSEY UNDER SEPARATE GOVERNMENT. MORRIS, BELCHER AND THE LAND RIOTS, 1738–1755

CHAPTER VI

PENNSYLVANIA DURING THE THIRD INTERCOLONIAL WAR.
ADMINISTRATIONS OF THOMAS AND HAMILTON

CHAPTER VII

CHAPTER IX

NORTH CAROLINA DURING THE ADMINISTRATION OF GABRIEL JOHNSTON,
1734–1752

CHAPTER X

Clinton's Adiministration in New York

CHAPTER XI

The Administration of Arthur Dobbs in North Carolina

CHAPTER XII

Virginia Politics during the Fourth Intercolonial War

CHAPTER XIII

SOUTH CAROLINA AND GEORGIA DURING THE FOURTH INTERCOLONIAL
WAR. INDIAN RELATIONS AND THE DEVELOPMENT OF
THE UP-COUNTRY

CHAPTER XIV

Westward Expansion and the Albany Congress of 1754

CHAPTER XV

THE FOURTH INTERCOLONIAL WAR. THE OPENING OF THE STRUGGLE,
1754–1756

CHAPTER XVI

The Fourth Intercolonial War. Success of the French during the Years 1756–1758

CHAPTER XVII

The Close of the War; the Triumph of the British

PART THREE

(Continued)

CHAPTER V

ON the death of Governor Cosby, Morris being absent in
England defending his rights against Cosby, John Anderson,
the eldest councillor who was then in the province, assumed
the presidency. But his death occurred soon after and John
Hamilton, the next on the list, succeeded.[1] He was son and
heir of the Andrew Hamilton who had been so prominent
as the last governor under the proprietors and also in Pennsylvania. The son was a prominent member of the Perth
Amboy group of proprietors in East Jersey and had long been
a member of the council of the royal province. Soon after
Hamilton became president Morris landed at New York and
insisted that he himself was entitled to this office. On
October 20, 1736, he appeared in council and demanded that
the administration should be turned over to him.[2] The immediate justification for this claim he based on an additional
instruction which had been addressed to him the previous
June under the title of president of the council. This was a
general instruction to all the governors and related to the
form of prayers for members of the royal family. Morris
issued two proclamations, one enjoining obedience to the
instruction and another adjourning the assembly to a later
date. Hamilton, supported by the entire council, refused to
yield and a counter proclamation was issued warning the
people to pay no regard or obedience to Morris and ordering
his arrest. Both claimants appealed to the home government, Morris in particular presenting labored arguments in
support of his claim. The contention of Hamilton was that,
in accordance with a standing instruction, a councillor who
without leave from the governor absented himself continuously

[1] N. J. Arch. V, 440, 445, 454; XIV, 521 *et seq.*; Tanner, 250.
[2] N. J. Arch. V, 455 *et seq.*; XIV, 536 *et seq.*

3

from his province for a twelvemonth, or for two years without the permission of the crown, thereby forfeited his place. Morris had been absent in England without leave for nearly two years and was therefore held to come under this rule. This contention, notwithstanding the fact that the additional instruction had been issued in the name of Morris as president, the crown upheld, and Hamilton retained his office until a separate governor for New Jersey was appointed.[1]

During the presidency of Anderson and Hamilton, though the assembly was not called together, efforts to bring about a complete separation from New York did not cease. Early in 1736 the president and council and various members of the assembly, as well as the grand jury of Middlesex county, petitioned the crown for the grant of this privilege. They set forth the evils that arose from long absences of the governors in New York and the preference which they gave to the business and interests of the larger province. Sir William Keith submitted a memorial and a long series of arguments in support of the same policy, coupling with the whole an application to Newcastle for appointment as governor.[2] Partridge, the agent, was also working steadily to persuade the British authorities that separation was desirable. Morris was authority for the report that at the time of the surrender he himself might have been appointed governor of New Jersey had it not been for the superior influence of the earl of Rochester in favor of his nephew, Lord Cornbury.[3] Though there was no boundary dispute, as in the case of New Hampshire, to promote ill feeling and hasten the decision, in the case of New Jersey a variety of disabilities were suffered by the smaller province which the advocates of separation were not slow to emphasize. As there was no resident naval officer, vessels could not be registered without going to New York. Trade, shipping and immigration, it was claimed, were injured by the connection. In order to secure the performance of a variety of administrative and judicial acts it was necessary for parties to visit the governor or other officers in New York. The tendency was for the higher officials generally, if there was any conflict or variety of interests, to

---

[1] The argument of Hamilton on the subject of the instruction is in N. J. Arch., V, 487.   [2] *Ibid.*, 440–454.   [3] *Ibid.*, 320.

prefer those of New York. The special and peculiar demands of New Jersey people could with difficulty find a hearing, and if they had officials who were wholly their own the assembly would be more inclined to give them an adequate support. These arguments prevailed, and in 1738 Lewis Morris was finally appointed royal governor of New Jersey.

Morris was now in his sixty-eighth year and he held the office to which he was appointed until his death in 1746. We have therefore reached the last stage in his chequered career. If from his opposition to Cornbury and Cosby the suspicion has arisen that he was in any sense a democrat, it will be dispelled by what is to follow. He was one of the most prominent aristocrats of his time, the founder of a family, one of the most prejudiced and dogmatic of men, outspoken and energetic, a foe of inefficiency and of dishonesty.[1] His experience was equally varied in two colonies as an elected representative in the assemblies, as member of the council, as judge and finally as governor. As a result of reading and a varied experience in business and politics, Morris had picked up some knowledge of law and government, and this on occasion he paraded at tiresome length. His opinions were typically Whig, with such variants as a life spent mostly in the colonies had produced. His only friendships which were long continued and give evidence of influence on his views were those with Robert Hunter and James Alexander. His visits to England appear to have afforded him only partial satisfaction. On the first of these he was instrumental in bringing proprietary government in New Jersey to an end, but the substitution of Cornbury made the last state of the province worse than the first.

When Morris went to England for the purpose of securing justice against Cosby, the opposition and delays which he met chafed his proud spirit and led him to confide to his friend Alexander some thoughts which are more instructive to the reader than flattering to British officials and courtiers. "You have very imperfect notions of the world on this side of the water," he wrote. "They are unconcerned at the sufferings of the people in America. . . . It is not the injus-

---

[1] He reminds one of the Adams family of a later date and especially of the first one of that honored tribe who bore the name of John.

tice of the thing [*i.e.*, of an oppressive governor's acts] that affects those concerned in recommending of him, provided it can be kept a secret and the people not clamor." "And who is there that is equal to the task of procuring redress? Changing the man is far from an adequate remedy, if the thing remains the same; and we had as well kéep an ill artless governor we know, as to change him for an equally ill with more art that we do not know." If possible, he was even less hopeful respecting applications to parliament. "We have a parliament and ministry," wrote Morris in the sarcastic tone which he naturally assumed, " some of whom, I am apt to believe, know that there are plantations and governors — but not quite so well as we do; like the frogs in the fable, the mad pranks of a plantation governor is sport to them, though death to us, and [they] seem less concerned in our contests than we are at those between crows and king birds. Governors are called the king's representatives; and when by repeated instances of avarice, cruelty and injustice, they extort complaints from the injured, . . . it must be termed a flying in the face of government; the king's representative must be treated with softness and decency — the thing complained of is nothing near so criminal in them as the manner of complaint in the injured."

In this passage Morris touched the source of the failure, or of the very qualified success, which has attended all imperialistic schemes, so far as they have involved real efforts to govern remote dependencies by means of bodies, executive or legislative, whose knowledge of and sympathy with the governed, because of remoteness and for various other reasons, must necessarily be either slight or absolutely nonexistent. It is true that Morris described colonial governors in harsher terms than the average among them deserved, but he had been brought into contact with two governors — Cornbury and Cosby — who deserved all he said about the class. And what he said about the difficulty of effectively lodging complaints against a governor was fully justified, notwithstanding the statute on the subject.

But when Morris turned to conditions as they existed in colonial assemblies and among their constituencies he was no better satisfied. His pessimistic views concerning them will appear in what follows. And just here, between the indifference, ignorance and superciliousness of the imperial authorities on the one side and the narrowness, poverty — real or assumed — and ingenuity of the colonists in devising methods of obstruction on the other, lay the problem of colonial government. When Morris was in England observation and experience sharpened his sense of the former.[1] When he received his commission and instructions and took the oaths as governor he began to realize his obligations on behalf of the crown. This silenced his criticism and made him a loyalist. He was naturally pugnacious and this quality was now intensified by age, and as he was met by the inevitable obstacles this man, whose earlier career had been a diversified opposition, now to colonial factions and now to the representative of the crown, became one of the most obstinate sticklers for the rights of the king and his governor who ever administered a colony. No one in the course of his life illustrated better the inconsistences and conflicts inherent in colonial relations than did Lewis Morris. Though he had spent most of his life in New Jersey and its immediate vicinity and knew its people as did scarcely any one else, his administration was an unbroken series of conflicts with their assemblies and brought discord rather than the expected peace. If the word " flat " could be used about anything which Morris did, his administration could be called a flat failure.

While Morris was governor six assemblies were elected and lived out their brief existence.[2] Shortly after he entered upon office the war with Spain began and questions connected with the raising and support of a contingent for the expedition to the West Indies arose. Events drifted on until France became involved and then came the even more insistent demand from Shirley that aid should be sent to the Louisbourg expedition. Clinton, the governor of New York, was at the same time corresponding with Morris about the

[1] And yet Morris acknowledges his large indebtedness to Newcastle. The favor of the duke, however, did not blind him to the essential spirit of the system.

[2] The authorities for this and later administrations are the N. J. Archives, Vols. VI and XV; The Papers of Lewis Morris, published by the N. J. Hist. Soc.; Ms. Journals of the Assembly; and Edgar J. Fisher's New Jersey as a Royal Province, being Vol. XLI of the Col. U. Studies in Hist., Econ. and Pub. Law.

Six Nations and the steps which should be taken to keep them faithful to the British cause. There were the usual alarms lest the enemy might descend upon the coast and find the colonists without any defence, for New Jersey, with its large Quaker population, was one of the most backward provinces in such matters. These were among the larger and more obvious issues with which Morris had to deal and the response with which his pleas for support were met were very disappointing. The management of the currency of the colony and the governor's support were other ever-present subjects in controversy.

The past experience of Morris had led him to formulate the relations between governors and assemblies as essentially contractual — so much support in return for assent to so many desirable laws. It was not original with him, but he was specially fond of it and used it more than anyone before his time. He brought it forward in the opening speech to his first assembly, and afterwards, in his letters and speeches, rang the changes on the same idea. On the first mentioned occasion, after emphasizing the contrast between the way of regarding laws as " Commodities to be purchased in Open Market " and the true view of them as the real basis of government and taking their rise from " well grounded views of Public benefit," he insisted that it was the privilege of the chief magistrate not only to assent to such laws but to propose them himself.[1] The passing of good and necessary laws and the raising of sufficient money for the support of the government in all its branches, he said, were the main correlative duties imposed upon assemblies and governors conjointly. Unless these were duly performed, magistracy would fall into contempt and, being left without power to execute the laws, would be tempted either to resort to violent measures or to use unbecoming arts to support itself. That was the dilemma in which Morris soon found himself, and while it led him to indulge in much violent speech, he preferred to go without support rather than bend to " unbecoming arts " in order to secure it.

With the separation from New York came also the retirement of the governor from the presidency of the council

[1] N. J. Arch., XV, 5.

when it was in legislative session. But this did not prevent the continuance of friendly relations between that body and Morris. These were doubly insured by the appointment of the governor's son, Robert Hunter Morris — who also succeeded Hooper as chief justice — to a seat in the council. Owing to the retirement or death of several of the older members, the remote residence of others and the appointment of several new men, there were many changes and attendance was often very meagre. But the council loyally supported the governor throughout and they together presented against the assembly such united front as was possible. Against the inherited custom of holding sessions of the assembly alternately at Perth Amboy and Burlington Morris never ceased to protest, and this was connected with his repeated demands that, now that New Jersey had its own governor, it should provide him with a fit and permanent residence. As the infirmities of age increased upon him, it became more necessary for Morris to meet the assembly at Trentown (Trenton), an intermediate point where was located one of the governor's estates. In this way arose the custom which was to give the province a new capital. Other changes also indicated that the old idea of maintaining the equality of the two divisions was disappearing.

The assembly in its first session under Morris did fully the average amount of work,[1] if not more, and its temper was conciliatory, as was to be expected after the prime object of separation from New York had been achieved. It granted Morris £500 to meet his expenses in procuring separate government for the province. It granted support to the government for three years,[2] the amount not being munificent and officials of lower grade coming off poorly. But that, under the circumstances, was no more than was to be expected. The assembly also refused to confer with the council over the terms of the money bill; but though this was flatly opposed to the governor's instructions it was in harmony with the

[1] Morris Papers, 39.

[2] Of this Morris received £1000 per year in currency, which as exchange then was the equivalent of about £550 sterling. As Morris was a rich man, he apparently had no personal reason to complain. *Ibid.*, 45, 49. For an account of the general character of support bills in New Jersey see Fisher, New Jersey as a Royal Province, 274.

attitude which by this time had been assumed in practically all the colonies. Upon this subject it was natural that Morris should protest.[1] But apart from that he lectured the assembly like a pack of school boys, on two occasions delivering long homilies which were intended as a reproof of their positive misdeeds or lack of good works. Never did the garrulity and pessimism of old age show to greater disadvantage from the practical standpoint. He also added injury to insult by ordering the treasurer not to pay the wages of the assemblymen. And yet Morris gave pungent expression to many truths and his effusions, as always, revealed a keen appreciation of the contradictions which existed in the political system they were trying to operate. At the close of his last homily Morris dissolved the assembly.

Not content with the addresses which he had already delivered, Morris repeatedly traversed the ground again in long communications to the board of trade and to his friend, Sir Charles Wager.[2] Of these the latter are the more illuminating and bring into prominence the fact that the dissolution was due to the differences between the council and the lower house and particularly to the claim of that house that it should have the sole disposition of the interest money arising from the bills of credit in circulation, though in the acts under which these were issued it was provided that the money should be disposed of jointly by the governor, council and assembly. Morris also reveals the fact that, though upon other subjects or earlier in the session " there grew so great a rancour among the members that they shunned the conversation of each other out of the house and could not preserve the rules of common decency in it, descending to downright scolding, giving the lie, threatening to spit in the face & were often very nigh getting together by the ears," when it came to the issue with the council the great majority of them ceased their quarreling in order to present a united front against the claims of that body and of the governor.[3] Against that resolve argument, that the money had been granted to the king or that it had never belonged to the people or in any other form, was useless. The surest way to

---

[1] N. J. Arch., XV, 54, 61, 80; Ms. Journal of Assembly, Jan. 31, 1738/9.
[2] Morris Papers.   [3] Ibid., 41.

obtain favor was to oppose the executive and few were willing to oppose the common current. A perfunctory expression of approval of his course and that of the council and condemnation of that of the assembly was all the support which Morris received from the board of trade and it was all he probably expected, for he wrote that it was the neglect of assemblies by the British government which had brought things to the present pass.

Though the election resulted in some changes of personnel, the governor's strength in the assembly was not increased.[1] This house was continued in existence about two years — 1740 to 1742 — when, at the close of its third session, it was dissolved by the governor. During the first two sessions a reasonable degree of harmony existed between the governor and the house. The two new subjects which were brought forward were the desirability of levying impost duties and fostering trade independent of New York and Pennsylvania, and the war with Spain. Impost duties New Jersey had never yet levied and while the assembly expressed itself as willing to consider the question it realized that time would be required to convince the people of the advantage of direct importation, and nothing was done. After some delay £2000 in currency was made available toward the support of the expedition to the West Indies.[2] With some difficulty in the management of this bill a renewal of the deadlock which had terminated the existence of the previous assembly was avoided. As the previous grant of support had expired, this had to be renewed in the next session. This was renewed to the nominal satisfaction of the governor,[3] though it was only for one year. Owing largely to Quaker influence, the assembly refused to revise the militia law. An effort to secure salaries for the members of the council also failed. A reflection of the feeling in many other colonies may be seen in the passage of a law to prevent actions involving less than £15 being brought into the supreme court. Morris assented to this and referred it to the authorities in England for consideration, where it was respited until the board of trade

[1] Fisher, 109; Morris Papers, 85.
[2] Ibid., 124; Ms. Journal of Ass.
[3] Morris Papers, 140, 149; Ms. Journal of Ass., October, 1741.

should know what effect it had. After many delays which the assembly considered unnecessary, Morris refused his assent to many of the assembly's bills. The selection of a fixed place for meetings of the assembly and the building there of a residence for the governor came up for discussion. The board of trade was specially interested in this for the reason that it would lead to a better preservation of the records of the province, and at this time an effort was being made to secure a copy of New Jersey laws. Partridge was still continued as agent and was supported by the assembly, though he was viewed askance by Morris.

Trouble began again in the session of October, 1742. Owing, it is supposed,[1] to the absence of R. H. Morris, the chief justice, from the council during this session, the two houses coöperated better than usual and several acts were passed which were offensive to the governor. Two of these, relating respectively to the extinguishment of the right or estate of a *femme covert* and to the acknowledging of deeds, were vetoed by the governor because they encroached upon the royal prerogative. A provision for the regulation of fees was also added to the support bill in the belief that the governor would assent to the whole. The ostensible purpose of the house in bringing up the subject of fees was to meet complaints of excessive charges on the part of attorneys, but Morris believed that the measure was really aimed at the fees of the secretary and other officers of the government. With difficulty he therefore got the provision concerning fees omitted. A bill for the issue of £40,000 in bills of credit was also particularly irritating to Morris and in the end he vetoed it. Besides carrying a grant of £500 to himself, which he angrily repudiated as an attempted bribe, it did not provide for the erection of a governor's residence and appropriate public buildings and therefore was considered by Morris as not properly providing for the support of the government. The house also tried to call before itself a case on appeal from the supreme court. This, in the eyes of the governor, was its final offence and, after reciting its misdeeds in a long address, he dissolved the assembly.[2] Out of the

---

[1] Fisher, 112.

[2] N. J. Arch., XV, 268–278; Morris Papers, 152.

eight bil's which reached him, Morris assented only to the one which provided for the support of the government.

A year later — October, 1743, — Morris met his next assembly. Ten new members, among them Samuel Nevill, had been elected, but the attitude of the body remained unchanged. Morris did not lecture them, but said that he was ready to assent to any laws in his power which were beneficial to the public. The house in its turn complained that many bills which previous assemblies had thought beneficial and not involving violations of the prerogative had been rejected.[1] This was discouraging, but they would again proceed with legislation and hoped the governor would prove his good intentions by assenting to some of their measures before the passage of the support bill. This he did by giving his assent to the bills respecting *femmes covert* and the acknowledgment of deeds. The support bill was then passed and the council rejected the bill for the issue of £40,000 in currency. But the subject of fees was again brought up in the form of a separate bill which received the governor's assent, partly because it contained a suspending clause. But the assembly passed a formal resolution the object of which was to put the measure immediately into execution in the courts and all the offices.[2] Jealousy was brewing also because the younger Morris held both a seat in the council and the chief justiceship of the supreme court, and it was believed to be partly due to this that sessions of the court had not been held with due regularity. It was certain that Morris was a political judge, as his father before him had been in New York. The governor, at any rate, was offended by the resolve of the house concerning fees and, calling its members before him, put to them a series of questions intended to challenge their right to pass it. After shuffling somewhat, like boys under the frowns of a pedagogue, they plucked up courage to say that they thought themselves "not accountable for that Opinion." They were therefore prorogued and did not meet again till the following June. Owing to a statement from Morris that the fees established by the assembly's bill were so small as to exclude all persons of ability from office, the

---

[1] N. J. Arch., XV, 280; Ms. Journal of Ass., Oct., 1743.
[2] N. J. Arch., XV, 318; Ms. Journal of Ass.; Fisher, 116.

measure was disallowed in England and fees were left wholly under executive control.

As war with France was then beginning, the attention of the assembly in its new session was directed to the strengthening of the militia law.[1] This no doubt was sadly needed if New Jersey was to take any effective part in the war. But the assembly expressed the opinion that the law was adequate for providing watches and the like and would enable the governor to send aid to the neighboring colonies. To this the governor replied with an overwhelming array of evidence of the neglect of militia officers in the counties to levy fines for failure to train, of the failure for years to call the companies together at all for training and of many other serious defects not only in the execution of the law but in the law itself. The house in its reply showed clearly that it did not intend to make any further provision for offensive war and that it disbelieved rumors of an impending invasion from the north and would not at present increase appropriations.[2] Although, as the course of the war proved, they pretty accurately sized up the situation so far as it affected New Jersey, it was far from satisfying the militarist governor and his friends and the assembly was dissolved.

An election was promptly held and the new assembly, with Nevill as speaker, met in August.[3] It was a busy season of the year and as the house saw no danger of an invasion and evidently was of the same opinion concerning the war as its predecessor, the best the governor could do was to prorogue it until October. Because of his illness they were then called to meet at Trenton and later at his nearby residence at Kingsbury. Such frequent removals and the fact that the governor was often too far away or too ill to be accessible, were perplexing and a great hindrance to business. The assembly was also becoming irritated by the long and fruitless sessions and attacked the council as a small body consisting of only six or seven active members, among whom chief justice

[1] N. J. Arch., XV, 322, 329, 335, 336; VI, 172, *et seq.*; Ms. Journal of Ass., June 23 to July 3, 1744.

[2] In the majority which voted that the existing militia law was adequate were eight professed Quakers. N. J. Arch., VI, 202.

[3] Ass. Journal; N. J. Arch., XV, 337, 339, 340, 369–372, 375, 377, 382; Fisher, 118 *et seq.*

Morris was a dominating influence. The money in the treasury must be frugally husbanded and they could not give so large support to government as in past years. This declaration of the house was first adopted in a committee of the whole on the state of the province and was occasioned by the discussion of the question of support. The spirit of the house was further shown by a cut in the governor's salary to £500 currency, while it was alarmed by the report that legislation in England was to be expected against issues of paper money in the colonies. A long and wordy dispute between the two houses was thus begun, the council finally addressing the governor at length in defence of its action in defeating certain bills. As a side issue came also a controversy over the election of loan office commissioners in Hunterdon county, in which the county justices were charged with illegally supplanting the freeholders in the choosing of these officials. Upon this subject the house came to an issue with the governor and in mutual disgust over a long and disturbed session all parties welcomed a dissolution.

The new house met at Perth Amboy in April, 1745. Though several new members had been elected, they did not lessen the spirit of opposition. Morris opened the session with one of his longest and most argumentative speeches in denunciation of the previous assembly.[1] He spoke as a defender of the *status quo,* so far as the legal powers and rights of governor, council and assembly were concerned, and cited abundant precedents in support of the practice of giving the chief justice a seat in the council. In referring to the militia and to the fact that promises of better support as a result of separation from New York had been proved false by the practice which was now followed of levying no taxes at all but making appropriations from the paper which was paid into the treasury as interest on the bills in circulation, he made telling points. But he was pleading the cause of vigorous government to be run by a coterie of officials, and toward this combination the assemblymen were indifferent or suspicious or both. He was insulting the men who listened to him who had voted with the opposition in the previous

[1] N. J. Arch., XV, 393–408, 410 *et seq.*; Ms. Ass. Journal; Morris Papers, 235.

assembly, and was proving how much of a stand-patter or reactionary a colonist could become when placed in the office of governor. Morris's attitude was one of narrow legality and so far as that was justified he is entitled to approval. But before his Whig doctrine of parlimentary absolutism [1] the colonists, if they understood it, might well have trembled for their liberties. The doctrine which Morris here expressed amounted practically to the same as that which Joseph Dudley had once scandalized the colonists by uttering. In its dignified reply the house disclaimed responsibility for the doings of former assemblies and reproved the governor for reopening old disputes. "We confess," they said, "that Former Assemblies, as well as the present, have been chiefly composed of Farmers and Plowmen, from whom could hardly be expected such Courtly Addresses or explicit Reasons as of men of more Polite Education and perhaps less sincerity might be capable of performing. But as Plainness and Truth are Companions, we are well content in their Company." Referring to the Governor's slur upon them as idiots, they assured him that the rights of assemblies in New Jersey, as defined by himself, were very well understood.

Governor Shirley's urgent calls for aid toward the Louisbourg expedition were already in the governor's hands and were laid before this assembly. But the most that could be obtained was a vote applying £2000 to the king's service, and this came altogether too late to be of use in the expedition. On the one side the governor declined to assent to the issue of £40,000 in bills of credit, especially in view of the expected legislation in England, and on the other the government was left without support for more than a year. The assembly was kept together by successive brief adjournments for some two months. Nothing was done except the interchange of long and ill-natured addresses with the governor. The assembly was then successively called for brief sessions at Trenton and Burlington, its spirit growing more restive and the governor no more conciliatory. Meantime reports of the first of the land riots, this one being at Newark, were received. The removals from place to place, which were due to the state of the governor's health, also occasioned criticism

[1] N. J. Arch., XV, 397.

and a questioning of his right to do this. Thus, in the midst of mutual recriminations, without practical result or the addition of new ideas, the year approached its close and with it came the dissolution of this assembly.[1]

In March, 1746, the last assembly which Morris was to meet gathered at Trenton, and mutually friendly expressions seemed to indicate a peaceful session. But news that the fee bill which they valued so highly was to be disallowed in England dampened the ardor of the assembly. They had again prepared three of their favorite bills, — for the issue of the accustomed amount of currency, to renew the act preventing actions under £15 being brought in the supreme court and to regulate the giving of security by sheriffs for the proper discharge of their duties.[2] A militia bill also had been passed. But the support bill was held up until they should receive assurance that the governor would assent to their favorite measures. He was in his last illness and was too weak to read any but the militia bill. But he sent the house an assurance that if it would grant the usual support, he would assent to its bills. The house, however, knew that the currency bill must contain a suspending clause and that Morris would very likely procure its disallowance. Hence they proposed to reduce the governor's salary one-half unless the royal assent should be given to the bill for the issue of £40,000 in currency. To this Morris, of course, refused to agree and gave his assent only to the militia bill. This was his last act, for in less than two weeks later he was dead. The administration of Morris had certainly not brought to New Jersey the full advantages which had been expected as a result of its separation from New York. So unpopular had Morris become that his heirs found it impossible to collect the arrears of salary which had been due him. When the demand for this payment was last presented — in October, 1749, — the assembly presented an able review of the deal-

[1] See, in addition to the sources usually referred to above, the Morris Papers, 270, 274–285.

[2] This act provided that sheriffs should take an oath or affirmation for the purpose indicated. When later this measure was scrutinized in England, Mathew Lamb reported that the limitation of the office of sheriffs in ways similar to this was not uncommon in the other colonies or in England, and the act was allowed to stand. N. J. Arch., VI, 330.

ings of Morris with the houses that met during his administration. So destructive was this, in their opinion, and so
strong throughout the province was the feeling of disgust at
the conduct of the late governor, that none except his imme-
date friends or those who were personally interested would
say one word in favor of the proposed reimbursement.[1] The
Morris heirs were receiving the same treatment which the
father had helped to mete out to Cornbury, and which we
have seen more deserving governors receive in those days of
loose habits in the payment of salaries and other legal dues.

From June, 1746, until August, 1747, the affairs of the
province were administered by a president and council.
Hamilton and Reading were the two incumbents of the presidency, the former dying in office after an illness which had
prevented his taking a very active share in the administration. And yet the necessity of raising its contingent of 500
men for the expedition of 1746 against Canada necessitated
several sessions of the assembly, a thing unusual during intervals between the governorships. Without opposition acts
were passed for the issue of £10,000 in bills of credit for fitting
out the expedition and a smaller sum later for victualling the
troops. Support of the government was also voted for a year.
A mutiny of the New Jersey troops, who were being kept over
winter at Albany after the abandonment of the expedition,
followed by the payment of their wages in full, occasioned
some correspondence with Governor Clinton. Land riots were
also spreading rapidly in northern New Jersey and this omi-
nous subject was repeatedly brought to the attention of the
two houses, but no action respecting them was taken by the
legislature.

Meanwhile Jonathan Belcher, former governor of Massachusetts, had secured in England the appointment to the
vacant office in New Jersey. Being aware of the failure of
Morris for several years to secure appropriations for the
support of the government for more than one year at a time,
and also of the compromise which he had secured for himself
in Massachusetts, Belcher petitioned for the same concession
again and it was not denied him. As he was to leave his
family in Massachusetts, he also desired leave to visit them

[1] N. J. Arch., VI, 335–343, 460, 464.

at intervals and at the same time to retain the half-salary which regularly went in such cases to the official who would fill his place;[1] but this request met with a denial. Belcher was about sixty-five years of age at the time of his appointment and he held the office until his death, ten years later. Thus New Jersey was again intrusted to the management of a man well advanced in years, of varied experience, but of very uncertain health. Though Belcher was a New Englander and was now placed in an environment very different from the one to which he had been accustomed, his religion and his earlier dealings with Quakers in Massachusetts fitted him in some respects for his new duties. His tolerant attitude toward the Quakers in their struggle for religious freedom in New England had won for him their support and this was extended to him during the years when he was in England looking for another appointment. His brother-in-law, Richard Partridge, a Quaker, had also been continuously active as agent in England and was to continue his support of Belcher while the latter was governor of New Jersey. As the bills of credit of New Jersey were issued by the government and on the whole were well managed, the policy of that province in regard to them met with Belcher's approval. The bitter animosity which appeared in his attacks on the land bank in Massachusetts played no part in his New Jersey career.[2] These influences, as well as Belcher's New England training in general, are to be borne in mind if one is to understand the very mild attitude which he assumed toward the assembly in New Jersey. The factions there were so hostile to one another and the relations between council and assembly so irreconcilable, that it would have required a genius to keep on good relations with both. Neither Morris nor Belcher attempted this. Morris, as his property interest and those of his family and friends indicated, sided with the council and in attempting to thwart the assembly succeeded in almost completely blocking the wheels of government. Belcher said and wrote little, and what he did express was of slight importance. The inferior calibre of the man appears even more clearly in this last stage of his career than it did in his earlier governorship. But in letting affairs take their course he was

[1] N. J. Arch., VI, 444, 449, 453.   [2] N. J. Arch., VII, 246.

playing into the hands of the assembly and of the constituencies back of it, and he probably intended to take this line of policy or regarded it as the only one that was possible for him. In either case the selection of such a man as Belcher to meet the crisis which existed in New Jersey was equivalent to the abandonment by the crown of all it was supposed to be contending for in that province. And it is significant that when he was appointed governor of Massachusetts the crown had yielded to the demands of that colony upon the salary question.

The relations between Belcher and the assemblies, apart from the question of the land riots which is reserved for later treatment, were of the ordinary and peaceable character. The assembly which he found in existence on his arrival was continued for nearly two years. No business of importance was done until November, 1747, when in a long session which continued until February, 1747/8, more was accomplished than in any session for several years. The business which at this time was brought before the assembly related, in addition to the land riots, to provision for the troops which were still in service on the New York frontier, the grant of support for the government and the punishment of certain alleged counterfeiters of New Jersey bills of credit.[1] It was not until the assembly had been in session nearly two months — on January 7, 1747/8 — that the house replied to the governor's speech and stated its attitude upon these questions. This it gave in the form of several bills which had already been passed or were in process of passage. The situation, so far as it affected the troops, had already been relieved in a measure by advances made toward their pay by Schuyler, their commander, and now was made quite tolerable by the prospect of reimbursement, to the amount of some £9000, which the governor was able to present to the assembly on the strength of despatches from Shirley and from England. No assistance could be procured from the assembly for Shirley's projected expedition against Crown Point. But peace came soon after and the difficulties which had been occasioned by the war were removed.

About the time of the beginning of the consideration of the

[1] N. J. Arch., XV, 527, 574.

support bill in the council the governor appeared and said he desired for his information to hear the bills to which he was expected to assent debated, but he did not intend to vote or otherwise participate.[1]. A committee was appointed on the subject, but it apparently was dropped by the governor's coming to see that his attendance would not best conserve the king's interest. Over the support bill the usual disputes between the houses arose. The council demanded vouchers for several accounts mentioned in the bill as sent from the house. The latter replied by asserting what had always been considered its exclusive privilege of judging what sums should be raised and paid for services rendered to the province. This they declared it was their determination never to give up. The council asserted in reply its right to amend money bills,[2] and, repeating the statement so often made by Morris, declared that this claim applied with special propriety to a case like the present, where no tax was levied but interest money, derived from the circulation of bills of credit authorized by all three branches of the legislature acting jointly, was applied to the payment of public debts. It was also easy to cite any number of rulings of the board of trade in support of this claim. But the council thought the occasion not favorable for renewing the old controversy and so refrained from pressing the point. The supply bill for a year therefore went through and received the governor's assent. The act which was passed against counterfeiters was disallowed because of certain improper provisions. The old measures concerning sheriffs and excluding the supreme court from jurisdiction over minor cases were passed, as was one regulating fees and one for the issue of £40,000 in bills of credit. The last-named act was disallowed in England, as was one for running the New York and New Jersey boundary line. This session had been unusually fruitful in legislation and this was a subject for congratulation at the close.

The next important session was held in November, 1748. By this time rioting had reached its height and, as always during these years, it occupied much of the attention of both houses. As there was still no law against counterfeiting and many references were made to that as flourishing, the general

---

[1] *Ibid.*, 565, 567 *et seq.*; Fisher, 48, 135.   [2] *Ibid.*, 635.

disordered condition of society resulting from the riots served as an encouragement and protection to this evil as well.[1] With reference to both these the attitude of the two houses was at variance, and by this time the conflict between them had reopened all along the line. While regretting counterfeiting, the lower house passed no bill against it and asked that the session might be short. Preparatory to raising a revenue, the quotas which the counties must contribute had to be fixed, but the houses fell out over their respective rights to determine what these might be.[2] It soon became impossible to hold conferences on any subject. The lower house resolved that the assumption by the council of the power to direct the methods of raising money was a manifest infringement of its privileges, and that it had the right to enjoy its sentiments on all matters and things without being accountable to or censured by the council. Under such a state of feeling it was useless to continue the session, and after a support bill for a year and a few minor bills had been passed, the assembly was dissolved and an election was ordered.

This resulted in some changes of personnel, but in no change of spirit.[3] Therefore in the session which began in February, 1748/9, the controversy was renewed. The two houses in discussing the quota bill came to an issue over the taxation of unprofitable lands, of which the proprietors held large tracts. The royal instructions forbade the taxation of such property and the lower house insisted that the bill which it drafted was in harmony with this principle. But the council insisted upon its amendment. Although the lower house pretended to be willing to refer the issue to the governor for decision, it, of course, was not done and the measure failed. At a later session in September the deadlock was continued and over the same question as before. The support bill failed and with it went the provision for the payment of the agent unless this was made on the authority of the house alone. It was at this time that the demand for the payment due to the Morris heirs received its final denial.

When the assembly was called together again, in the winter

---

[1] N. J. Arch., XVI, 3, 25, 38, 43, 46, 48

[2] *Ibid.*, 24, 64, *et seq.* On the system of property taxes in New Jersey see Fisher, 284.   [3] Fisher, 143.

of 1749/50, the house declared that the cause of the trouble was the infringement of the council upon its rights by amending money bills, thus attempting to deprive them of the appointment of an agent and assuming too much control over the disposal of the public money.[1] In no province was this issue more definitely drawn and stoutly maintained by the lower house than in New Jersey. During this session, however, a little variety was given to the conflict by an episode which involved certain justices of Burlington county and their assumed right to impose a local levy without the consent of a majority of the freeholders. Upon this also the two houses divided, the council upholding the conduct of the justices and the governor, on its advice, refusing to remove them.[2] Throughout a final session, in February, 1750/51, practically the same questions were fought over without result. Only one act was passed. At the close Belcher dissolved the assembly. In the first brief session of its successor — in May, 1751 — the deadlock was broken by a compromise on the subject of quotas which made possible the passage of a support act.[3] Seven attempts had previously been made to pass this measure, the council insisting that land should be taxed according to quality and the lower house according to quantity. Now they compromised by combining the two principles and Belcher prematurely inferred that peace was assured. The quotas, however, for the several counties were not prepared till the following September when the assembly was called together to pass the tax bill.[4] A genuine bill for levying a tax for the support of the government by quotas upon property in the counties was prepared by the house. But it was amended by the council in several points. These were not accepted by the house and a conference also was refused. The house now proposed to deliver all support bills directly to the governor, giving him an opportunity to peruse them in cases where the council refused to act. But this plan he did not accept and the session ended without an agreement.[5]

In the session of January, 1751/2, the council changed its tactics and refrained from attempting to amend the supply

---

[1] N. J. Arch., XVI, 215.

[2] Ibid., 222 et seq.

[3] Ibid., 291–309; VII, 598.

[4] Ibid., XVI, 311, 342.

[5] Fisher, 154.

bill. By some in the assembly it was again proposed to send the bill directly to the governor, but this was voted down. And so the government was again fortunate enough to receive temporary support. Disorder in the province was also gradually abating, and the council had to accept the inevitable and yield the supremacy in the fiscal domain at least to the assembly. Signs, which were multiplying, of the approach of a more serious struggle with the French than any which had preceded served as a warning against unnecessary domestic strife. During the years 1753 to 1755 the subject of paper money was again brought prominently to the front. An able report in support of the policy was made by a committee of the lower house, of which Leaming and Spicer were members. The governor approved of the views expressed and the crown was petitioned for a grant of permission for new issues and, though this was not given, the bill was not disallowed. The war soon decided the question for the present by necessitating many emissions to meet its cost.[1] Under these conditions we approach the conclusion of all that was specially significant for the history of New Jersey alone in the general relations between Belcher and his assemblies.

We now come to the consideration of the land riots, which were of prime importance in the history of New Jersey during Belcher's administration. And they are important not simply for New Jersey history, but as a symptom of the feeling of impatience mingled with contempt which was steadily growing among the rank and file of the colonists in reference to the territorial policy generally followed in the provinces. In this connection appeared the survivals of European feudalism which had found a permanent place in the American colonial system. Their origin and character have been fully described in treating of the seventeenth century.[2] In the present work it has not been possible to trace through the later development of the territorial system as connected with the advance of settlement. That is a subject which must await further investigation. But especially in New York, the Carolinas and Virginia abundant evidences have appeared of land spec-

---

[1] *Ibid.*, 294 *et seq.*

[2] Osgood, Am. Colonies in the 17th Century— references running through all three of the volumes.

ulation and frauds, or at least favoritism, on a large scale, by means of which a landed aristocracy was built up, social inequality was promoted, the advance of settlement was to an extent hindered and a sinister and corrupt influence was continually exerted on the political and social life of these provinces. We have also seen how the imposition of quit rents was everywhere opposed and their payment avoided by all possible means. Such survivals of tenant right as these, imported from Europe, were not welcomed in the colonies and perhaps were the most generally unpopular of all features of imperial policy.

But in the royal provinces these impositions were made in the name of the king and it was under the direct authority of the crown that territorial affairs were administered. That gave to them a certain dignity and compelling force which without it they would never have had. This mystical influence which went with the word " crown " was to an extent lacking in the proprietary provinces. Though land titles in those colonies were ultimately derived from the crown, they had their immediate origin in its grantee, the proprietor or group of proprietors. The proprietor was only a subject, with very limited power and resources, and about him there could be no breath or suspicion of divinity. In practice also the proprietorships were the weakest and on the whole the least satisfactory of the three forms of colonial government. They had always been a chief object of attack on the part of parliament and the British officials, and the disappearance or modification of so many of them clearly showed how insubstantial they were. In the case of a political overturn, whether it came from Great Britain or from the people of the colonies, it might be expected that they would be among the first to fall. The term proprietorship comes with the idea of a small, privately managed, unprogressive establishment, and such on the whole these provinces were. Nothwithstanding the vigorous growth of Pennsylvania, the spirit and policy of the Penn family furnishes no exception to the rule.

And of the proprietorships none was weaker and certainly none other so poorly organized as that of New Jersey. Its proprietors were so numerous and so divided into factions that they were almost useless for administrative purposes.

They never enjoyed undisputed right of government and their claim to a large part of the soil of the province was vigorously contested and frequently in litigation. As was the case with all proprietors, they were speculators in land, though under a title that was legal and respectable and, originally at least, backed by powers of government which had their origin in England. Their exclusive right to extinguish the claims of the natives to land was necessary to the preservation of peace on the frontier and to the maintenance of any semblance of order in such relations. It was analogous to the exclusive rights of traffic with the natives which were bestowed by Great Britain on the trading companies. In both cases it involved the creation of a monopoly, with the opportunity which such grants always offer for the enrichment of a few. But that was in harmony with the aristocratic policies upon which all empires have thriven, and it was claimed that the rewards offered were only a fair — and sometimes an inadequate — compensation for the risk and loss involved. Inevitably such grants provoked jealousy, and the interloper was always the present or prospective foe of the monopolistic trading company. Corresponding to the interloper in trade was the settler or trader on the American frontier who ignored the rules of the proprietors and dealt with the Indians directly for their land, giving them the few goods which they demanded and taking their deeds in return as furnishing a sufficiently valid title. As we have seen, Roger Williams, in Massachusetts, was the first to formulate the view according to which justification was sought for this line of conduct. It was based implicitly on the conception of the natural man, irrespective of race or social status, and of his right to such of the gifts of nature as he might reasonably appropriate and which were necessary for his support. This was set up in opposition to the claims based on real or assumed discovery and occupation by white men from Europe, who asserted that they came as the representatives of a Christian, and therefore a superior, civilization. The view of the white European, with his Roman and imperialistic ideas, received elaborate formulation in innumerable charters, deeds, treaties, commissions, instructions, statutes and all the array of documents which lawyers, judges and government officials are continually occupied in multiplying.[1] On the other side few, if any, gave definite expression to the ideas of Williams or knew that he had uttered them. But every squatter on the frontier or on any large and unimproved grant of land, whether or not he sought to strengthen his claim by an Indian deed, acted in accordance with this theory. In this line of conduct the original anarchistic tendencies of American democracy have always found one of their chief expressions. Governments, in the colonial period especially, were continually struggling against this but never succeeded in more than establishing a virtual compromise with it by which it was to an extent held in check. In New Jersey at the time of which we are speaking occurred the most serious outbreak of this spirit which appeared during the colonial period, and the purpose of what has just been said is to show in part why conditions were specially favorable for such an outbreak there and at that time.

The disturbances originated and had their continuance chiefly in East Jersey, where a background for them was furnished by the long-standing controversy between the proprietors and the Elizabethtown and Monmouth patentees. Though the assumption of government by the crown had deprived the proprietors of their political authority, they gained thereby the full support of the crown and its officials in these disputes. All the royal governors until Belcher actively interested themselves in upholding the proprietary claims and interests. The judges and council were on the same side, especially during the administration of Morris, and the home government always upheld vested property rights. Hunter declared as one of his principles that questions of land title should be left to the courts. Therefore, in 1714, the first of a series of test cases, intended to reach a decision upon the claims in dispute between the proprietors and the Elizabethtown patentees, was tried.[2] This involved rights in the so-called Clinker Lot Division of the Elizabethtown tract, which had been surveyed and distributed in total disregard of the

---

[1] To these correspond in the realm of religion the creeds and formularies of the churches, and both proceed from a common impulse.

[2] The Elizabethtown Bill in Chancery, and Answer to the Elizabethtown Bill in Chancery, in Hatfield, Hist. of Elizabeth, New Jersey; Tanner, *op. cit.* 80, 497, 632, 662; Fisher, *op. cit.* 182 *et seq.*

rights of the proprietors. This case — of Vaughan *vs.* Woodruff — was decided in favor of the proprietors, David Jamison being the judge. But later, in 1730 and while Hooper was chief justice, several ejectment suits were brought in the name of Patrick Lithgow against Clinker Lot men and in these the defendants won. The trial of the test case — Lithgow *vs.* Robinson — lasted for the unusual time of nineteen hours, the ablest lawyers of New York and New Jersey acting as counsel and the chief justice summing up the evidence at five o'clock in the morning. This verdict renewed the courage of the Elizabethtown patentees. They appointed a committee and surveyed and sold tracts outside the Clinker Lot survey to help pay the cost of litigation. In other cases which were brought to trial the proprietors won, and so the issue, which affected the claims of the Monmouth patentees as well as those of Elizabethtown, remained undecided. In 1744 the patentees petitioned the crown for a hearing. The petition was received and referred to the board of trade, but there is no evidence that further action was taken.[1]

In the course of the administration of Morris the effect of the extension of settlement into the hilly region back of Newark[2] and into other remoter districts of the province began to be felt. Early residents and squatters in increasing numbers had bought up Indian claims in these regions and occupied land without recognition of the superior rights of the proprietors. They were in part a rough frontier folk, with primitive ideas, but their leaders and many of the rank and file of the rioters were members in good standing of the Presbyterian churches of Elizabethtown, Newark and the towns of the Monmouth purchase. They were people of New England and Scotch origin and descent, men with substantial properties, as intelligent and socially as respectable as were the Anglicans or the proprietors and their supporters. A little further northwest people of the same sort, but with more of Dutch descent, were concerned in the disturbances

---

[1] N. J. Arch., VI, 205–215.

[2] This is the region now occupied by the Oranges, Montclair and the adjoining townships. Wickes, History of the Oranges, gives the best account of the origin and development of these outgrowths from the old town of Newark. From this book and the study of the records and histories of the other towns concerned, the status of many of the rioters may be ascertained.

which gave variety and interest to the boundary dispute that was in progress between New Jersey and New York. By these trespassers timber was cut down and other havoc wrought upon tracts which had been surveyed for the proprietors and was designed for formal occupation. By such men as Ogden, Alexander and Morris, father and son, such proceedings could not be tolerated. The proprietors, with their legal counsel, began to resort to writs of ejectment and the governor to talk of strengthening the militia law. The squatters and those in the community who sympathized with them and disliked the proprietary régime, began to appeal in the New York press and elsewhere to the natural rights of white man and Indian to the use of the soil.[1] They declared that, though they had bought the land they were occupying from the native owners and had long been in possession, the proprietors had lately been surveying large tracts along the Passaic and elsewhere and were proceeding to dispossess them unless they would pay rent and submit generally to their regulations. A "Brief Vindication of the Purchasers against the Proprietors"[2] was published, in which, as in the fulminations of the Levellers of a hundred years before, much religious enthusiasm, even in lyric form, was mingled with a strong defence of the rights of Indians and squatters. This was all quite horrifying to the proprietors and their lawyer friends. They were ready to brand it as treason and to bring the entire resources of government to bear for its suppression.[3] Several verdicts were rendered against the Elizabethtown people by juries that they said were far from impartial. But in New Jersey such was the mixed character of the population that sympathy with the squatters was widespread. In general they belonged to the Elizabethtown and Monmouth party and the cause for which the two were contending was essentially the same. The squatters were simply bringing primitive ideas to bear on the issue and making it as broad as humanity itself. Under these conditions, the proprietors could not count on much

[1] N. J. Arch., VI, 266–296.

[2] The pen name of Griffin Jenkins was signed to this, but Wickes, in his History of the Oranges, states that it was generally attributed to Rev. Daniel Taylor, pastor of the "Mountain Society" of Newark: Wickes, 94, 104.

[3] See Statement of proprietors, Arch., VI, 297–323.

support from the assembly. This was the situation when the opponents of the proprietors began to defy the courts, officials and jails and to meet prosecutions and ejectments by rioting and general disorder.

In September, 1745, Samuel Baldwin, a member of the commitee of Essex county which had been appointed to protect the interests of the people against the proprietors, was arrested for cutting trees on a proprietary tract. A body of Baldwin's sympathizers broke open the county jail at Newark and released him.[1] Governor Morris appealed to the assembly to strengthen the militia law, but without result, and had to content himself with ordering the attorney general to prosecute and the county officers to do their duty. Three of the rioters were arrested, but all were rescued by the mob. The governor appealed again to the assembly, but could not bring it to any action so decisive as the passage of the English riot act. The rioters, on the other hand, asked the assembly to pass an act staying all processes against them until the king's pleasure could be known. These petitions were made the subject of a long and highly denunciatory speech by Samuel Nevill, one of the proprietors, judge and at various times speaker of the assembly.[2] At its close he moved that they be rejected, but that the governor should proclaim a general pardon under such restrictions as seemed to him proper. Nevill's vote and that of one other proprietor were the only ones cast in the house against sending the petitions to the governor. Meantime the "Infection of the Newark Riots" was spreading into Hunterdon county in West Jersey and meetings were held there by tenants on one of the large proprietary tracts.

About the time of the death of Morris some of the rioters revived the former proposals of a test case to end in a settlement of the issue in the law courts. But a question arose over the assignment of counsel and after months of delay the idea was dropped. The rioters, at any rate, could not believe that such a solution was possible or that the decision of the courts could ultimately fail to be against them. During the interim of council government between the death of Morris

[1] N. J. Arch., VI, 292, 397 et seq.; Fisher, op. cit., 187 et seq.
[2] N. J. Arch., VI, 324–348, 408.

and the arrival of Belcher, the adoption of vigorous measures against the rioters could not be expected, and there were outbreaks in Bergen, Middlesex and Somerset counties, accompanied in some places with the breaking open of jails.[1] In July, 1747, Robert Hunter Morris wrote to James Alexander that he had little hope of the assembly doing anything effective, or even that juries could be relied on; their chief reliance must be on the council, the members of which must stand together and avoid giving cause for suspensions.

Judging from the high-handed policy which Belcher followed in suppressing the land bank in Massachusetts, it might have been inferred that he would have been equally strenuous against the rioters in New Jersey. The supporters of the former were not guilty of illegal acts or of breaches of the peace, while the rioters of New Jersey were guilty of both and that in specially pronounced fashion. But Belcher, though his first utterances both to committees of the rioters and to the assembly indicated a vigorous line of action for the purpose of suppressing disorder, did not advance beyond an anxious tolerance of what was going on, culminating in appeals to the British government for advice and help. In addition to the facts which have already been stated in explanation of Belcher's dealings with the assembly and council, it should be noted that he early connected himself with the Presbyterian church at Elizabethtown, of which the able Jonathan Dickinson was pastor.[2] This connection doubtless contributed strongly toward the interest which Belcher took in the founding of the College of New Jersey — the most important and praiseworthy act of his administration. But Dickinson was also an active supporter of the Elizabethtown patentees and the governor was brought directly into their circle. As a New Englander he naturally would be opposed to tenant right and the payment of rent, but he was surpassed by none in his love for the rich and powerful, the class with whom all proprietors were affiliated. If the influence of old age and ill health is added to these tendencies, we have the explanation of the neutral attitude which Belcher took toward the question of the land riots. If the British authorities realized at the time of his appointment — as they

[1] *Ibid.*, 397–422, 426 *et seq.*, 471.   [2] Hatfield, Hist. of Elizabeth.

probably did not — the danger that lay ahead and wished to have the disorder promply checked, he was about the poorest selection they could have made for the office of governor.

The assembly and council early appointed a joint committee to consider means for the suppression of riots. But it was not until near the close of 1747, and after much urging by the council, that meetings of the committee were held.[1] A large amount of evidence of rioting was laid before this body and the houses. They were also presently informed that the rioters, who by this time were definitely organized under leaders, were coming in force to lay their grievances before the general assembly. But this was too clearly an attempt to overawe the legislature to be allowed and it did not occur. In January, 1747/8, the council, under the title of "A Brief State of Facts,"[2] submitted an account of the riots thus far and of the steps which had been taken to bring them to an end. Bacon's Rebellion and the Porteous riot in Edinburgh were the precedents which naturally occurred to their minds in trying to judge what course the British government might take toward the province if the disorders did not cease.

Two acts were also passed at this session, one modeled on the riot act of Great Britain and intended to suppress riots, tumults and disorders by declaring it a felony for twelve or more tumultuously to assemble together and refuse to disperse when ordered to do so by proper authority. This act was to be read once every session in all the courts of the province and was to continue in force five years. The other act, like those which were commonly passed for the suppression of piracy, provided for the pardon of those who had participated in the disorders on their expressing sorrow for their conduct, applying for relief and taking the oaths. But no applications for pardon were made for six months, and then only nine rioters gave bond and took the oaths prescribed by law.[3]

---

[1] N. J. Arch., XV, 530, 539 et seq., 549, 598.

[2] Ibid., 585; VII, 207–226. The history of the riots and of the attitude of the governors and the two houses of assembly toward them, as reported to and formulated by the board of trade, may be followed in its representation to the privy council, June 11, 1750. N. J. Arch., VII, 466–528. This gives the official view of the affair.

N. J. Arch., XVI, 12, 53.

This clearly indicated a confidence that the government would do nothing effective and amounted to contempt of its power. Riotous outbreaks continued to be frequent, and individuals throughout the northern parts of the province who offended or ignored the rioters might expect to have their houses destroyed or other outrages committed upon themselves or their property. Lust for plunder had now begun to appear as an increasing motive among them while at the same time they were becoming better organized and were able to levy on their supporters to meet the cost of the agitation. The council advised the governor to keep the present assembly in existence, as it would not be safe to hold an election. The East Jersey board of proprietors presented a memorial in which they argued that the rioters were preparing to throw off the king's authority. The lower house, however, insisted that the laws were sufficient and that the trouble was due to weak execution. There was, of course, much truth in this, but it drew from the council a warm protest in which the failure to make fit appropriations for the pay of officials came in for emphasis. This was hotly answered by the assembly. When the council tried to advise Belcher to turn from the assembly and apply at once to the king he told them that he would hold one session more, and also that when he wanted the advice of the council he would ask for it. The council, however, insisted upon his obligation to receive its advice and sent an address of its own to the secretary of State. The council of proprietors also petitioned through Ferdinand John Paris, their agent, that the king would protect their property since the laws were too weak and could not be executed.

The new assembly which was convened in February, 1748/9, continued the same attitude as its predecessors. Its dispute with the council over the money bill was as serious as ever. It would not raise money to guard the jails and, insisting that the riots were caused by private controversies about land, tried again to arrange for trials of test cases and the settlement of the question in court. But this could not be arranged. Belcher formally laid the case before later sessions of the assembly. In general his language was sufficiently strong, but his appeals and those of the council fell on deaf

ears. No action followed. This gave rise to charges on the
part of Alexander and Morris against the governor in England, which in turn drew out brief replies from Belcher.[1]
In the interest of the proprietors Morris was sent to England.

The only resort left was to solicit action by the British
government. Official papers concerning the riots had long
been accumulating in the hands of the board of trade, and
now the information which they contained had been ably
supplemented by the personal statements of R. H. Morris.
In June, 1750, it submitted to the privy council one of its
elaborate résumés. As was done about a year later in reference to the controversies of Clinton's administration in New
York, so here the board prepared a detailed and highly docu-
mented chronological review of the riots in New Jersey and
of the action of its government occasioned by them. This was
almost wholly drawn from official sources and of course was
heavily weighted on the proprietary and legal side. It was
essentially an *ex parte* document. The proprietary system as
a whole was accepted as an original and unalterable fact, like
a dogma in the mind of a rigid Calvinist or Anglican, and no
attempt whatever was made, or imagined as possible, to inquire into its expediency or justice. In one of the early
paragraphs of the report the party of the rioters was described as consisting chiefly of the dregs of the people, many
of them Irish, wicked men who, as usual, had taken advantage
of the weakness of the local government and of a foreign
war and the invasion of the Pretender at home, to subvert the
laws and carry out their nefarious designs. At the close of
the review of facts the conclusion was drawn that the province
was in a state of entire disobedience to all authority of government and law and that circumstances manifested a disposition to revolt from dependence on the crown of Great
Britain. But, on the other hand, we know that the rioters
were not of the disreputable character which is here stated
and also that they always professed complete loyalty to
the crown. Moreover, there is not the slightest evidence that
they had timed their operations so as to take any advantage
either of the foreign war or of the rebellion in Great Britain.
From such pseudo-investigations as this and others of the

---

[1] N. J. Arch., VII, 379, 571, 573, 594.

board of trade only coercion — if the government was strong enough to enforce it — could result or, if the government was too weak for that, the continuance of resistance and disorder until the claims and practices of those who had broken the law were tacitly recognized in order that quiet might once more be enjoyed. Such was the course pursued in this case.

With a view to coercion in some form, the board of trade, partly it is possible at the instance of Morris, suggested a choice among three courses of action. One was to send over a sufficient military force under a commander from England, to establish order and submission with the strong hand. The second was to make use of the four independent companies of New York for that purpose, either under an officer appointed for the purpose or under the command of a proper governor of New Jersey. The third was to reunite New Jersey and New York as they were before 1738 and order the governor of the two to go to New Jersey with the four companies, or such of them as should be deemed necessary, and reduce the rioters to obedience.[1] This report was signed by Dunk, earl of Halifax, James Lord Grenville, Dupplin and Charles Townshend, and toward the close the statement was made that in their books they had found many useful precedents for reducing or pacifying a province by pardons, indemnities and the like, " which happen to have been formed upon a great Occasion of a like Nature." This was Bacon's Rebellion; the land riots of New Jersey were an event in some respects as significant and important as the earlier convulsion in Virginia, and for purposes of pacification they might lend themselves to similar treatment.

But the committee of the privy council ignored the three proposals of the board of trade and took steps for the appointment of a commission of inquiry and also for preparing an instruction to the governor to express the king's displeasure at the conduct of the assembly and his expectation that hereafter it would contribute its best endeavors to supporting the government and reëstablishing peace and tranquillity;[2] also that the governor should inform the people of the commission that was to be appointed and that he had

---

[1] N. J. Arch., VII, 522; VIII, 90.
[2] Acts P. C. Col., 1745–1766, pp. 76–80.

under consideration an act of indemnity the terms of which would be available for all who merited it. Ryder and Murray, the law officers, drafted a commission for the purpose of inquiry into the origin and progress of the disturbances in New Jersey.[1] It was realized that as full information as was likely to be obtained was in the report on the subject which had been submitted by the board of trade to the privy council. The law officers, on the other hand, were of the opinion that, as the questions involved related to titles to property, they could best be settled in the courts, provided full right of appeal to the privy council and final adjudication there was allowed. The result of such trials in the province courts had not been especially reassuring and an appeal to England would be both costly and uncertain in its outcome for the rioters. The board of trade, however, at once fell in with the suggestion of the law officers and the plan of a commission was dropped. With considerable difficulty the proprietors, in 1752, induced the committee of the rioters to join in an action to be tried before a jury in Middlesex county. As the riots were still in progress in several of the counties, it was not difficult to find material for a test case. But the suit was never brought to trial. All that was done toward reaching a judicial settlement in New Jersey was the filing, in 1751, by the committee of the Elizabethtown patentees of "An Answer to a Bill in the Chancery of New Jersey." The bill to which this was an answer had been filed by the proprietors in 1745, in the later months of the administration of Morris, and is known as the "Elizabethtown Bill." This was drawn by James Alexander and Joseph Murray and the "Answer" to it by William Livingston and William Smith, these four men, leading lawyers of New York and New Jersey, being counsel for the parties concerned. It was the intention that the case should be heard by the governor of New Jersey sitting as chancellor. But Morris died more than five years before the answer was prepared. Belcher, of course, would hardly be an acceptable judge to the proprietors. Parties to the case died. The Fourth Intercolonial War diverted attention to other and more pressing issues. Under its influence rioting gradually ceased and

[1] N. J. Arch., VIII, 53–59, 90.

energies, so far as possible, were devoted to the task of repelling the French advance and later of conquering Canada. For these reasons the case never came to a hearing and the points involved in it remained undecided. Until the war began Belcher was the object of criticism on the part of the proprietors and their sympathizers, but he was always able to show that the assembly was chiefly responsible for the condition of weakness in the government. Therefore the governor was not interfered with by the authorities in England, except so far as his nominations for places in the council were concerned, and was allowed to finish his life in office.

Another subject which occupied much of the attention of the East Jersey proprietors during these years and until a much later date was that of the dispute between New Jersey and New York over that part of their boundary line which lay west of the Hudson River.[1] This was more than a mere territorial question and therefore involved the governments of the two provinces. It was also a dispute of long continuance, but, as it raised no political question of importance, it demands only a brief reference here. Attempts had been made in 1686 and 1719 to fix this line. At the latter date an indenture had been signed declaring that the Fish-Kill was the northernmost branch of the Delaware, but as to the point on the Hudson at the other end of the line the surveyors disagreed. By 1740 Morris county in New Jersey and Orange county in New York were steadily filling with settlers and attempts of officials to exercise jurisdiction within the disputed region led to clashes, while the confusion was increased by the strife of borderers who were too much disposed to the violent assertion of their claims.[2] The New Yorkers were specially aggressive and lawsuits, ejectments, assaults upon settlers, surveyors and others became chronic in the region between the upper Delaware and the Palisades of the Hudson. Such conflicts occurred wherever boundary disputes became acute. The East Jersey proprietors appealed to Governor Morris and he took the matter up with Clinton. Efforts were made to secure legislation and New Jersey passed an act, in

[1] See the full account in Fisher, *op. cit.*, 210, and references.
[2] In 1753 Sussex county was also erected from the upper part of Morris county.

the winter of 1747/8, for running the line *ex parte*. But New York appointed Robert Charles as agent in England, the first agent it had had for ten years, to oppose this measure. Paris was actively enlisted on the other side. After long delay, at the close of 1752 the board of trade pronounced in favor of a resort to judicial procedure or that all parties should join in running the line, and the New Jersey act was not approved. The proprietors were then able to induce the board to support the fixing of a temporary boundary line, meaning that of 1719.[1] But upon this it was found impossible to agree. New York then passed an act to submit the question to the king for final determination, but this was disallowed as unfair to the New Jersey contestants. The contest drifted on until 1762, when the parties began to agree upon a royal commission. After much delay it was appointed and met in 1769. A decision favorable to New Jersey was reached. From this New York appealed, but failed to prosecute the appeal and the line was finally run.

[1] Advocated in an elaborate report to the governor, N. J. Arch., VIII, pt. 1, 202–286.

CHAPTER VI

PENNSYLVANIA DURING THE THIRD INTERCOLONIAL WAR.
ADMINISTRATIONS OF THOMAS AND HAMILTON

WE have now fully entered upon the period of Pennsylvania
under the " young proprietors." For some years prior to 1741
Thomas Penn resided in the province, but in that year he
returned to England. There the brothers resided until long
after the period we are considering. In 1746 John Penn died
without issue. His share of Pennsylvania was bequeathed to
Thomas for life, with succession to his sons and in default
of these to the descendants of Richard Penn.[1] Thomas Penn
was thus the brother most interested in the proprietorship
and this interest was shown not only while he was in the
province, but by an active correspondence with the governor,
with Richard Peters and others, after his return to England.
This insured a unity of management analagous to that which
existed in the Calvert family and helped to extricate the
Penns from the embarrassments into which they had fallen
during the latter years of the founder. In due time it could
be stated that the debts of William Penn had been paid, and
under prudent management,[2] strengthened by the growth of
wealth and population in the province, prosperity returned to
the family of the Quaker philanthropist and proprietor.
But the sons were very different from the father. Of them
John was the only one who retained even a nominal connection with Quakerism until his death. Richard joined the
Church of England early in life, and Thomas entered that
communion in 1758.[3] The benevolent spirit and idealism of

[1] Shepherd, op. cit., 203.
[2] On September 17, 1742, Thomas Penn wrote to Clement Plumstead,
"Our affairs I thank God, as to money matters are in a pretty easy situation."
They could use large sums due in Pennsylvania, "Yet as we owe none here,
the not recovering so much as we could wish gives us no great uneasiness, and
we can't be disappointed of having all we want." Penn Letter Book, II, 11.
See also ibid., I, 302 et seq. J. to T. Penn, July 9, 1739.
[3] Ibid., 267.

the father was not reflected in them. They were English gentlemen and aristocrats of the mid-eighteenth century and nothing more. Respectable they were and honest, as the times went, but, especially in the case of Thomas, bent upon the securing of such profits as were due under their territorial rights in Pennsylvania and upon maintaining through their governors, councillors and other officials such influence over the government of the province as was possible under the concessions which had been made by their father.

Thomas Penn in particular always professed to wish well to the people of the province and to have nothing more at heart than their welfare. The proprietors individually and jointly gave expression on occasion in their letters to the desire to do all they could to strengthen and improve the province. Thomas, on one occasion, wrote that he felt under obligation to serve the public both personally and with contributions of money, and a few gifts to institutions testified to the reality of this feeling. These gifts are to be estimated on the scale of the very few and meagre offerings of that time and with an eye to the impression produced on the mind of the giver by the losses which the carelessness of his father in money matters had brought on the family. In those days the social motive with its resulting policy of uplift had not found a place in the creeds of governments and, had it done so, the resources of any proprietary family were far too small for achieving results along such lines. It may be conceded that the young proprietors were an improvement on those who made a faint pretence of governing the Carolinas, and certainly they were in a position to effect more than the mere land speculators who went under the name of proprietors in the Jerseys — though the Penns were among those who shared in that investment. Their administration stands on a par with that which the Calverts in their later days developed in Maryland. But, like all their kind, they were for the most part absentees and their correspondence, which is quite abundant, was almost entirely concerned with affairs of property and with those features of their governors' conduct which immediately concerned the proprietary interests. The survey, laying out and sale of lands throughout the province, the levy and collection of quit rents, the extension and care of manors and other proprietary estates in the province, the formation of rent rolls, the revenue which accrued from these various sources and the conduct of the commissioners of property which had these interests especially in charge, formed the staple of correspondence which has been left by the young proprietors and especially by Thomas Penn.[1] At a much later time, when two of the third generation of proprietors assumed the governorship, their duties extended throughout the entire sphere of government.

But it should also be said that at the time of which we are now speaking, that is, during the fourth, fifth and sixth decades of the century, proprietary interests in Pennsylvania involved questions of larger moment than merely those of laying out estates and grants and collecting the revenue therefrom. The rapid influx of settlers from Germany and the British Isles pushed settlements out into the Indian country and down to or across what was supposed to be the border of Maryland. Thanks to the liberal policy of the great founder and of the Society of Friends, Pennsylvania, beyond all other colonies, appeared as a haven of rest to the oppressed of Europe. They flocked to it and freely occupied its territory, often in calm disregard of the rights and dues of the proprietors. This raised not merely territorial questions but political as well. The naturalization of aliens, the extension to them of electoral privileges and the effect which this would have on the control of the province by Quakers, relations with the Indians and above all with Maryland along the border, all these subjects of prime political importance arose directly out of territorial relations and the extension of settlement.

Beginning in 1731, the question of the Maryland boundary was almost continually agitated until its final adjustment more than two decades later.[2] With this was closely involved the title of the two proprietors to the Lower Counties and the continuance of the latter under the executive control of Pennsylvania. Now, as at earlier dates, the Calverts took the initiative and sought to oust the Pennsylvania authorities

[1] These letters are in the collection of Penn Papers in the possession of the Hist. Soc. of Pa.

[2] Shepherd, op. cit., 133 et seq.; Penn Mss , Penn vs. Baltimore.

from the disputed territory. They threatened to renew the claim to the Lower Counties if the Maryland boundary was not extended northward to points about fifteen miles south of Philadelphia. They also insisted that the boundary should be definitely settled or they would appeal to the crown for a final decision. In May, 1732, an agreement was reached for the running of a line due west from Cape Henlopen to the centre of the peninsula and of another due north from the end of the first line and to extend to a point fifteen statute miles south of Philadelphia. From that point a due westerly line should ultimately be drawn across the Susquehanna to the limit of longitude.[1] The drawing of a circle about Newcastle at a distance of twelve statute miles therefrom, as provided in the charter of Pennsylvania and the deeds of enfeoffment, constituted another feature of this process. Commissioners were to be appointed by the two provinces to join in running these lines and they were to be marked on exact plans and surveys and these deposited in the public offices of the two parties concerned. The parties also should renounce all territorial claims not consonant with the boundaries as thus defined. The chief result intended to be reached by this agreement, apart from fixing the southern boundary of Pennsylvania, was the division of the peninsula between the Delaware and Chesapeake bays, into two parts, the western going to Maryland and the eastern remaining under the jurisdiction of Pennsylvania.

The commissioners, however, failed to agree upon the location of the circle to be drawn about Newcastle, and Baltimore in a petition to the king renewed his claim to the Lower Counties. The board of trade made a non-committal report, leaving a loophole open for a possible assertion of the right of the crown to this territory as superior to that of both contestants. The order in council, which followed in May, 1735, recommended that a decision should be postponed and in the meantime the Penns should seek relief on the articles of agreement in a court of equity. As a result of this, proceedings were transferred to the court of chancery in England, and for years thereafter the letters of the proprietors

---

[1] For the present, because of the unsettled state of the country, this line should not be extended more than twenty-five miles west of the Susquehanna.

contain frequent references to the progress of the suit before that court and the delays incident thereto. The Penns presented an elaborate statement of their case. Baltimore, in an answer which he was forced with difficulty to give, denied the allegations and insisted that his commissioners had acted fairly under the agreement of 1732, though fraud had been committed in drafting its articles. He also insisted that the agreement had become invalid through lapse of time and should be cancelled and that either he should be put in possession of the lower counties or a royal governor appointed over them. In harmony, however, with its usual course of action, the board of trade reported in favor of continuing the Penns in their accustomed control while the suit was pending. As outrages were from time to time occurring along the border, an order in council was issued in August, 1737, commanding the governors of both provinces to join in measures for their suppression and to forbid settlement and cease the issue of grants in the disputed territory until the king's pleasure should be known. But this had little effect, and in May, 1738, the two parties made another provisional agreement, the purpose of which was to preserve a semblance of peace along the border west of Newcastle, while grants of land within specified limits might be continued there, subject to readjustment when the boundary should finally be settled. Baltimore also injected into the controversy various minor questions, one involving the location of the fortieth degree of latitude. So the case was continued before the chancery for more than a decade longer, to the great cost of both parties in the fees of counsel and witnesses. Finally, in May, 1750,[1] Lord Chancellor Hardwicke pronounced a decree which required substantially the enforcement of the agreement of 1732. Commissioners must be appointed and the lines duly surveyed by the close of April, 1752, and minor points which then remained in dispute should be referred to a master in

[1] See T. P. to Gov. Hamilton, May 16, 1750, P. L. B. II, 304, for a good account by the Pennsylvania proprietor of the way the trial went and of the decision of the Chancellor. The Maryland case broke down through lack of adequate proof against the validity of the agreement of 1732. The Chancellor praised the merit of William Penn in settling the Lower Counties and said that it amounted to a very valuable purchase. He also regarded the duke of York as virtually a trustee for Penn and that the crown was now a royal trustee and had no other right than the duke of York had.

chancery. The decision had gone against Maryland and Baltimore was required to pay the entire costs of the suit, the Penns repaying to Earl Powlett the sum which as trustee he had expended in connection with the suit. Various obstacles were imposed by the defeated party to delay or prevent the execution of the decree, but the circle about Newcastle and the east and west and north and south lines in the peninsula were duly located. It was not, however, until 1767 that the surveyors, Mason and Dixon, completed the surveying of these lines and also of the southern boundary of Pennsylvania for a distance of 230 miles west from the tangent near Newcastle. All the proceedings were ratified by an order in council under date of January 11, 1769, and proclamations were duly issued for quieting settlers in their possessions along the entire boundary. Thus the most important boundary dispute in which Pennsylvania and Maryland were concerned and one of the most involved and persistently contested in the entire history of the colonies was settled. Such hold as the Penns had on the Lower Counties remained unimpaired and about 1745 the name Delaware began occasionally to be applied to that district.

These transactions went on under the young proprietors, as did the very important treaties and other negotiations with the Indian tribes, both within and without Pennsylvania, of which an account has been given in other chapters of this work. It was during these years that Pennsylvania was assuming a leading place among the continental colonies. The interests involved and the volume of business done in its collective activities were coming decidedly to exceed those of the sister proprietorship to the south. This was not due to any special merit on the part of the young proprietors, though the development was not hindered by them. They fell in with it naturally, profited in a quiet and assured way by it and formed a dignified figure-head for it all. Their alignment, sooner or later, with Anglicanism was a disappointment to the Quakers and proved a root of bitterness to many. Not a little of the intense party feeling of the later time was due to it. It contributed to the formation of a strong antiproprietary party and to the circulation of exaggerated charges concerning the wealth which the Penns were supposed to be accumulating from their province. But this alignment brought the young proprietors, so far as their influence and facilities for dealing with the British government went, into harmony with the conditions of the time. In spite of the fact that the Great Awakening was contemporary with the events of which we are now speaking and that it met with a notable response in Pennsylvania, the spirit of the age had come to be largely foreign to that in which, a century before, William Penn had been reared. Religious enthusiasm, except during the spasm of a revival, had cooled and hidden itself under the crust of habit, of inherited beliefs and forms. Though Pennsylvania was the home of religious enthusiasts of many names, this change was slowly affecting even them. Trade, industry, secular affairs were taking the place of prime interest in society which had been held by religion when the colonies were founded. In a deep and real sense Penn's "Holy Experiment" was proving, and was to continue to prove, a success. But his sons keenly felt how disastrous it had proved to the family fortune and were not minded to commit their father's mistakes. Logan still survived, an old man and a relic of the age of the founder. He had discharged the duties of president of the council during the interval between the close of Gordon's governorship and the appointment of his successor. Occasionally thereafter appears one of his letters, filled with the accustomed wise and penetrating observations on men and things, and then silence falls upon the last contemporary and friend of William Penn, the founder. Richard Peters, himself an Anglican clergyman as well as an administrator and public man of extraordinary gifts and versatility, succeeded to Logan's place as proprietary secretary and chief correspondent of the Penn family in reference to their special interests in the province. Peters and the young proprietors, like Dudley and Belcher in Massachusetts, were mediating between the old and the new age, men of the secularized eighteenth century set to administer colonies which had been founded to express the politico-religious ideals of the seventeenth. They drifted with the tide without breaking entirely away from the ancient moorings and Pennsylvania with its new leaders reaped rewards from both the old and the new time. The same cannot be so truly said of Massachusetts, because the founders had built upon a less broad and humane foundation and the spirit which they showed was more harsh and repellent.

We have seen that on the death of Gordon the young proprietors were in doubt as to the advisability of the governorship being assumed by one of them. Thomas would have been the natural choice, but the matter of the oath stood in the way. Had his zeal to serve the province been sufficiently strong it is possible that this difficulty might have been overcome, as also the excuse that the Maryland boundary case was demanding too much attention. But it was not, and proposals for the appointment of one George Thomas were entertained. He was a wealthy planter of Antigua, who had property also in Pennsylvania and had gained a favorable idea of that province. When he heard of the vacancy in the governorship he applied to the proprietors for the place, representing that his independent fortune would raise him above the temptation to corrupt bargains.[1] It was not until after the beginning of Evans's administration that the assembly had begun to vote salaries to the governors with considerable regularity. It had been the custom of William Penn and the later proprietors down to the close of Gordon's administration to demand from the governors a part of their receipts, including under this term both their salary and their perquisites, but the response to this demand had never been at all regular or satisfactory. In the case of Thomas a definite contract was made for four years with permission to quit on a year's notice, and on the request of the appointee it was kept secret lest the people might consider it disreputable. It provided that out of the salary and perquisites, which were expected to amount to £2000 a year, Thomas should pay the proprietors £500 sterling, or, if not that sum clear, at least one-half the perquisites. The people would have preferred one of the proprietors as governor, but it was said that Baltimore would strongly oppose the confirmation of such an appointment. As it was, owing to Baltimore's

[1] See a variety of letters exchanged between the Penn brothers and their friends during 1736 and 1737. These are in various parts of the Penn Mss. The correspondence of Thomas with the proprietors reveals his side of the story. Shepherd, 206.

opposition to the continuance of the Lower Counties under the control of the Penns, the confirmation of Thomas was delayed for some months.[1] At length it was granted and he was able to reach Philadelphia and begin his administration of both the province and the Lower Counties in the summer of 1738.[2]

As the administration progressed, Thomas showed himself to be a man of firm and well-balanced judgment. In ability he surpassed any of the recent governors of Pennsylvania except Keith. He lacked the originality of Keith and showed nothing of the spirit of the adventurer or political agitator. He therefore fitted well into the proprietary traditions of government and made a good impression upon the conservatives. Logan after a time praised him in high terms and the part which Thomas played, especially in Indian affairs, won him repute in more than one colony. His bearing contrasted favorably with what some Pennsylvanians considered the stupid blundering of Clinton in New York.[3] But the attention of Thomas was also fixed on the expected salary and perquisites, and the bargain into which he had entered with the proprietors was so definite as to affect deeply the spirit of his administration. Never before, so far as we know, even in any proprietary province, had the relations between a governor and the authority which appointed him been expressed so clearly in the terms of the cash nexus. Such a definition would have been inconceivable in the corporate colonies of New England. In most of the royal provinces, though salaries were fixed as the result of much virtual bargaining between assemblies and governors, the fact, so far as possible, was concealed under the thin disguise of regard for the liberties of Englishmen on the one side and loyalty to the crown on the other. So far as the British crown itself was concerned, the idea of such remuneration being determined by bargains or contracts was never tolerated for a moment. So inconsistent was such a thing with any tolerable conceptions of sovereignty that a proprietor who had yielded to it as the Penns had now done, whether from necessity or from business astuteness, might well be condemned in the strongest

---

[1] For an account of this see Acts P. C. Col., 1720–1745, pp. 337, 564. Concerning Cresap and outrages on the border much material is in Pa. Arch I.

[2] Pa. Col. Recs., IV, *et seq.*; Votes of Pa. Ass., III, 301 *et seq.*

[3] Logan to Thomas, Dec. 11, 1745, Off. Corr., IV, 58.

terms. It went far to justify bribe taking and private under-
standings of all sorts, against which oaths and sureties were
no effective protection. Wittingly or unwittingly, the Penns
and Thomas had furnished a vivid illustration of the spirit
of the proprietorship and had dealt a body blow to British
sovereignty as exercised through such institutions and by
such methods as these. The sinister influence of this bargain
and of other analogous doings upon government and opinion
in Pennsylvania was to appear in the future to the serious
disadvantage of proprietary interests. This also was a time
when the council, never so influential in Pennsylvania as in
many other provinces, was weak both in personnel and in the
numbers who usually attended its sessions.

Andrew Hamilton, the famous lawyer, now advanced in
years and approaching the close of his public career, was
speaker of the assembly and a member for Bucks county.[1]
Among the other prominent members were John Kinsey, Jonathan Robison, William Allen and Isaac Norris from Philadelphia county, Israel Pemberton from Philadelphia city,
Jeremiah Langhorne and Lawrence Growdon from Bucks. The
assembly numbered thirty members, eight each from the three
original counties of Philadelphia, Bucks and Chester, two
from the city of Philadelphia and four from Lancaster
county. From the general list and names which appear on
important committees one would infer that practically every
one was a working member and that together they formed
a compact and experienced body of Quakers, of British descent, representing chiefly the eastern section of the province
and the counties which were first settled. The past record of
this body, as well as its conduct during the administration of
Thomas and later, shows that it was committed to a simple
and well understood policy of opposition to war and aggressive imperialism. This half consciously was the attitude of
all the colonists — at least outside of New England — who
did not have some official or commercial interest to serve by
the policy to which Great Britain was committing herself.
Among those who maintained this quietist attitude the
Quakers occupied the left; they were the only group whose

[1] Hamilton had recently pleaded his professional duties as an excuse for
declining a seat in the council: Col Recs., IV, 293, 295.

views and course of action in reference to it were systematic
and fully self-consistent. In their case these views determined their attitude toward the Indians as well as toward
the French and Spanish. They would not make their religion,
though Christian and Protestant, a cause for war with either
the heathen or the Catholics. It is true that they based their
views on literal reading of Scripture texts and thus far shared
in the narrow mental habits of their time. But beneath this
procedure lay a true consciousness of the essentials of humanity which transcended all differences of color, race, nation
or creed. Quakers shared in the movement westward toward
the interior of the continent so far as was a necessary consequence of the growth of population. But with the artificial
stimulations of these tendencies by military and commercial
exploitation, accompanied with the partial or complete destruction of native peoples, they had no sympathy. Under
the conditions and to the great majority of people in their
time, this attitude seemed perverse and purely obstructionist.
But to the modern man it appears worthy of all honor as a
dim foreshadowing of what human relations should everywhere be. Of the superiority of the Quaker ideal to that of
the Calvinist, even when viewed from the standpoint of the
New Testament alone, there can be no doubt whatever.

The appropriateness of these statements at this point in
the narrative will appear when we consider that immediately
ahead of us lie the last two intercolonial wars and that during
their continuance Quaker principles were to be put even more
severely to the test than was the case in the earlier struggles.
The result of this was their reassertion, not so much as previously by a great leader like William Penn as by native
Pennsylvanians in their assembly and elsewhere and under
changed conditions and those made more pressing by the
growing intensity of the conflict. It was during the two
decades that we are now to consider that Quaker principles
as to war became a question of large significance in general
colonial politics, for the frontier and the struggle to maintain
and defend it had now so far developed that Pennsylvania
had become in a true sense a keystone of the structure.

But before Governor Thomas was compelled to take up
with the assembly the question of war and military service he

found himself confronted with the related question of paper currency. That body, after making considerable changes in the board of trustees of the loan office, laid before him a bill for continuing in circulation such bills of credit as by former acts were appointed to be redeemed and destroyed and for the striking of an additional sum.[1] As both of the preceding governors had been so favorable to continued issues of paper, the assembly had become accustomed to a smooth passage for measures of this kind. But the cautious tone in which Thomas replied to their first suggestion of this policy indicated the possibility of executive opposition. He referred to the bill as too important to be hastily passed, to the attitude of the board of trade toward former bills of this nature, to its possible effect on British trade and debts, to the possibility that the province did not need so large an amount of currency and to the low credit into which those colonies had fallen which had resorted to too frequent emissions. In view of these considerations the governor trusted that the assembly would not blame his disinterested caution or his insistence on such delay as would insure a well-digested measure. Thomas spoke not only as a business man but as an official who was bound by the instructions regularly given by the British government at this time respecting this subject and under the restraint of a special instruction which he had received from the proprietors. This provided that the governor should not assent to any law within the province or the counties respecting the issue of bills of credit unless there was inserted in it a provision that the quit rents and other rents due them should be paid in accordance with the true rate of exchange between Philadelphia and London at the time of such payments.[2]

The assembly replied that haste was not required or intended and the matter went over till the next session. Then the bill was again brought forward with the definite provision that the additional issue should be to the amount of £11,110 and that the whole amount in circulation should be £80,000. The term during which it should be outstanding was fixed at sixteen years, the rate of interest at which it should be loaned

[1] Votes, III, 305, 306, 311, 312.
[2] Col. Recs., IV, 318.

at 5% and the amount that should be loaned to any person should not be less than £12 or more than £100.[1] When the bill was passed in this general form and came before the governor some amendments were insisted upon by him in connection with the council and in a message he came out with a frank criticism of the policy of the measure in general. He laid before them a copy of his instruction from the proprietors, though in a letter to Paris, the agent, he expressed the wish that he had been left more free, so that the course to be followed might have been settled in conference with Thomas Penn who was then in the province.[2] To the assembly, however, he presented a firm countenance, protesting in the name of justice and truth against their effort to make their currency equivalent to proclamation money when exchange on London, measuring the amount of depreciation, was at 70% and proclamation money was only about 30% below sterling. He did not veto the bill but told the house how likely it was that it would be disallowed by the crown and that it was impossible for him to do otherwise than oppose it unless he was to expose himself to the imputation of injustice and breach of trust.

In a conference between a committee of the house and the governor he proposed that ˙debts and dues to the crown, sterling debts and all rents due the proprietors be excepted from the terms of the bill, but to these the house for a variety of reasons refused to consent.[3] The most important of these, especially as substantiated by a statement from the speaker, was that the policy urged would lessen the credit of the currency by insisting upon a rate of exchange which was more unfavorable than actually existed in the province and was going beyond what the proprietors had a right to claim. The governor, however, kept the discussion close to fact and reality by insisting that when an English shilling was mentioned in a law or contract or resolution of the assembly the coin referred to was really meant and that justice to creditors, even if they were proprietors or British merchants, required that the shilling or its equivalent should be paid. Had the

---

[1] Votes, III, 326 *et seq.*; Col. Recs., IV, 319 *et seq.*
[2] P. L. B., I, 278, J. Penn to T. Penn, Jan. 6, 1738/9.
[3] Votes, III, 330 *et seq.*; Col. Recs., IV, 323 *et seq.*

bills of credit been really equal to proclamation money, the rate of exchange would have shown it.

The controversy was continued until May, 1739, when as the result of a concession by the house the bill was accepted by the governor and became law. The concession was that two payments should be made to the proprietors, one of £1200 as compensation for unpaid arrearages of quit rent, they receiving them in bills of credit instead of silver, and the other an annual payment of £130 during the continuance of the bill as law.[1] Though Thomas informed the house that the arrears of quit rents amounted to more than £11,000 sterling it was felt — and the result justified the assurance — that the proprietors would be placated by the offer and allow the law to stand though it nullified their instruction. Indeed, letters which at the time were exchanged between the Penns and the governor show that, though they considered the instruction just, they would not refuse to change it if such change accorded with the judgment of those residing in Pennsylvania.[2] In his statement in the conference above referred to, Hamilton had added one more to the many testimonies from colonials that instructions, because framed in England and by persons who had little acquaintance with conditions in the plantations, were often ill-adapted to secure the ends sought.[3] The agreement did not affect the Lower Counties, where scarcely any rents had been paid for twenty years or more. As the two houses of parliament were just addressing the crown for information concerning issues of bills of credit in the colonies since 1700 and also as to the rates at which such notes exchanged for gold and silver, the Pennsylvania law reached England at an unfavorable time and Thomas thought it would be best to wait awhile before presenting it for confirmation.[4] But this and another act for better preserving the credit of paper money were duly submitted and

[1] Votes, III, 339. Recs. of Council, IV, 330–336. Pownall, in his "Administration of the Colonies," explained the main features of this act, as "containing all the improvements which experience had from time to time suggested in the execution of preceding acts."

[2] J. Penn to Thomas, Mar. 29, 1738/9, P. L. B., I, 294; J. Penn to T. Penn, July 9, 1739, P. L. B., I, 301.

[3] Votes, III, 333.

[4] Col. Recs., IV, 357; Thomas to J. Penn, Nov. 5, 1739, Penn Mss.; Off. Corresp., III, 89.

after a brief inquiry by the board of trade from two merchants and Fane, the counsel, were duly approved.[1] The
statements demanded by parliament were duly prepared by
the assembly and defended against criticism by the governor.[2]
They took occasion to state that their issues had always been
secured by land to double the value of the sums emitted, that
their credit had been otherwise supported, and they believed
that the policy would be found to be absolutely necessary for
carrying on the trade of the province but also of great advantage to Great Britain. With this opinion Thomas now
expressed his agreement, provided issues were kept within due
bounds. With this the paper money issue was laid to rest
in Pennsylvania.

But meantime two or more sessions of the assembly had
passed and Thomas had received a grant of only £600, made
on his arrival, and £200 from the Lower Counties.[3] The
assembly was proceeding from session to session without
referring to the subject of his support. Since his arrival he
had spent £1300 and was bound to make the payments for
which he had agreed in his bargain with the proprietors.
Under these circumstances Thomas soon began to complain
to the proprietors. Though he was determined to support
both his character and his instructions, he had met with more
opposition than he expected. He questioned the fairness of
the bargain he had made and gave the first intimation that
he should renounce it and leave the province. If he did, he
felt tempted to write a history of the wretched inhabitants
of a country where the head was governed by the tail. Later
he wrote that he was £900 a year out of pocket and, unless
things improved, was planning to send his family to England
in May.[4] The sum of £1000, however, was voted him in
May and he resolved to keep his family with him a year
longer.[5]

It was at this juncture, just before the beginning of the
third intercolonial war, that Andrew Hamilton, because of
age and infirmities, resigned the speakership and retired from

[1] Stats. at Large of Pa., IV, 322, 344, 479–483.
[2] Col. Recs., IV, 359 *et seq.*
[3] Thomas to J. Penn, Jan. 29, 1738/9. Orig. Corresp., III, 77.
[4] *Ibid.*, March 15, 1738/9.
[5] Votes, III, 343; Thomas to J. Penn, Nov. 5, 1739. Off. Corresp., III, 89.

public life. In his valedictory address to the assembly [1] he attributed the great progress which Pennsylvania was making not to natural advantages of soil and rivers but to the excellence of its constitution. In support of this he referred to its annual assemblies, to their right of self-adjournment, to the fact that the province had no unnecessary or overpaid officials and that the authority of nearly all of them came directly from the people or their representatives. Trade and shipping were free from all imposts except those levied under the laws of Great Britain and internal taxes were inconsiderable, while the assembly appointed the treasurer and controlled the finances of the province. This simple constitution was crowned by freedom of religion, the whole being the work of William Penn and fulfilling the Quaker ideal of what a free government should be. The only danger which he saw confronting it was that of factional strife caused by men ambitious of power. But at the present this peril seemed slight and Hamilton could look forward with confidence to the future. But before a year had passed the Quaker principle of pacifism was put to the test and a new controversy was opened with the governor. John Kinsey, a man of ability and prolonged experience both in New Jersey and in Pennsylvania, had then succeeded to the speakership.

In October, 1739, Thomas first sounded a warning to the assembly that the threatening aspect of affairs in Europe made it the part of wisdom to see danger at a distance and make timely provision against it.[2] A committee of which Robert Jones, Israel Pemberton, Thomas Kirkbride, Joseph Harvey and John Wright were the members was appointed to draft the message of the assembly in reply. Later, when it became necessary to draft other messages, Isaac Norris was added to the committee. The position assumed by the assembly and defined by this committee was that they were loyal subjects of Great Britain but protected by the clause in the royal charter which permanently guaranteed liberty of conscience. Following the same line of argument which was

---

[1] Votes, III, 349. This was published in the "Pennsylvania Gazette," in its weekly issue of Sept. 20–27, 1739.

[2] Ibid., 354; Col. Recs., IV, 355. See the following pages of both these journals for the messages exchanged between the governor and assembly which set forth the arguments used in this discussion.

so often used in New England, they declared that without the guaranty of this and other kindred privileges their ancestors could not have been induced to leave England and settle the province. But since its founding large numbers had made a home within its borders who believed it their duty to fight in defence of their country. Adequate authority for such procedure had also been granted in the royal charter and with the aid that was necessary from the mother country it was believed that their efforts would be adequate to the public need. But to attempt to force those to fight whose principles forbade it would be not only to violate the royal charter and charter of privileges of 1701 but to commence persecution against all Quakers in the province. It would also be impossible, they added, for an assembly the majority of which were Quakers to pass a law which, though exempting them-, selves, should compel others to fight. Thomas in his reply said that he had grouped the Quakers in with the whole body of Protestants as moved by a common opposition to " the bloody Religion of France and Spain." He necessarily disclaimed all intention of resorting to persecution — against which they were fully protected — but appealed to them on the ground of the political motive — the danger of invasion by the enemy, the fact that they had been chosen as representatives of all the freeholders of the province, many of whom had already petitioned for the adoption of measures of defence, and the recognition by the founder of the necessity of armed defence as shown in the military provisions of the charter.[1] Voluntaryism in such matters he dismissed as utterly futile, as it had been shown to be so in the administration of Evans, and in the existing state of the world would prove as fatal as it would be for a crew to abandon the navigation of a vessel at sea in the midst of a storm.

The assembly met this argument by endeavoring to belittle the danger, showing an attitude of mind which was very common throughout the colonies. It was the inertia born of this non-militaristic temper against which officials

[1] On Jan. 5, 1739/40, a petition from a great number of the inhabitants of Philadelphia to this effect was read in the assembly and it was resolved that the sentiments of the house on this subject were fully expressed in its reply to the governor's speech. Votes, III, 362.

and militarists generally found it so hard to contend. Penn-sylvania, the assembly agreed, was distant from the sea and sheltered by colonies to the north and south of it whose inhabitants, unlike so many of its own people, were inured to war. The Canadians were hundreds of miles away and too weak in numbers to hope for success in any enterprise against the English. Also, war with France was not yet declared. Why be so solicitous about an event which might never happen? The building of forts, they believed, would be of no use and of the effectiveness of a militia as shown in all the colonies they had a poor opinion. If the non-milita-rists should petition they would far exceed those who were clamoring for defence. As they were sure that the sentiments of William Penn were in agreement with those they now pro-fessed, so were they confident that the British government would continue to indulge them in their present attitude. That it was consistent with Christianity to defend themselves at the expense of the lives of their fellow creatures, though enemies, was not evident to them, though they would not interfere with the liberty of those who held that view. The governor, of course, was able to show them that Delaware Bay was navigable and that the French and Indians could easily reach the frontier of Pennsylvania from the northwest. He could also refer them to official documents by means of which William Penn had authorized action of a military nature, and in many other ways could show them how absurdly imprudent their attitude was. But the assembly was not to be moved, and if the argument could have been resumed at the close of the war which was then beginning they could have proved to the governor that their estimate of the probable course of events was more reliable than his own. Indeed, it agreed well with the policy of Walpole, though the British prime minister based his action purely on expediency and not on any idealistic principles. The war which the British were then beginning with Spain was the result to a considerable extent of the misconduct of their own seamen toward that power, while the share of the British in the so-called War of the Austrian Succession was as destitute of plan and result as could well be imagined. So far as the American side of the affair was concerned, with the possible exception of the New England enterprise at Louisbourg, it was partly a hideous and partly a laughable fiasco. In connection with the events and personages of that time the old régime, as embodied in the British empire, touched the nadir. One can imagine the serene content and contempt with which the Quakers viewed the costly and futile plans of 1746 and 1747 for expeditions against Canada and Crown Point, duplicates of similar efforts in the previous war, which were coolly nullified by conditions or officials in Europe, three thousand miles away. And then at the end of the war came the crowning absurdity, if there were any who had been sincere in its prosecution, of the mutual restoration of all conquests. The peace of Pennsylvania had not been disturbed except by rumors of war, and, in view of the issue as a whole, who could have desired a more complete justification of the Quaker argument?

But long before these more general results had become apparent the issue was again brought squarely before the assembly by the instructions from the crown which were followed by the despatch of contingents to the West Indies in 1740.[1] The assembly desired to see the original of the instruction but, as usual, this was denied. Thomas told them that they were only expected to provide victuals, transports and other necessities for the troops until their arrival at the general rendezvous, and this they might do from money in the treasury without the levy of a shilling on the people. But the assembly replied that, though they considered it their duty to pay tribute to Caesar and obey the powers that God had set over them, they could not " preserve good Consciences and come into the Levying of Money and appropriating it to the uses recommended," because it was repugnant to the religious principles of the majority of them. This was early in July and, on the plea that it was harvest time and that a report had arrived of a peace with Spain, the assembly adjourned until the following month. But at the instance of Colonel Gooch and Blakeney and because of the progress of enlistments it became necessary for the governor to call them together again before the close of July. He then laid before them the royal instruction and an extract from Newcastle's

[1] Votes, III, 389 *et seq.*; Col. Recs., IV, 422 *et seq.*

letter. Seven companies, he told them, were already enlisted
in the province and were billeted in adjacent villages; the
need of an appropriation for their support was imperative.
But in reply Thomas received the strongest protest which
had yet been addressed to him, in which not only the general
attitude of the assembly toward war was again affirmed, but
the treasury and accounts were stated to be in an unsatisfactory condition. The bulk of the address, however, was
occupied with the enlistment of servants by recruiting officers
and the unjustifiable way in which they not only were reducing the labor supply of the province, but also were undermining the relation of servant and master, an institution
which the British government evidently promoted, by con-
cealing the names of servants who enlisted, encouraging them
to escape and by the severe treatment which masters who
applied for their servants received at the hands of recruiting
officers.[1] In the name of liberty and property, for which the
king had always shown such regard, the assembly demanded
that the enlistment of servants be stopped and that those
already enlisted, 276 in number, be returned to their masters.[2]
The extent to which enlistments had exceeded the proportion
due from Pennsylvania seemed, in the opinion of the assembly, to justify this.

Meantime an opinion [3] had been also secured from John
Kinsey, who, in addition to being speaker, was attorney general of the province, upon the law affecting this issue. He
was a Quaker and in full agreement with the policy of the
house, and in the opinion which he rendered this attitude
was reflected by such an interpretation of the law as to
make apparent a direct conflict of rights under it. On the
one side, he said, the king had a right to the personal service
of every subject in time of war and no one could by engage-
ment with another deprive the king of that right, though he

[1] In May petitions from sundry inhabitants of Chester county and the city
of Philadelphia against this practice were received by the assembly. Votes,
III, 378, 381, 402.

[2] Peters to J. Penn, July 31, 1740, Penn Mss.; Off. Corresp., III, 123.

[3] Penn Mss.; Ass. & Prov. C. of Pa., 41, Apr. 21, 1740. For references to
earlier and later claims in reference to this subject, see Shepherd, *op. cit.*, 523
et seq. Root, *op. cit.*, 281, gives an account of the controversy. In addition to
the references below, see Thomas' review of the question in his message of
Aug. 17, 1742, to the assembly. Col. Recs., IV, 590–600.

might so tie up his hands that he could not lawfully enlist. This he implied that indentured servants had done. They might not enlist without their masters' consent and were liable, if they did so, for suits for non-performance. They might be arrested and detained by a civil officer, and enlisting officers concerned in such cases, if they exceeded their commissions, would subject themselves to an action at law.

As the controversy progressed, the parties showed themselves as opposed to one another as were the two alternatives of this opinion, though suits apparently were not resorted to by Quaker masters either against servants who had enlisted or for the recovery of damages from officers who had received their enlistments. There was no law of the province upon which the Quakers could safely fall back and they doubtless were well enough aware that their contention would not receive the support of the British government or courts. In the proclamation which the governor issued calling for recruits, only the word " subjects " had been used and he was receiving legal advice that it included servants. The assembly, however, resolved that it was not legal under its terms to enlist servants without the consent of their masters.[1] Some servants probably took advantage of the opportunity to escape from their masters and enlist and the recruiting officers eagerly availed themselves of the offer of servants as well as freemen. The Quakers were making the war a distinct political issue and by appealing to the self-interest of the Germans had secured almost the unanimous support of the assembly. It voted £3000 for the king's use, but added the stipulation, among others, that payment should be withheld until the enlisted servants were released and the governor promised not to enroll any more.[2] But the recruits had already been raised and the time had arrived or was near when they should sail. All who were responsible for the success of the government declared that mutiny would result if the servants were dismissed.[3] As there was now no hope

[1] Col. Recs., IV, 396, 453.

[2] Votes, III, 409; Col. Recs., IV, 459, 461. The warrant also provided that, if the king should not direct the disposal of the money within nine months, it should remain in the treasury.

[3] See a resolve of the council on this, Col. Recs., IV, 466–469.

of an appropriation by the assembly, the proprietors and merchants subscribed £6600 and ships were offered as transports on condition of reimbursement by the home government, Thomas drawing on the navy board for the purpose. The assembly then stopped his salary and threatened to appeal against him, which led him in turn to write to the board of trade in strong condemnation of the Quaker tactics.[1] Of this letter Partridge, who had been appointed its agent by the assembly to the exclusion of Paris, procured a copy, circulated it among the Quakers in England and sent it to Pennsylvania, where it served still further to widen the breach between the assembly and the governor. The board called on Partridge to explain how he got the letter, and on his refusing to do so he was forbidden to appear before it on behalf of any colony until he made satisfaction. The Quakers did not secure the return of their servants, but in 1741 appropriated £2354 to compensate the masters for the loss of their services.[2] The Lower Counties meantime gratified the entire proprietary and royal interest by passing a militia act.[3]

The governor, council and the proprietors were greatly scandalized by this episode. When, early in August, the assembly addressed the resident proprietor, Thomas Penn,[4] and asked him to use his influence with the governor to induce him to assist them in transmitting an appeal to the crown for justice, he contrasted the governor's loyalty with theirs and reproved them for trying to avoid assisting the king in the present undertaking. They should first, he said, compensate all for the loss they had suffered by the enlistment of their servants and then, if they were convinced that the governor had acted an improper part, they could more safely seek redress. The two non-resident proprietors regarded the conduct of the assembly as contemptible and in their irritation expressed the wild idea that the British government would expel the Quakers from the assembly or make

[1] Stats. at Large of Pa., IV, 468; J. P. to Thomas, Mar. 7, 1740/1, P. L. B., I, 364.

[2] Votes, III, 429–431.

[3] Pa. Arch., I, 628.

[4] Votes, III, 407–409. The completion of the petition to the king and the appointment of Paris are entered on p. 422. See also p. 425.

laws which would effectually prevent such doings. Thomas Penn praised the governor highly and considered that he must be retained in office, especially as he (Thomas) expected soon to visit England.[1] Conrad Weiser, in 1741, reproved the Germans for repeatedly choosing assemblymen who would make no appropriation for war and who quarrelled with the governor and withheld his salary.[2] But he forgot how much there was in the religious beliefs of these same Germans and especially in their European experiences to make them hate the very name of war. Thomas again complained of his inability to secure support and obtained from the proprietors a release from the money article in their agreement with him.[3] There was some talk of his accepting an appointment in the West Indies, but that blew over. Thomas took a long look into the future when he wrote to John Penn, " if You do not part with them [the Quaker majority in the assembly] they will in the end part with you, for they publickly avow their design to throw the government into the hands of the crown, and from hence the more confusion the better, as that is the most probable way of bringing it about." [4] William Allen wrote that the province had been taken by surprise by the union of the Germans with the Quakers, and on the issue of military preparation the coalition was likely to be permanent. The leaders among the Quakers he considered to be Norris and Kinsley.[5]

No colony better illustrated the extreme individualism, with its opposing ideals, which was characteristic of the time, than did Pennsylvania. Never were a governor and an assembly more completely at loggerheads than were Thomas and the representatives with whom he was contending. While the discussion over war and defence was in progress another warm controversy arose, though it was not so prolonged, over the way in which the governor treated the assembly in expressing his dissent to a bill for levying money on the

[1] J. & T. Penn to T. P., Nov. 26, 1740, P. L. B., I, 338, 340–342. See also ibid., 360.

[2] Walten, Life of Weiser, 604. Logan supported this appeal.

[3] T. P. to J. P., Nov. 11, 1740, J. & R. P. to T. P., Nov. 26, 1740.

[4] Thomas to J. P., Mar. 25, 1741, Off. Corresp., III, 139. T. P. to Paris, ibid, 141.

[5] Allen to J. P., Mar. 27, 1741, Off. Corresp., III, 143.

inhabitants of Philadelphia.[1]   Young Israel Pemberton also
in a conversation which was promptly noised about, charged
the governor with an intention when he came over of reducing Pennsylvania to the condition of a royal province.[2]   This
led to an inquiry before the council, an attempt on the governor's part to arrest Pemberton and his taking refuge for
a time to avoid arrest.   A restriction which, at the instance
of Great Britain, was laid on the export of provisions little
suited the taste of the assembly.[3]   Though Spanish privateers
were infesting the coast, the assembly doubted the veracity
of the reports concerning them,[4] insisted that the ships of
war of other colonies furnished sufficient protection and declined to provide for fitting out vessels.   But in October,
1741, in view of the extraordinary taxes to which the people
of Great Britain were being subjected, the newly elected
assembly did appropriate £3000, current money, as an expression of their loyalty and ordered that it be remitted to
the British government through the agent.[5]   A representation of the state of the province was ordered at the same
time to be sent to the proprietors.   The method of making
appropriations, as was done in this case, by resolution was
disapproved by the governor, but was rather difficult to
avoid in a province where the council had no legislative power.
Thomas also interpreted the grant as a bribe to secure his
removal,[6] but the proprietors, of course, in their reply to
the assembly and in their correspondence stood by him.   So
absurd seemed the appropriation made by the assembly and
the way in which it was sent to England that William Allen
thought it would be treated as a joke in the clubs of London.
Equally petty on the other side was the handle which was
made of a report that there were a few Catholics among the
Germans and the activity of priests there was sufficient to
justify special efforts at suppression.[7]

When, in 1741, the assembly presented Kinsey again as

---

[1] Col. Recs., IV, 389, 398 et seq. and entries for corresponding dates in the
Votes.

[2] Col. Recs., IV, 389 et seq.   [4] Ibid., 494, et seq.

[3] Ibid., 492.   [5] Votes, III, 446.

[6] Thomas to J. P., Oct. 27, 1741, Off. Corresp., III, 197.

[7] Penn Mss., Ass. & C., 46; Off. Corresp., III, 201, 227, 275, Letters of
William Allen to T. Penn.

speaker, Thomas so severely reflected on his conduct in former assemblies that it was not thought best to repeat his language when the house resumed its session, and the committee of grievances was again appointed.[1] A resolution in defence of Kinsey and criticising the governor was also passed. The governor and council on the one side and the assembly on the other also fell into a long altercation over the visitation of ships which were landing immigrants in the province [2] and the building of a pest house as a protection against contagious diseases. With this the question of the governor's salary and perquisites became involved. He then began to hold up bills in order to force the house to terms.[3] So the factional fight went on, neither party yielding, the one asserting that they were working for liberty and the other for normal principles of government and the dignity of the executive. In the fall election of 1742 the government party, of which William Allen was a very active leader, redoubled its efforts to break the alliance between the Quakers and the Germans and thus weaken or destroy their majority. The passions which were aroused culminated in an election riot in Philadelphia, in which sailors with clubs participated on the side of the anti-Quaker party and heads were broken. The city magistrates, who were in sympathy with the government, were charged with failure to suppress the disorder, many affidavits were taken and much recrimination followed. But the political situation was not changed.[4] Kinsey was re-elected speaker and the committee of grievances was given power to send for persons and papers. Thomas wrote to John Penn, " The party here is too obstinate to be convinced or reformed by any thing that has or can come from the Lords of Trade or from the King, Himself; and as the leaders have long since laid aside all shame or regard for character, they would sacrifice the Proprietors, the province or their own Society to justify the dic-

[1] Votes, III, 344.
[2] Votes, III, 450 et seq.; Col. Recs., IV, 509 et seq.
[3] Col. Recs., IV, 558 et seq.
[4] App. to Vol. III, of Votes; ibid., 501, 504, 506; Col. Recs., IV, 620, 623; Hockley to T. P., Nov. 1, 1742; Penn Mss., Off. Corresp., III, 241; Remonstrance of Mayor Plumstead and others to Ass., ibid., 289; Allen to T. P., ibid., 263; Logan to T. P., Nov. 20, 1742, P. L. B., IV.

tates of their unbounded malice. These sons of humility expect a submission for all others, and though they talk of peace, it is very far from their hearts and I fear is not to be obtained without licking the dust off their feet." [1]   When it came to the question of trying the offenders, the government even attempted to show that the city courts alone would have jurisdiction and that the cases could not be called before the higher courts of the province.   The assembly also took the matter in hand and after a report from a committee on the remonstrances of the magistrates, resolved that the charter of the city did not exempt its officials from the concurrent jurisdiction of the county court,[2] which would bring the case directly into the line of appeal to the highest courts of the province.   It also declared that the magistrates had neglected their duty and that it was the right of the assembly to inquire respecting riots and to offer advice to the governor touching the manner in which offenders in such cases should be proceeded against so as to protect freemen in their liberties. The minutes of the assembly and the examinations it had taken respecting the riot were ordered printed, " a parcel of *ex parte* affirmations," wrote Allen, " taken when people were in a heat " and characterized by the grossest falsehoods and suppressions of the truth.

Meantime the committee of the council in England, moved by a petition of merchants and others of Pennsylvania concerning the importance and at the same time the defencelessness of that province, and having also considered a petition of the Quakers in which they claimed to have been unjustly attacked, ordered that a special instruction be sent to the governor to put the colony into the best posture of defence that was possible and that he stand constantly on guard against surprise.[3]   All that could be done was for the governor to issue a proclamation requiring the inhabitants to prepare themselves as best they could to repel attack and to commission the best qualified men to levy, muster and train them; the power to grant money for military supplies and expenses of all sorts rested wholly with the assembly.   When, in

---

[1] Thomas to J. P., Nov. 17, 1742, Off. Corresp., III, 245; also *ibid.*, 247, 289.

[2] Col. Recs., IV, 626, 628, 638; Votes, III, 520, 527–530.

[3] Acts P. C. Col., 1720–1745, pp. 709–713; Pa. Arch., I, 633; Col. Recs., IV, 670.

December, 1743, Thomas laid this instruction before the assembly, it expressed thanks to their lordships for their tenderness and care toward these remote parts, but calmly observed that the prospect of continued peace with France was better than it had been and there was reason to hope that the storm would blow over.[1] They then adjourned until May. Since the previous assembly, near the close of its winter session, had voted Thomas £1000 and he in return had assented to six of its bills, relations had improved and the worst seemed to have passed.[2] In the session of May, 1744, further evidence of improved relations was afforded by an additional grant of support to the governor and his assent to an excise law and an act designating trustees of the loan office and providing for the issue of £10,000 in bills of credit.[3] Thomas also acceded to the request of the house that he attend the Indian conference soon to be held at Lancaster.

In June the forecast last made by the Quakers was proved false by the arrival of the declaration of war against the French king and the issue of a proclamation in due form by the governor.[4] The fitting out of privateers at once began and the assembly was called to meet at the close of July. During the sessions which followed, this body maintained the same negative attitude toward military preparation that its predecessors had done. They quietly recognized what was done by others in Pennsylvania or on the offensive or defensive in other colonies, but would make no provision for raising troops or furnishing military supplies. Toward Indian relations, however, they were fairly attentive. When appeals came from Shirley and others for aid to the Louisbourg expedition,[5] the assembly remarked that it had been planned without consulting the colonies at large and hence they could hardly be expected to contribute; the advantage and glory of its success came chiefly or wholly to those who were immediately concerned and the Quakers were content that it should be so. But when, after the capture of Louisbourg, requests came for supplies for its garrison, the assembly appropriated £4000 to be expended by commissioners named in the resolu-

---

[1] Col. Recs., IV, 671–674.
[2] Ibid., 626, 628, 638.
[3] Votes, III, 552; Col. Recs., IV, 687, 688.
[4] Ibid., 689–697.
[5] Ibid., 740, 749, 754 et seq.

tion, and under direction of the governor, for articles of food to be used in the king's service.[1] Thomas from time to time received grants toward his support, though arrears remained unpaid, and he assented to a few rather unimportant bills. In the spring of 1746, however, his arrears were paid in full and several additional bills were signed.[2] He had learned, and it was so understood by the proprietors, that it was useless to contend with the combination which controlled the assembly. Neither was there any prospect that by the working of internal causes it would soon be broken up. The only hope for the present, therefore, was in appeals to the British government. Such a representation from the governor of the defenceless condition of the province was referred to the law officers in England. Their opinion [3] was that the province was obliged to provide for its own defence and that the assembly should pass appropriate laws for the purpose. But, they added, as the assembly was a part of the legislature, its members were the only immediate judges of the methods to be taken for this purpose, and it was not clear how they could be compelled to do more than they should think fit unless forced to act under rules prescribed by an act of parliament. To this the board of trade added nothing and it was referred to the committee of the council. At the lord president's request Paris had given him a history of the question at issue, but business was pressing and the ministry did not care to ask the assistance of parliament.

When the summons came for the colonial contingents toward the expedition of 1746 for the reduction of Canada, the assembly made its usual plea, which in this case was followed by an appropriation of £5000.[4] No general tax had been levied in Pennsylvania for some twenty years and, as the assembly now stated, the fund for contingent charges arose from the interest on the bills and the excise, and during the last year these had fallen off, so that there was a balance against the province, increased by expenditures on the state

---

[1] Col. Recs., IV, 769.

[2] Votes, IV, 34, 35; Col. Recs., V, 35; Thomas to T. P., April 26, 1746. Off. Corresp., IV, 65.

[3] T. P. to Thomas, Mar. 7, 1744/5, P. L. B., II, 118.

[4] Col. Recs., V, 37, 39, 43, 46 *et seq.*; Votes, IV, 39, 40; Penn Mss., Off. Corresp., IV, 67, 69.

house. On account of the recent activities in parliament against colonial paper money, an additional issue of that seemed impracticable. For these reasons the house limited its appropriation to the sum named, but £5000 in new bills were issued, to be redeemed in quotas of £500 per annum from the excise. With much compunction Thomas assented to this, for the assembly was demanding issues of £20,000 to £30,000 and there were reports that in other colonies there would be large emissions notwithstanding instructions. " Better to make this small stretch than that you should not have the reputation of doing something." Though the money granted was not deemed sufficient for more than three companies, the governor ventured to raise four. He was therefore obliged to advance money himself, which he thought a hardship as he received no salary from the crown and the proprietors had no consideration for his additional fatigue or expense. " I am taught," he wrote, " to give some check to my public spirit." As the levies had to remain in Albany over winter, the governor was forced to make further advances, amounting to several hundred pounds.[1] The usual delays and general muddle arose over payments and reimbursements for these expenditures, the soldiers and governor being the chief sufferers. During these years also the management of Indian affairs, including attendance on conferences, greatly increased the duties of the governor. As the result of it all, though the province was perfectly tranquil and Thomas was greatly respected and now the relations between him and the assembly were friendly; his health became impaired and he laid down his office, returning to England in the summer of 1747. His retirement was much regretted by the proprietors. John Penn had recently died. Thomas Penn, though considering the advisability of assuming the governorship, was not yet ready to return to Pennsylvania and undertake it. He desired the aged Logan to serve again as president of the council, but this Logan absolutely declined to do. Therefore a period of government by the council followed, lasting nearly a year and a half, with Anthony Palmer as its president, until the arrival of James Hamilton as lieutenant governor, in November, 1748. In England,

[1] Votes, IV, 49, 50, 52; Col. Recs., V, 56, 57, 58.

meantime, the ex-governor and Thomas Penn quarreled over the refusal of the latter to cancel the bond by which Thomas had bound himself for payments to the proprietor and to return a part of the money which he had paid. Thomas seized the opportunity to tell the proprietor by letter [1] that his services to him in affairs of the land office alone, involving the receipt of applications and determining of differences, often by hearing counsel, was worth £500 a year. He had also secured more in quit rents than his predecessor had been able to collect, and had advanced money for the support of the king's troops. As the result of a laborious and successful administration he had undermined his health and received no financial gain. With this sordid incident terminated the custom of bargaining between proprietors and their governors in Pennsylvania.

Of late the council had played an insignificant part in the affairs of the province. Seats in that body were filled largely by old men or those of inferior ability and attendance at meetings was small. In 1741 Thomas had expressed a very low opinion [2] of its importance and of the way in which it was regarded in the province. Since it was not a part of the legislature and was treated with such contempt by the assembly, men of ability were not willing to accept seats in it. Shortly before the close of his administration Thomas therefore strengthened it by the addition of three new members, Turner, Hopkinson and Growdon. As the duties of the executive were now to fall wholly upon the council, Thomas Penn who, in disgust at the attitude of the assembly toward defence, had already put aside everything but the name of Quaker, relied chiefly upon the Anglican, Richard Peters, for the management of affairs.[3] Palmer was not regarded as a desirable head of the government, but as he could act only with the consent of four of the council it was felt that nothing improper would be done. Palmer was the only councillor to whom authority over the granting of land was given, but he

[1] Penn Mss., Off. Corresp., IV, 111, 117, 121, 135; Shepherd, 208.

[2] Thomas to J. Penn, July 14, 1741, Off. Corresp., III, 185; IV, 77; Col. Recs., V, 65. In 1739 Logan wrote that the board then was the weakest by much he had ever known it. Logan L. B., IV.

[3] See T. P. to Peters, Mar. 5, 1746/7, P. L. B., II, 183, and the correspondence between the two during the months that followed.

could not sign any patent which was not drawn by Peters, the secretary of the proprietors. Peters also could be called to account only by the proprietors, and it was hoped that the president would depend largely on him for advice.

During the months when the council was in control, the province was more agitated over the subject of defence than at any earlier period of the war. This was due to the activity of hostile privateers off the coast and about the entrance to Delaware Bay. No guardship had been stationed there, though the dispatch of one had been requested. The demand was now pressed through the proprietor more urgently and finally the "Otter" was sent. Another more threatening phase of hostile activity was the coming of vessels up the bay under flags of truce.[1] In July, 1747, a small body of the enemy also landed and plundered a few houses and farms near Lewes. Much uneasiness was caused in Philadelphia by these events and people began to imagine that the enemy was already before their doors. As time passed, reports kept circulating that an expedition from Havana might be expected to attack the coast. The council was called and with them conferred Kinsey, the speaker, and a few other members of the assembly. As the majority of the council were not Quakers, it was proposed to fit out a vessel. Kinsey would not bind the assembly to provide for the cost of this, but thought that the president and council would not suffer for what they might do for the good of the province.

The assembly, therefore, was called and met in August. Before it were laid not only the perils and insults down the bay, but the desirability, as it had been urged in letters from Shirley and Clinton, of encouraging the Indians in the north, perhaps by means of a joint conference at Albany. Weiser had been sent to sound the Indians on the subject and those living on Lake Erie wished to be taken into friendship.[2] The conclusion was that for the security of his majesty's dominions and protection against invasion some measures should be taken for the defence of the province. The assembly showed that its attitude had not been changed by referring at the beginning of its reply to a law of the 10th of Anne which took from them, in the absence of a governor, the

---

[1] Col. Recs., V, 80, 87, 90 et seq.   [2] Ibid., 96–98.

power of legislation.[1] As to the situation in the north, they were convinced that offensive operations against Canada had been laid aside and therefore that no special harm was to bq expected from the Indians. They refused also to take seriously the threats made against the city of Philadelphia and considered it impossible to prevent such " accidents " as the late raid in the Lower Counties, while such pointed references to the defenceless condition of the province seemed rather to increase the danger. Their opinions as formerly expressed were reaffirmed and attention was called to the burden of expense which would have been imposed on the province had those applications for money been complied with. The temper of the assembly as shown in a later session in October was even more pacific.[2] A largely signed petition from inhabitants of Philadelphia urging the assembly to put the province into a state of defence proved ineffective.

At this juncture the non-Quaker part of the population, especially in the more exposed parts of Pennsylvania, began to form an association and arm for defence.[3] A leader in this movement was Benjamin Franklin. For years he had been a growing influence in the business and social life of Philadelphia, as printer, editor and writer, as well as a genial promoter of clubs, literary and learned societies, and beneficent social and scientific activities of every conceivable sort. To his hospitable mind nothing that was human was foreign. Born in New England, but removed in early manhood to Pennsylvania, he shared in the qualities of both. He was a blend of the fighting qualities of the New Englander with the persistence and quiet dignity and poise of the Quaker. The practical shrewdness, as well as what was most available and useful in the moral ideals of the two sections, Franklin inherited or mastered to the full. Hence came his remarkable diplomatic skill, which was shown during many years on the narrow stage of business and politics in Pennsylvania before there was occasion for its exhibition in Europe. Since 1736 he had been clerk of the assembly. This, as well as his earlier activities as a printer, brought him into connection with the group of Quaker leaders and his keen powers of observation were active in arriving at an estimate of the

---

[1] *Ibid.*, 101–104.   [2] *Ibid.*, 126.   [3] *Ibid.*, 158, 161.

course they pursued in disputes with Thomas. Upon the money question Franklin was with them. But upon the subject of defence he was their most dangerous opponent. He saw their frequent embarrassment when applications for grants were made to them from the crown, caused by their unwillingness to offend the British government on the one side and the body of the Quakers on the other.

Soon after the war had been greatly increased in seriousness by the entrance of the French into it, Franklin published his " Plain Truth or Serious Considerations " on the current state of Philadelphia and Pennsylvania.[1] Writing as a tradesman he appealed to " the middling people," who found themselves in danger of invasion and ruin, on the one hand through the mistaken religious principles and love of power of the ruling party and on the other through the envy and hatred with which the Quakers were viewed by the rich, who would not contribute toward defence because thereby they would be protecting the property and trade of that hated sect. Starting from the city and extending his view to the province and the surrounding colonies, considering also the perils from the Indians as well as those from Europe, Franklin, in language more fervent than he was wont to use, painted the horrors of armed invasion and told his fellow citizens that in a voluntary association lay their only safety. He appealed to the fighting qualities of the English as recently shown in New England after their removal for a hundred years from England, and to the even greater spirit shown by the Scotch Irish at Londonderry and Enniskillen. Neither did he omit " the brave and steady Germans," numbers of whom had actually borne arms under their respective princes. All that was needed was united action, discipline and a few cannon.

The pamphlet circulated widely and was eagerly read. Alarmist reports, alleged to come from some who had been prisoners on enemy privateers, were circulated to the effect that in the spring of 1748 a concerted attack would be made on the city by these craft. Some families actually prepared to remove. It was at about this time that a public meeting was held, at which Franklin spoke and circulated copies of

[1] Sparks, Franklin, III.

an association. About 1200 signatures were at once obtained
and these were increased to 10,000 when the agreement was
circulated through the province.[1] These men formed themselves into companies and regiments, chose their own officers,
while the women made and decorated silk colors which they
distributed to the companies. Franklin's assistance was welcomed by the council and at his suggestion — a reminiscence
of New England — the first fast ever held in Pennsylvania
was proclaimed. The Quakers, on the other hand, did not
break with him for, as he had observed, they were not so
averse to measures of defence provided others than themselves
undertook them and bore the responsibility.

It was proposed to erect one or more batteries on the river
and to petition the proprietors for a supply of cannon and
small arms. The merchants of Philadelphia also petitioned
the admiralty for a man-of-war. For immediate purposes,
however, cannon from Cape Breton were sought and some
were finally borrowed, as the result of a visit of Franklin
and others, from Governor Clinton at New York. An account
of these defensive measures was sent to the proprietors and
their favorable reception of various addresses sent to them
was bespoken. A lottery was started to raise £7000. On
April 12 a city regiment of associators, duly armed, was reviewed by the president and council and it was hoped that
the public [2] would now feel somewhat reassured. Peters
wrote to Penn that the large and well organized body of
associators redounded to the proprietary interest and made it
possible to overcome or escape from Quaker control. But
Penn, writing from England,[3] expressed the fear that "Plain
Truth" had done much mischief by raising a dangerous
spirit among the people. The people of America were too
ready to act in defiance of government without associating
themselves for that purpose. They might at least have
asked the president and council to appoint their officers, but
to establish a military commonwealth was little less than
treason. The president and council were repeatedly re-

[1] See Franklin's Autobiography.

[2] Col. Recs., V, 161, 174, 223; Off. Corresp., IV, 93, Peters to T. P., Mar. 25,
1747/8, May 11, 1748. A battery was built at Wicoco for 20 or 24 guns; N. Y.
Col. Docs., VI, 531.

[3] P. L. B., II, 223, 225, 227.

proved for allowing military authority to be derived from any but themselves. Later, when the danger, if there had been any, had been removed by the certainty of a speedy peace, Penn gave Peters his opinion of Franklin. The latter's statement in " Plain Truth " that obedience to governors is no more due than protection to the people, Penn declared, was not fit to be in the hands of the wild, unthinking multitude. Franklin he pronounced a " dangerous man," " a very uneasy spirit," and he should be glad if he inhabited any other country. " But as he is a sort of tribune of the people he must be treated with regard." [1] But Peters assured the proprietor that the associators acted only under orders from the president and council, and their choice of officers was only a recommendation, their commissions being revocable at any time by the board. Allen had informed Peters that they all were hearty friends of the proprietors, and they certainly behaved with remarkable dutifulness.

The president and council also wrote to the proprietors that it was a mistake to think that the associators acted independently of the government, for the tenor of the officers' commissions showed this to be false. The superior officers received their orders from the board and passed them on to those of inferior rank. The military council had no power to decide upon courses of action, but was only a bond of union for the different regiments, to draft such regulations as were usually embodied in military laws, such as times and places of training, spreading of alarms, the rendezvous of regiments and the like, these not to be operative without the sanction of the president or governor and council. Military orders in action were expected only from the governor as commander-in-chief. After receiving such reports as these Thomas Penn expressed approval of the association as a necessity and was pleased that it had been so careful to avoid even the appearance of illegality.[2] He confessed that in such a time he should have been an associator, as he actually was in England, but there an act of parliament had been passed to indemnify the associators. Under the charter measures of

---

[1] P. L. B., II, 231, T. P. to Peters, June 9, 1748; Shepherd, 222, 529. Off. Corr., IV, 95, Peters to T. P., June 13, 1748; Col. Recs., V, 319.

[2] P. L. B., II, 242, T. P. to Peters, Aug. 31, 1748.

defence could not be undertaken except by order of the executive. Penn expressed the hope that before another war something effective might be done. But a further exchange of amenities between the president and council,[1] in which they firmly adhered to their previous opinions and reproached one another for their action concerning the fitting out of a colony sloop, afforded little hope that such would be the case. The view which the assembly now expressed was that efforts to make the colonies defensible without large assistance from England were futile. Therefore, the more the colonies attempted to do unaided, the more hopeless their condition became. England must be convinced that she would have to shoulder the chief burden. Therefore, by withholding the sum needed for an armed vessel they did not intend to prove that nothing should be done, but to show that the province had reason to expect greater assistance and that otherwise all that could be done would be insufficient. This statement, of course, is to be taken as a specimen of finesse on the part of the Quaker politicians. But, in view of the situation in the colonies as a whole and of the course of events in the wars down to that time, this must be taken also as an unusually truthful statement. Upon the subject of militarism and patriotism, as exhibited at that time in the colonies, the Quakers were the realists and the New Englanders, with Shirley at their head, were the idealists. The static and the dynamic were well illustrated in their respective attitudes. After the election in October, 1748, Peters wrote to the proprietors that the former members had been returned to the assembly without opposition and were now crowing over their opponents unmercifully. Peace had come without any of the dire incidents of war which Franklin and the associators had foretold as probable, and now the Quakers were more firmly intrenched in power than ever and apparently could not be removed unless they quarreled with one another.[2]

In the interest of harmony it is probable that no better selection could have been made for the office of governor than James Hamilton. He was the son of Andrew Hamilton, the famous lawyer who, though not a Quaker, so won the

---

[1] Col. Recs., V, 277, 333, 339, 341, June and September, 1748.
[2] Peters to Proprietors, Oct. 20, 1748, Off. Corresp., IV, 158.

respect of that body as to become speaker of the assembly while, from the hands of the executive, he received numerous prominent offices. The son had already been mayor of Philadelphia and later had absented himself for some years in Europe. Like his father, he was a genuine Pennsylvanian, fitted to sympathize with what was best in the Quaker spirit and policy. He entered upon office, too, just after the close of the war, when for a few years at least the question upon which the issue between a governor and the assembly least admitted of compromise could not be raised. At the request of the proprietors the council was strengthened by the addition of Richard Peters, he also being permitted, as was the case in Logan's time, to retain the office of secretary.[1] Though the assembly in the first sessions after Hamilton's arrival, among a number of bills of local interest only, submitted one for the addition of £20,000 to the bills of credit then current, the need was not pressing and the governor felt justified in reserving this for further consideration.[2] With the exception of £5000, provision for which was made in a law designating a new board of trustees for the loan office, no more bills were made current until the beginning of the next war.[3] Meantime the Penns and Baltimore by a strong representation, supported by Partridge and by some London merchants, convinced the leading members of the committee of parliament that the issue of some currency as legal tender must be permitted, and the houses, because of lack of information, finally deferred action till the next session.

But in Pennsylvania the assembly had long since attained even more than the usual degree of ascendency, and in maintaining its claims it had the support of the great majority of the inhabitants of the province. This was shown in its stubborn opposition to the existence of a chancery court, or any other tribunal, which rested on any but statutory authority. This and other characteristics of its attitude appeared in 1750 in a bill relating to the office of register general and affecting the probate of wills. Another bill regulating the watch of the city of Philadelphia gave offence to the execu-

[1] T. P. to Hamilton, Oct. 15, 1748, P. L. B., II, 251.
[2] Col. Recs., V, 370, 374.
[3] Stats. at Large, V, 58; T. P. to Hamilton, June 6, 1749, P. L. B., II, 267, 269; Col. Recs., V, 417.

tive because it ignored the existing magistrates and placed
the watch under the control of elected wardens. This bill
Hamilton accepted, though much against his will and that
of the council. The same issue came up in a bill for building
work-houses in the counties of Lancaster, York and Cumberland, and in this case also the executive was forced to yield.[1]
In the letters which were exchanged between the governor,
Peters and Thomas Penn appear the gloomy views which
these measures inspired in the minds of all supporters of the
proprietary interests. The government, wrote Peters, is weak
and a want of decency is shown where proprietary rights or
interests are mentioned. The governor had no man independent of the people to advise him on questions of law and
felt the lack keenly. It was inconceivable, wrote Hamilton,
what an inveterate dislike the people had toward appointive
magistrates, so that many whom he had commissioned refused to qualify lest they might lose their popularity. So
strongly impressed was Hamilton with the difficulties of his
position that he was tempted to resign.[2] It seemed necessary
that the proprietors should come over and assume the government, while Thomas Penn deplored the fact that opposition
should be so general among the people to a government that
could do them no harm.

Now that the war was ended, attention could be given to
internal conditions as affected by the large immigration which
had been steadily proceeding and the expansion of settlement
which was its immediate result. In response to petitions
which for some time had been before the assembly, several
new counties to the westward were now created. York county
was formed from that part of Lancaster which lay west of
the Susquehanna river and southeast of South Mountain and
extending to the limits of the province.[3] A similar region
lying north and west of York was formed into Cumberland
county and the boundary between the two was fixed. These
counties were erected in the session of 1749/50. Two years

[1] Stats. at Large, V, 33, 115.

[2] Peters to Proprietors, Jan. 30, 1750/1, Off. Corresp., V, 121, 123; Feb. 4,
1750/1, *ibid.*, 125. Hamilton to T. P., Feb. 22, 1750/1, *ibid.*, 127; T. P. to
Hamilton, March 30, 1751, P. L. B., III, 66; T. P. to Peters, March 31, 1751,
ibid., III, 67.

[3] *Ibid.*, 71, 88, 105.

later a part of the counties of Philadelphia, Chester and Lancaster,[1] lying to the west and northwest, was formed into Berks county and the town of Reading was settled. In this business Peters, the secretary to the proprietors, was much occupied, for lots had to be granted in the new towns that were being settled as well as in the country at large, and the rights of the proprietors secured. By repeated purchases Indian rights were eliminated farther and farther westward. The territory steadily filled with immigrants, squatters' claims forming always a difficult question as they affected both relations with the Indians and the rights of the proprietors.

Peters was apprehensive of the growing German influence, writing that they carried elections in all the counties except Chester. He thought it a pity that there was not a law incapacitating any persons from sitting in the assembly who could not speak English and read it well enough to understand the laws and proceedings in the courts. As to Moravians, he was opposed to permitting their settling near the frontier because they were exempt by act of parliament from bearing arms.[2] The adoption of measures to check immigration was discussed, but the proprietors, who were aware of its great importance to the empire and of the value which the British government set upon the additions thus made to the labor power of the province from the continent of Europe, could not be brought to favor such a policy.[3] A solution for the difficulty which bore a more distinctly modern aspect than any of the others was the simple gerrymander proposed by Thomas Grocene to Thomas Penn. He said that if they would divide the large counties of Philadelphia and Bucks, the former by a line extending sixteen or eighteen miles south of Reading and the latter by a line extending about the same distance south of the Forks, in the new counties thus made would be included nearly all the Germans in the eastern part of the province. Allowing two members to a county and

[1] *Ibid.*, 133; Penn Mss., Off. Corresp., IV, 193, 197, 205, 219; Pa. Arch., II, T. P. to Peters, Aug. 2, 1749; Penn. Mss., L. Counties, 35; Peters to Proprietors, Sept. 11, 1749, Off. Corresp., IV, 237; T. P. to Peters, Oct. 9, 1749, P. L. B., II, 283.

[2] Off. Corresp., IV, 195, 245.

[3] P. L. B., II, 313, T. P. to Peters, May 30, 1750.

with Lancaster, York and two new western counties returning only Germans, they would number only ten in an assembly of thirty-eight. Governor Hamilton and the proprietor
also approved of this plan, but its execution was not attempted.[1]

The advance of settlement westward not only made the
running of the Maryland line throughout its entire length
a necessity within a few years after the suit in chancery had
been decided, but occasioned a controversy with Virginia
which was to be of long continuance respecting the extreme
western bounds of Pennsylvania and their possible infraction
of the claims of Virginia in the region of the upper Ohio. In
July, 1748, Peters wrote to Thomas Penn,[2] that " that vile
fellow Cressap had proposed a scheme to Colonel Lee and
other great men in Virginia to make trading houses at
Alleghenny " and so open traffic with the Indians of that
region. Peters believed they had already gone to make settlements there, and that they would not hesitate to settle lands
which might be within the limits of Pennsylvania and so
create new squabbles. He had also been told that Colonel
Lee, " who has a plotting head," had sent a scheme to the
ministry to build forts on some of the waters of the Ohio,
" as if thereby all the country might be secured to His
Majesty up to the Mississippi." He was also advised that
Lord Fairfax and his friends were hurrying an agent with
goods to the Ohio and might have joined with the council
of Virginia in a representation to the crown. Penn was
advised by his secretary to inquire at the council board or
board of trade respecting these matters. Penn found on inquiry that the Ohio Company had procured a grant between
the forks of the Ohio, which he believed lay to " the southward of Pennsylvania." But if it should prove otherwise
he would seek to have it recalled. A year later Peters wrote[3]
that he believed the greatest part of the 500,000 acres of this
grant lay within Pennsylvania, and made suggestions concerning the running of the line so as to correct this. The

[1] G. to T. P., Nov. 6, 1750, Off. Corr., V, 83; T. P. to Hamilton, Feb. 25,
1750/1, P. L. B., III, 57.

[2] Off. Corr., IV, 143.

[3] T. P. to Peters, Aug. 2, 1749; Peters to Proprs., July 5, 1749, Off. Corr.,
IV, 219.

Indians, he was sure, would not sell that part of the country to the Virginians and, if they attempted to settle there, he thought there would be an Indian war.   In November, 1749,[1] the council of Virginia wrote to Hamilton respecting the Ohio purchase and complained that traders from Pennsylvania were misrepresenting their intentions and prejudicing the Indians against them; they therefore had found it necessary to apply to the king to have the line run.   Hamilton favored this and suggested that it be done by a joint commission. But Penn thought he was proceeding too hastily and should wait for an initiation of this measure from England.   Mr. Hanbury, also, of the Ohio Company thought that, to avoid irritating the Indians, the building of a fort in the Ohio country should be deferred till they consented, as they might think the two provinces intended to take their country and share it between them.[2]   Thus the discussion of this issue was begun and in its early stages went on while the Maryland-Pennsylvania boundary was being settled.

The encroachments of British settlers on Indian lands from the east and the advance of the French from the north caused an increasing ferment among the natives.   This made the subject of Indian relations one of increasing importance.   In order to quiet the complaints of the Six Nations, a large purchase or repurchase was made by the proprietors in 1749 of land east of the Susquehanna river and north of the Kittochtinny Hills.[3]   This was a part of their policy of extinguishing all Indian claims east of the Susquehanna and of opening the country for settlement.   But, as we have seen, settlers were pushing west of the Susquehanna and squatting on Indian lands.   The creation of the new counties in that region was a recognition of that fact.   But Indian claims had not by any means been fully extinguished in that region, and, now that the war was over, the Six Nations were complaining of that fact with renewed emphasis.   In the summer of 1749 two delegations of their chiefs visited Philadelphia and spoke with great plainness about these encroachments.[4]   The offenders were largely Scotch Irish, who were pushing up the

---

[1] Col. Recs., V, 422, 423, 424.
[2] T. P. to Hamilton, May 1, 1750, P. L. B., II.
[3] Shepherd, 103.
[4] Col. Recs., V, 388–403.

Juniata and into the valleys just north of the Maryland boundary. A proclamation was issued by the governor warning any who had settled west of the Blue Hills to remove with their families and effects on penalty of eviction by the magistrates. Conrad Weiser and George Croghan, as usual, were intimately connected with affairs along the frontier, and Weiser seemed too thrifty in the matter of securing land for himself and laying the foundation of a fortune for his family to suit the taste of the proprietors. But his influence over the Indians was too great and his services too valuable to be dispensed with at this time of crisis.[1] In 1750 Peters and Weiser accordingly were sent into the western country to check the inroads of the squatters, and with the aid of the magistrates of the new counties several families were induced to retire or were dispossessed and their cabins burned.[2] But this was only a palliative; the movement continued and doubtless was not hindered, in the minds of those who knew of it, by the view which Weiser expressed of the richness of the country beyond the Alleghanies.

These were the elements of the situation along the frontier, as viewed from the standpoint of Pennsylvania, at the beginning of the second half of the century. The Indians were being squeezed into narrower limits by the advance of the English and French. Already a tendency had been observed of Pennsylvania Indians to move further westward. This meant that they would escape from English control if they did not fall under that of the French. Hamilton expected that the western Indians would soon be as numerous and powerful as the Six Nations and would no longer be content to take the law from them. Over the western cantons of the Six Nations French influence seemed predominant. The friendship of the Shawnees toward the English was doubtful. In view of these probabilities, strengthened by the report of Kalm, the Swedish traveller, Peters concluded that the present method of treating with the Indians, giving them presents and listening to professions of their friendship, was of little avail. Better openly insist, he thought, that the

[1] Peters to Proprietors, Feb. 16, 1749/50, Off. Corr., IV, 189; Peters to T. P., Sept. 28, 1750; Off. Corr., V, 59, Hamilton to T. P., *ibid.*, 27.
[2] Col. Recs., V, 440–449, 454; Watson, Life of Weiser, 198 *et seq.*

friendly tribes join in opposing the measures of the French.[1] Alarming letters from Clinton and Johnson in New York increased the fear that the French would draw the Indians generally away from alliance with the English. But when Hamilton suggested this to the assembly,[2] it expressed the opinion that New York was more directly concerned in the growth of French influence, while the large gains which the proprietors were making from western lands made it proper that they should contribute more liberally toward the expense of negotiations with the Indians. Under the pressure of necessity the proprietors did expend a little more on the frontier, but were pleading that the Penn family was able to lay by only a small annual surplus. In the council Peters was the only member who could be relied on to give valuable and weighty advice to the governor in a crisis of this nature. As to securing the coöperation of neighboring provinces, the jealousy of Governor Ogle, growing out of the heated boundary controversy with Maryland, and the difficulties which were arising with Virginia did not make the prospect hopeful.

[1] Peters to Proprietors, Oct. 15, 1750, Off. Corr., V, 73; Hamilton to T. P., Oct. 13, 1750, *ibid.*, 69.
[2] Col. Recs., V, 484, 486.

CHAPTER VII

THE period indicated by the title of this chapter covers more than twenty-five years — from 1722 to 1748. At first sight it would seem scarcely possible to give adequate treatment in a single chapter to the history for so long a time of a province so important as Virginia. The number and variety of events in most other colonies have necessitated the treatment of them under much briefer subdivisions of time. But Virginia, like Connecticut, was a land of steady habits, and in the case of both colonies this was largely due to their possession of an homogeneous people with a normal and well-balanced political and social organization. Though their political and social systems differed as widely as any which appeared among the colonies, they were in both cases the result of natural and steady development from the first and fitted well the spirit of the people. No enemy of consequence had yet crossed the border of either of them, and their financial systems were so ordered as to work smoothly. In Connecticut the last-mentioned advantage was secured by the complete control which was held by the general court over appropriations, and in Virginia it was due chiefly to the payment of the governor's salary from the quit rents and the revenue from the export of tobacco, a procedure which kept the question of his support out of politics. The last few years of Spotswood's administration also had passed in quiet, the governor having carried his main point with the council and later being occupied with his Indian policy and plans for public improvement in the upper districts of the province.

Concerning the reasons for the sudden close of Spotswood's administration and the appointment of Hugh Drysdale as his successor, the sources are even more than usually silent. No complaints or requests to be relieved or to return appear on either side or from any quarter. No clear reason appears for such an event at the time when it occurred, for everything was working smoothly, especially when viewed from the standpoint of the home government, and Spotswood, after a prolonged visit to England, returned in 1729 to Virginia, where he spent the rest of his days superintending his estates and performing the duties of his office as deputy postmaster general of America. But the change inaugurated, or rather made permanent, an era of good feeling which was to continue until near the outbreak of the last colonial war. Drysdale and Gooch, the former during a rather brief administration (1722–1726), and the latter during one of the longest in colonial annals (1727–1749), fell in completely with Virginia conditions and tendencies and thus insured internal peace. This meant that the leadership of the prominent Virginia families, as represented in local government, council and assembly, a leadership which had been challenged by Spotswood and in an even less effective fashion by a few earlier governors, now continued unopposed. Drysdale and Gooch — conspicuously the latter — were men of mild speech and manners, who said little about the prerogative and had no pet schemes of policy to advocate which were likely to run counter to the customs or prejudices of Virginians. And yet they were faithful officials and satisfied all reasonable requirements, whether of the home government or of the province. Gooch in particular was like Shirley of Massachusetts, though without Shirley's early experience in colonial life and his tireless zeal in the invention and promotion of plans for the advancement of colonial interests. While many of the other colonies were being disturbed by factional or sectional strife, the quiet of Virginia was scarcely disturbed except by fear of slave insurrections. It was a period of slow expansion westward to the mountains, but of slight internal change. Of Indian troubles there was none of consequence and of European wars Virginia felt only remote effects. The period in hand coincided with the administration of Robert Walpole in England and that implied a minimum of interference with colonial development except along commercial lines. The early correspondence of Gooch with Newcastle would indicate that his appointment was due to that minister and that they were on somewhat familiar terms.[1]

A minor proposal which had been favorably discussed for some years in both Maryland and Virginia was rejected at the very beginning of Drysdale's administration. This was that a lighthouse should be built at Cape Henry. Both Spotswood and the board of trade had favored the project, and its utility for all mariners on the coast no man could deny. But as the duties levied for its support would chiefly come from British merchants, they opposed it, and therefore the board wrote Drysdale that if an act was passed for the purpose he should have a suspending clause introduced on the familiar ground that it affected British trade.[2] An act on the subject was passed in Virginia in 1727, but the structure seems not to have been erected, presumably because the opposition of the merchants prevented the crown from giving its consent. Gooch finally wrote in 1730 that he resigned himself to the decision upon the question of the lighthouse, but kept his opinion of its utility.

Among the subjects which were inherited from the previous administration was the disallowance of an act of 1720[3] for the better discovery and payment of quit rents. A long argument against the measure was submitted by Walpole, the auditor general, his chief objection being to the provision which allowed payment to be made in current money instead of sterling. The option given in the act was between tobacco and current money,[4] and as the latter fluctuated considerably in value, it was correctly inferred that the planters would always pay in the cheaper medium and the crown would therefore in all cases be the loser. No effort was made by the assembly to pass another act on this subject and quit rents continued to be paid in tobacco. The analogy between the position of the crown on this occasion and that of the Virginia clergy in the famous parsons' case of a later day

[1] C. O. 5/1337, Va., Letters from Governors to Secretaries of State.

[2] C. O. 5/1365, B. T. E. B., Va., June 19, 1723; Hening, IV, 182; C. O. 5/1320, B. T. O. P., Feb. 15, 1727/8; Dec., 1728; Nov. 26, 1729; Journal of the Board, 1727/8.

[3] Hening, IV, 79; C. O. 5/1319, O. P. Va., June 12 and Aug. 27, 1723.

[4] This of course was a common alternative in the tobacco colonies. Another instance of it may be found in the law of 1732 imposing a duty on slaves: Hening, IV, 318.

is obvious. We also learn from another source [1] that the finance officers of the crown were finding a difficulty in disposing of tobacco received in payment of quit rents which was analogous to the perplexities of the parsons in selling the weed in which their salaries were paid. The quit-rent tobacco had usually been sold during the session of the general court in April, but by that time the ships had received their lading or sailed, and by a combination of the few purchasers who attended at the sales the price was lowered, to the detriment of his majesty's revenue. Whether the quality of that paid to the king was equal to the average we are not told. But it was ordered that sales by auction and at any time, as had previously been the practice, be revived.

The close connection between defence, finance and current trade policy is well illustrated by the reactions which were occasioned by the passage of the act of 1723 imposing a duty on the importation of liquors and slaves. The motive behind this arose from the need of arming the militia as a protection against the Indians and against what was coming to be the more dreaded peril of slave insurrections. We have now reached the time when the importation of negroes had become large and the interests of the Royal African Company, combined with the demands of mercantilism as connected with the production of colonial staples, imposed negro slavery on a large scale upon the colonies south of Pennsylvania. Planters and New England skippers, of course, shared in the enterprise, for almost all who were concerned viewed the slave traffic in those days simply as a good business. Tobacco and slaves were intimately connected and both had most direct fiscal implications for the colonies which produced the tropical or semi-tropical staples. A duty similar to this one had been imposed during the years 1710 to 1718 and it had then met with no special opposition. It offered a ready source of relief when the poll tax threatened to reach too high a rate, while a suspending clause was introduced to bring it within the terms of the royal instruction concerning laws affecting British trade.

But since the passage of the earlier law the importation of negroes had increased and the interest of the Royal African

[1] C. O. 5/1418; Ex. C. of Va., Dec. 11, 1723.

Company in opposition to such laws had grown stronger. Its views also were shared in general by British merchants who were engaged in colonial trade. The mercantilist views on the subject were well expressed by Fane, the special counsel of the board of trade, in his report on the act. He declared that what Virginia really needed was a large and constant supply of negroes at the easiest rates, and that the dearer and scarcer negroes were the less would be the quantity of tobacco produced and the smaller the revenue of the crown from Virginia. He even went so far as to state that, since the negroes were bought in Africa in exchange for British manufactures, the passage of this measure was equivalent to laying a duty on British goods, and was inconsistent with the dependence of Virginia on Great Britain. Of course the measure was disallowed. But the fiscal motive in Virginia continued strong and in 1732, by passing a law which stated that the duty should be paid by the buyer instead of the importer, they secured a measure which was allowed to stand.[1] As the demand was strong and slaves were seldom sold on credit, but for ready money or bills of exchange, it was believed that the buyer would not be able to force the importer to share the duty with him, and from later statements by Governor Gooch one would infer that in the main this was the case.[2] The governor then wrote that he had never heard it pretended that the traders in slaves had not cleared as much by their cargoes since, as for several years before, the buyer was made liable to the duty. Motives for buying slaves were imperative and buyers could not expect to beat down the price because a duty had been imposed upon them. But another reason for the continued prosperity of all classes under the law, to which Gooch also had to confess, arose from the fact that the duty was so poorly collected. It failed by far to bring in the sum expected from it.

At the time when the above-mentioned policy was under consideration, a step forward was taken in the regulation of the production of tobacco itself in Virginia. Various meas-

[1] Hening, IV, 118, 182; C. O. 5/1319, O. P. Va., June 29, 1723; C. O. 5/1365; E. B. Va., Jan. 29, 1723/4; May 19, 1724; Cal. Va. State Papers, I, 206; C. O. 5/1366, May 23, 1729; Journal of Board, May 12, 1726; C. O. 5/1321, O. P. Va., Dec. 10, 1728.

[2] C. O. 5/1325; O. P. Va., Aug. 29, 1740.

ures had been passed in previous years for the improvement
of the crop, as acts against false packing or the tending of
seconds, and for the appointment of inspectors, and the like.
But these had not proved effective to prevent the attempt to
raise tobaco on poor land or under such conditions that an
inferior quality was produced, as well as an excessive quantity.   Much of this trash was sent to England and actually
paid duty there, though afterward it had to be burned.[1]   In
order, if possible, to prevent this abuse and to check the fall
of the price of Virginia tobacco, in 1723 and again in 1727/8,
in each case for a term of three years, a restriction was laid
upon the number of plants which any person could cultivate.
This necessitated inspectors, lists of tithables, reports and
other elaborate administrative regulations.   But as the number
of plants which any tithable or laborer could tend was fixed
high — at three, six and ten thousand — the measure could
not have been intended greatly to reduce the crop, though it
did provide for the destruction in Virginia of the poorest
quality of tobacco.[2]   But in their efforts to insure the quality
of the staple and prevent its price from falling lower, a strin-
gent inspection law was passed in 1730.[3]   This provided
that all tobacco should be brought to public warehouses and
inspected, that of good quality stamped and packed in hogsheads of a prescribed size and the poor burned.   The commissioners objected against this measure because of the cost
entailed by inspection and because it would exclude all the
poorer quality from the market, where it sold well because
of its cheapness.   The board of trade called attention to an
attempt less than twenty years before to enforce a similar
policy but it had not kept the trash from reaching the market.
The present act was allowed to stand on probation because
of the earnest letters of Gooch in its support.   But the Virginians soon found the restriction of the number of plants to
be " inconvenient " and the act was repealed.   The governor
and general assembly then limited themselves to a series of
measures for the regulation of the tobacco culture, this being

---

[1] C. O. 5/1412; Va. Ex. C. Min., June 20, 1723.

[2] Va. Mag. of Hist., XX, 158–178.   The date of the second act is wrong in
this publication.

[3] Hening, IV, 247; C. O. 5/1366; E. B. Va., May 19 and 27, 1731.

in accordance with a plan which Gooch had already sent to England for approval. The perfecting of these occupied much of its attention until 1742,[1] when they were brought together into a comprehensive statute upon which, with favorable results, was based the policy of the province for years to come. This policy consisted in the building of a large number of warehouses at convenient places, to which the entire product must be brought for inspection. The inspectors were annually appointed by the governor and council on the recommendation of the county magistrates, and were laid under strict obligations to exclude and destroy all poor tobacco and see that only that of good quality was sent to market. The shipping of tobacco in bulk was rigidly prohibited and the dimensions and content of the hogsheads to be used were specified in their final form. In return for the deposit of tobacco at warehouses in discharge of private or public debts or contracts, notes or receipts under the hands of the inspectors were issued, which had a limited circulation within the respective counties where they were issued. Successive enactments show that inspectors were often proved unfit for their tasks and therefore that the detailed administrative provisions of the acts were to the usual extent ineffective. But it was under this system that the quality and amount of the tobacco crop of Virginia was thenceforth guaranteed. It helped to confirm the reputation of that province for producing better tobacco than its rivals on the north and the south.

Among the questions which occupied the attention of the Virginia government at this time none was more important than the settlement of Brunswick and Spotsylvania, the two new frontier counties, and the territorial arrangements which were made in connection therewith. Spotswood, as we know, was deeply interested in this enterprise and from it arose the last controversy in which he was involved in Virginia. Upon representation of the board of trade, occasioned by an address from the Virginia assembly, the lords justices, in August, 1723, granted for seven years remission of quit rents to purchasers

---

[1] C. O. 5/1337, Gooch to Newcastle, July 24, 1730, July 19, 1731, July 20, 1732, July 13, 1733; Hening, IV, 241, 247, acts of 1730; *ibid.*, V, 124 *et seq.*, the act of 1742.

of rights in those counties and also ordered that no one grantee should take up more than 1000 acres in either of the counties.[1] When this order was received in Virginia, the council expressed the opinion that it might discourage settlement and suggested that the king should be applied to for more explicit directions.[2] They especially desired that the restriction placed upon the size of grants should be removed.

This suggests at once the attitude which Spotswood and those who had been associated with him during the last years of his administration took toward the question of land grants in the new counties. Spotswood's visit to Albany and treaty with the Five Nations had resulted in their abandonment of the shadowy claims they had made to several million acres in northern Virginia. This measure was preparatory to the execution of a grandiose scheme of Spotswood's for the production of naval stores on a large scale in the new counties and especially in Spotsylvania. Deposits of iron at Germanna and in its neighborhood he had already begun to work. The bringing of immigrants from the continent of Europe to work the mines was also a part of the plan which was promptly put into execution. The erection of the new counties was only a part of this comprehensive scheme. Scarcely had the bill for their erection passed the assembly when a number of patents were issued for large grants of land, especially in Spotsylvania county. John Grymes, the receiver general, stated at a later time that this procedure was facilitated by the fact that for a time just before the arrival of Drysdale as governor Spotswood acted as secretary, that office having been left vacant by the death of its incumbent. At any rate, before the issue of the order of the lords justices, Spotswood had taken out grants aggregating many thousands of acres, while others also were profiting greatly by concessions in the same region. These grants aggregated, ten, twenty or forty thousand acres apiece, and the episode as a whole suggests some of the features of Fletcher's doings in New York.[3]

When the order from England arrived, Drysdale awoke to

[1] C. O. 5/1319; O. P. Va., Aug. 6, 1723; C. O. 5/1365, E. B. Va., May 12, 1727; J. of B. Dec. 13, 1720.
[2] C. O. 5/1418; Ex. C. J. Va., Apr. 23, 1724.
[3] C. O. 5/1319, O. P. Va., June 6, 1724, *et seq.*

the situation and realized that his predecessor had "made haste to be beforehand with any instructions that should come in hither of that nature," and that already much or all of the good land, especially in Spotsylvania, had been "parcelled out and patented in a manner directly opposed to these orders." The ex-governor, Drysdale wrote, had also neglected to call on the patentees to produce head rights or certificates from the officers of the revenue that they had paid the 5s. sterling for every fifty acres, one or the other of which was the condition the fulfillment of which the law required before land could be patented in Virginia. In a very few cases bonds for the required purchase money were given, but their discharge was never enforced. By this means the patentees were enabled to hold the grants for several years without payment of any kind, and then to surrender them if they proved likely to be unprofitable. With his letter giving an account of these doings, Drysdale sent to the board of trade certain queries, which were submitted to the law officers and were intended to draw from them a report on the legal bearings of the case. Spotswood now, as was necessary, went to England to protect his interests and answer the charges which were thus formulated against him. There, with the grand air of which he was such a master, he ascribed the course which he had pursued wholly to his patriotism and zeal for the production of naval stores. He, with partners, had imported 300 persons for carrying on his undertakings and had shipped the first pig iron and hemp of Virginia production ever sent to England, besides proving that tar could not be made according to the directions of the act of parliament without the aid of skilled tar-burners from Finland. Hemp of good quality also could not be raised from English or East County seed. On the other hand, his new iron was growing in demand with all English ironmasters who had tried it and his new hemp was considered superior to the best Russian and equal in strength to the best Riga, as appeared from a recent report from the officers of Woolwich yard to the commissioners of the navy. In taking up the remote lands from which all these valuable products were being extracted, Spotswood claimed to have conformed to the law of the colony, while the expenses of his journey to Albany and the cost of extinguish-

ing prior rights and of guarding the territory were thrown into
the scale as added justification of his course.[1]

All of these considerations appealed directly to British
officials — including Walpole and Newcastle — as in harmony
with their most cherished policies, and the extent to which
this was true became evident when the law officers made their
report on the queries which related to the case. In reference
to all his leading contentions the report was favorable to
Spotswood. It declared that where the grants were made
the only restrictions upon their size were those to be found
in the laws of the colony and that the limitation to 1000 acres
was conditioned upon the exemption of the grantees from the
payment of quit rents for seven years. Patents were not void
because they had not been recorded, but in cases where they
had been received and enjoyed without the payment of purchase money or the submission of head rights deceit had been
practiced upon the king. If security was given, grants might
be held subject to payment at a later time, or, even when no
security was given, the king, if he chose, might accept a later
payment and thus relieve the grantees from the necessity of
taking out a new patent. The conclusion was that if the
king saw fit to accept from Colonel Spotswood the customary head rights and purchase money for his grants, he
could make them good.

In harmony with this opinion the board of trade reported
in favor of the retention by Spotswood of his land, new
patents being made out for nearly 60,000 acres,[2] the patents
of which were considered defective, the ex-governor himself
having offered to pay the government all such demands.
The period of seven years during which quit rents were to
be remitted having expired, that concession also was made to
him and, no opposition coming from the colony, the whole
was confirmed to him by order of council in 1729. The
chief motive which led to this action was expressly stated to
have been that the fiscal advantage to the crown would be
greater if Spotswood was allowed to retain his lands than

---

[1] The substance of this, as stated by Spotswood before the board of trade,
and in its relation to the general policy of the British government, has been
stated in another connection.

[2] C. O. 5/1365, E. B. Va., May 12, 1727, May 20, and Aug. 14, 1729; Acts
P. C. Col., 1720–1745, p. 168, *etc.*

it would be if they were granted to other persons, while it was considered to be a proper recognition of his services in the production of naval stores, in the extension of settlement and providing for the defence of the frontier.

By this time Governor Gooch was writing about the difficulty of preparing a rent roll for the new counties, due to a resolution of the Virginia council that no quit rents or purchase money should be received for lands granted there, lest the acceptance of these might be construed as an allowance of the large grants which had been made there before the king's instructions were known. In response to this the committee of the privy council on colonial affairs reported that some measure of indulgence might be permitted to grantees other than Spotswood. The concession agreed upon, and also embodied in an order of council, was that holders of tracts in the new counties which did not exceed 6000 acres each might be exempt from the payment of purchase money provided they paid the quit rent which was now seven years in arrear.[1] In this way the granting of land in the new counties, notwithstanding the order of the lords justices in 1723, was brought into conformity with conditions which prevailed generally in Virginia. When, in 1732, William Byrd visited Colonel Spotswood and his family at Germanna, he found him, now some years back from England, as enthusiastic as ever in the improvement of his estates and ready to talk at any length upon the production of iron, tar and hemp.[2] Politics he referred to only briefly and in relation to issues of a general nature. His days of political strife in Virginia were ended and his activities during the few years which remained — until the very close — were those of a landed proprietor and an entrepreneur of the eighteenth century in the production of iron and naval stores.

The question of the Northern Neck had been a thorn in the side of Virginia since the Restoration, and during the years of which we are now speaking it became more promi-

[1] Acts P. C. Col., *ibid.*, 244–247; C. O. 5/1366, May 20, and Aug. 14, 1729.
[2] A Progress to the Mines, in Bassett's edition of the Writings of William Byrd. Two years before, the governor had reported that five furnaces for smelting iron had been set up in the province, and a copper mine had been discovered in Spotsylvania and two in the Northern Neck. C. O. 5/1322, O. P. Va., July 23, 1730.

nent than it had been since the last decade of the seventeenth century. It was a territorial question which did not admit of so prompt a settlement as that of the border counties. And yet the two were connected, for the prominence of both at this time was due to the westward trend of settlement and discovery. This, among other things, made it necessary to establish the location of the headwaters and branches of the Rappahannock and Potomac rivers. Over this a long controversy developed with the patentee of the Northern Neck.

At the close of the reign of Charles II it seemed altogether likely that the unity of Virginia would be restored by the total surrender and extinction of the Culpeper claim. But by an unwise act of favoritism in the fourth year of James II the grant of of the Northern Neck was renewed,[1] and this time it was declared that it should extend to the head springs of the Potomac and Rappahannock rivers, the grantee being also entitled to fines and forfeitures and the goods of felons and fugitives within this territory.[2] After the death, in 1690, of Lord Culpeper, the original grantee, by process of marriage and inheritance the Northern Neck soon passed into the possession of the Yorkshire family of Lord Fairfax, who continued to hold it as long as Virginia remained under English rule. They administered it through agents, the first of whom was the elder Philip Ludwell.[3] Virginians were offended by the grant of James II and, in 1691, its assembly petitioned the crown that, for the encouragement of settlers, the Neck might be fully incorporated with the province. But the heirs presented a counter petition, upon which Sir John Sowers, as attorney general and, as Virginians thought, without "true information of the case," rendered an opinion that the grant was regular, with the exception that it had not been submitted to the lords of trade, and that there seemed no good reason for vacating it. It therefore stood and for several years the relations between its proprietor and the province continued undisturbed.

[1] An abstract of this patent is contained in a Virginia law of 1736 confirming titles to land in the Northern Neck. Hening, IV, 520.

[2] J. of B., June 30, 1730; Address of H. of B. to the King.

[3] C. O. 5/1320, O. P. Va., Report of attorney and solicitor general, Aug. 12, 1727.

But in 1705, when Nott was governor, Robert Carter, who was already agent for the Northern Neck, raised objection before the executive council of Virginia against the issue of certain patents for land. He submitted the grant of James II and tried to prove from it and perhaps other alleged evidence that the proprietor had been given all the land below the first heads and springs of the Potomac and Rappahannock rivers. But the location of these points was wholly unknown at the time of the grant and was not to be determined until many years after Carter set up the claim. At this time settlement had advanced only to the falls of the rivers or a little above, and the Virginians contended that the western boundary of the grant should not extend beyond the points where the branches of the two rivers united to form the lower or main streams. This point on the Rappahannock was at its junction with the Rapidan, and on the Potomac was at its junction with the Shenandoah, near the point where it passes through the Blue Ridge. Above this place the river was known to the Indians not by the name Potomac but as Cohongoronta. The Virginians came to insist that the western boundary of the Northern Neck should not be located west of a line connecting those points, or at least that it should not lie west of the Blue Ridge. But the surveyors who were appointed in 1705 reported that they were unable to decide whether the Rappahannock or its southern branch was the larger stream and therefore which should determine the boundary. Carter also betrayed his own uncertainty, as well as his greed for land, by soon after taking out patents from Virginia for two tracts which were located at the very fork which he claimed belonged rightfully to Lord Fairfax.[1]

During the administration of Spotswood a dispute arose concerning the right to fines and forfeitures within the grant. This was passed on, undecided, to Drysdale. In 1726 he asked the authorities in England for a legal opinion, especially on the right of the governor to pardon offences and remit forfeitures arising in the Northern Neck. In the following year the opinion was rendered, to the effect that, with certain minor exceptions, goods of felons convicted within the grant

[1] C. O. 5/1412, Min. of Ex. C. Va., May 2, 1706; C. O. 5/1366, E. B. Va., July 27, 1739; Bassett, *op. cit.*, 407.

passed to the proprietor, as did also fines imposed by king's courts held in the territory and forfeitures resulting from convictions in a variety of cases. The governor, however, in the king's name might pardon offences and remit forfeitures within the Northern Neck.[1] This opinion, which by the admission of the Virginians was in harmony with the terms of the patent, made clear the large extent of the rights which had been granted.

But it was the advance of settlement northwest to the mountains and across the first range into what was to be known as the Valley of Virginia which brought the question of the Northern Neck directly to an issue. It came, as has been suggested, in the form of a boundary dispute between the province under Governor Gooch and Lord Fairfax. The latter had the very effective aid of his agent Robert Carter, who because of the large estates which he secured in Virginia and the wide influence which he exerted was popularly known as " King Carter." On the death of Governor Drysdale, Carter, as senior member of the council, had been the head of government during the few months which passed before the arrival of Governor Gooch. Thomas, Lord Fairfax, who was now the proprietor of the Northern Neck, was the sixth to bear the baronial title in that family. He continued to reside in England until about 1745,[2] when he removed to Virginia, passing the last years of his bachelor existence, until his death in 1782, at Greenway Court near Winchester in the Valley of Virginia.

As we have seen, the possibility of the westward extension of the territories of Lord Fairfax had been greatly increased by the provision in the patent of James II that they should extend to the head springs of the rivers Rappahannock and Potomac. As exploration and settlement advanced, especially up the Potomac, it was found not only that this river extended far beyond the Blue Ridge, but that its branches, which might be interpreted to contain the " first springs " of that river, would lead one well into the midst of the Alleghanies. Before 1733 Carter and Lord Fairfax had become fully

[1] C. O. 5/1320, O. P. Va., Apr. 20, 1726, Aug. 12, 1727.
[2] A letter from Newcastle to Gooch, Mar. 18, 1734/5, states that Fairfax was then going to Virginia to settle the bounds. C. O. 5/1337.

aware of this and were expanding their claims accordingly. In 1728 and later, when grants were made by the Virginia government to pioneer settlers along the course of the Shenandoah river, beyond the first mountain barrier, they were met by protests from Carter on behalf of his principal.[1] If all the territory which was drained by the two rivers mentioned were included in the claim, as was quite possible and as often happened in cases where river systems gave rise to boundary disputes, Lord Fairfax's possessions might be made to include parts of Maryland and Pennsylvania, as well as the best part of Virginia. In fact, as the dispute progressed, Pennsylvania, and to a slight extent Maryland, was drawn into it and it thus formed a prelude to that later controversy which culminated in Dunmore's War.

The settlement of the Valley of Virginia proceeded from two centres, the tidewater region of Virginia itself and Pennsylvania. Its bearing upon colonial development in general can be seen only in connection with the history of immigration in the eighteenth century and the social and political effects which followed therefrom. But in Virginia history proper this westward expansion not only gave new force to the claims which in the ppoular mind had survived from the early grants of James I, but made necessary some decision as to the westward limits of the Northern Neck. It was the leaders of various tidewater families, the Carters, Beverleys, Pages, Robinsons and others, who secured grants beyond the first ridge of mountains.[2] Very little, if any, westward migration resulted from these grants, but they served to confirm the connection between Virginia and this region and to secure it against the pretensions of Lord Fairfax. These grants, the issue of which was followed by the influx of German and Scotch Irish settlers from the north, lay in the valley of the Shenandoah river, the most important southern tributary of the Potomac. Spotswood's expedition of 1716 had penetrated to that region and about ten years later the issue of Virginia grants there had begun. Immediately Robert Carter entered a caveat against such proceedings as an encroachment on the

---

[1] Va. Mag. of Hist., XIII, 114 *et seq.*; Cal. of State Papers I, 215.

[2] See a valuable series of papers on The Westward Movement in Virginia, in the Va. Mag. of Hist., Vol. 13, 1905–6.

territorial rights of Lord Fairfax, whose agent he was. At
this very time, however, he was a member of the council of
Virginia and had just been acting as president of the province.

As no Indians of consequence inhabited the Valley, though
it was the chief highway through which they were accustomed
to pass on their raids from north to south, the process of
settlement could go on without disturbance from the natives.
The Virginia government persisted in the issue of grants, and
by 1734 some settlers were actually established under its
authority in that region. Litigation now began between some
of these and Lord Fairfax. Under such circumstances the
questions at issue must necessarily come before the British
government. As early as 1727 [1] the submission to the board
of trade of letters and papers from Colonel Carter occasioned
the drafting of a report on the case by the attorney general.
John Clayton and Micajah Perry also appeared at a hearing
on the subject. The letters of Governor Gooch show that by
1729 or earlier Carter was asserting that the Northern Neck
rightfully included all the lands which were drained by the
tributaries of the Rappahannock and Potomac. The conclusion of the governor was that, if this was true, there would be
little left for Virginia to grant.[2] In the fall of 1731 Mr.
Ochs, who was petitioning for a grant on which to settle a
colony of Swiss, presented a memorial on the boundaries of
Maryland and of the Northern Neck, with the purpose of
showing that the claims of Lord Fairfax should not extend
beyond the Shenandoah. At the beginning of the following
February both Lord Baltimore [3] and Lord Fairfax appeared
before the board and declared that the land which Ochs
applied for lay partly within their territories. In September,
1732, the board of trade wrote to Gooch implying that it
approved of his promotion of settlement west of the mountains since it would strengthen the barrier against the French,
but as the proprietors concerned had entered caveats against

[1] Journal of B. T., Sept. and Oct., 1727. The report of the attorney general
has not been found. The Clayton referred to was the attorney general of
Virginia.

[2] C. O. 5/1322, O. P. Va., June 29, 1729, July 24, and Nov. 21, 1734.

[3] *Ibid.*, Oct. 28, 1731; J. of B. T., same date and Feb. 1, 1731/2. Sir William
Keith, ex-governor of Pennsylvania, seems to have been interested in this
scheme.

this course, the board had proposed to the king to have their claims settled before approving the requests of other petitioners for land.[1]

About a year later Lord Fairfax petitioned the privy council that a commission might be appointed for ascertaining the bounds of his lands in Virginia, and as the board of trade reported favorably upon this an order in council was issued directing the appointment of the commission in Virginia.[2] Three men were appointed to represent each of the parties concerned and surveyors were chosen to run the lines. But Lord Fairfax refused to leave the decision of the controversy to these or any other commissioners, and therefore nothing could be done except to make such explorations and surveys as were possible.[3] At the close the Virginia commissioners refused to unite in a joint report, and therefore two separate reports were made in 1737. At this time it was ascertained that the head springs of the Rappahannock were not located beyond the first ridge of mountains, while the upper course of the Potomac was pretty thoroughly explored. This latter search made it perfectly evident how enormous would be the territory of Lord Fairfax if his pretensions were allowed to stand.

Delay then followed, whether it was owing to the need of preparing some accurate maps or to other more general causes, until 1745. Then a decision was reached by the committee of the privy council on plantation affairs, which was confirmed by orders in council. It was based on a literal interpretation of the patent of James II, combined with the view that the headwaters of the Rapidan marked the true source of the Rappahannock and that the name Potomac rightfully belonged to that river throughout its entire course. The orders provided that a northwesterly line should be run between these two points and that it should constitute the

---

[1] C. O. 5/1366, E. B. Va., Sept. 13, 1732.

[2] *Ibid.*, Oct. 16, 1733; Feb. 21, 1733/4; J. of B. T., Sept. 26, 27 and Dec. 20, 1733; C. O. 5/1323, O. P. Va., July 25 and Nov. 29, 1733.

[3] Cal. of Va. State Papers, I, 223–231; C. O. 5/1420. Min. of Ex. C. of Va., Aug. 11 and Sept. 10, 1736; C. O. 5/1324, O. P. Va., Jan. 8, 1736/7; Acts of P. C. Col., 1720–1745, p. 386 *et seq.*; Bassett, Writings of William Byrd, 401, *et seq.* Carter had now died and Edward Barrodall was his lordship's agent.

inner boundary of the Northern Neck.[1] Like the decision
of all such questions, this proceeded from purely legal considerations and was far different from what statesmanship
demanded. It left in the hands of a proprietor 6,000,000
acres of the most fertile land of Virginia and thus at a late
period of our colonial development perpetuated the results of
some of the least justifiable acts of royal favoritism of which
any of the English monarchs were guilty in America. During
the critical years when the Fairfax claim was in litigation
it operated as a steady check upon immigration into the
Valley of Virginia and thus prevented the establishment of
an effective barrier against the French.[2] To secure such a
barrier was, of course, one of the most important objects of
imperial policy, but in this case, as in many others, ill considered acts of an earlier period were allowed to stand in
the way of measures the need of which all intelligent men
had come to acknowledge. But such is the warp and woof
not only of our colonial history but of all history as well.

The share borne by Virginia and its governors, in common
with several other colonies, in the expeditions to the West
Indies which formed the prelude to the third intercolonial
war, is elsewhere described. The legislation of the province at
about that time reveals the virtual ineffectiveness of its
militia system and the difference between what it appeared to
be on paper and what it was in reality. Like other colonies
which had had no real experience of war, Virginia was
peopled by a body of untrained civilians and its coast and
frontier defences were scarcely worth consideration. It had
militia laws with detailed provisions which implied efficiency,
but they proved in most respects a dead letter. When, in
1738, war with Spain was seen to be imminent, a new statute
was added to the list,[3] the preamble of which declared that
the laws previously made on this subject had proved " very
ineffectual." The provisions for maintaining discipline at
musters were made somewhat more strict and a section was
introduced which showed that the dread of slave insurrections

[1] Acts of P. C. Col., *ibid.*, 389; Va. Mag. of Hist. 13, p. 115.
[2] A number of the letters of Governor Gooch are eloquent upon this subject.
See especially his letter of May 24, 1734, to the board of trade. C. O. 5/1323,
O. P. Va.
[3] Hening, V, 16.

was quite as strong and impelling a force as the fear of war. The promptness with which results from the act were expected is indicated by the provision which allowed each soldier eighteen months in which to provide himself with arms. This indicates that arms fit for use were scarcely to be found in the colony and time requisite for procuring a supply from England must be allowed. But that the supply was not procured is shown by an appropriation of £2000 two years later for the purpose of providing arms for the colony.[1] In commenting on this act Gooch wrote that the officers of the militia had always been so aware of the incapacity of the poorer people to provide themselves with arms that they had neglected to hold annual musters because they did not wish to fine them for appearing unarmed. In 1736 Gooch had urged the assembly to establish a fund from which to provide arms for the poor, but no expedient for this could be found except a poll tax, which was thought too burdensome and the bill failed to pass.[2] So also did a proposal, which was embodied in an additional instruction to the governor, that a bill should be passed requiring that the tonnage duty on incoming vessels should be paid wholly in powder, except in instances where from the necessity of the case the governor and council ruled otherwise. The object of this measure was to supply the magazine of the colony with powder which might be used in resisting the Spanish privateers which were then infesting the coasts.[3]

The expedition of 1740 necessitated the levy of an additional impost duty of five per cent on slaves, the same to be paid by the buyer.[4] A part of the revenue from this source was to be expended in providing arms for the poorer inhabitants and relief for those who should be disabled and for the widows and children of those who might lose their lives in the West Indies. For some years after the close of the disastrous expeditions applications for the relief of survivors occasionally appeared on the records of the burgesses,[5] but

[1] *Ibid.*, 90.

[2] C. O. 5/1325, O. P. Va., Aug. 29, 1740.

[3] C. O. 5/1325, O. P. Va., July 16, 1741; C. O. 5/1366, E. B. Va., June 18, 1741; J. of B., May 11, 1742; Ex. C. Min. in Va. Mag. of Hist., XV, 123, 127.

[4] Hening, V, 92.

[5] For example, in J. of B., Sept. 10, 1744.

they must have fallen far short of the numbers who under the law were entitled to relief. As the duration of the law was limited to four years, applications of this sort had to be made promptly in order to be effective.

While the enlisted force of 1740 was waiting in its quarters prior to embarkation for the West Indies, some desertions occurred. After several advertisements kindly inviting the absentees to return had been published in the *Gazette* without effect, the governor issued a proclamation for the arrest of the offenders and their transfer, under an order from a justice of the peace, from constable to constable till they should be imprisoned at Williamsburg. In view of the hazardous prospect of the expedition and especially of its actual fate, it can scarcely be a cause of surprise that some repented of their enlistment and sought to escape, but it was a grave offence for the aid or concealment of which parties were threatened with prosecution to the utmost extent of the law. The desertion of seamen from the ships of war called forth a similar proclamation which threatened like treatment to offenders.

Gooch was surpassed by no other governor in the strength of his orthodoxy and in his determination to hold vice, disorder and all unusual opinions in check. This comported well with the spirit of the ruling class in Virginia and in the colonies generally at that time. When, for example, news came of the Jacobite uprising of 1745, Gooch delivered to the assembly an attack on Catholicism and an exhortation to support the altar and throne, the religion and liberties of England, the equal of which in fervor can scarcely be found elsewhere in colonial literature.[1] As a result of this appeal, an association to support the Hanoverian dynasty was signed by the members of the two houses and a loyal address was sent to the king. In illustration of contemporary attitude toward dissenters of another type, reference should be made to a declaration of the council of Virginia in 1747 against the followers of Whitefield. They viewed with concern the spirit of enthusiasm which had been introduced among the people by itinerant preachers, a spirit, they said, which was productive of confusion and of those most wicked and destructive

[1] J. of B., Feb. 20, March 6, 1745/6.

doctrines and practices which in the previous century had subverted the constitution of both church and state in England. In accordance with this spirit Gooch issued a proclamation warning all magistrates to prohibit, so far as they legally could, all itinerant preachers, whether New Lights, Moravians or Methodists, from traveling, preaching or holding meetings in Virginia, and all persons were warned to give their assistance for this purpose.[1] It was in accordance with the efforts of such men as Nicholson and Gooch to suppress vice and its effects by governmental action that laws were passed and proclamations issued for this purpose. In 1740 Gooch issued a proclamation for the arrest of vagrants and in 1744 acts were passed for the suppression of vice and especially in restraint of gambling.[2] Acts like these, if they were more than dead letters, fell in appropriately with the laws for defence and for the repelling of invasions by the side of which they stand on the pages of the statute book.

With the exception of sending its contingent to the West Indies at the beginning of the war, a few alarms from Spanish privateers off the coast in 1741, the efforts which it made to contribute to the futile demonstration against Canada in 1746 and the brief visit, in the winter of 1746, of two regiments which were on their way to garrison Louisbourg,[3] Virginia had no experience of the third intercolonial war. It did not even disturb the Indians to the north or south of her and their quiet for the time was insured by an embassy to the Cherokees[4] and by the famous treaty of 1744 at Lancaster, Pennsylvania. As affairs were correspondingly quiet in the neighboring provinces of Maryland and North Carolina, there was no need of intervention in those quarters.

During the decade between 1740 and 1750, therefore, the history of Virginia consisted almost exclusively of the record of local happenings. In the entire administration of Gooch only one controversy occurred in the legislature, and that was the dispute of 1747 and 1748 over the proposal to remove the capital from Williamsburg. The occasion of this was the

---

[1] C. O. 5/1326, O. P. Va., Apr. 3 and June 10, 1747.
[2] Hening, V, 225, 229; C. O. 5/1325, O. P. Va., Apr. and Aug., 1740.
[3] J. of B., Feb. 20, 1745/6, July 11, 1746 *et seq.*
[4] Ex. C. Min., June 11, 1741, Va. Mag. of Hist., XV, 235.

destruction of the capitol building by fire. Thereupon dissatisfaction with the location was at once expressed by the burgesses. In reply to a statement by the governor they proposed that a new site upon navigable water should be selected for the capital. In later resolutions they insisted that a site should be chosen which should be not only upon one of the rivers but less remote from the majority of the inhabitants of the colony. Their preference was for a location on the Pamunkey, a branch of the York river. They prepared a bill estimating the expense of removal, building a capitol, governor's house, church, prison and magazine at £12,000 and the time which would be required for finishing these at six or seven years. In order to meet the expense they proposed an additional tax of one shilling per hogshead on the export of tobacco and an assessment on wheel carriages. The minority in the burgesses which was opposed to this plan was large but not sufficient to defeat it. The council, according to the governor, was about equally divided in sentiment, but through two or three conferences retained a majority in favor of the Williamsburg site. The burgesses were so irritated by this that the session ended without any provision being made for housing the legislature or the officials of the government, and they had to accept for several years the courtesies of the college.[1]

On account of the feeling which existed Gooch finally dissolved the assembly and a warmly contested election, turning on the question of the capital, was held. The membership of the house was somewhat changed, but its feeling on the question at issue was much the same as that of its predecessor. At first resolutions were adopted in favor of a Pamunkey site and a bitter personal quarrel was threatened between John Blair of the council and John Robinson, the speaker of the burgesses. This however was avoided by the tact and spirit of concession of the councillors, and the house, though by a small majority, soon abandoned its insistence upon the new site and passed the acts which were necessary for rebuilding the capitol at Williamsburg.[2] It was duly signed by the

[1] J. of B., Apr. 1, 6, 10, 16, 1747; C. O. 5/1326, P. O. Va., June 10, 1747; C. O. 5/1425, J. of C. in Ass., March and April, 1747.

[2] J. of B., Oct. 27, Nov. 11, 16, 18, 23, Dec. 17, 1748; C. O. 5/1327, O. P. Va., Dec. 5, 1748. The act in question is not printed in Hening.

governor. In the spring session of 1749 a majority was actually obtained in the burgesses in support of a bill which would have reversed this decision, but it was rejected by the council. Again in 1761, as the result of the extension of settlement westward, this measure was considered four times by the house in committee of the whole and failed of passage there by only one vote. Then, owing to the lack of any other suitable town, the proposal was abandoned and Williamsburg continued to be the capital of Virginia until after the Revolution.[1]

While this assembly was in its first adjourned session, in March, 1749, and before the feeling between the houses had wholly abated, the burgesses were guilty of a breach of good usage by appointing a committee to search the journals of the council for the purpose of ascertaining the existing status of a bill for dividing two of the western counties. This abrupt procedure, as well as the personnel of the committee, was offensive to the council and it replied that it expected to be informed by the burgesses of their desire and object before it granted permission for the search of its records. Its clerk was also instructed to deny the request. The house then claimed that it was its right to search the journal of the council for proceedings upon any bill or other matter which they had sent up to the council, and condemned the attitude of that body as a high infringement of their privileges and as tending to interrupt the harmony which ought to exist between the two branches of the legislature. The council then informed the burgesses that it was willing to keep up a good correspondence and recommended to that end that both houses erase from their journals the irritating utterances to which they had just been giving expression.[2] This was done.

But near the close of the discussion the council had prepared a defence of its conduct in the premises and was able to show from certain precedents which were not very remote that the burgesses, in applying to the upper house, had exactly conformed to what it was now claimed their conduct should be.[3] In order to justify itself in the eyes of the public

[1] J. of B, Apr. 10–13, 1749; Mar, 1, 1761, et seq.
[2] J. of B., Mar. 10, 1748/9, et seq.
[3] Cal. of Va. State Papers, I, 241.

and clearly to show where right lay, the council also ordered this statement published in the *Virginia Gazette*. The publication was delayed until May, but when it appeared William Parks, the public printer, was summoned before the bar of the assembly. There he explained that he had printed the statement upon the positive order of the council. That body assumed at once full responsibility for what had been done. The burgesses were clearly in the wrong, but would probably have somewhat prolonged the dispute if it had not been immediately cut short by the end of the session.[1]

Unlike most disputes between the houses of colonial legislatures, the governor did not share in this either as partisan or as political manager. Though his sympathies were with the council, his attitude was simply that of the interested observer. This was in harmony with the part played by Gooch in Virginia affairs throughout his administration. His views and influence as governor were never unduly obtruded and yet his ability as an administrator was such that he always enjoyed the respect of the province. His selection as commander of the colonists on the West India expedition of 1740-1 not only testifies to the esteem in which he was held by British officials but gave him a certain prestige during the rest of his career.

A strong impression is given not only of the firmness of Gooch but of his acquaintance with official usage by a letter which he wrote in 1739 to the duke of Albemarle, who was the absentee governor of Virginia and therefore his immediate superior. On the death of the adjutant general of the province Gooch had appointed one of the Randolphs to the place without informing the duke. The appointment was confirmed, but Newcastle expressed his surprise and wrote to Gooch that the like must not occur again. The lieutenant governor thereupon wrote in explanation to Albemarle that the appointee was well known and esteemed by Mr. Hornbury, who was in his lordship's favor.[2] He then went on to say that for sixty years back there had not been an instance of a lieutenant governor being controlled by the governor in the appointment to an office of trust on a vacancy. Albemarle, he continued,

---

[1] J. of B., May 11, 1749, *et seq.*
[2] C. O. 5/1337, Aug. 5, 1737, Oct. 3, 1739.

could not perform any act of government or give any commission of trust or profit *in absentia*. The consent of the
council to appointments must also be obtained, and how an
absentee could secure such was worth considering. Gooch
then went on to enlarge on the necessity of rewards as well
as punishments as a means of carrying on government and
that it subverted first principles to take from the officiating
magistrate the power to reward merit. It would make ciphers
of governor and council to give them merely the power
to appoint provisionally. The governor was put under bond
of £1000 to be answerable for the conduct of officials, but
how could he be so without the power of appointment or
removal? Consider also the few places which the governor
had to dispose of compared with the many granted to the
college and to the secretary. He had had not more than five
in his time and therefore there was little reason to deprive him
of these as means with which to serve the king and influence
the assembly. " As Your Lordship was never informed to
whom this Power is Committed, . . . and as it is impossible
to carry on the King's Business under the Restriction mentioned by the Duke of Newcastle, I trust your Lordship,
. . . will not insist on having anything done so destructive
to His Majesty's Service."

In the light of this letter the strength of the governor's
character appears much more clearly than it does in many
of his speeches to the legislature. It reveals the strength and
balance which enabled him to discharge the duties of his
office so long and successfully. Like Sir William Berkeley,
in the later stages of his career Gooch became, as it were,
an institution, an organic part of that aristocratic, orthodox,
planter régime, stagnant in appearance yet full of potential
life and power, which constituted the essence of what we
call Virginia in the eighteenth century. His administration
was the last one which was to pass undisturbed by the conflicts of the frontier and by opposition which came from
settlers in that and the Piedmont regions.

The lately elected and last assembly of Gooch's administration, which was in session during much of 1748 and the early
months of 1749, accomplished much in the way of legislation.
A joint committee of the two houses which had been appointed

in 1746 for the revision of the laws of the province and which, according to the terms of the act creating it, was to survive a dissolution, now made its report.[1] By this the laws were divided into three classes, those that were obsolete and ought to be repealed, those that should remain as they at present stood, those which had been changed and amended by the committee and were recommended by it for passage in their revised form. The committee on courts of justice was immediately ordered to bring in a bill for the repeal of the laws which were reported to be useless or obsolete. Those in the second class remained in force as they were reported. To the bills of the third class the attention of the houses was devoted, as the demands of other business permitted, throughout the prolonged session. A large amount of work was devoted to this task, resulting in a notable body of legislation, adapting the code of Virginia to the needs of the province as they were then apprehended to be by its body of aristocratic legislators. It was a crowning work and formed a suitable ending of Gooch's long administration of twenty-two years.[2]

Unlike the practice of many governors, Gooch, when he sent acts to England, referred to them in itemized order and arranged his criticisms or explanatory remarks under the heads of the respective bills upon which he was commenting. He had little occasion to fill his letters with caustic reflections on the conduct of his assemblies, for he had no opposing group or factious conduct to contend with. Therefore his concise and somewhat dry comments were devoted in an impersonal spirit to explanations of the changes intended by the new legislation and the improvements which were expected from it. Like similar revisals in the past, this body of laws prescribed the rules for settling titles and bounds of lands — deeds and their recording, surplus and lapsed land, improvements, processioning of bounds, penalties for unlawful fishing and fowling. It declared slaves to be personal estate and repealed laws which provided that they should be treated as realty. It regulated the distribution of intestates' estates, the probate of wills and the care of orphans

---

[1] J. of B., 1742–1749, pp. 217–220, 277–279. Editor's introduction to this volume.

[2] *Ibid.*, 406; Hening, V, 408–558, VI, 9–214.

and their property. The second group of laws dealt with the organization, jurisdiction and procedure of the courts, civil and criminal, doing this in great detail and renewing the provisions concerning that much discussed subject in the colonies generally, the jurisdiction of the county courts. A statute of limitations was also included and provisions against frivolous and vexatious suits. The duties of sheriffs and their method of appointment, as well as the method of selecting jurors and rules for the practice of attorneys, were prescribed. A special act provided for the method of holding courts in the sparsely settled counties on the western border. Detailed provision was made concerning writs of execution against insolvent debtors and the disposition of the property seized; also against the transporting of debtors and their movable property out of the colony. Distress for non-payment of rent and fraudulent practices of tenants was made the subject of a special enactment. A long act concerning the regulation of servants and slaves of course found a place. Ferries, roads, bridges and promoting communication came in for a certain attention. Surveyors of land were strictly regulated. There was much legislation on the tobacco trade, the use of tobacco notes issued by inspectors, public storehouses and on the foreign trade of the province in general, under the conditions laid down by parliament. The support of the college and the church received attention. Iron works were encouraged, as was the production of hemp. Rules were laid down for the inspection of important exports of the province other than tobacco, namely, pork, beef, flour, tar, pitch and turpentine. In an act against invasions and insurrections some provision was made concerning the militia. A treasurer was designated. Various acts were also included for the establishment of new towns and the division of counties and parishes. This list, though not exhaustive, will indicate the general scope of Virginia legislation as shown in the revision of 1748.

In transmitting this body of legislation to England Gooch commented more or less at length on a large number of the acts.[1] In most cases his comments were confined to explanations of their relation to the laws for which they were in-

[1] C. O. 5/1327;   O. P. Va., May 1750.

tended to be substituted and the ways in which they were adapted to the existing needs of Virginia. In reference to the tobacco act he told how inspection was to be more strict and the passing of trash made more difficult. The rebuilding of the capitol at Williamsburg, the cost of reprinting the laws and the old debt of £4000 raised toward the expense of the futile Canadian expedition together necessitated the addition of a penny per gallon to the impost duty on wine and liquors. The increase of the allowance to the province treasurer was due to the increase in the number of warehouses and consequent trouble in settling with inspectors. A provision for the opening of roads through gaps in the mountains originated in an effort to induce the new settlers in the valley to send their cattle, butter and cheese to tidewater Virginia rather than to Pennsylvania. Gooch explained fully the scattered settlements and the dearth of lawyers which necessitated special legislation concerning the courts of the frontier counties. Three laws, he said, had already been made respecting tar and hemp, but they had been of little use. The back inhabitants were now falling into the way of raising hemp and this induced the assembly to continue the premium and reduce the laws into one act with certain alterations. The additional regulations intended to elevate the character of attorneys were also explained. To the land laws much attention was given. And so the governor went on through the list.

But when he came to the act declaring slaves to be personal estate, he told how by the law of 1705 and a later act they had been declared to be real estate and it was probably due to them that Virginia had so increased in wealth and population. The orthodox view of the connection of the African trade with all of this was expressed, while the annexation of negroes to land had enabled the planters to keep estates in their families, make marriage settlements for their daughters and improve Virginia in all ways. Gooch had assented to this measure because it had passed both houses and he thought it would gratify them, but he was of the opinion that it ought to be disallowed. As the act concerning the distribution of intestates' estates depended upon this view concerning the nature of property in slaves, that also he thought should be

disallowed.   As to the law establishing the general court,
Gooch thought it made the previous one not better but worse.
As the county courts were for the most part constituted of
very weak men, he thought that the prohibition of bringing
suits in the general court where the debt or demand was
under £20 might result in great oppression.   In the prohibition of appeals from the inferior courts also he saw the prospect of mischief to many traders.   Therefore he preferred
the old law.   The old law concerning servants and slaves he
considered better than the new one and advised its repeal.
These were the only cases in which Gooch recommended this
action.

When this body of laws reached England, and was referred
to Counsellor Lamb, he supported the objections of Gooch
to four of the acts and thought that too exclusive power over
breaches of the penal laws was given to the county courts.
He also noted the fact that the instructions were violated
by the repeal of many acts without reference to their titles
and without a suspending clause.   The board of trade, in its
report to the king,[1] explained that the revisal arose from the
necessity of having a new edition of the laws of Virginia
printed and, as in recent years many acts had been wholly or
in part repealed and others had expired or been amended, the
work had been carried through.   Such a practice it would
be glad to see followed in all the colonies.   As they all repealed or changed existing laws, they should in all cases have
contained a suspending clause.   Though this had not been inserted, the board did not propose their repeal because it was
necessary that they should go into force at once.   But the acts
that repealed laws which had been confirmed by the crown
and were still without the suspending clause, it proposed
should be repealed.   The failure to observe this requirement
in such cases, it said, was " a deviation and departing from
your Majesty's instructions which no circumstances or necessity can justify."   To this the committee of the council on
plantation affairs added the statement that, if the acts were
not repealed, " that power which the Crown has so wisely
and properly reserved to itself of rejecting such laws passed

---

[1] C. O. 5/1366, E. B. Va., Jan. 1750/1, Aug. 6, 1751; C. O. 5/1367, Report
of Committee of Council, Feb. 14, 1753.

in the Colonies as shall upon due consideration be thought improper or liable to objection [would be forfeited and it] would destroy that check which was established not only to preserve the just and proper influence and authority which the Crown ought to have in the Government of its Colonies, . . . but also to secure to its subjects their just liberties and privileges. . . ." For this reason it was that ten of the acts were disallowed. Of these the most important were the ones declaring slaves to be personal estates, regulating the distribution of the estates of intestates, establishing the proceedings of the general court, for the limitation of actions and avoidance of suits, concerning servants and slaves and to prevent the tending of seconds — a provision of the law concerning tobacco culture — and an act for the better support of the College of William and Mary. The other acts were local in character, relating to towns, fairs and similar matters. Certain of the acts also were ordered to lie by probationary and were reserved for further consideration by the treasury board or others.

The repeal of these acts was announced in Virginia by proclamation after the arrival of Dinwiddie as governor, in 1752. It brought home to the colonists more clearly than ever before the extent to which, by the instructions above, the freedom of legislating in their assemblies was restricted. Without leave first obtained no law to which the king had once refused his assent could be re-enacted. And also, when a law had once been passed in the province and ratified by the crown it could not be revised without the use of the suspending clause. As that left the discretion in the hands of the crown, it seemed effectually to tie the hands of the colonists so far as the most important part of their legislation was concerned. This seemed to them to be a dangerous extension of the sphere of royal instructions. Their hands seemed to be tied and the initiative of their assemblies largely to be taken away, and that at a time when the interests of the colonies were widening and the volume of their legislation was becoming larger. As they compared this situation with the freedom of earlier times, when the undefined term repugnancy, as used in the charters, expressed the only restriction of which they were conscious, they were filled with dismay.

This feeling was expressed by the legislature of Virginia in an address of protest which they at once prepared and sent to the king.[1] In this they urged a reconsideration of the acts which had been repealed and expressed their deep concern at the prospect that the large number of laws which the king had ratified could not be revised to suit the changing needs of the province except under the difficult conditions which had been specified. They then briefly defended the measures which had been repealed as normal specimens of Virginia legislation. Acts establishing towns and authorizing the holding of fairs were passed at every session and were for the public benefit. The lowering of the duty on the export of raw hides, as provided in the act concerning the college, would result in an increase of their export and thus enlarge the income of that institution. The object of the law concerning tobacco was to save a part of crops which were so often destroyed by tempests and yet not to overstock the market with a product of poor quality. The act concerning the general court was held to have improved its status by placing a higher limitation on cases which could be brought before it by original process, and the good effects of the few changes which had been made in earlier practice had begun to appear even during the few months it had been in force. Naturally greater stress was laid upon the acts changing the status of slaves as property than on any of the others. Attention was called to the fact that, until the 4th of Anne, they had been treated in Virginia as personal estate. The legislation of that year and later had partially changed their status, making them real estate for certain purposes and leaving them personal for others. That had occasioned confusion, which it was thought desirable to remove by reducing them wholly to the status in which they originally were. Neither was it beneficial to continue entailing negroes any longer, for in time they overstocked the plantations and could be worked to better advantage on fee simple lands than on those which were entailed. Emphasis also was laid upon the injury which it was claimed had come to the credit of Virginia with British merchants from the entailing of slaves. The advantages which were claimed for this treatment of slaves in cases of intestacy were also explained.

[1] Hening, V, 432 et seq.; C. O. 5/1327, O. P. Va., Jan., 1753.

Such arguments as these in support of the expediency of the acts in question of course did not touch the reason which had been assigned by the British government for their repeal. In their passage a positive instruction of the king had been disregarded and until conformity upon that point had been reached it was useless to discuss the merits of the acts themselves. That was the position taken by the board of trade in its representation to the king on the protest of the Virginia legislature. The substance of this was embodied in an order in council and an additional instruction, by which, for special reasons, permission was given the governor to reenact the law affecting William and Mary College and also a part of one of the acts affecting a locality, but against the rest of the legislation the original objection was reasserted with all force.[1]

[1] *Ibid.*, March 7, 1753; C. O. 5/1367, E. B. Va., Apr. 5, 1753. In 1754 a similar course was pursued in reference to another of the group of acts passed in 1749. This related to executions and the relief of insolvent debtors. British merchants trading to Virginia objected to this because it fixed the rate of exchange for Virginia currency at 25% below sterling, which was too high. The act was first approved and then on further knowledge the governor was instructed to procure its reenactment without this provision. C. O. 5/1367, E. B. Va., June 27 and Aug. 6, 1754; C. O. 5/1327 and 1328, O. P. Va.

CHAPTER VIII

THE contrast between the course of events in the Carolinas in 1729 and that in Maryland in 1715 is sufficient to justify comment. In the case of Maryland the step which had been taken years before toward the establishment of royal government was retraced and the proprietary régime was restored. In the Carolinas the opposite course was followed, though after delay and without vigorous initiative on the part of the British government. The act of 1729 brought to an end the confused and uncertain condition which had come about as the result of protracted neglect in the northern province and of the revolt of 1719 at Charlestown. The Carolinas now became in the full sense of the word royal provinces, and this decisive result may be attributed mainly to the fact that they lay adjacent to the southern and southwestern frontier. Maryland was so protected, toward the coast as well as to the west, that in her case such a change did not seem so imperative.

Robert Johnson, the last of the proprietary governors, was selected as the first fully equipped royal appointee. For some years he had been in England trying to supplant Nicholson and to secure this post for himself. Toward the close of 1729 he succeeded. The board of trade realized that the problem which must be faced in Carolina was a difficult one. It had before it addresses from the lower house and a long representation from the council of the province explaining the controversy over bills of credit. A number of British merchants added their testimony on the subject. Johnson himself presented a paper on the state of the currency. A few months later Sir Alexander Cuming gave a very gloomy view of the situation. It was known that disorder was chronic, that arbitrary acts had been committed, that most of the laws

114

of the province had expired and that tax bills had not been passed. The province was suffering politically and socially from the effects of a prolonged and bitter partisan conflict.[1]

More than usual care seems therefore to have been given to the drafting of those special clauses of Johnson's instructions which referred to the existing crisis.[2] A general revision of the laws of the province was ordered, but this was not carried into effect. The necessity for fixed salaries was emphasized, while the need of a certain amount of currency in the province was recognized. In pursuance of these suggestions, Johnson secured from his first assembly, in 1731, a law authorizing the issue of public orders to the amount of £104,775 for the payment of the public debt which had accumulated since 1727, the date of the last appropriation bill. It was planned that this issue should be redeemed in seven years, but this result was not attained until 1750.[3] The sinking fund law of 1723 was also suspended for seven years and provision was made for the use of the stated revenue and accumulated funds for redeeming the outstanding paper. The sum of £106,500 in paper was left permanently in circulation, provision being made for the printing of new bills to take the place of the old ones as they became worn. Owing to the provision for an impost duty on negroes in the appropriation act of 1731 and to the suspension of the sinking fund law, considerable opposition to this act was made by English merchants. But it was defended by council, assembly and agents and was not disallowed.[4] No increase in the amount of bills of credit was allowed at this time and later efforts to secure such a result met with the steady disapproval of the British government. The check which was thus given to the soft money craze was the direct result of bringing South Carolina into line as a royal province and thus subjecting its

[1] C. O. 5/360, O. P.; S. C., July 15, 1729, July 15, 1730; Colls. of S. C. Hist. Soc., I, 300.

[2] C. O. 5/361, O. P. S. C. July, 1729–July, 1730; C. O. 5/400, E. B. S. C., June, 1730; Acts of P. C. Col. 1720–1745, p. 266 *et seq.*

[3] State of S. C., III, 301, 334–341; Smith, S. C. as a Royal Province, 272 *et seq.*

[4] C. O. 5/401, E. B. S. C., July 11, 1735; C. O. 5/363, O. P. S. C. Mar. 22, July 23 and 30, Sept. 10, Dec. 3, 1734. Under date of Aug. 20, 1735, in O. P. is a valuable report of receipts and payments by the public treasurer from 1731 to 1734.

laws to the veto power of the crown. With this a distinct phase in the financial history of this province was brought to an end and the way was opened for the development of another somewhat related issue.

The leading controversy of Johnson's administration had reference to the irregular and fraudulent grants of land which had been made between 1719 and the date of his arrival in the province. It was intensified and brought to an issue by the continuance of enormous grants under the lead of Johnson and the council. Though the provincial nobility disappeared after the establishment of royal government, the policy of large speculative grants continued. During the revolt of 1719 the proprietors closed their land office and no grants were made by the crown until near the close of 1731.[1] But during this interval there was a strong demand for land and by reviving rights which had originated when the patents were granted to landgraves, caciques and other prominent men of the colony in its earlier days, about 800,000 acres of the most valuable land near the coast was appropriated. These grants had usually been made without limitation of the place where or the time when the land was to be settled, and when in 1730 the board of trade submitted to the law officers a typical case from among them, the opinion rendered was that they were void in law. Several other opinions upon the grants of this period were rendered at later dates, the purpose of some of which was to smooth the way to the acquirement of title notwithstanding the defects which appeared in them all.[2]

Among Johnson's instructions when he came to the province was the requirement that he should assent to a law remitting quit rents — which were greatly in arrears — provided the assembly would repeal the act of 1696 regulating conveyances and conditions of payment and provide for the complete registration of grants and future payment of quit rents in proclamation money.[3] Grantees were also to be

[1] C. O. 5/370, O. P. S. C., McCulloh to Whitaker, Jan. 23, 1742, with enclosures. Smith, op. cit., 36 et seq. A list of grants between 1713 and 1727, as made out by the proprietors, is in C. O. 5/363. O. P. S. C., Jan. 23, 1734. This is probably not exhaustive.

[2] Chalmers, Colonial Opinions, 171–178.

[3] Smith, op. cit., 56.

required to record their deeds and promptly to settle and cultivate their lands. In August, 1731, an act was passed which contained these provisions and several points in addition.[1] One was a section which guaranteed the validity of all grants that had been made by the proprietors, whatever were the defects in describing the land, provided they had been surveyed by a sworn surveyor. By this was meant the surveyor general and his deputies appointed by the proprietors. By this and other loose provisions in the statute all the grants which had been made to landgraves and caciques were legalized. When this act came before the treasury in England objection was made to its approval on the ground that it was prejudicial to the crown and by confirming large and pretended grants of land discouraged private settling in the colony.[2] By such means, the English government said, the intention of the home government, as expressed in its instruction to Johnson, was defeated.[3] Meantime James St. John had come to South Carolina with an appointment from the crown as surveyor general and also one from Horatio Walpole as deputy auditor. Grants of varying extent were then made in large numbers, that constituting for years to come the chief business of the executive council.

If South Carolina be considered from the physiographic standpoint, like all the colonies of the Atlantic seaboard from Virginia southward it consisted of three belts or terraces, the low country, the middle country and the up-country or piedmont region. All of these are traversed by numerous rivers, navigable for small craft to the falls, which are usually found in the second belt or terrace. This succession of terraces is better defined in South Carolina and Georgia than in the colonies to the north of them, but it appears in all. The land on the coast is only a few feet above the sea-level. In the pine belt, red hills and sandy hills of the middle region

---

[1] Stats. of S. C., III, 289–304; Seven-eighths of existing arrears were remitted, but some rigid provisions were inserted concerning payments in the future. As was to be expected, these were not enforced.

[2] In 1729 the well known Thomas Lowndes held five baronies which he had come into possession of in various ways and most of which were held in other names than his own. C. O. 5/371, O. P. S. C., Feb. 21, 1746; C. O. 5/401, Nov., 1732.

[3] C. O. 5/369, O. P. S. C., Feb. 16, 1742/3.

the elevation varies from 130 to 700 feet. The up-country, rising into the foothills of the Appalachian ranges, reaches in some parts an elevation of 3000 feet. Settlement progressed successively through those regions, the original native occupiers of the soil being pushed back as the Europeans advanced. In the tidewater or coast belt there developed colonial societies in the form which they first took after being transplanted from Europe. Estates were large and upon them were produced chiefly the staples — tobacco, rice and later indigo — which it was the object of the British government to encourage. Foodstuffs for the support of the population and also large quantities of naval stores were produced. Trade upon a considerable scale with Europe and the island colonies was carried on. Society was aristocratic, with a population of slaves and white servants which came soon far to outnumber the free whites. The planter aristocracy was as tenacious of its privileges in government and society as were the nobles of England or the citizens of a Greek commonwealth. These characteristics appear in clearer relief in South Carolina and Virginia than in the other southern colonies on the continent.[1]

In the history of South Carolina we have now reached the time when the settlement of the middle section began. Among the projects favored by the crown and embodied in Governor Johnson's instructions was the laying out and settling of eleven townships on the rivers of the colony, extending from the Altamaha on the south to the Pedee on the north and at a distance of about sixty miles from Charlestown. This plan, however, was executed only in part. Of the towns which were actually founded, the one of which most was heard at the time was Purrysburg, on the lower Savannah, which was settled by a colony of Swiss under Jean Pierre Purry, a grant of 40,000 acres being made to them. New Windsor was settled on the Savannah nearly opposite the site of the city of Augusta. On the Pedee, within the Welsh Tract granted to immigrants from Pennsylvania, Queensborough was laid out. On the Santee Amelia was founded, and farther up, where the name Congaree was given to the river, Saxe-Gotha

[1] These facts are well stated by Schaper, Sectionalism in South Carolina, Reports of Am. Hist. Ass., 1900, I, 253 et seq.

was settled by Germans. In the same region, on the north fork of the Edisto, Orangeburg was founded, and, south of the Great Pedee, Williamsburg. Such towns as were founded were not of the New England type, but originated in proprietary grants and owing to natural and social conditions never developed much community life. Some developed into parishes or election districts and others never became more than names. But the experiment shows that during the third decade of the century South Carolina began to feel anew the influx of immigration from Europe and from other colonies and as the result of it the middle section of the colony was settled, and the frontier was pushed to the upper courses of the rivers. As yet the immigrants from the north who were to settle the up-country had not appeared.

In the baronial and other grants made by the proprietors, large parts of the middle section had been included, reaching in certain cases as high as twelve, twenty-four, or even forty-eight thousand acres, and now the claims of these land monopolists stood in the way of healthful development of the colony.[1] The interests of both crown and colony were obstructed by them and it was this fact that soon attracted the attention of St. John. He therefore began to attack the land speculators, having as his supporter Benjamin Whitaker, who at the first was deputy surveyor but later became attorney general and chief justice and was probably the best lawyer of his time in the province. The grantees were the large planters, the aristocrats of the coast region, and their friends. In their hands was centred the political control of the province, for they constituted the leading element in council and assembly. The situation was similar in its essentials to that which existed in New York and Virginia, only political power was even more concentrated. The only leverage against it must be through the British government, and that in such a matter offered only an uncertain support. Therefore, as we shall see, there occurred a long struggle which passed through various phases with no clear result.

In 1732 St. John wrote at length to the board of trade against the quit rent act. Enclosed in his letter was a report

---

[1] See *e.g.*, a representative of the board of trade on the petition of certain inhabitants of S. C., C. O. 5/401 E. B. S. C., Dec. 19, 1734.

from Whitaker on the same subject.[1] Their contention was a correct inference from the indefinite language of the grants themselves and from the opinion of the law officers in reference to them. From the strictly legal aspects of the case, Whitaker argued that, as most of the original grantees had died before their lands had been surveyed or seizin of them had been taken, their heirs could not have inherited them and neither original nor present claims to them were valid. A recent decision in the court of chancery of the province that these grants were valid he disputed and also insisted that it would be better policy to throw open the vast tracts to settlement than to confirm them simply in order to protect innocent purchasers. The councillors, assemblymen and officials were among the largest holders of these grants and therefore were especially anxious not to have the quit rent act disapproved in England. As to the evils which would result from the ratification of the act, St. John called attention to the large loss which the crown would suffer in the matter of arrears of rent, while, owing to the indefinite bounds and location of the grants, the patentees had been able to take all the best lands along the navigable rivers and, in many cases, after cutting off the timber to move on to other tracts. Settlers who now wanted such lands had to move on to other colonies. The old planters had also abused the institution of head rights to increase their monopoly, while under a reservation authorized by a resolve of the provincial council the grantees considered themselves absolved from the necessity of securing warrants from the governor or deputations from the surveyor general and had taken up land without surveys and wherever and to what extent they chose.

As soon as the parties concerned learned of the attacks which St. John was making on their policy they began to annoy him in all possible ways. As usual, the fees charged in the surveyor general's office proved to be his vulnerable point, and particularly in the executive council a prolonged and bitter controversy with him over this matter was raised.[2]

[1] Smith, 38, 39; C. O. 5/362, O. P. S. C., Sept. 21, and Dec. 6, 1732, June 5, 1733.

[2] C. O. 5/434, Ex. C. J., S. C., 1732–1733; C. O. 5/431, U. H. J., 1731, S.1733; C. Stat., III, 343.

It was charged that his fees for the surveys required in laying out the townships were excessive and an act was passed in 1733 limiting them in all cases to 4d currency per acre, which St. John was required to share equally with his deputies. From the contradictory statements which appear in the disputes with St. John which preceded this act it would seem that he had been taking 4d per acre for himself and allowing his deputies to take fees in addition to this. Charges of unfairness and extortion were bandied about on both sides. Complaints were also made against St. John because he had unduly delayed to produce his patent and take the oath for the office of deputy auditor and had treated the council and assembly with contempt. In a succession of stormy interviews with the governor and council St. John parried their threats as well as he could, but after a while refused to answer except in writing.[1]

The next step in the controversy was the imprisonment of Thomas Cooper, an assistant judge of the court of pleas, and two others for surveying land in certain tracts about Port Royal which it was claimed that the speculators had appropriated to the exclusion of intending settlers. Cooper's object in this was to bring the case into court and test the validity of titles.[2] But instead of seeking a judicial decision, the landlords applied to the assembly and it ordered Cooper and two of his assistants into the custody of its messenger, where he remained for five weeks. He sued out a writ of *habeas corpus*, but the messenger refused to obey. A second and a third writ, issued by other parties, met with the same reception. Cooper then petitioned the governor and council and the governor separately, but these petitions were disregarded and the two merchants who carried the petition to Johnson were ordered into custody, and were released only after paying heavy fees and asking pardon. Several other merchants and lawyers were imprisoned for carrying petitions to members of the house who were justices of the peace, and regained their liberty only after similar humiliation. The extreme and arbitrary attitude of the assembly now brought

[1] Colls. of S. C. Hist. Soc., II, 131–135; C. O. 5/364, O. P. S. C. Jan. 29 and Apr. 23, 1733.

[2] C. O. 5/365, O. P. S. C., May 12, 1733.

on a conflict with the courts. Robert Wright, the chief justice, issued the writs to the messenger of the house requiring the release of the accused. He also addressed the executive council on the bold attack which was being made upon the laws. By mere resolutions of its own, he said, the assembly was attempting to set aside the laws and to supersede the writ of *habeas corpus,* which was the chief guaranty of English liberty.[1]

The next step of the group of land speculators was to introduce and pass a bill, the object of which was to indemnify the messenger of the house, and, as a means to this end, to assert the doctrine of legislative absolutism. It declared that no public officer should be liable to suit or penalty for refusing obedience to writs of *habeas corpus* which were sought on behalf of persons who were imprisoned under order of either house of assembly for violating its privileges. The debate on this bill in the upper house was distinguished by two speeches, one by Francis Yonge in its favor, and the other by Wright in opposition.[2] Yonge claimed that the lower house possessed all the privileges of the house of commons, and cited the cases of Manwaring (in the time of Charles I), Sacheverell, the directors of the South Sea Company, and the like, for the purpose of showing that on many occasions the commons had pursued a course similar to that of the present assembly. It was not until the upper house had expressed its full concurrence with the argument of Yonge, approved of the course of the assembly and had rejected the appeal of Cooper and his associates for relief that Wright delivered his speech. He claimed for the judges the right to issue writs to any officer requiring him to show cause for arrest or commitment, this being necessary as a protection against arbitrary violence. Parliament, he reminded his hearers, had declared by statute in 13 Charles II that all who affirmed that either or both houses had legislative power without the king were guilty of a *præmunire,* and the tendency of this bill was to strengthen resolves of that kind, which were likely to lead to high offences.

[1] C. O. 5/434, Ex. C. J., Apr. 13, 1733; Smith, *op. cit.,* 45.

[2] C. O. 5/431, J. of U. H., Apr. 14 and 27, 1733. Yonge's speech was published in the S. C. Gazette. See also L. H. J.

Yonge was again sent to England as agent,[1] and Johnson, in transmitting the act which was in the dispute, urged its approval by the home government in order to put a stop to the litigious proceedings of some lawyers who had aided in procuring their own commitment in order to raise contributions from the magistrates.   But the petition of Cooper and his associates revealed the true nature of their troubles and Fane, the counsel of the board of trade, reported that the object of the act seemed to be to secure its supporters from the just resentment of those whom they had injured.   Therefore, on report from the board of trade, an order in council was issued, in April, 1734, for the disallowance of the act.[2]

But meantime the lower house at Charlestown had made a direct attack upon Chief Justice Wright by refusing to provide for his salary in the estimates for 1734.   So strong was their feeling against him that they declared, if his salary had been established by statute, they would have introduced a bill to disqualify him.[3]   As another feature of the policy of reprisal, St. John was arrested and detained as a prisoner until, as the result of the petition of his to the board of trade, he was released by order of that body, he having been imprisoned on a slight and frivolous pretense.[4]   Cooper was also removed from his judgeship by Johnson on the ground that his assuming to survey lands and publishing the same was a contempt of royal authority, the power to order survey resting only with the governor and council.[5]   The dominant faction on various pretexts refused to admit to their seats friends of Cooper and St. John, when returned to the assembly. But though the governor and council agreed with the majority of the lower house on the main points at issue, they were

[1] There he was for a time associated with Peregrine Fury, who was resident agent for South Carolina from 1731 to 1749.   Fury was chosen by the assembly on the recommendation of the duke of Newcastle, it being considered necessary to have one who was acceptable to the duke.   C. O. 5/431, U. H. J., July 15, 1731; Smith, 416.

[2] C. O. 5/363, O. P. S. C. May 4 and Dec. 6, 1733, Jan. 19, 1733/4;   C. O. 5/401, E. B. S. C. Feb. 15, 1733/4;   Stat. of S. C., III, 348.

[3] L. H. J. and U. H. J., May, 1733.   Wright was son of Sir James Wright, whose services to the cause of James II ended with the Trial of the Seven Bishops, over which he presided.   The son of the chief justice of South Carolina was the famous Sir James Wright who was so successful as governor of Georgia.

[4] Colls. of S. C. Hist. Soc., II, 137;   C. O. 5/401, E. B. S. C., June 7, 1733.

[5] C. O. 5/363, O. P. S. C., May 16, 1734.

opposed to the witholding of the salary of the chief justice as a policy which might at any time be used to cripple the executive. They were especially impressed with this danger because at this time Middleton was trying to recover the salary which was due him for the time when he was acting governor. The case dragged on for years and in the end Middleton received only a part of what was due him.[1] It required an order from the crown to secure for the chief justice even a third of the salary which was his due. In 1735 by royal warrant his salary was charged against the quit rent fund and in this way his support passed from under the control of the assembly.[2]

The attacks upon the chief justice were not limited to his salary. His official authority was also assailed. By laws of 1731 and 1732 the judicial system of South Carolina was reëstablished after the confusion of Middleton's administration, during a large part of which the courts had been closed.[3] Full provision was made in these for jury trial and for a superior criminal court of the province under the title of court of general sessions of the peace, oyer and terminer, assize and general gaol delivery. It was to meet twice a year at Charlestown and to be presided over by the chief justice and two or more assistants. A notable advance was made in a provision that every person who was accused of a capital crime should have a copy of the indictment against him, have counsel learned in the law to defend him and be allowed to summon witnesses. By another statute it was provided that a court of common pleas, with jurisdiction over civil cases, should meet quarterly and be presided over also by the chief justice and assistants, he being empowered to act in their absence. By an act of 1727, which was disallowed by the privy council in 1732, the first step of the process in civil actions was changed from a summons to a *capias*.[4] The former might be left at a man's house, but the latter must be served upon him personally. The British merchants, who had debts due them in the

---

[1] L. H. J. ,March, 1734.

[2] C. O. 5401, E. B. S. C., June 13, 1735; Acts of P. C. Col., 1720–1745, p. 459.

[3] Stat. of S. C., III, 274–287, 323–326, VII, 184–189; Smith, 126 *et seq.*

[4] C. O. 5/401 E. B. S. C., Apr. 2, 1731, Mar. 7, 1731/2.

colonies, strongly objected to this because the colonists were so remote from home and because of the distance at which many of them lived from Charlestown. For these reasons the board of trade, after learning from Governor Johnson that the assembly probably could not be induced to change the provision, recommended the disallowance of the act and an order to the effect was issued by the privy council.

The next change which was attempted in the judicial system was directed against the chief justice and originated with the land speculators whom he had been opposing. In April, 1734, an act was passed reversing completely the position which assistants regularly held toward the chief justice. It provided that they should have an equal voice with him and authorized them to hold court in his absence.[1] Hitherto they could only adjourn the court until he came. Wright and his friends petitioned the crown for the repeal not only of this act but also of that establishing the court of common pleas, in 1732. The reason for the latter request was that under his authority, given in that law, to appoint two assistant justices, Johnson had appointed two men who not only were ignorant of the law but were declared opponents of the chief justice, ready to override his acts and to take a part of his fees.[2] The objection to the latter act lay in the unwarranted position given by it to the assistants, the petitioners urging that they should be reduced to the position of puisne judges in English courts. This representation prevailed and the two acts were disallowed. After the death of Governor Johnson, in 1735, an additional instruction was sent to Thomas Broughton, who succeeded as acting governor, that he should appoint two assistant judges in each provincial court who should have the same powers as puisne judges in England. Benjamin Whitaker, a man whom we have already seen as an active opponent of the land speculators and who, as successor of Chief Justice Wright, was to leave behind him some most valuable statements concerning the judicial system of South Carolina, addressed to Lieutenant Governor Bull in 1742 a valuable memorial in which he reviewed the history of the office of assistant judges

[1] S. C. Stats., VII, 184–189.
[2] C. O. 5/401, E. B. S. C., Aug. 14, 1735.

and urged that they be kept in due subordination to the chief justice.[1] As from the nature of the case they could not be trained lawyers, this course was now followed.

Before the question of the salary of the chief justice passed finally from view a spirited discussion arose between the two houses over the right of the council to amend money bills. In February, 1735, the council reminded the lower house that the salary of the chief justice was nearly three years in arrears and that the subject should be considered. After voting down two motions in which sums were specified as proper to be granted him, the lower house excluded his name from the estimate altogether. The upper house then stated that they could not read the tax bill a second time until provision was made for the chief justice. When, on special request for the tax bill that it might be finished before the Easter holidays, the assembly found that the upper house had inserted an item of £2100 — £700 per annum for three years — as the salary of the chief justice, the bill was unanimously rejected. A strong set of resolutions was then sent to the council, with a message denying its right to amend money bills.[2]

After a prorogation of two weeks the assembly read for the first time a new tax bill and sent it to the council. In reply the council cited the governor's instructions as they were in Nicholson's time, and still continued, which sought to put the two houses on an equality so far as the framing and amending of money bills was concerned. A committee of the lower house then searched for precedents and verbally reported that the position which it now claimed had been asserted and maintained in 1725 when Middleton was beginning his administration. In a message to the upper house [3] the hope was expressed that its regard for the liberty of the people would prevent it from insisting upon the governor's instruction, never assented to by the assembly, to the serious injury of the rights of the lower house. To this body, as to the representative assemblies generally in the colonies, the practice of parliament with reference to money bills furnished an ideal precedent against the influence of which royal in-

[1] C. O. 5/441, Ex. C. J. Oct., 5, 1742; Smith, 129.
[2] L. H. J. and U. H. J., Feb. and March, 1735; Smith, *op. cit.*, 296 *et seq.*
[3] L. H. J., Apr. 23, 1735.

structions were cited in vain. To this procedure the colonists clung, as they did to the principles of the *habeas corpus* act, of the bill of rights and the toleration act — though they did not mention the dominions — because they made for the liberty of the subject. In this instance, as in so many others, the upper house gave way and the bill was passed without change.

Chief Justice Wright now carried his claim before the administrative boards in England. The board of trade listened to statements from Fury and Yonge, the agents of South Carolina, from Hume, a former speaker of the assembly, and from Shelton, the secretary of the late board of proprietors. In this way it learned that under the proprietors the salary of the chief justice had been paid from the quit rents, but since the crown took control it had been subject to grant by the assembly. Adopting this as a way of escape from the present difficulty, a royal warrant was issued for the payment of an annual salary to the chief justice of £1000 currency from the quit rents.[1]

This, however, did not free the chief justice from dependence upon the assembly for the appropriation of this sum, as well as his arrears and his salary for years to come. Broughton was now lieutenant governor and he joined with the council in the winter and spring of 1736 in efforts to secure obedience to the royal warrant. The assembly refused to obey this on the ground — which was doubtless true — that the chief justice had never been paid a regular salary but only allowances for special services. This they claimed in a later message to be the general practice in the colonies, also a statement which was to a large extent true. For these reasons they at first voted down every proposal to give the chief justice anything. But finally, as a result of persistent efforts on the part of Broughton and the council, £700 was allowed to Wright in full of all his services and this was incorporated in the appropriation act.[2]

As a triennial act was in force in South Carolina and the life of the existing assembly had nearly expired, a new house was elected in the fall of 1736. Of this Charles Pinckney

---

[1] C. O. 5/401, E. B. S. C., June 13, 1735; Smith, 299.
[2] L. H. J., Jan.–May, 1736; Smith, 301.

was chosen speaker. He was the man who in the previous assembly had drafted the resolutions which so vigorously asserted the exclusive control of the lower house over appropriations. When the house appeared before the governor, Pinckney demanded the preservation of its known privileges. Henceforward this became the custom. When, therefore, Broughton again brought forward the claim of the chief justice for arrears to the amount of £3600 and that a salary of £1000 a year be provided for the future, in obedience to the royal warrant, it was vain to hope for a reply different from that which had been given by the previous assembly. It refused to reopen the question and both the royal warrant and the just claims of the chief justice were totally ignored.[1]

But the controversy between the two houses over the share of the council in formulating appropriation bills continued much longer. It is probable that in 1735 the lower house began to insist that those who had claims against the government for services should present their accounts to its committee only. Prior to that time estimates had been formed by a joint committee of the two houses on petitions and accounts. In accordance with this practice, on February 23, 1736/7, the upper house sent down a request for a conference committee on a tax bill.[2] To this the lower house declined to accede. The council in reply referred in general terms to earlier South Carolina precedents which were favorable to its claim. But the lower house insisted in reply that no colonial precedents could supersede the rights to which all English subjects were entitled from the ancient and fundamental constitution of the country on which they depended. The council sent down a protest against this view, but at the same time read the bill for the second time and a few days later passed it. But in the interval another dispute had arisen over the title which should be given in the estimates to Hammerton, the secretary of the province, and over a witticism which had been used at his expense. As the secretary was a member of the council, it insisted that the assembly should punish the author of the witticism. The latter body, in true colonial style, interpreted this as an infringement of the rights

---

[1] L. H. J., Nov. and Dec., 1737; Smith, 302.
[2] L. H. J., Feb. 23, 1736/7, *et seq.*

of its members to freedom of speech, and sent to the council a stoutly worded series of resolutions on this subject. As Broughton was involved with the council in this matter, he too was denounced by the house for violating its privileges and he had to state that he had no intention of invading its rights before it would proceed with business.

Following, though unconsciously, in the wake of New York and other colonies, the lower house now proceeded at once to assume control of expenditure. As war was becoming imminent with the Spanish, the opportunity for such tactics was favorable. The royal instruction on this subject, to the effect that all payments from the treasury should be made under the governor's warrant, was ignored as the royal warrant for the payment of the salary of the chief justice had been. It was provided that the sum of £6000, which was appropriated in 1737 for an expedition against the Spaniards and Indians, should be paid out only under orders drawn by the governor, council and a committee of the assembly. In response to a protest against this from the chief justice, the house ordered that its committee for the purpose of the bill should consist of the members who resided in or near Charlestown, that the delay in issuing money should be as slight as possible.[1]

As Broughton died in November, 1737, and Middleton had passed away in the previous September,[2] the government now devolved on another Carolinian, William Bull, who as president of the council, and afterward as lieutenant governor, stood at the head of affairs until the arrival of the next royal appointee, James Glen, in 1743.[3] William Bull, as Indian commissioner and member of the council, had long been in official life and was to be closely followed in this career by his son of the same name, who was elected speaker of the assembly in 1740. The Bulls were quiet, tactful, efficient men, thoroughly familiar with South Carolina affairs and sympathetic with its spirit; duly regardful also of the interests and rights of the home government. In due time the

[1] L. H. J. Mar., 1736/7.
[2] C. O. 5/366, O. B. S. C., Dec. 10, 1737.
[3] McCrady, op. cit., 177 et seq.; C. O. 5/440, Ex. C. J., Apr. 3, 1739. In the board of trade papers are many entries in reference to the appointment of Samuel Horsey, who did not live to assume the governorship.

son succeeded to the lieutenant governorship which had been held by his father and was acting in that capacity during the troubles which immediately preceded the Declaration of Independence in 1776. As the later thirties were a time of threatened or actual war, the opportunity was favorable for the lower house to maintain and extend its claims, and steady progress in this direction was made. In April, 1739, it struck out certain amendments which the council had made in an explanatory bill for maintaining a watch in Charlestown. The council asked for a conference in which to discuss what they charged to be unparliamentary conduct in this matter. The assembly in its reply asserted that, as this was a tax bill, it was the council which was guilty of unparliamentary conduct, because it should never have proposed any amendments. Their sole power to fix the terms of money bills at all stages of their progress was again asserted to its fullest extent.

Meantime the general duty bill, including rates on the importation of negroes, liquors and merchandise, came up for consideration. The upper house found that it lacked specific statements of claims with vouchers and was drawn for a lump sum. In order to check possible extravagances it asked for a conference committee. The lower house replied that it had already passed the treasurer's accounts separately and the council might do the same. Then in a long series of messages the discussion drifted off into a repetition of the exclusive claims of the lower house in reference to money bills which had been emphasized a few months before. The council asserted that it would allow no measure to pass until it had been subjected to such alterations as it thought necessary for his majesty's service. As an incident of this controversy, the council insisted that Bull should absent himself while they were engaged in debate, and to this he seems to have acceded without opposition. During the rest of his administration the council as upper house conducted its business without the presence of the acting governor, though he continued to preside in the executive councils.

Returning to the controversy over money bills about the middle of April, 1739, it was interrupted by a recess of about six weeks. But when the session was resumed it began again, and effectually blocked action on both bills. A most detailed report was made by a committee of the lower house in support of the contentions of that body in which it was again asserted that a royal instruction could not set aside fundamental rights of the people which had been handed down from their ancestors. Though the council urged Bull to prorogue or dissolve the assembly, he declined to interfere. Finally he permitted an adjournment until September, and before that time came dissolved the assembly and ordered a new election. Pinckney and Whitaker, who had probably been the leaders in the last assembly, were reëlected and the former again chosen speaker. A severe visitation of smallpox delayed the meeting of the assembly for two months, and when it met for business in November, Oglethorpe was calling earnestly for aid against St. Augustine and the need for defence at home both on the coast and against the Indians was pressing.

The tax bill was at once read for the first time by the lower house and sent to the council. This body demanded a joint committee on petitions and accounts, but the lower house insisted that they could not concede this without giving up their rights as Englishmen. A deadlock followed, the upper house keeping the bill for a month.[1] Then an urgent message was sent from the assembly and as a result a joint committee on procedure in passing bills was appointed. Its report was accepted, which, in respect to money bills, was to the effect that the upper house should make out a schedule of amendments which it thought necessary and send them down with the bills; these, if approved by the lower house, should be passed by it, added to the bills and sent to the upper house to receive its final confirmation. After some further discussion between the houses this plan was accepted provisionally by the council because of the pressure of war, and nineteen amendments to the duty bill which it desired were accepted by the lower house. It also insisted that this was no precedent and that a sole control over money bills continued as its right. The arrangement, however, was expressly continued by succeeding assemblies until 1745, after which by tacit agreement it was kept in force till the close

[1] L. H. J. and U. H. J., Nov. and Dec., 1739; Smith, 106, 311.

of the colonial period. A working agreement was thus reached under which the upper house retained to a degree the share in framing money bills which it had originally claimed. During Bull's administration no further controversy occurred between the houses except a brief one in 1743 as to the person who should be designated as treasurer.[1]

The rapid extension of settlement in both the Carolinas, and the consequent importance of the land question, led the British government in 1739 to appoint Henry McCulloh, a London merchant, commissioner for inspecting and controlling his majesty's revenues and grants of land in North and South Carolina. In the persons of this man and his son, and in the two-fold capacity of royal commissioners and large investors in colonial lands on their own account, the McCullohs were destined to important careers in the Carolinas which were to continue during the remainder of the colonial period. The abuses which the elder McCulloh was sent over to correct were those against which we have seen St. John vainly struggling. The object of the appointments was, if possible, to prevent the wholesale granting of township lands to parties who had no intention of settling them and to restrict head rights to fifty acres for every member of a grantee's household. McCulloh was also to secure a better collection of the quit rents and in general an abatement of the frauds as a result of which the crown was suffering and land, especially in the middle section of the province, was being monopolized in large tracts to the exclusion of actual settlers.[2] His instructions required the applicant for land to prove his claims before the governor and council when at least four members of the council were present who had no interest in the land petitioned for. On the granting of a petition a warrant describing the land was drawn and signed by governor and council and made returnable by the surveyor within a year from date. On the return of the warrant the grant was issued and recorded in the secretary's office, a docket of the same being entered in the office of the deputy auditor. Within

[1] L. H. J. and U. H. J., March and April, 1743; Smith, 313.

[2] Smith, *op. cit.* 48, 57; C. O. 5/368, O. P. S. C., Aug. 14, 1740. One of the best accounts of the policy which McCulloh was sent over to execute and of the obstacles which he vainly tried to overcome is in his letter to Governor Bull, Feb. 16, 1742/3, C. O. 5/369; O. P. S. C.

twelve months copies of all these entries were required to be sent to the treasury board or the board of trade in England. Requirements such as these had been in force in Maryland almost from the date of settlement and were necessary in all the colonies if a systematic territorial policy was to be followed so as to conserve the interests of crown or proprietor, as well as those of the ordinary colonist. But so different was it from the loose practices which prevailed, not only in the Carolinas but in the colonies generally, that the efforts of a royal commissioner to enforce it, though well intentioned, were doomed to failure from the outset.

As soon as he arrived at Charlestown, McCulloh [1] had his errand stated to the assembly and issued a circular letter to the freeholders asking for their coöperation. Notice was also given to all who had not registered their lands in the office of the deputy auditor to do so at once, and all were warned that land would be declared forfeited after a delay of five years in the payment of quit rents. McCulloh also began to labor for the passage of a law which would enable him to secure a rent roll of the province. But he had no independent authority and was forced to depend upon the aid of other officials, and especially of the governor, to accomplish anything. He tried to secure admission to the council, but failed. The board of trade favored his admission, though no order was issued upon the subject, as had been done in the case of the surveyor general of customs.[2] As was to be expected, McCulloh found himself opposed by the united influence of the council, though the assembly seemed a little more inclined to his ideas. After an attempted slave insurrection at Stono a bill for increasing the number of white servants was proposed, but the council refused even to read it, lest it might occasion an inquiry into the amount of land which was held by its members. Settlers of Williamsburg, one of the eleven townships which the crown had ordered to be established, appealed to McCulloh in vain to secure the return of tracts within their limits which had been wrongfully

---

[1] Concerning the policy and experiences of McCulloh in South Carolina, see the entries in O. P. S. C. beginning in May and Aug., 1739, continued in Nov., 1741, and especially during the years 1743 and 1744. There are also many entries concerning McCulloh in N. C. Col. Recs., IV.

[2] C. O. 5/402, E. B. S. C., Aug. 30, 1739.

granted to others. These complaints were continued for a long time and came from other townships as well.[1]

As a part of his plan for securing a rent roll McCulloh made great efforts to secure lists of mesne conveyances, or the records of purchases and sales of land once granted, but he found it impossible to do so. He urged that the offices of receiver of quit rents and treasurer be united in order that the first-named official might avail himself of the lists of holdings which had to be submitted as the basis of levy of the land tax; but this of course was not done. The governor and council persisted in the former method of granting lands in disregard of the instructions which had been given to McCulloh. He was somewhat officious and interfered in some cases with affairs which lay outside his sphere. In this way he offended the governor for though Bull was a man of easy temper he was a Carolinian; he resented some of the doings of the royal commissioner and could not be induced to break with his friends in the council.

As McCulloh was unable to secure any increase in the amount of quit rents, he failed to obtain a salary. Shortly before he came to South Carolina the establishment of a court of exchequer had been somewhat discussed. McCulloh now urged the measure as an aid to himself, but, though supported by the board of trade, the step was not taken.[2] He also asked that power be given him to stop the support of all disobedient crown officials, a request which manifestly would not be granted. Becoming at length discouraged by his lack of success, McCulloh retired for a time to North Carolina, where he obtained large tracts of land on the strength of promises to bring over colonists and enter upon the production of naval stores. He thus became to an extent an imitator of the policy which he was laboring to check in the southern province.

The extent to which the crown had suffered is indicated by a memorial submitted to the governor and council in 1743

---

[1] C. O. 5/369, O. P. S. C., Mar. 17, 1742/3, with inclosures. For a similar experience of the grantees of Purrysburg, a little earlier, see C. O. 5, E. B. S. C., July 16, Sept. 5 and Dec. 19, 1734. C. O. 5/363, O. P. S. C. Apr. 8 and July 13, 1734.

[2] C. O. 5/401, E. B. S. C., July 25, 1738. See C. O. 5/364, O. P. S. C., Nov. 21 1732, for an earlier move of Governor Johnson for a court of exchequer.

by George Hunter, who was then surveyor general. This contained a list of 291 plots (114,584 acres) of land surveyed under common warrants, and of 156 plots (61,865 acres) surveyed under township warrants, all of which Hunter proposed should be vacated after suitable notification on the ground that the grants had not been settled or quit rents paid on them.[1] The land then might be sold to actual settlers. In 1744 some response was made to the efforts of McCulloh and Whitaker in the passage of an act providing for the deposit in the office of the deputy auditor of descriptions of all lands held outside of townships and of rents due thereon. This act also empowered persons to resign to the crown lands which they held in excess of what they had been able to cultivate and so to escape future assessment for quit rents upon them.[2] Some improvement in conditions seems to have accompanied the passage of this law.

In a controversy like this, had the province possessed an efficient judicial system, with trained judges, McCulloh might have resorted to the courts as against the council. But in South Carolina, as in other colonies, the judiciary was not sufficiently independent or intelligent for action of this sort. The chancery consisted of the governor and council. It, as well as the other courts, had been established by acts of the assembly and their powers were subject to further change by the same authority. The two common law courts did not possess all the powers of either king's bench or common pleas in England, and certain forms of English procedure were excluded. The chancery had proceeded only on the equity side, while no officers had been appointed on the plea side, where lay the ordinary jurisdiction of the chancery court in England affecting matters of property. The lack of a court of exchequer was also a very important defect. For these reasons the officials and people of South Carolina could not avail themselves of all the common law for securing the objects they sought. As to statute law, the act of 1712 had declared a long list of British statutes to be in force in South Carolina to the exclusion of all others, while the laws

[1] C. O. 5/370, O. P. S. C., Apr. 29, 1743.
[2] Stats. of S. C., III, 633; C. O. 5/370, O. P. S. C., June 25, 1744, Whitaker, to board of trade, with inclosures.

which had been passed for the establishment of courts forbade them to put into force any statutes of Great Britain which did not mention the dominions or which did not necessarily extend thither.

In 1743 Benjamin Whitaker, who easily had one of the best legal minds in the colonies, reasoned after this fashion about the courts in their relation to the battle which he and McCulloh were waging. And at the close of his very important paper he threw out what is apparently the earliest suggestion ever made that the courts ought to pass on the constitutionality of acts of the general assembly. He was brought to this idea by observing that the laws of the province were often inconsistent with those of Great Britain. The provincial acts were extremely defective and Whitaker had seen the late chief justice hampered by them in his efforts to administer justice, as his commission required, in accordance with the laws of Great Britain. He, too, faced the same difficulty. Were laws, then, which not alone contradicted the royal instructions but violated the prerogative to be voidable only by disallowance, or were they void *ab initio?* Were they enforceable until repealed, or might judges, when cases involving them came up, pronounce them void? Was repugnancy to be understood as related to the common law or only to it as modified by statutes? These were questions about which Whitaker was pondering before the middle of the eighteenth century. But the procedure which he had in mind involved too great a departure from English practice to receive attention at that time, and the idea is interesting only as the remote anticipation of a practice which later became a corner stone of American federalism.[1]

While these internal controversies were in progress and the settlement of South Carolina was steadily advancing, as is evidenced by the multitude of land grants which passed the executive council, events of a wider significance were occurring which helped to define its position as a border province. The central event of this nature was the founding of Georgia in 1732. Like the grants of Maryland and the Carolinas in their relation to Virginia, this also furnished a good

[1] C. O. 5/442, Ex. C. J., Mar. 29, 1743; C. O. 5369, O. P. S. C., Mar. 25, 1743; Smith, 132.

illustration of the way in which the crown disposed of its unsettled domain, though it had lain within the original charter limits of a province. The southern boundary of the Carolina grant of 1665 was fixed at the beginning of the twenty-ninth degree of latitude, which lay south of the present limits of Florida. When royal government was fully established at Charlestown, settlements on the south had scarcely reached the Savannah river. The unsuccessful attempt to establish Fort King George on the Atlamaha river has already been described. The original Georgia grant comprised that part of this unsettled region which lay between the Savannah and the Altamaha. A broad belt of territory between the Altamaha and Florida was left ungranted and therefore for some thirty years might possibly be regarded as a part of South Carolina.

The effect which the founding of Georgia had on relations with the Spaniards and as an event which contributed to the outbreak of war in 1739 is considered in another connection. South Carolina was drawn into that war as itself a border province and bound in honor and interest to assist its weaker neighbor on the south. Both before and after the war, also, the relations between these provinces on the whole were friendly, thus presenting a contrast to those which early existed between Virginia and Maryland, to say nothing of the many jealousies and the slight coöperation which existed between New York and New England in affairs which concerned the northern frontier. No opposition was made by South Carolina to the Georgia grant, and when Oglethorpe and his colonists reached Port Royal both the executive council and the legislature extended to them their assistance.[1] They were allowed the use of the barracks at Port Royal, a scout boat was sent to assist, and a small body of troops was detailed to escort the newcomers to their place of settlement. Colonel William Bull accompanied Oglethorpe to the Savannah river to aid in selecting a site for the new town. Influence was exerted to induce the Indians to aid the new settlers. Not only was this in harmony with instructions

[1] C. O. 5/434 Ex. C. S. C., Jan. 12, 1732/3; C. O. 5/431; U. H. J., Jan. 19, 1732/3; C. O. 5/401, E. B. S. C., Sept. 6, 1732; Harris, Memorials of Oglethorpe, 353.

from the privy council to Governor Johnson, but it was also a natural expression of good will on the part of the South Carolinians themselves. When Oglethorpe returned on his first visit to England a South Carolinian was associated with a Georgian in the management of many of the affairs of the province.[1] In cases when it might be necessary for the militia of the two provinces to take the field together it must be under the command of an officer from South Carolina.

Beginning in 1735, however, harmony between the two colonies was somewhat disturbed by a controversy over Indian trade. As had been the case with Virginia years before, South Carolina inferred that her traders would continue after the settlement of Georgia to enjoy freedom of access to the tribes south of the Savannah river. But as Georgia, like most of the colonies, adopted a license system, this was not the case. Captain Patrick Mackay, who was sent by Georgia into the country of the Creeks as Indian agent and also to build a post there, undertook without authority to displace certain traders and put in others, threatening any who should return later with only South Carolina licenses. The prohibition by Georgia of traffic in rum and threats of her officials to seize craft on the Savannah river which had liquor on board added to the irritation.[2] Mackay was removed from his post and much correspondence followed between the two colonies. A special session of the South Carolina assembly was called and a committee was sent to Savannah to confer with Oglethorpe on the subject. The question whether any province could wholly exclude colonists or British merchants from the Indian trade was referred to the law officers in England. Their opinion, delivered in July, 1737, was that such a course would be illegal, but the requirement of a license was no more than a proper regulation of trade within a province.[3] This was rather noncommittal and implied the necessity of considerate action

---

[1] Ga. Col. Recs., II, 43, 45; C. O. 5/364, O. P. S. C., Dec. 1735.

[2] C. O. 5/364, O. P. S. C., July 4 and Dec., 1735; C. O. 5/366, ibid., July 28, 1737; C. O. 5/401, E. B. S. C., May 21 and Sept. 14, 1737. Journals of executive council and of the two houses of the South Carolina legisture, beginning in April and July of that year. There is also much material in the Georgia Col. Recs., V, XXI. Smith, 218.

[3] Chalmers, Colonial Opinions, 591.

on both sides. At the same time the board of trade was listening to testimony and arguments of counsel on behalf of both the colonies which were concerned. Its opinion, as reported to the privy council, was that, because of its importance and of the danger that the French and Spaniards might profit by the dispute, the Indian trade should be free and the Georgia law should not be strictly interpreted. South Carolina licenses, issued at Charlestown, should be accepted as well as those issued by Georgia at Savannah. Trade on the Savannah river should be free and no vessels stopped unless they attempted to land rum in Georgia. In the following year an instruction was issued to the Georgia trustees that an act should be prepared which would be mutually satisfactory to the two provinces, that the imposing of a special fee on Carolina traders should cease and licenses be granted to such of them as brought certificates from the governor at Charlestown.[1] This was followed by a series of experiments in reciprocal trade relations which were continued with diminishing friction until 1750 or later.[2]

If we consider Robert Johnson to have been virtually a South Carolinian by 1743 when James Glen took office as governor, the province for nearly two decades had been under the administration of men who were either colonists themselves or pretty fully identified with the aristocracy which governed at Charlestown. On the whole this had been favorable to growth of the spirit of independence within the colony. Glen had received his appointment in 1738, but for five years his removal to America had been delayed and during that interval the traditions of colonial self-government had been slowly strengthened under the quiet and successful rule of William Bull. Glen administered his office for thirteen years, from 1743 to 1756, and effectually broke the tradition of government by Carolinians. He was a Scotchman, trained in the university and not in the army, and had had some experience in civil administration in his own country. He soon became well informed concerning his own province and colonial affairs generally. This knowledge he obtained not only by official and social intercourse

[1] C. O. 5/401, E. B. S. C., Sept. 14, 1727 and June 21, 1728.
[2] Ga. Recs., V, 546.

and repeated journeys through the province and into the Indian country, but apparently by the study of historical materials. He wrote and spoke well, though profusely and sometimes rhetorically, and for a colonial official made an unusual display of learning.[1] He possessed energy and showed it by his activity in office and the faithful performance of its duties. Tactful he was and socially agreeable, but somewhat vain and therefore susceptible to flattery. Of this the assembly became aware and on occasion skilfully played upon his weakness to their own advantage. Though a loyal supporter of the prerogative, Glen was not blind to the colonial point of view, and for his yielding to that and a certain looseness in some matters of official routine, he was sharply criticised by the board of trade after it fell under the influence of the earl of Halifax. Glen seems to have been fonder of Indian affairs and of the study of general American conditions to which they naturally led than of any other phase of his work, and it was due to him that detailed records of correspondence and acts of the executive council in reference to these matters were first kept at Charlestown.

Now that war was beginning with the French, South Carolina and the colonies near by would need protection toward the west as well as the south, and peril from the sea was redoubled. At last the British government had been moved to respond, though feebly, to a petition which two years before had been sent by the assembly at Charlestown to the king for aid. This petition had been supported by various persons from the province and England, among them Colonel Vanderdussen, James Abercromby, the attorney general, and merchants who were engaged in the South Carolina trade.[2]

---

[1] An example of this may be found in his letter to the board of trade, dated in Feb., 1750/1, on the boundaries of South Carolina and on the history of its discovery and of the way in which British secured their right to it. Another example of his comprehensive knowledge of the province appeared in 1761, in his published, but anonymous, "Description of South Carolina," Carroll's Hist. Colls., II, 191–272. An earlier version of this has been reprinted by Weston, "Docs. Connected with the Hist. of S. C.," London, 1856. As this originated in answers to queries of the board of trade, it was submitted to the assembly and criticised by it. C. O. 5/461, U. H. J., May 5, 1749. What appears to be the original of the answers to the queries is in C. O. 5/392, O. P. S. C., under date of July 19, 1749.

[2] C. O. 5/443, U. H. J., June 31, 1742; C. O. 5/448, Feb., 1744; C. O. 5/370,

In the summer of 1744 an order was issued, as requested, for the raising of three independent companies, but it was not until the beginning of 1746 that the sixty recruits and their officers reached Charlestown. The majority of the men, therefore, who were to constitute the force had to be raised in the northern colonies. This was done, and by the beginning of 1748 the companies were full. The war was then nearly over, but they were retained in garrison service at various points and were not disbanded until the close of the last intercolonial war. The province bore all, or by far the chief part, of the cost of maintaining this force, including their pay and provision for their barracks.

The attack of the Spaniards upon Georgia in 1742 had occasioned the expenditure of about £6000 currency on the fortifications of Charlestown.[1] Upon the opening of the war with France reports were circulated that another attack from the south might be expected. Under the influence of these, after discussing elaborate plans of defence for the town, a summons was sent to the Bahamas for Captain Bruce, an engineer. He arrived at the beginning of 1745. After inspecting the harbor and town he recommended a work for the protection of Hog Island Creek, a minor entrance to the harbor, and a costly series of defensive works to extend across the neck on which the town is situated for its protection toward the land. Because the cost of these works was greater than the province could bear, this plan had to be abandoned. A moat commanded by one or two bastions, and a horseshoe battery were, however, constructed on the neck, according to a cheaper plan recommended by the commissioners of fortifications. The credit of the province was pledged for their cost by the issue of the so-called fortification orders to the amount of £20,000. The securing and keeping of guardships sufficient for protection against the numerous privateers off the coast and against minor attacks from hostile colonies was another object of solicitude, and to meet these dangers it is not strange that Glen should suggest the sending of forces from the British West Indies; but no attention

O. P. May 9 and July 19, 1744; C. O. 5/371, Feb. 11, 1745/6. Smith, S. C. as a Royal Province, 193.

[1] Council and Assembly Journals; Smith, 199 *et seq.*

was paid to such suggestions. To the efforts which it was necessary to make to keep peace with the Indians and ward off renewed attacks by the French and their savage allies from the west reference has elsewhere been made. Though the weak defences of the southern colonies were not put to further tests during the war we are now considering, rumors of danger continued until hostilities ceased in Europe and on the sea and these gave special emphasis to problems of government which South Carolina shared with all other provinces.

For several years before Glen's arrival William Bull and the council, all Carolinians, in administering the government had conformed in most things to the preferences of their fellow colonists. The new incumbent therefore, as was usual in such cases, found much to criticise.[1] He found " the whole frame of Government unhinged." Bull, he thought, had spent too much time on his plantations away from Charlestown and the absence or indolence of earlier governors had allowed too much power to slip into the hands of the council. The exclusion of the governor, since 1739, from participation in the business of the legislative council troubled him much and he does not seem to have been aware that this had come to be the practice in several other provinces. The best that he could do was to obtain the privilege of being present, though without speaking a word or being able to tell them he had an instruction relative to any business which was before them.[2] The parceling out of the governor's powers among a number of elected officials aroused the anxious attention of Glen, as it did of many other executives. Besides the treasurer the assembly also appointed the commissary, the Indian commissioner, the controller of duties and the powder receiver. In addition special duties were assigned by the assembly to a commissioner of the market, of the workhouse, of pilots, of fortifications and the like. To this he might have added that the employment of

---

[1] Glen to B. T. Feb. 6, 1743/4, C. O. 5/370. Again, at much greater length, Oct. 10, 1748, C. O. 5/372; Colls. S. C. Hist. Soc., II, 286, 303; C. O. 5/449, U. H. J., Jan. 20, 1744/5.

[2] That Glen indirectly joined in the business of the upper house, his name being entered on the journal, is stated in the report of its committee on style of legislation, May 7, 1745, U. H. J.

a variety of standing committees by the lower house added to its efficiency and enabled it to assume many functions which were quasi-executive in their nature.

"The crown," wrote Glen with one of his characteristic rhetorical flourishes, "is by various laws despoiled of its principal flowers and brightest jewels." The governor "can neither reward the virtuous and deserving, nor displace or punish those that offend." The effect of this on defence he cited as an example of the disastrous tendency which was at work. One of the earlier governors, he said, had written to the assembly asking them not only to raise money for the repair of Fort Johnson on Sullivan's Island, but to take charge of the work itself. Such messages, added Glen, led assemblies to arrogate to themselves the right of directing everything and they would not listen when afterwards told that all castles and forts belonged to the king and could not be erected, repaired or demolished without proper authority. Assemblies, he continued, often threw away money to little purpose, as in the case of a fort recently built at Port Royal, on which £1100 st. had been expended. This fort, he claimed, was injudiciously situated, "monstrously constructed, and made of oyster shells, and is called a fort but a garden fence is just as strong." The assembly, however, was in good temper and continued so during Glen's administration. At the beginning it voted him ample house rent and a salary of £500 st. per year, and he never became involved in a serious controversy with either house.

In time of war, especially when the danger from all quarters seemed so great as it did at this time in South Carolina, a governor and assembly would in most cases be forced to avoid disputes, the effect of which would be to block public business. But in addition to the force of this motive, we have also the conciliatory attitude which Glen uniformly maintained toward the assembly. In spite of his criticisms of Carolina government to which reference has been made, Glen in his dealings with the assembly accepted things as they were. His speeches were smooth and persuasive in tone and he often expressed sympathy with colonial policies which were frowned upon by the British government. At the close of the seventh year of his office he publicly commended the character of the laws which had been sent him to sign.[1] It was the adaptability, added to his diligence in the public service, which insured the success of Glen's administration. He became involved in no controversies of importance.

At the time when he assumed office the struggle of the council to retain its right to amend money bills was already in its later stage. In May, 1745, a very full report was submitted by a committee of the council on the style of legislation and the respective shares of the two houses in framing the money bills.[2] Its conclusion as to existing practice was that the power of the council in framing money bills had become a shadow, the liberty barely of reading such bills. The entries in the journals during Glen's administration bear out the truth of this statement. When messages were sent down with amendments or asking for conferences, no answers were returned. The council must approve or reject tax bills outright, and for the sake of the public welfare they had yielded. The assembly had improved every concession to win others, "till they have pushed us quite out. They are pushing the governor out of his executive power in the same way." Under such conditions a conciliatory attitude was as necessary for Glen as it was for his contemporary, Shirley, in Massachusetts.

In one respect the two houses of the South Carolina legislature imitated the practice of parliament more closely than did those of other colonies, and that to the relief of the provincial exchequer, their members served without pay, and in 1746 they defeated a bill the object of which was to provide them with wages for this service.[3] In 1745 the law concerning elections was changed for the first time since 1721.[4] A prolonged discussion occurred between the two houses over a proposal to raise the property qualification required for voting and over the form of taking the oath.

---

[1] C. O. 5/463, L. H. J., Nov., 1750.

[2] C. O. 5/453, U. H. J., May, 7, 1745.

[3] C. O. 5/401, E. B. S. C., July 19, 1739; Smith, 115.

[4] S. C. Stats., III, 136, 657; C. O. 5/453, U. H. J., May, 1745. L. H. J., Sept., 1745. The Fundamental Constitutions, as well as earlier statutes of the province, were cited to show that the English form of taking the oath had not prevailed in South Carolina.

Charles Pinckney on the question of the oath defended the cause of the Protestant dissenters and of civil liberty with great vigor, but was temporarily defeated. Two other provisions were introduced which provoked opposition in England. These were a clause excluding from membership all holders of offices of profit under the government, and another providing for annual elections and sessions of assembly. Because of these provisions and of the fact that it repealed parts of a former act without the insertion of a suspending clause, this measure was disallowed. By a supplementary act passed two years later a system of biennial elections was substituted and those who scrupled to take the oath on the Evangelists were permitted to affirm.[1]

In 1747 an act, like several which had previously been in force, was passed for regulating the duties of justices of the peace in the trials of small causes. By this law their jurisdiction was extended to include cases of debt involving as much as £75 currency, which was equal to £15 proclamation money.[2] The object of this act, as was so frequently the case when similar legislation was passed in many of the colonies, was to provide a cheap method of settling minor disputes for those who lived in the remote sections of the province and save them the labor and expense of coming to Charlestown for such purposes. But the measure was attacked in South Carolina on the ground that it would greatly curtail the jurisdiction of the court of common pleas. The chief party in interest, however, was the provost marshal, who saw in prospect a serious diminution of his fees. A representation therefore was sent to the king against the measure, alleging that the sum was placed so high that it would transfer to the summary jurisdiction of the justices a large proportion of the suits of the province and thus would seriously curtail trials by jury. The act was referred by the board of trade to Counsellor Lamb and he approved of the cited objections,[3] adding that the king's debts would hardly be secure under such jurisdiction and that the act did not

[1] *Ibid.*, 672; Acts P. C. Col., 1745–1766, p. 50; C. O. 5/402. E. B. S. C., Aug. 13, 1747.

[2] *Ibid.*, 701. The court was to consist of two justices and three freeholders or a majority of the same.

[3] Chalmers, Colonial Opinions, 476; Acts P. C. Col., 1745–1766, p. 59.

contain a suspending clause, as was required by the governor's instructions. The board of trade also severely criticised the measure and it was disallowed, Glen being censured for having assented to it.

The currency was still, of course, a very live issue in South Carolina. The war necessitated a continuance of issues, though on a more conservative scale than in earlier times. The high rates of insurance and freight at sea, caused by the presence of so many hostile privateers and the other risks of war, hindered the export trade of the province while it kept the prices of imported European goods high. This caused more or less stringency and suffering and kept alive the demand for more issues of paper, the generally adopted panacea for social evils. Some form of relief for debtors was widely urged.[1] In June, 1746, an act was passed for the emission of £210,000 in bills of credit to be legal tender and loaned out at 8% interest payable in gold and silver on good mortgage security. It was calculated that the fund which would accrue from the interest payments in twenty years would be sufficient for the redemption of all the outstanding bills, with a surplus for helping poor immigrants to establish themselves in the province. By the operation of this bountiful scheme it was claimed that in twenty years South Carolina would be brought to a specie basis, and this claim was made on behalf of the bill by the agents, Fenwick and Fury, in England.[2] The encouragement of the production of indigo as well as an increase in the exportation of rice were depended upon to help produce this result. The debtor class and supporters of the demand for more bills of credit were also interested in the act for extending the jurisdiction of the justices of the peace and lower courts of the localities, so that these two pieces of legislation were connected. That the demand for larger issues of currency was not so widespread as was claimed and that some sharp political practice may have been resorted to in its support, is indicated by the fact that many of the petitions in favor of it — and they all came from the remoter country parishes — were identical

[1] See an article entitled, "An Overture and Proposal concerning Carolina," in the S. C. Gazette, Aug. 23, 1746. A scattering reply to this, signed "Freeholder," approved of the issue of Jan. 6, 1748. This dealt also with other though related issues.

[2] S. C. Stats., III, 671; C. O. 5/371, B. T. O. P., Feb., 1746/7 and 1747/8.

in language and it was charged that it was often the case that the names were written in by the same hand.[1] But we know that conservatives as well as radicals, creditors as well as debtors, were capable of tricks like this.

During this period the British government was considering the passage of an act of parliament to prevent further issues of bills of credit in the colonies. In 1744 and again in 1750 reports to this effect reached South Carolina.[2] This always occasioned great activity in the assembly, drafting reports and addresses, employing and instructing agents to oppose such measures in England. The fact that Glen had opposed the measure just referred to proves that, like not a few other governors, he sympathized to a large extent with the colonial point of view. On one occasion he declared in a message that the passage of such an act as was contemplated in England would be a " deadly blow to us." Glen also had signed the other acts mentioned above, which met with serious objections in England and some of which were disallowed. Some goods, also, which were sent over as presents to the Indians and which seem to have been intrusted by Glen to certain traders for delivery, were lost and this especially irritated the officials at Westminster. This accumulation of objectionable acts or oversights on his part drew from the board of trade a number of letters sharply criticising the governor.[3] As these were written near the beginning of the administration of the earl of Halifax as president of the board, they may be viewed as examples of the increased rigor and demand for efficiency which were then appearing in that office. The board told him that, though he seemed to be aware of the encroachments of the assembly on the executive, they could scarcely reconcile it with his approval of the bills concerning the franchise and the enlargement of the jurisdiction of the justices' courts. They were totally inconsistent with his instructions, involved an attack on the prerogative and all order in government, and seemed to the board quite inconsistent with views which Glen had previously expressed. They criticised the arrangement of subjects in his letters, his submission to the assembly of queries

[1] S. C. Gazette, Jan. 6, 1748; C. O. 5/455, U. H. J., Nov. 1746.
[2] C. O. 5/452, L. H. J., Dec., 1744; C. O. 5/461, U. H. J., Dec., 1750.
[3] C. O. 5/402. B. T. E. B. S. C. B. T. to Glen, Dec. 20, 1748, Dec. 2, 1749 and Nov. 15, 1750.

from the board as being very improper, and corrected at great length a report of a conference committee of the houses on the amount of currency outstanding. The omission of suspending clauses in acts, the whole system of specific appropriations and many other things came in for sharp criticism. The board declared that it would urge the king to forbid Glen to assent to any more acts for the issue of bills of credit. "We cannot help saying with some concern that we have seldom opportunity of writing to you upon the affairs of your province without being obliged at the same time to complain of some departure from your instructions and often of a notorious breach of prerogative."

Glen, in defence, was able to give a more or less reasonable explanation for everything that he had done and to show that, if he had erred, it had been due to errors of judgment and not to evil intentions.[1] The loss of the Indian presents was due to a difference of judgment between the board and himself in reference to the advantage or even the feasibility of having the natives come to Charlestown for conferences. The distance from the remoter tribes was so great and the danger on the way so serious that it was the firm opinion of the governor that they ought never to be brought so far. They themselves did not desire to come and unless forts could be built in or near their country it would be better to send presents to them, as in this instance he had tried to do. As to the acts which had been disallowed Glen claimed that he had acted in accordance with previous legislation or — in the case of the justices of the peace — with a practice he had known in Ireland. The board of trade did not pursue the matter further and its outburst may be regarded as a warning that more strict obedience of instructions was expected. But under conditions which had long been established in South Carolina, as elsewhere, the most that could be expected was a compromise between the ideals of Halifax and his associates and those of the colonists, and governors of the mild temper of Glen, though fully satisfying neither party, were best fitted to preserve the peace and keep the machine moving along its accustomed course.

[1] C. O. 5/372, O. P., Dec. 23, 1749, July 15, 1750.

CHAPTER IX

NORTH CAROLINA DURING THE ADMINISTRATION OF GABRIEL JOHNSTON, 1734-1752

UNLIKE most royal governors, Gabriel Johnston did not come from the army or from a court office. He was a university man and had held a chair of Oriental languages at St. Andrew's. Later he had removed to London, where as a political writer he had won the favor of Spencer Compton, the earl of Wilmington, to whose influence he probably owed in large measure his appointment to the governorship of North Carolina.[1] The city of Wilmington, on Cape Fear river, owes its name to this connection. It was at Brunswick near the mouth of this river, the settlement of the Moores from South Carolina and their friends, that Johnston landed and had his commission read. His rival — for Burrington was long to be active in that capacity — was at the same time holding his last assembly at Edenton in the opposite northeasterly corner of the province.

Johnston even in his first measures declared war upon his predecessor, thus indicating that the administration which was to follow would be far from a peaceful one. He at once issued a proclamation recalling to office those who had lately been suspended or removed. Smith, the chief justice; Rice, the secretary; Halton and Edmund Porter, all opponents of Burrington, now took their places at the council board.[2] Matthew Rowan and Edward Moseley were among the new appointees, the latter being thus removed from the lower house. Because of the disorders which prevailed, a court

[1] In one of his letters Johnston wrote, "For the last seven years before I came abroad, I lived almost continually with the late Lord President Wilmington, and have the honour to be known for many years by the Earl of Bath, Lord Anson, the Bishop of Worcester and several other persons of distinction . . . ." This Johnston wrote in 1749 in answer to a charge that he was a Jacobite. N. C. Recs., IV, 918, 926, 931, 933.

[2] N. C. Recs., IV, 2, 3; Ashe, Hist. of N. C., I, 248 *et seq.*

of oyer and terminer was at once called, Smith presiding, and Rice, Pollock and Porter being among its justices. Steps were also taken for holding an election and the meeting of a new assembly. Previous to its meeting Johnston journeyed in state from Brunswick to Edenton, receiving in general a cordial welcome. Burrington, seeing his friends put out and his enemies restored, soon left for England where he long kept up opposition to the new governor.

In his opening speech to the general assembly, Johnston took up the refrain of Burrington's critics in the assembly of 1733, and stated that he found affairs in great disorder, judges and other officials violently displaced, and appointees of very inferior character put in their places, the inferior courts in some places discontinued, and in others put to oppressive uses. In their replies both houses joined in denouncing Burrington and his rule as oppressive and arbitrary in the extreme.[1] Not only did Smith, Porter and Rice, who had previously been enemies of Burrington, utter these sentiments, but Moseley, who had been somewhat in sympathy with the spirit if not with the utterances of the ex-governor, now joined in the general criticism of him. For the moment the new governor seemed to be facing a united province and to have in prospect a successful and progressive administration. The appropriations which were made and laws which were passed by this assembly seemed also to indicate almost unanimous support. Toward the governor's expenses since his arrival an allowance of £1300 was made, and to provide for a list of other claims there was a general appropriation of £14,000, the sum to be raised in part by a tax on the inhabitants. To meet these demands and rid the province of the old outstanding bills of credit, most of which had been counterfeited, £40,000 were issued in bills to be exchanged, and £10,000 in new bills to be added to the total then in circulation. All the outstanding paper was called in. An import duty was imposed on liquors, partly to make the poll tax on the poorer inhabitants more easy. This all indicated that some attention was to be paid to revenue and appropriations, a phenomenon which had not been much in evidence in the past. In accordance with the

[1] N. C. Recs., IV, 77, 81, 119.

governor's instructions, the clause in the election law which had extended the suffrage to all freemen was repealed and a freeholder suffrage was substituted. Two new precincts were established and given representation, while roads, ferries and bridges received some attention.

But a proclamation, which Johnston had issued, that quit rents should be paid in sterling money or in bills of credit at such discount as the governor and council should determine, drew a protest from the lower house and a reassertion of the permanent binding force of the " great deed." To this the governor replied at great length and with considerable show of spirit, and prorogued the assembly.[1] The attitude which Johnston now assumed in reference to quit rents, and to many other subjects as well, was determined by information which Chief Justice Smith had secured, while recently in England, that the proprietors, years before, had issued an order that all acts of assembly should be certified to them and that such as were not confirmed by them should expire at the end of two years; this order had not been obeyed by the colonial officials, and of the whole body of laws only six had been confirmed. Smith was so impressed by this and by the possibility that nearly all the legislation of the pro-prietary period might be declared invalid that he had the question submitted to the law officers in England, but they had not yet rendered an opinion on the subject. Johnston, however, stated this as law to the assembly and applied it to the acts which permitted the payment of quit rents in commodities. He also denied that the " great deed " had been in force more than two years and that elsewhere than in the district north of Albemarle Sound. With this view the ma-jority of the council agreed, as did the chief justice. Moseley, the leading defender of the " great deed " and all existing practices relating to land, was so enraged by these views that he struck the chief justice and was put under bond to appear before the general court.[2] In accordance with his instruc-tions, and with the approval of the council, the governor established a court of exchequer, of which he made Smith the chief baron, and issued proclamations requiring the pay-ment of arrears of quit rent, the taking out of warrants for

---

[1] N. C. Recs., IV, 108–114, 147, 155.   [2] Ibid., 33; Ashe, 249, 250.

all land which had not yet been surveyed or settled, and forbidding the making of tar or turpentine from trees on the king's ungranted lands. As the receiver general of the Carolinas resided in the southern province, Eleazer Allen was appointed to that office for North Carolina, subject to the king's approval. A committee of the council was also designated to inquire into abuses connected with the issue of blank patents.[1] These measures show with what vigor Johnston was attacking irregularities which had been inherited from the proprietary period and was seeking to establish policies which better agreed with the principles of royal government. The fact that his own salary depended upon the amount of quit rents collected furnished the element of personal interest which gave point to his resolution.

Throughout the period of Johnston's governorship, immigration was active, as is evidenced by the very large number of land grants which were issued. The chief regular business[2] of the governor in executive council, as is shown by the journal of that body, was the issue of these grants. The new settlers, some of whom came in from the colonies to the north and others direct from Europe, established themselves on the middle and upper courses of the rivers, especially of those in the Cape Fear region. New precincts or parishes were established and the province began perceptibly to emerge from its previous weak condition. The capacity of this province for producing pitch, tar and potash, and for raising flax, hemp and other staples which were desired by Great Britain, served as a continuous attraction to all parties that were interested in colonization. Before the end of 1735, Arthur Dobbs and other gentlemen of prominence in Ireland, and Henry McCulloh, a London merchant and a relative of Johnston, had begun to make inquiries about facilities for settling poor Protestant families in the province. Through their attorney, Captain Woodward, a tract of 60,000 acres was selected on Black river in New Hanover county. Early the following year McCulloh petitioned the board of trade

[1] N. C. Recs., IV, 36–43.

[2] The business of the executive council, from Feb. to Oct., 1736, related almost wholly to land grants. Very many petitions for grants were acted on. N. C. Recs., IV, 216–225. The same was true during much of the period we are now considering.

for two other tracts, comprising together 132,000 acres, and the grant was made.[1] At the same time Burrington, who was then in England, and Jenner and Ochs became interested in the establishment of a colony of Swiss in the province. McCulloh, in conjunction with Crymble and Huey, two London merchants, also petitioned for grants, to the extent of about a million and a quarter of acres, to be surveyed for settlements near the heads of the Pedee, Cape Fear and Neuse rivers. An order in council was issued for the governor to grant and the surveyor general to lay out those lands.

It was the declared purpose of McCulloh to set his Scotch-Irish colonists at the production of potash and naval stores, and something of this kind was probably put forward as an inducement in favor of all such grants, though in the end they proved to be the schemes of ordinary land monopolists. As the unoccupied area in North Carolina east of the mountains was now known to be so large and the encouragement of immigration was considered desirable, it was comparatively easy to secure grants in England for large tracts, the bounds of which were very loosely determined by the surveyors, and which in extent were far larger than the grantees could reasonably hope to settle. This became the occasion for prolonged disputes and litigation in the future and helped to keep territorial questions very prominent in North Carolina till the close of the colonial period. The connection of the Mc-Cullohs, father and son, with this province, a connection which originated in the way just explained, and was later to result in the appointment of the elder McCulloh as agent and a special royal commissioner, was to continue until their speculative ventures merged in the hopeless loyalist claims after the the Revolution.[2]

In the scramble for accessible open land which had been in progress during recent administrations and was still going on, many blank patents had been issued. They had been signed by the governors in advance of surveys and to them the province seal had not been affixed. But possession

[1] *Ibid.*, 72–74, 156, 209–215; Acts of P. C. Col., 1720–1745, pp. 490, 501, 504–506.

[2] N. C. Recs., IV, 72–74, 156, 162, 209–215, 248, 253–263, 684; Acts of P. C. Col., 1720–1745, pp. 490, 501, 504–506; Ashe, *op. cit.*

of the land had been assumed by the grantees to the extent, Johnston said, of half a million acres, and on this either no quit rent at all was paid or sums very much less than the amount required by royal instruction, which was 4s. per hundred acres in proclamation money. It was partly in grants of this kind that the commissioners who ran the Virginia line received their payment. It may have been in that connection that Edward Moseley became interested in this form of speculation, for Johnston states that in his time Moseley and the Moore family were "the principall proprietors of the blank patents." The rich land grantees got such land as they wanted to hold for 6s. per hundred acres, and that part of it which was covered with the poorer quality of pine they made unfit for further use by burning the lightwood and extracting the tar and pitch from the trees.

It was to remedy evils of this nature that Johnston caused a bill to be introduced into his first assembly to provide for a rent roll and for the more regular payment of quit rents.[1] Though Moseley was now in the council, the feeling against such regulations as the governor desired was naturally strong in the lower house. The persons who held blank patents tried hard to introduce a clause confirming them, but the governor would not consent. The forms and places of payment of quit rents also came up for discussion and upon these there was disagreement. The people and members of the lower house insisted, as of course was the practice in Virginia, upon payment in kind, but in North Carolina, as we have seen, a variety of products were tendered instead of the one staple, tobacco. As to places of payment, the practice of Virginia, according to which rents were paid on the plantations where the crop was raised, had also been followed. In the bill in question the Carolinians thought they had improved on Virginia conditions by insisting only that payments should be made in a few of their best commodities, such as tobacco, rice, deerskins, hemp and flax, and those in a limited number of places. But the governor and council called the attention of the assembly to the fact, or perhaps the report, that the burgesses of Virginia made up to the king the amount which their expensive method of collection had cost.

[1] N. C. Recs., IV, 8, 30, 77, 93, 110, 134, 147.

In view of these differences of opinion, it is not strange that the first attempt under Johnston to pass a law relating to quit rents failed. His order for the collection of arrears occasioned general complaint, and he put the militia into such hands as would, if possible, prevent the king's officers from being insulted. The feelings with which the frontiersmen viewed this process were well expressed in an address to the governor from the loyal Protestant inhabitants of Bertie and Edgecombe precincts.[1] Their poor and mean estates, they said, had first been honestly paid for, and then settled with much hard labor under the violent heat of the sun, with the flesh of the deer, bear or the raccoon for food. During the process, also, many had fallen at the hands of the savages. These lands they regarded as their own, subject to the payment of the moderate quit rent which had been prescribed in what they considered the permanent concessions of the proprietors. They asked the governor to withdraw his proclamation or at least not to fix upon the month of June as the time for the first payment of arrears, as then they had no commodities which were fit for sale in the Virginia market, and that was the only place whence they could hope for returns for what they had to offer. As the governor had stated that their lands belonged to the king and that thousands of industrious Protestants stood ready to take them on the king's terms; if so, when they were paid for their labor and improvements, they would readily quit the province and seek out lands in neighboring colonies where they could call the fruits of their labor their own, and where resort was not had to collusions between the rich and powerful for the undoing of the poor.

By other parties the establishment of the court of exchequer was met by the objection that such a court could be established only by act of assembly. The acquaintance of certain Carolinians also with very recent history in the neighboring provinces was evidenced by their citing a " book " on this subject " published by Mr. Morris, late Chief Justice of New York."

Because of his attitude on these questions, as well as his dislike of the biennial act, Johnston dissolved his first

[1] *Ibid.*, 18–22.

assembly and met a new one in September, 1736. During its first session signs appeared of opposition to the governor. When in his vigorous opening speech Johnston referred to his services in protecting actual settlers against holders of blank patents for their lands, Moseley and one of the Pollocks dissented from the favorable reply which was made by the assembly. Petitions later came in from various precincts against their inhabitants being compelled to go to certain points to pay their quit rents, this being contrary to the custom under the proprietors. It was also said that collectors were illegally exacting " seven for one " and, from such as did not bring their rents to the specified places, " eight for one." To those charges the governor replied[1] that when, in the time of the proprietors, collectors visited the houses of the settlers, they demanded specie but accepted province bills at a ratio of 7 to 1 in sterling if the rents were paid at the court houses. There was, however, an express understanding between the proprietor and the assembly, when bills of credit were first issued, that they should not be received for quit rents except on such terms as were acceptable to the proprietors. In view of the present demands of the people, Johnston inferred that they were trying to drive a harder bargain with the king than with the proprietors.

This assembly passed a fee bill and also a bill for a rent roll, the collection of quit rents and quieting of titles.[2] Both of these were rejected by the governor, the latter in particular because it contained some provisions declaring valid every claim and practice which he had condemned, blank patents, the " great deed," and payment in commodities. In addition to this it provided that the rate of exchange for bills of credit should annually be fixed by a commission selected by the lower house. The council joined with the governor in rejecting this measure. The house remained obstinate and when two futile efforts had been made to hold a session and

---

[1] N. C. Recs., IV, 236–239, 266. According to all available accounts, in these estimates, the currency was over-valued, *i.e.*, terms of payment were made more favorable for the people than the actual value of their currency would justify. It was passing at 9 or 10 to 1 in Virginia. The salaries of officials were also paid in currency at 7 to 1, and thereby they, as well as the king, lost about 30%.

[2] *Ibid.*, 180–200.

it had ordered officials into custody who were distraining for quit rents, Johnston dissolved this assembly in March, 1737.[1]

Though the temper indicated by these acts was, we know, widely diffused among the people, not only of North Carolina but of all the colonies, Johnston was able to report in October, 1736,[2] that more progress was being made in collecting arrears of quit rent than at any time in the entire history of the province. The collection of £4200 since 1729 may not have been much, but it was more than had resulted from the total ineffectiveness of the proprietary period in such matters. However reactionary the quit rent policy as a whole might be, the fact that arrears were slowly coming in reveals a certain increase in the force and efficiency of government since it had come under the control of the crown. The existence of an exchequer court may have moved some to payment. As many patents for land were being taken out, the governor appointed a deputy auditor and surveyor of the king's quit rents and other revenues, the first appearance of such an official in North Carolina.

While Johnston was working in North Carolina with these objects in view, Burrington, the ex-governor, was opposing him in England. Notwithstanding his violent quarrels, Burrington's reputation as a man who fell in with the Carolina spirit and traditions was still strongly felt in the province. The Bertie and Edgecombe memorialists, to whom reference has just been made, spoke in terms of the greatest admiration of his fatiguing journeys on foot through the back woods for the ostensible purpose of knowing and aiding the remote settlers, though prospecting for land was doubtless also a most practicable feature of his errand. As, according to Johnston, he held 50,000 acres under blank patents in the province,[3] he yielded to a natural temptation when he now caused to be circulated among the settlers both written and printed protests against declaring these void, as well as against the reduction of the number of places where quit rents might be paid. Burrington also sought to strengthen the impression he was making by representing, though falsely, that the board of trade was in sympathy with him,[4] and that the king was in-

[1] *Ibid.*, 272.
[2] *Ibid.*, 177.
[3] *Ibid.*, 203, 265.
[4] *Ibid.*, 207, 215, 243.

different to the payment of his rents. But Burrington's activities at this time were not all factional or partisan, for he was urging upon the board the need of a port and of the development of a direct sea-going trade with the islands and with ports in Europe, so that North Carolina might no longer be forced to depend upon indirect traffic through Virginia and New England. The products from the farms of North Carolina for export — tobacco, rice, cattle, corn, pork, pulse — were now becoming large and valuable in the aggregate and Carolinians were losing a large part of their natural profit by the unnecessary employment of Virginians and New Englanders as middlemen.

Under these conditions Johnston was very desirious of support, and definite instructions from England. Both he and McCulloh, the agent, urged that such be promptly given. This they regarded as necessary, not only because the governor was being charged by Burrington's partisans with arbitrary conduct, but because North Carolina had always been in such a disturbed and lawless condition. They also called attention to the fact that it had no effective militia law. The need of such a law was brought home to the authorities when, on the occasion of a meeting of the general court at Edenton in 1737, the people of Bertie and Edgecombe precincts, to the number, it was said, of 500, rose in arms and came to within five miles of the town to rescue a man who, they erroneously thought, had been called in question about his quit rents. By this event the weakness of the government was revealed in the clearest manner, for " how to quell them I cannot tell," wrote the governor, " if they should attempt an insurrection against next collection." When the assembly met in March, 1736/7, the lower house ordered some of the province officials into custody because they were distraining for quit rents, and thereupon the governor at once dissolved it.[1] With the assent of the council, a table of fees for the officials of the court of exchequer was then published.

During the first half of 1738 the general subject of blank patents and quit rents in North Carolina was discussed at many sessions of the board of trade. Representations from the assembly as well as from the governor, through their re-

[1] *Ibid.*, 272, 276.

spective agents, were heard, and also a statement from the secretary of the late board of proprietors. Queries were submitted to the law officers, and in February they rendered an opinion in which were laid down the principles which the home government was to follow in dealing with this question.[1] The opinion was a compromise between the policy which Johnston had so emphatically affirmed and the claims of the colonists, leaning rather in its practical consequences to the latter. As to blank patents the opinion was that, though they had been issued after the proprietors had closed their land office, if the proprietors had been informed concerning them and had received the consideration money, they would be good. So also if the bounds of the grants were not specified in them, or if they had not been registered, but had been followed by long possession, and if no evidence of fraud was discernible in connection with them. Those issued after notice was received of the king's purchase were not good, though in certain cases consideration should even then be shown. In almost every point the intent of the opinion was to guard the interests of actual holders of the patents, provided they had come into possession of them with honest intent. The only method which it recognized of declaring a grant invalid was by information before the courts, a procedure which certainly would result in little change in North Carolina.

In another opinion [2] rendered at the same time, the law officers declared that the " great deed " could have been revoked by the instruction to Governor Sayle in 1669 only if Albemarle lay within Sayle's territory, which it did not as he was expressly limited to the territory south and west of Cape Carteret. Failure to observe even the terms of the later grant would be remedied by long possession. As to the form of payments, they might be in specie or commodities rated at the market price. In general, laws which had long been in use among the people and had been acquiesced in by the proprietors could not be declared void by the crown on account of such defects as had been mentioned. An exception, however, strangely was made of the act legalizing biennial elections, and it actually was annulled for special reasons.

In 1739, in an assembly held at Newbern, the first sign of

[1] N. C. Recs., IV, 318–323, 325–328, 339–342.   [2] Ibid., 286–291.

a compromise on the subject of land and rents appeared in the province itself. A law was passed which made provision for a rent roll, and that the rents should be paid in a limited number of commodities — tobacco, hemp, flax, deer skins, and beeswax. But Johnston was forced to yield somewhat on the subject of blank patents, they being confirmed to the extent of 150,000 acres, provided they were duly registered. As in the previous bill, a commission was designated to fix yearly the rates of exchange between bills of credit and sterling and proclamation money. The modernizing of the province was advanced by converting its precincts into counties, and substituting sheriffs in the place of marshals.[1] The passage of the quit rent bill opened the way for the payment of salaries, now heavily in arrears, and it was sent to England with the hope that it would be approved. Johnston considered the act favorable to the crown and congratulated himself on having ended a four years' struggle so advantageously.

The opinions of the law officers, to which reference has just been made, and which were rendered in 1738, were retained in the office of the board of trade or elsewhere for more than two years and the knowledge that they had been rendered did not reach North Carolina until 1741. Meantime Henry McCulloh presented to the board a long adverse criticism of the quit rent bill which Johnston had sent over for approval. He was heard repeatedly on the subject and brought with him a number of merchants who were also opposed. The result was that the board reported adversely on the act and it was disallowed. The point on which the disallowance was based was the provision which gave to a body of provincial office-holders and assemblymen power to fix the rate of exchange at which bills of credit should be received in payment of quit rents.[2] Thus, owing to the unfortunate connection which existed between quit rents and the currency, between the dues of the crown and the inferior medium in which they must largely be paid, this important measure was lost. As a result royal officials in North Carolina were deprived of their chief permanent support.

When this is viewed in connection with the opinions of

---

[1] *Ibid.*, 368, 400, 415, 424, 921; Ashe, *op. cit.*, 257.

[2] *Ibid.*, 368, 400, 415, 424–439, 921.

the attorney and solicitor general, which more nearly harmonized with the views of Moseley than of Johnston, the governor might well consider his territorial policy defeated at every point. He had not been sustained by the home authorities, at least, though he might well have considered the lines on which he started out to be such as were in harmony with the principles of royal government. In view of the long delay in reaching a decision and of its nature, it can not seem altogether strange that Johnston himself, as he was charged with doing, should have neglected his duty in writing home. In 1746 he wrote that his salary was eight years in arrears, and the salaries of other officials in proportion. A regular grant from the crown to be met from the quit rents had been made, but payments were largely in arrears, especially in Lord Granville's share of the province.[1] In 1741 Johnston labored hard to secure the passage of a quit rent bill and that in an assembly at Wilmington and under generally favorable conditions. McCulloh also gave his aid. But the members of the assembly " still wanted to crowd in more commoditys, and at higher prices, so that after trying all methods for four weeks together I was forced to prorogue them without bringing this matter to a conclusion." [2] The revenue from quit rents continued to be small during the years 1745 to 1748, rising to £400 in one year and in another falling as low as £146. The result was that at his death in 1752 the salary of Governor Johnston, which was £1000 a year, was in arrears to the amount of more than £13,000.[3]

While the quit rent troubles were in progress new grants of land were being issued in large numbers. Both the Carolinas at the time were increasing steadily in population, and immigrants were pushing into the interior. It was with a view to the better regulation of these matters, and of their currency, that the king, in 1739, appointed Henry McCulloh commissioner for supervising and controlling the revenues and grants of land of the two Carolinas, with authority to inspect their records and from time to time to report not only what he found to be actually existing but his view as to possible reforms.[4] Of his efforts in South Carolina, which for the most

---

[1] *Ibid.*, 792.
[2] *Ibid.*, 585.
[3] *Ibid.*, V, 19, 77.
[4] N. C. Recs., IV, 1076, 1130–1133.

part were unsuccessful, an account has already been given. In the northern province, in conjunction with the English merchants Crymble and Huey, he secured very large grants of land. But a controversy arose between the grantees of these tracts and Mathew Rowan, the surveyor general, over their location.[1] It was alleged on the one side, but denied on the other, that before the grantees had time to give instructions as to the location and subdivisions of the grants, a deal was entered into by Rowan, Governor Johnston and Woodward, the collector of the Cape Fear district, for a division of the fees of £2000 and more which would accrue from this large survey.[2] The survey did not accord with the plans of McCulloh and his associates. A complaint was made to the governor and council, and in 1745 it was carried before the board of trade.[3] The board told McCulloh that, as it was his private affair, they could give him no help and referred him to the council. This prolonged controversy, which gave rise to many voluminous documents of some historic value, finally merged with the general complaints against Governor Johnston and his defense, with which the administration closed. From the statements which were made in that connection it seems certain that Johnston himself was a speculator in land and possible that on accasion he was guilty of irregularities in the granting of land which were similar to those with which he charged Moseley and the earlier governors.[4] As to the direct purpose of his commission, McCulloh seems to have accomplished nothing, and what he was able to report concerning irregularities came only as an incident of the controversies in which he was perpetually involved. Among the standing grievances of the lower house was the monopolizing of large tracts of land, such as McCulloh held, to the prevention of actual settlement.[5]

One of Governor Johnston's early recommendations to the board of trade was the repeal of the existing acts for ascertaining officers' fees, because they gave too large a power to the lower house to establish them and because the fees established either could not be collected or were not at all ade-

---

[1] *Ibid.*, 644, 648.
[2] *Ibid.*, 1107, 1115.
[3] *Ibid.*, 666, 668, 690, 757–758.
[4] *Ibid.*, 1101 *et seq.*
[5] *Ibid.*, 744, 824.

quate for the support of officials of the higher rank.[1] In 1736, however, he told the assembly that, if it would prepare a reasonable fee bill it should not want his assent. No bill relating to fees was passed that session and in the following spring a new table of fees for some of the officials was proclaimed by order of the governor and council.[2] In February, 1739/40, the assembly passed a fee bill; but it was rejected by the upper house, and by advice of the council the governor directed officials to continue taking fees at the rates prescribed in the old table, estimating them, when paid in currency, at the customary rate of 4 to 1 in lieu of proclamation money, until fees should be regulated by statute.[3] In 1744 and again in 1746 the fact that fees were being collected on the sole authority of an ordinance of the governor and council was included in the list of grievances of the lower house.[4] A new act of assembly regulating fees was finally passed in 1748. It stated the amounts in proclamation money, but made them payable in either proclamation money or bills of credit, and was silent as to the relative value of the two.

By 1730 North Carolina was surpassing its southern neighbor in the number of its population. But owing to the lack of a port its trade with Europe and its direct trade with the remoter colonies was very small.[5] Its backwardness in all that constituted social and economic development was to a great extent due to its unfavorable coast line. With the development of the Cape Fear region, however, a port and navigable water extending some distance into a fertile interior country were secured. The opening up of this part of the province and the settlement of the interior to the west and northwest of it were the leading features in the general development of this province during Johnston's administration. He at once interested himself in this and promoted in all possible ways the growth of Newton, a settlement which was started above Brunswick on the Cape Fear river. He and his political friends took up land there; a land office was opened and courts were called to meet there. In 1736 a bill for the incorporation of the new settlement was introduced

---

[1] *Ibid.*, 26.
[2] *Ibid.*, 229, 275.
[3] *Ibid.*, 446, 513.
[4] *Ibid.*, 745, 824, 825.
[5] N. C. Recs., IV, 156.

into the assembly, but it was defeated through the influence of the Moore family and their friends, who were the proprietors in the rival town of Brunswick. A session or two later, by the sharp practice of Chief Justice Smith in the council, and by prompt action in the house before the Moores had time to muster their forces, the bill was passed and the town was incorporated under the name of Wilmington. It was in connection with this stroke of policy that Johnston lost the support of the Moores.[1] The appointment of commissioners in 1735 to run the boundary line of South Carolina was a natural outgrowth of this policy and Eleazer Allen, a supporter of Johnston, was one of those men. The boundary was fixed just south of the Cape Fear region and the line was run a considerable distance into the interior during this administration.

A considerable export and import trade developed on the Cape Fear river. Swiss, Scotch, and Irish settlers came in steadily growing numbers and pushing northward and northwestward necessitated the founding of several new counties. After the defeat of the second pretender, in 1745, large numbers of the Scotch Highlanders settled on the upper Cape Fear. Settlers also pushed up the course of the Pedee from South Carolina. By this process, as well as by additions from or through Virginia and by the natural expansion of the Albemarle region, the middle and southern parts of North Carolina were settled. An unfortunate hindrance to the unification of the province, analogous to the distinct existence of the Northern Neck in Virginia, came after 1743 in the setting off to Lord Carteret, now Earl Granville, of his share of the original Carolina grant. As this was taken wholly from North Carolina, it included nearly two-thirds of that province. The line was run from Hatteras through Bath and thence due west and the entire broad strip of the province north of that line was left, so far as the right to its territorial revenue was concerned, under Granville as sole proprietor.[2]

Closely connected with this expansion of settlement was the controversy upon land grants and quit rents which has just been described. The other great controversy of John-

[1] N. C. Recs., IV, 43, 45; Ashe, 252.
[2] Ashe, 264 et seq.

ston's administration was a sectional one, the struggle on the part of the newly settled Cape Fear region, with the large district formerly known as Bath county which lay just north of it, to secure equal representation in the assembly with the nucleus of the colony that lay north of Albemarle Sound. In most of the colonies settlement proceeded along east and west lines and therefore conflicts of this nature arose between east and west sections. But in North Carolina the current of population first turned southward before it took its final western trend, and that gave rise to north and south sections and to a prolonged struggle between them.

An early and prominent object of Johnston's dislike in North Carolina was the law of 1715 providing for biennial elections. It legalized the holdings of elections and of one session of the legislature annually without the intervention of the governor's writ. It also gave the suffrage to freemen. Another clause of the act provided that the precincts of Albemarle county should be represented by five members each, while those of other counties, "that now or hereafter shall be erected," should each choose only two members. While North Carolina was confined almost wholly to the settlements north of Albemarle Sound this was perhaps a tolerable arrangement, at least it was one the origin of which can be understood. There were somewhat similar inequalities in other colonies though none was so extreme as this. As the regions about Bath, Newbern and Cape Fear, with the broad stretches of territory to the west, began to fill up and questions arose in which the settlers there were interested, this inequality of representation was felt, and protests against it were raised. Johnston especially felt it as an obstacle to his territorial policy and to his plans for the development of the Cape Fear region. As the originators and defenders of the "great deed" were men of Albemarle, it will be seen how valuable to them would be the maintenance of a system of representation which gave to that section, with its four or five precincts, a majority, or at least fully one half of the members of the lower house. The territorial questions of Johnston's administration therefore inevitably led to a sectional struggle to secure equality of representation for the province as a whole. It was the first important conflict of this character to develop in the colonies, but by no means the last.

The royal instructions required the governor to see to it that members of the assembly were elected only by free-holders.[1] The fact that the election law of 1715 gave the suffrage to all freemen brought it into conflict with this instruction. Along with its other implications relating to procedure, this feature had, indeed, provoked the criticisms of Burrington in his administration. He had insisted in his letters to the board of trade that the act ought to be repealed. Among the arguments which he used were these,[2] that the frequent elections robbed members of their independence, for they were in constant fear of failing to be returned at the next election, and that two of the Albemarle precincts did not have inhabitants who were fit to be magistrates or burgesses. He thought that its repeal would insure more orderly elections. Secretary Popple wrote to Burrington in 1732 that no change should be made in the act until the attorney and solicitor general reported on the North Carolina laws and then the change could be more properly effected by an instruction than by act of assembly.

At the beginning of Johnston's administration he, with the advice of the council, ordered writs to be issued requiring freeholders to meet at their usual places for the election of burgesses. He also criticised the existing law, as Burrington had done.[3] Early in 1735 an act was passed repealing the clause in the biennial act which empowered freemen to vote and imposed a freehold requirement.[4] But in his letters Johnston continued to criticise the remaining features of the law. In 1736 he wrote that he had recently dissolved the assembly because it insisted on following the, to him, unreasonable course of meeting without the king's writ. Moreover, elections every two years kept the province in confusion and led to continuous obstruction of government. As to the inequality of representation, he said that the six Albemarle precincts, as they then were, with a population of less than 15,000 had 30 out of a total of 46 members in the lower house. Johnston gives no estimate of the population outside

[1] *Ibid.*, III, 93.
[2] *Ibid.*, 180, 207, 335, 344, 355.
[3] *Ibid.*, IV, 3, 4, 25.
[4] *Ibid.*, 108.

of Albemarle, for his general contention was that the representation should be cut down, probably to two from each precinct, because, in his opinion, it was impossible to find 46 men in the whole province who were fit to do legislative business.

In July, 1737, the biennial act, after it had been in force for more than twenty years, was disallowed by order in council. This left the governor free to follow his instructions in reference to times of calling, proroguing, and dissolving the assembly. There had never been a definite limitation as to the place where the assembly should meet. The process was soon begun of removing the legislature from Edenton to points nearer the southern part of the province. Johnston resided most of the time on the Cape Fear river. The executive council met with considerable regularity there. In 1739 the legislature was called at Newbern, which was conveniently located for both sections, and there it met nearly every year until the close of Johnston's administration.[1] In 1742 and 1743 only it met at Edenton,[2] and on one or two occasions at Bath. During most of his governorship Johnston complained, at intervals, that there were no public offices, that the records were scattered or lost and kept insisting that there ought to be some centre of government with suitable offices. As the legislature came to meet more regularly at Newbern, the executive council also met there oftener. But as late as 1744 Johnston insisted, in his opening speech to the assembly, that it was high time to fix on a proper place for the capital of the province. When all settlements, he continued, were near the Virginia line, and even that region thinly peopled, officials might keep records in their houses. But now the province was settled nearly to the head of the Pedee river and the population and trade of the southern section had so increased that a place for courts and offices nearer the centre of the province should be selected. People were being hindered from moving west by their remoteness from the offices. At a later time the governor described North Carolina as a " Province where there is not one Publick Office, nor one place to keep any record or Public Papers. They all lye

[1] *Ibid.*, IV, 355, 470, 770, 814, 898, 971, 1256.
[2] *Ibid.*, 651, 714, 719.

disperst in private Houses and we must often send a hundred miles for a Paper that is wanted. . . . It is a wonder to me we have been able to observe any regularity at all or indeed to keep up the face of Government." [1] This was the need as it appeared from the purely administrative point of view. But politically the effort to move the official centre of gravity of the province showed some far more interesting features.

At the assembly held in Newbern in 1739 an act was passed incorporating Johnston's favorite new town, on Cape Fear river, under the name of Wilmington. The passage of this bill through the council was effected by Chief Justice Smith, who was presiding, voting twice, his first vote as a member resulting in a tie and his second vote being cast as the presiding officer in order to break the tie. This act was scandalous and it provoked much discussion, but the chief point in Smith's defence was that in case of tie votes, a decisive vote must be lodged somewhere and in general practice it was placed in the first person who was acting under the commission [2]; if any were dissatisfied, let them appeal to the authorities in England. The act of incorporation, however, stood as passed, though it caused much sharp discussion over the relative advantages of Wilmington and Brunswick as ports and the alleged harsh discrimination against the last mentioned town by the governor and his supporters. Twice this same year, also, attempts were made to impeach Smith because of his irregularities in the courts, as well as his sharp practices as a political ally of the governor. [3] On one of these occasions Smith thwarted the plan of his opponents by inducing four members to absent themselves, and thus defeating the efforts to make a quorum. At the next session he won over a majority by promising to increase the number of commodities in which quit rents could be paid and to raise their rating. [4] Not only was impeachment thus avoided, but Smith was able by prosecution to humble one of his chief opponents and to spend the few remaining years on the bench. Throughout these disputes the council was split into contending factions — the governor and Smith leading on the

---

[1] *Ibid.*, 720, 735, 1075.　　　　[3] *Ibid.*, 466, 503.
[2] *Ibid.*, 449, 455–460, 462–470.　　[4] Ashe, 259.

one side and Moseley, Roger Moore and Eleazer Allen on the other.

Tactics similar to those which saved Smith from impeachment at Newbern were tried by the governor upon an assembly at Wilmington in 1741. He called it to meet there in order to prevent the northern members from attending, and some of their most troublesome leaders were prevailed upon to be absent. Only two more than the number required for a quorum were present. The measure which Johnston hoped to persuade this body to pass was an acceptable quit rent bill, but so set were their minds on payment in commodities, and that at high prices, that he found it impossible to bring them to satisfactory terms.[1]

These were only skirmishes preliminary to the sectional conflict, which began in earnest in 1746. Then, after two prorogations, the assembly was called in Wilmington, in November.[2] The representatives from Albemarle, hoping to break a quorum, agreed to stay away. Fifteen from other counties of the province attended and since the biennial act, which required a quorum of one half the members, had been repealed, it was held, in accordance with the rule of the house of commons in England, that a quorum was present. Two important bills were passed, one fixing the seat of government permanently at Newbern and establishing circuit courts throughout the province, and the other allowing to each county two representatives, and no more.[3] The claims of the northern section were thus challenged in the most direct fashion. Insisting on the rule of the biennial act that it required a majority of the members to make a quorum, they totally denied the validity of the acts and declared that they had been carried by a trick. They refused to attend future assemblies at Newbern. The governor's writs calling for the election of two members were disregarded and five were chosen, as previously in each of the Albemarle counties. By the assembly these elections were declared void, and writs for new ones were issued, but all the electors refrained from voting.[4] The governor continued the assembly of 1747 in existence by successive prorogations until the close of his

[1] Ibid., 584.
[2] Ibid., 1154.
[3] Ibid., 838, 843, 870; Ashe, 268.
[4] Ibid., IV, 857, 860, 864, 865, 1152, 1156, 1163.

administration. Albemarle refused to send representatives and the assembly therefore represented only the southern part of the province, and there alone were its acts accepted as valid. The northern counties refused to pay taxes, and as the burden of supporting the government was soon declared by the assembly to be too heavy for its constituents alone, taxes ceased generally to be paid throughout the province. The administration of justice practically ceased in the northern counties, and anarchy in the sense of absence of government existed, with much accompanying outrage and disorder.[1]

In this controversy McCulloh supported the northern counties and became their agent in proceedings before the board of trade in England. James Abercromby was agent for the governor and the province. In 1747 the case was carried before the privy council on petition from the northern counties and with preliminary statements from both parties. It was referred to the committee of the council for plantation affairs.[2] In July, 1748, this committee ordered that free and full testimony bearing on the subject should be taken by both sides in North Carolina and transmitted to England. This was done under the direction of two agents who were appointed for the purpose. The testimony of the northern counties went to show that they had acted in accordance with precedents which had existed since the time of the Fundamental Constitutions, while Johnston claimed that for years prior to 1746 the northern representatives had systematically obstructed or defeated the measures of government by threatening to withdraw from the assemblies and that the final break was not only legal, but a necessity. Since then some valuable laws had been passed, as an act for a rent roll and for revising and printing the laws of the colony.[3] It was not until 1751 that this evidence was received in England and hearings begun before the board of trade.[4] A decision of the question had not been reached in England when Johnston died, in July, 1752.

So far as extant records indicate, Johnston, during the last half of his administration, was remiss in his correspondence with the offices in England. For nearly five years, between

---

[1] *Ibid.*, 1165, 1311.
[2] *Ibid.*, 1152–1163.
[3] *Ibid.*, 1168–1225.
[4] *Ibid.*, 1225 *et seq.*

1742 and 1747, no letter from him was received by the board of trade. When they began to reprove him for this neglect, he persisted in stating that he had regularly sent letters and packets to the board but that they must have miscarried. Probably in some cases the captains of merchant vessels to whom his letters and packages were entrusted neglected to deliver them. Judging, however, from what occurred in the case of the other colonies, and making all allowance for the chances of loss which were involved and the necessity under which he lay, of sending his mail through posts in other colonies, we must infer that Johnston was guilty of much neglect. Among his excuses, also, he hints at the probable explanation of this, for it began just after the disallowance of his quit rent bill and the transfer of a large part of the territory of the province of Lord Granville. These events to a large extent defeated Johnston's policy of developing the territorial revenue, which was entirely independent of appropriations by the legislature, and, by means of this, of securing salaries and of gradually introducing better order and system into the government.

He was greatly chagrined by this defeat and perhaps especially so, because the disallowance of the act was made to hinge, not on the main issue, but on a question which was largely distinct from that issue. He wrote the board that after this defeat he had almost nothing of which to inform them except the miseries and hardships under which he and other North Carolina officials labored. If, when he received communications from England, he could have met the council and secretary promptly, in many cases he would have been able to return more satisfactory answers, but that in these circumstances this was impossible. " It is with great difficulty we make a shift to meet twice in a year. All the rest of our time is spent at our own little plantations which are some fifty, some one hundred and some two hundred miles distant from one another: and this will always be our case until our salaries are regularly paid. Mine is now eight years in arrears, and those of the other Officers in proportion, and our fees [are] but very trifling, which makes it impossible for us to remain long in any of the Towns of this Province where, small and despicable as they are, living is dearer than in London." [1] Somewhat later, in 1747, Johnston wrote to much the same effect, adding that as a result of the recent passage of the act for the establishment of the seat of government at Newbern, and laying of a tax for public buildings, he hoped to bring officials and the public papers together and be more regular in his correspondence in the future. But his neglect continued and the following year he was again reproved for it by the board of trade.[2]

Under such conditions complaints were naturally made in England against the governor. Soon after the defeat of the second pretender, he was charged with being a Jacobite and it was said that he had excluded Palatine immigrants from their lands in order to make room for Scotch exiles of that party.[3] These charges he explicitly denied, though his nationality and the settlement in the province of many who had been concerned in the uprisings of both 1715 and 1745 continued to give some occasion to his opponents to repeat the complaint. Early in 1749 Francis Corbin, who for a short time had been attorney general in North Carolina, and a number of other persons who had various interests in the province, among these McCulloh and Arthur Dobbs, preferred complaints against Johnston. These were referred by the duke of Bedford, the secretary of state, to the board of trade for inquiry and report.[4] Hearings were held at which James Abercromby as agent for the province appeared on the governor's behalf. The charges had to do with his alleged sympathy with Jacobites, as indicated, among other things, by his appointment of one McGregor, who had been concerned in the rebellion of 1715, to the offices of captain of the militia and justice of the peace; with his approval of measures for the issue of bills of credit which contained no suspending clauses; that, though very rarely holding sessions of the chancery court, he often granted injunctions, orders of *nolle prosequi* and appeals to chancery, whereby many cases lay suspended and the course of justice was interrupted. The fact that so important a law as that reducing the representation of the northern counties had been passed without a suspending clause, also came in for adverse criticism. Aber-

---

[1] *Ibid.*, 792, 797, 844.　　　[3] *Ibid.*, 9, 18, 935.
[2] *Ibid.*, 870.　　　　　　　　[4] *Ibid.*, 925, 936, 940.

cromby insisted that these charges originated in England and
were not supported by documents; that they were presented
by parties who had not been interested in North Carolina,
and who had not been injured, and therefore asked that
copies of them be sent to Johnston and the legislature before
action was taken. The board of trade, in its report to the
duke of Bedford,[1] summed up the evidence in the case and
submitted it to the secretary with the brief comment that it
indicated the existence of great disorder and confusion in the
province.

Meantime letters of self-defence had begun to come in from
Johnston himself. The case was therefore kept open, and
was before the board of trade at intervals through 1750.
McCulloh then came to act definitely as agent for the party
of the northern counties, as well as an opponent of bills of
credit, and those subjects were much under discussion.[2] Abercromby continued to act under definite instructions from the
assembly to defend the policy of the governor and the southern counties on all controverted points. The controversy
dragged on and a settlement of the general points at issue
was not reached until the next administration.

[1] *Ibid.*, 930–935.   [2] *Ibid.*, 1020, 1028 *et seq.*

CHAPTER X

The part of Clinton's administration of New York which concerns us here began in the spring of 1746, when he quarrelled with James De Lancey and called Cadwallader Colden back from the country to be his chief adviser. Though Colden had been an active member of the council as long ago as the time of Burnet, since the departure of that governor he had devoted his attention chiefly to his favorite scientific pursuits, to his estate in Ulster County, and to the duties of his office of surveyor general.[1] In his earlier career he had fully sympathized with the Indian policy of Burnet and especially with his hostile attitude toward the Canadian trade interests which centered at Albany. His official duties had long made him familiar with the system of granting land in New York and with the social and political interests which sprang from this and rested upon it. He and his family were profiting in a very substantial way from this system and from the marriage relations which followed naturally in the wake of property and office. Colden himself was well advanced in middle life and when, about this time, George Clarke returned finally to England, he was left as the senior member of the council, and, as such, possibly the next in succession to the government. And yet, in the inner circle of political management Colden was a new man, comparatively a stranger. He was far less experienced than De Lancey, whom he now innocently displaced and who for that reason was to be henceforth his unscrupulous rival. De Lancey was also his superior in craft and subtlety, socially more brilliant; Colden's power lay in his learning, his solid and logical un-

---

[1] Alice M. Keys, Cadwallader Colden, A Representative Eighteenth Century Official. See a long letter of Colden to Collinson, May, 1742, which abounds in personal details; Ms. Colden Papers in Library of N. Y. Hist. Soc. It is in this letter also that one will find a very frank expression of opinion by Colden of the Indian Commissioners at Albany and their policy.

derstanding and in the force with which he set forth his views. With tact he was not plentifully endowed. With other than the official views of government or any attitude which indicated hostility to the crown or its representative in the province he had no sympathy. To the illiterate Clinton he became an invaluable assistant, for he wrote all his important state papers and addresses, gave him valuable counsel, and shared with him not only the burden of government business but the unpopularity which his administration so abundantly incurred.

The pressure of war and its expenditures had already provoked hard feeling between Clinton and the assembly; now that he had broken with the chief justice the majority of the council was almost sure to be arrayed against him. Under these conditions to hope for more than annual appropriations was vain, while all acts of the executive which involved the spending of money were viewed with suspicion. De Lancey's position had been greatly strengthened by an appointment as chief justice during good behavior which he had received from Clinton. The good fortune and merits of Sir Peter Warren, who had married a sister of De Lancey, and who was now rapidly rising to the rank of admiral in the British navy, notably increased the prestige of the family. But the governor obtained about this time the support of William Johnson, a nephew of Warren, who was now taking an important place as a landed proprietor in the Mohawk valley and whose influence as a trader and negotiator among the Indians was soon to exceed that which any other British subject ever gained. To the conference of 1746 Johnson came with the Mohawks, into which tribe he was adopted, and on this occasion, owing to the indisposition of the governor, Colden delivered the opening speech. In Johnson, Colden and the governor were presently to find one whom they could oppose as a rival to the Indian commissioners at Albany. This, together with the emphasis which all three of these men laid on the importance of vigorous Indian policy and the steady extension of the frontier as the best method of opposing the French, was but a revival of Governor Burnet's course of action, the same, too, which Colden had supported at the beginning of his career.

It was in the autumn of 1746, after it had been necessary to abandon the operations in the region of Lake Champlain which had been planned for that year, that the foes of Clinton, in both council and assembly, declared open war upon him. When the fall session of the assembly opened, October 17, the governor was again indisposed and asked the speaker to lay his speech before the house.[1] That body, already in an ill-tempered mood, criticized this procedure as unprecedented, but received the speech, though they did not condescend at once to reply to it. The speech itself was elaborate and well written, and it is not unlikely that it was the first of such messages to come from the pen of Colden.[2] With a tone of assurance, such as a really strong executive should have used, it told of the liberal appropriation which was needed for the winter camp, for the establishment of which Clinton had left orders at Albany, and for the forts and blockhouses which must be built to guard the frontier and maintain communication with the army. Statements of this nature were followed by an unfortunate reference to parsimony as something the bare mention of which in the house at such a time would be indecent. The address closed with an exhortation to harmony, a condition which was often destroyed by " the private views of artful and designing men."

An act had been passed the previous July for the intended expedition against Canada which contained provisions deemed by the assembly to be suitable for the purposes desired by the governor. The house therefore at once set at work upon a bill extending the time during which this act should be in force.[3] Two commissioners were named in the act for the purchase of the provisions and two at Albany for receiving and delivering the same. While this bill was under consideration, the governor sent the assembly a message to the effect [4] that he understood provision was to be made by it for transporting the supplies to Albany and their actual delivery to

[1] Ass. J., II, 124 et seq.

[2] Among the Ms. Colden Papers are several drafts in the hand of Colden of papers which were issued by the governor or in his interest, and these sufficiently prove the general fact that Colden was the author of many of Clinton's papers.

[3] Col. Laws, III, 577 (Chap. 832); 634 (Chap. 847).

[4] Ass. J., II, 126.

the captains of the troops.[1] They should be delivered, he said, from time to time and in quantities needed. A radical defect in the earlier act was pointed out when the governor added, " I must . . . tell you that the provisions for the army are so necessary a part of all warlike enterprises, that any . . . obstruction in the daily supply of them may defeat the best concerted measures; and that, if the provisions for the army are not subject to the orders of the general, or commanding officer, it is in the power of those persons who have the direction of furnishing provisions to defeat any enterprise." He therefore urged that provision be made for transporting the supplies along with the troops and that the independent companies, a part of whom he proposed to detach for winter service, be put on the same footing in this respect as the militia. But the new measure, which, however, was not passed until December, does not show that the provisions suggested were introduced. On the other hand, the resolutions of the house under which the supplies were actually procured clearly implied that they were to be used for the militia and to be transported to Albany.[2]

Before Clinton had left Albany, and as soon as it had become evident that there would be no expedition to Canada that season, he had issued orders for the forming of a winter camp at the Carrying Place (now Fort Edward) between the Hudson river and Lake Champlain,[3] and the supplies under discussion were intended by him chiefly for the troops to be stationed there, and among them a part of the four independent companies was included. A warrant had been issued by the governor, September 29, requiring the commissioners at Albany to supply the independent companies in like manner as they did the militia.[4] This introduced conditions essentially different from those contemplated in the resolutions of the house. And as soon as Clinton became aware of the intentions of the assembly, he sent in a special message, in which he insisted that the act of the previous year be so

[1] The language of the clause implied this, though it was possible to give it a different interpretation, Col. Laws, III, 584.

[2] Ass. J., II, 126.

[3] See the narrative of this in its final form, in an address by the governor to the assembly, Aug. 4, 1749; Ass. J, II, 272. In an earlier and more detailed form it is in *ibid.*, 137.   [4] *Ibid.*, 128, 130, 132–135.

amended as to provide that the supplies be carried along with the forces and to the places where the captains with their companies should be on duty and there delivered as needed.[1] But this appeal produced no effect on the assembly, and already before it was made a clash between the military and civil authorities had occurred at Albany.

When, on the day of its issue, the governor's warrant for the delivery of provisions was presented by Colonel Marshall, the commissioners declared that they did not think themselves empowered by the act to deliver them.[2] Their reason for this was that the language of the statute, " for the forces raised in this colony," seemed to limit their activities strictly to the militia and to exclude the independent companies. On the other point at issue — the transport of provisions beyond Albany — they also pleaded the language of the statute as most narrowly interpreted, and refused to act. Having repeated this refusal before the local officers met in council of war, on October 16, an order was issued by Colonel Roberts to Holland, the sheriff, under which the storehouse was broken open and the supplies which it contained were taken entirely out of the hands of the commissioners. Roberts offered to give his personal receipt, but it was refused. The plea urged in justification of this course was that it was necessary for the defence of the frontier, the prosecution of which was being thwarted by the commissioners. It also appeared that Colden, under instructions from the governor, had said that, if the commissioners did not transport the provisions with the troops, they would be removed and others appointed in their places.[3] The conditions were thus delicately posed for another violent factional conflict. Viewing the subject broadly, one's sympathy must be with the executive, for its measures were well calculated to meet the crisis on the frontier, and it needed liberal discretion. But it was as clearly bound by the resolutions of the house, the body which controlled the purse, and these resolutions had been rudely violated. The Albany officials, who disliked Colden and all who were connected with him, were ready to obstruct the governor by insisting on the strictest possible interpretation of their duties in the case as set forth in the statutes.

[1] Ass. J., II, 126.   [2] Ass. J., II, 132 et seq., 138.   [3] Ibid., 272.

As soon as the assembly learned what had occurred,[1] it resolved to investigate the affair in committee of the whole. While this was progressing it made an angry reply to the message with which the governor had opened the session.[2] Referring to that speech, they professed themselves ignorant of the alleged bad disposition of the Six Nations and of the poor administration which was bringing it about. In the hope of entrapping the executive, they expressed a willingness to investigate the management of Indian affairs, if the governor would lay before them all the papers bearing on that subject. They deprecated the governor's proposal to establish a winter camp on the remoter frontier, because of the deaths and desertions which would be likely to result. Speaking of alleged parsimony, they claimed to have done even more than the crown had recommended or expected. Replying to the need of a good understanding between the different branches of the government, they struck by implication at Colden as one of the " artful and designing men," " not friends to their country," who were trying to gain the support of the governor for their own " private views." The political interest attaching to this representation is also shown by the fact that it was at once printed and circulated.

On receiving the report of the committee of the whole concerning the seizure of provisions, the assembly resolved that the governor was ill advised in granting a warrant for provisions for the independent companies, that the commissioners in refusing to obey that warrant had conformed with the terms of the statute, that Colonel Roberts' warrant was arbitrary and illegal and that in issuing it he was guilty of a high misdemeanor; that Holland and Colden had incurred similar guilt, while the breaking open of the storehouse was a gross violation of the rights of the subject, and finally that the governor be desired to order the attorney general to prosecute the offenders. The practical conclusion of the assembly was, that it was vain to furnish more provisions until proper assurances were given that a stop would be put to such proceedings.[1]

---

[1] *Ibid.*, 128, 132 *et seq.*   [2] *Ibid.*, 130.
[3] *Ibid.*, 134; N. Y. Docs., VI, 657. Archibald Kennedy wrote to Colden, probably about this representation: "This thing is not to be printed. Where

In the two replies which were made by Clinton and Colden to these deliverances of the house it was declared to be notorious that the discontent of the Six Nations was due to ill usage by traders, most of whom were employed in the conduct of Indian affairs.[1] In proof of this the governor declared himself ready to submit all his correspondence with the Indian commissioners, an offer which was at once accepted. As to the seizure of provisions, Clinton further informed the assembly that he had offered to pay for or replace the provisions needed for the independent companies, and had also offered to pay for the transport of provisions from Albany northward, a proposal with which the commissioners there had expressed themselves satisfied. This would seem to establish beyond doubt the purely factious nature of their opposition. As the conduct of all the subordinate officers had been regular, Clinton declined to order their prosecution, but he was ready to submit the question to the king. Colden's conduct he justified. The house resolved that this answer was unsatisfactory and that those who had advised it had tried to create dissensions between the different branches of the legislature, had encouraged a breach of the laws and were enemies of the constitution of the colonies; and finally that, until assurances were given that these abuses would cease, they could grant no further allowance nor proceed to any business whatever.[2]

The De Lancey faction, which was stirring up this trouble, felt even more strongly against Colden than it did against Clinton. Both parties now resorted to the press and articles began to appear in the newspapers. The proceedings of the Indian conference at Albany during the previous August and September were issued in pamphlet form and distributed.[3] To this was prefixed an introductory note, stating that in holding the conference, the purpose of which was to engage the Indians in the proposed expedition, the governor had de-

it was hatched you may guess, but it was licked into shape at the Cart and Horse, where I hear they had many meetings." Ms. Colden Papers, Kennedy to Colden, Dec. 22, 1746.

[1] Colden must be held largely responsible for all important official utterances at this time.

[2] Ass. J., II, 139.

[3] N. Y. Docs., VI, 330, 332, 659; Journal of Leg. C., II, 957.

sired the assistance of as many of the council as was possible. But they all declined to attend except Mr. Colden, Mr. Livingston and Captain Rutherford, the last two being already at or near Albany. The governor therefore was obliged to act with the smallest number of the council which would make a quorum.

In the session of the legislative council of December 4, De Lancey read this paragraph, saying he conceived that it contained a misrepresentation of facts and an invidious reflection on the members who did not attend the conference. He therefore moved that the printer be examined for the purpose of ascertaining who had directed that the paragraph should be printed. Murray seconded this motion. Colden was in the chair, and by following these tactics a confession was extorted from him that he was the author of the paragraph and was responsible for its being printed. The council then resolved, in harmony with the declaration made by De Lancey when he introduced the subject, that its proceedings on the subject be printed.[1] A strong representation against Colden was also sent to the governor by his opponents in the council.[2] In this they made chief use of an expression Colden had used in his opening address at the recent Indian conference, when in the absence of the governor he had referred to himself as the next person in the administration. In view of this and of many other instances of his vanity, they warned Clinton against his new favorite as one who probably intended to supplant him and who had already changed the relations between the governor and the legislature.

From his country residence in Ulster county Colden sent to Clinton a long defence of his course at Albany in answer to this representation.[3] Barring one or two errors in details, this was an able and convincing plea. He left it to the governor to judge whether the break between him and the legislature had not come previous to his (Colden's) return to active service, and whether his troubles had not resulted from the advice he had received when he first came into the province, to the effect that he should make De Lancey his

[1] They were printed in the New York Post Boy, Dec. 8, 1746.
[2] Keys, *op. cit.*, 157.
[3] N. Y. Docs., VI, 331 *et seq.*; Ms. Colden Papers; Keys, 159.

chief councillor. Colden admitted his share of vanity, but truly observed that it grew luxuriantly on American soil. Clinton, of course, fully accepted this defence, and was prepared to urge upon Newcastle the removal of Horsmanden, who had supported De Lancey in his attack in the council, and other changes which would be favorable to Colden's prospects. The "faction," on their part, through Sir Peter Warren were urging Colden's removal and were making such bitter attacks upon him that Clinton especially urged him to reply and promised to give him his own full support.[1] Never before in New York, and very rarely if at all elsewhere, had a situation arisen which was so suggestive of the favorite or chief minister as was this one. Before the opening of the spring session Colden was back in town actively coöperating with the governor.

During the winter of 1746-7 Clinton and Shirley had planned another expedition for the following summer against Crown Point.[2] At first the council approved of this, provided Connecticut would join, but finally it decided that it was impracticable. It was in reference to this project and related enterprises that the controversy between Clinton and the assembly was reopened in the spring session.[3] It began over a resolution of the house that, as the new levies raised the previous year had remained unemployed, one hundred fit men from them be used as scouts in the country about Albany, and the assembly would allow them one shilling daily above their regular pay. This was formulated as a bill which received the assent of council and assembly and was submitted to the governor. The assembly later stated that by referring to the levies as unemployed it only meant that they were not yet designated for service on the expedition against Canada, and hence that part of them might be temporarily utilized for scouting.[4] But the reference touched the governor's sensibilities as a military man and these were acute. It drew from him a long explanation and defence of his care for the frontier during the previous campaign, and proved his fidelity, energy and good judgment, so far as

[1] Ms. Colden Papers, Clinton to Colden, March 11, 1746/7.
[2] N. Y. Docs., VI, 659.
[3] Ass. J., II, 141.   [4] Ibid., 149.

military problems were concerned.[1] It brought out his preference for the Carrying Place over Saratoga as the central
point of defence on the extreme frontier toward Crown Point.
The assembly tried to uphold the advantages of Saratoga in
spite of assurances that a fort there could be commanded
from the surrounding hills. The point was repeatedly in
dispute as the controversy progressed, and one wonders if
it was not the Schuyler interest that led the assembly to favor
Saratoga.

But Clinton in this paper hopelessly reopened the breach
with the assembly by charging them with " declining every
expence that seems necessary for the security of the British
colonies and the well being of this province at this time."
A reference to the appropriation acts of the past year will
show that this was a gross exaggeration. But he made it the
justification for an onslaught on the traders and Indian commissioners of Albany, holding them responsible for the alleged
inactivity of the assembly. Because of the gain they reaped
from trade with the French and Indians, he declared, they
" do not wish well to any expedition against Canada." Here
we have the views of Colden and Burnet, their explanation of
the attitude of Albany ever since the long period of neutrality
during the second French war. So savage was this attack
that it could never be forgiven by the powerful element
against which it was directed.

In its answer to the governor, which was prepared by the
members from New York, Westchester and Suffolk counties
acting as a special committee,[2] the assembly reviewed its
record on appropriation as Clinton had done his record on
measures of defence, and with a similar justifying result.[3]
They also questioned the right of the three members of the
council who had accompanied Clinton to Albany, with commissioners from Massachusetts alone, to bind this or other
colonies to provide for forts at the Carrying Place and for
attacking Crown Point. They chose to wait for orders from
England and experienced officers. But the governor's savage
attack on Albany furnished an occasion for an equally vig-

[1] *Ibid.*, 144 *et seq.*
[2] These were Clarkson, Van Horne, Richard, Cruger, F. Philipse, Thomas,
Morris, Pierson and Nicoll.   [3] *Ibid.*, 149 *et seq.*

orous counter thrust at Colden,[1] and also at the son of
Lydius, the Dutch minister at Albany, whom they held responsible for the alleged calumnious charges. They declared
that the conduct of affairs had not been steady and successful since confidence had been placed in Colden, " a person
obnoxious to and censured by this house." They held him
responsible for the reopening of the controversy between the
legislature and the executive. They also complained that
private persons — meaning Johnson — were appointed to
transact business with the Indians without the knowledge of
the commissioners.

Clinton made no reply to this manifesto except to state
that he would lay it before the home government. This he
did, accompanied by extended comments.[2] Few and unimportant communications had been received from England since
the beginning of Clinton's term, and the difficulties in which
he and Colden were now becoming involved led the governor from this time to write more frequently and urgently
for support. As time progressed, the financial pressure on
Clinton became more severe and his pleas to Newcastle for
help became correspondingly insistent. The burden of these
letters was an elaboration of Clinton's defence of his conduct
of the war and of Indian affairs, and the constant insistence
on the charge that under the lead of the De Lancey faction
the control of the province was wrested from the governor's
hands and the king's authority treated with contempt. So far
had this gone that Clinton now began calling for the direct
interposition of the crown or parliament, without which he
could not answer for the safety or continued loyalty of the
province. The calm with which Colden bore the attacks of
his rivals, as shown by his unpublished letters, reveals the
exaggeration in Clinton's appeals to the home government.

At the time of which we are speaking, some New Jersey
troops, as well as Pennsylvania Germans, were in service on

[1] " Your Excellency will permit us to say, that whoever has had Influence
enough to instil such Notions into your Excellency's Mind, has, in our Opinion,
most grossly abused that Confidence you have thought fit to repose in him."
As to rumors of intrigues at Albany to betray English interests to the French,
they declared in the strongest terms their belief that there was not the least
shadow of truth in such suspicions.

[2] N. Y. Docs., VI, 365, 662.

the northern frontier. They had been held in garrison there since the previous year, and now attempts were being made to concert arrangements with Massachusetts and Connecticut for a joint expedition against Canada in 1747. In May Schuyler, who was in command in the north, paid the New Jersey men in full.[1] Clinton condemned this course as certain to provoke jealousy among the rest of the troops, from whom for the usual reasons of economy arrears of pay were being withheld as long as possible. This proved to be the result, and it was promoted by certain mischief makers among the Dutch at Albany, who told the Pennsylvanians that they would probably be cheated out of the greater part of their pay, as had occurred on the previous expedition; and that the officers were actually withholding a part of the sum which the governor had recently sent. The result was some mutinous demonstrations at Saratoga about the close of May, which drew Clinton to Albany. They soon subsided and it is not improbable that the importance of the affair was exaggerated for the purpose of embarrassing the assembly. Colden expressed the idle fear that his family might be molested in Ulster, and was not slow to avail himself of the event for the promotion of one of his sons to the office of muster-master.

It was at this time that the British government was beginning to commit itself to the policy of compensating the colonies in part for their expenditures in the wars. In April of the previous year Newcastle had written that both officers and soldiers who should then engage in the service would receive the king's pay.[2] The assembly understood this to mean that they would be held responsible for the subsistence of the force raised in New York, and in addition for the pay of such scouting parties as should from time to time be sent out. They thought the independent companies should be subsisted out of their own pay except where they were in service at Oswego. As to presents for the Indians, they thought that the home government should pay at least largely for these, while New York felt that it should not be expected

[1] Ex. C. Min. for May, 1747; N. Y. Docs., VI, 351, 357, 363, 367; Smith, II, 101; Keys, 169 *et seq.*
[2] Ass. J., II, 157, 160, 164.

to pay any of the levies which came from other colonies. As no funds adequate to these expenditures had been sent from England, Clinton had heavily to pledge his own credit to provide the necessary means. When the assembly met, June 2, he stated this fact and insisted that, if he drew more bills, the assembly should agree to indemnify his family. To this they made the replies just outlined indicating that they had faithfully performed their duty. They told the governor that he should continue to draw bills on the assurances of the duke's letter and, if he did not do so, he would show unreasonable distrust of the home government and make himself responsible for the evil which might ensue.

The plan of Shirley and Clinton for an expedition against Crown Point failed to receive the coöperation of England.[1] The ministry decided instead to turn its chief attention toward Nova Scotia. By the middle of August it had become evident that what was done must be accomplished by colonial troops. It also became impossible for commissioners from Massachusetts and New York to meet, and this fact the governor stated to the assembly when it met early in August. But he urged them to provide the £14,000 which was needed for the expedition as planned. He believed he could promise the hearty coöperation of the Six Nations, to whose encouragement Massachusetts and Connecticut had advanced considerable sums. The house, with its habitual distrust, replied that it would aid in any well-concerted plan, but, if they should raise money without knowing the reasons therefor, they would be false to the trust reposed in them by their constituents. They did not know how much Massachusetts and Connecticut had contributed toward the support of the Indians, but in any case they were sure that New York had surpassed them in liberality. They felt that in any joint scheme New York should not bear more than one-third of the expense and that the colonies to the south should also contribute a proportional share. This was the form in which the claims of New York, about which so much was heard in the first two years, were formulated at this time.[2]

Finally, at the close of August, Clinton informed the assembly that he could no longer endure the expense which he

[1] N. Y. Docs., VI, 384.   [2] Ass. J., II, 159–160; N. Y. Docs., VI, 668.

had undertaken at the charge of the crown, and therefore urged it to provide the necessary supplies for those purposes for two months, before the expiration of which time he hoped to learn the king's pleasure through Shirley and Knowles at Boston.[1] The objects for which he desired this temporary provision were supplies for the independent companies, presents for the Indians and support for the levies from the southern colonies. He also told them that they must henceforth provide for the relief and support of the garrisons at Saratoga and Oswego. The cost of transporting provisions to the latter post had been doubled by the panic caused by the recent attack of the French and Indians on Burnet's Field (German Flats). In committee of the whole the house reaffirmed its former policy and expressed a willingness to grant only what was necessary to pay and subsist 150 men as scouts for fifty days.[2] Their feeling toward Johnson was shown by the resolve that he should be held to his contract to supply Oswego with provisions, however much the cost of their transport had been increased. They also asked the governor to provide at once for the relief of Saratoga by posting there 100 of the regulars and some New York men, if the New Jersey troops had to be withdrawn. The governor replied that it was impossible for him to do any of these things and, after the fruitless discussion had been continued for some days longer, the assembly was adjourned and by successive adjournments was kept from further business until the sixth of October. It was at this juncture also that Clinton suspended Horsmanden from the council because of his pernicious activity as a member of the De Lancey faction. For a similar reason Stephen Bayard followed him into retirement.[3]

As soon as the assembly came together it again appointed the members from the counties of New York, Queens and Westchester a committee to prepare a remonstrance against such frequent adjournments. But before its report was made a message came from the governor containing the agreement which had been reached between the commissioners of New York, Massachusetts and Connecticut for a joint expedition

[1] Ass. J., II, 162.   [2] Ibid., 163–165.
[3] N. Y. Docs., VI, 380, 404, 671.

against the French.[1] This stated the contingent which New York should raise and asked for supplies. But it contained no special provision for the defence of the New York frontier or for preserving the Indian alliance. Clinton therefore repeated in substance his demands of the previous summer, with the addition of a specific demand that a fort be built in each of the cantons of the Six Nations. To this program the assembly in substance assented, ordering the appropriation of £800, to be expended among the Indians, and agreeing to provide for the Canadian expedition and for the defence of the New York frontier. But it included a criticism of the governor for expending such large sums upon the Indians and an emphatic reference to the necessity of keeping up the fort and garrison at Saratoga. This irritated Clinton and, by sharply informing the house that he would receive nothing from it except what related to the message he had just sent, he threw away all chance of coming to terms with this assembly.[2]

The flood of controversy was at once reopened. With an exaggerated sense of the gravity of the crisis, the assembly ordered the door to be locked and the key laid on the table. Then in a series of resolutions, after the manner of the Long Parliament, it reaffirmed the right of freedom of speech and action and pronounced the attempt of the governor to restrict them in this to be irregular and unprecedented and a breach of their privileges. " Whoever advised his Excellency to send this message," they added, " has attempted to . . . subvert the Constitution of this Colony, and is an Enemy to the inhabitants thereof." During the same session in which these resolutions were adopted Clarkson, from the committee which had been appointed at the beginning of the session, presented a remonstrance which fills seven of the printed folio pages of the *Journal*, and which in return was replied to in an equally long and violent message from Clinton.[3] The house made it plain that it held Colden chiefly responsible as the governor's adviser. It mercilessly criticised the neglect of Saratoga, the management of Indian relations, and

[1] Ass. J., II, 169 *et seq.*   [3] Ass. J., II, 173.
[2] *Ibid.*, II, 173–180, 181–187. The governor's reply was drafted by Colden; see Ms. Colden Papers.

the harsh and false terms in which he had characterized the assembly. His frequent adjournments of the house for the purpose of harassing it into submission came in for a scathing review.

In his reply the governor taunted the assembly with its lack of knowledge of executive affairs, especially of what he received from the crown. He dwelt upon what must always be the independent prerogatives of the crown, especially in military affairs. In view of this his course in reference to Indian and military affairs was defended. Then, in language which might have been borrowed from Cornbury, he declared that the assembly depended for its existence upon the governor's commission and instructions, both of which were alterable at pleasure. They were therefore a dependent body and were not entitled to the rights of the house of commons, though they had just laid claim to them. He denounced them also for their lack of respect for him by sending him messages through committees instead of by the speaker.

In a week after Clinton had fired this broadside, he had to inform the house that the crown had ordered the expedition against Canada laid aside and the forces levied for that purpose to be discharged,[1] except such as were thought necessary for the defence of Nova Scotia. Steps to this end were taken, when another outburst of anger occurred. This was occasioned by the governor's issuing an order to James Parker, the public printer, forbidding him to print the last remonstrance of the house.[2] When news of this reached the house, Clarkson, chairman of the committee which had drawn the remonstrance, who had carried it to the governor and whom Clinton in his reply had charged with bad manners on that occasion, brought up the subject and related what occurred. Parker was called in and produced the governor's warrant forbidding him to print. This was followed by the unanimous adoption of a series of resolutions asserting, in the face of the fact that the proceedings of the house were secret and were as a rule not published, the principle that constitutents had the fullest right to know what their representatives were doing and, to this end, that no obstruction should be put in the way of the printing of its proceedings. The action of the governor in the

---

[1] *Ibid.*, 190.   [2] *Ibid.*, 191 *et seq.*

premises was pronounced arbitrary and illegal. A few days later Parker was ordered by the house to print the remonstrance and deliver ten copies to each of the members.

Just before the Parker episode Clinton had informed the assembly that he was directed to ask it for such money or credit as was necessary for the payment of the New York forces now to be discharged from the projected Canadian expedition until their pay should be provided for by parliament. He also desired to know the proportion of these forces which they would retain under pay and at what rates. In response to this the house first resolved to continue 800 men in pay for the defence of the frontier until the next August. It then declared that exhaustion of the province from the war was so great and its treasury so depleted that it could not make the payment or advance of credit requested to cover the expenditures of the previous year. Clinton then, in a brief message, told them that it would soon be necessary for him to order a large draft or detachment from the militia and he asked that an appropriation be made for this purpose. At this the assembly expressed astonishment in view of its very recent vote to retain in service 800 of the existing levies. It could find no explanation for this except the " unsteady counsels " by which the governor had been guided since he had given his confidence to Colden. They professed themselves unable to make any provision for the frontiers so long as such ambiguous and vacillating messages were sent.[1]

The reply of the governor to this was that the assembly had fulfilled none of the conditions which he had mentioned as necessary to taking the existing levies into colony pay and implied that provision for their arrears of pay, pending action by parliament, was one of these conditions. The uncertainty about an advance by parliament was again proving the stumbling block. The speaker also had told Clinton that the house would reduce the pay of the officers to less than one-half the British rates, amounts for which none of them could serve. " I now repeat," he said, " that I have no hope of retaining them except in the manner I proposed." Widespread discontent and even mutiny might be expected if the existing levies, or a part of them, were disbanded without their

[1] *Ibid.*, 190–194.

arrears being paid and their rate of pay kept up. The house now charged the governor, and rightly, with placing the advance of the arrears of pay as a new condition upon the retention of the men in service. This he had not done in his original message. The house had therefore proposed that both officers and men, to the number of 800, should be retained, the men on their former rate of pay, with the addition of clothing, and the officers at reduced rates because the house considered their former pay too high. When the speaker first communicated this resolve to Clinton he had expressed doubt and had said that he must consult Shirley and Knowles. The house had awaited impatiently the result only to receive the announcement of the heavier condition at the end. From it they inferred that the governor intended to drive the men to desert and leave the frontier defenceless.

This subject, together with the conduct of the New York commissioners in their failure to procure help from New England toward the defence of the northern frontier, came up for consideration in the legislative council. Before the council in executive session Clinton read a letter from Shirley about the pay of the levies when discharged, its author suggesting the issue to the men of certificates of what was due them on a loan from merchants, if the assembly refused the credit demanded.[1] The advice of the council was to apply to the merchants for an advance of the pay.

Meantime, as November advanced, the assembly sent repeated messages to the governor urging that volunteers be called for, in companies of 50 or 60 men each, and they voted the issue of £25,000 in bills of credit for provisions and supplies for these men. Clinton expressed his consent to this arrangement, provided no clauses were introduced into the bill which were derogatory to the prerogative and precautions were duly taken to prevent the embezzlement of the supplies.[2]

---

[1] C. J., II, 994; Ex. C. Min., Nov. 6 and context.

[2] The desirability of such provision and their execution is shown by letters and papers of Colden. In these he told of beef and pork so bad that the troops could not eat them; barrels of bread with layers of good quality at the top and bottom and the middle filled with stuff which was fit only for the hogs; of kegs of rum stated in accounts to hold 6½ gallons each, but on being tested they proved to have a capacity of only 5½ or 6 gallons. Reports also stated that supplies had been sold at Albany and converted to private use. Many of these statements Colden printed. Ms. Colden Papers.

As the militia of New York City had refused to obey the governor's order for a draft and word had come from Johnson that his men were very rapidly deserting, the governor had to accept the assembly's measure. He then dissolved it in an angry speech and reported the state of affairs to Newcastle and the board of trade.[1] The burden of these utterances was to prove a persistent intention on the part of the assembly " to assume the superiority in the administration." " For this purpose you throw out all the aspersions on your Governor's conduct that malice can invent, that thereby you might disable him in retaining that authority over the people of this Province which the king has intrusted him with." To the board of trade Clinton insisted that the root of the trouble lay in the power of the assemblies to issue bills of credit, by means of which they secured resources and then assumed the right to nominate for all offices and reward all services. Thereby the crown was stripped of all power to support itself against any attempts to weaken the government. " I must observe once more to Your Lordships that popular faction and power are become so very prevalent, not only in this but in all the northern colonies, that unless some extraordinary assistance is given to His Majesty's Governors, I am humbly of opinion it will not be in their power to support His Majesty's authority, as one [colony] takes example from another." An adequate and permanent revenue must in some way be secured. After its dissolution the assembly in turn published a long review and defence of its course in which it redoubled its assaults on Colden.[2]

In the election which soon followed nearly all the old members were returned and Jones was again elected speaker. Clinton could therefore expect no change of policy.[3] Yet the early sessions passed without a recurrence of conflict. The reason for this was that, though some attention at the beginning was given to a renewal of the project for a joint Cana-

---

[1] Ass. J., II, 202; C. J., II, 999; N. Y. Docs., VI, 412; Col. Laws., III, 660.

[2] Ass. J., II, 206–221. This and the governor's last speech Smith calls "further specimens of the scribbling talents of Dr. Colden and Mr. Horsmanden, the latter having held the pen for the assembly." Smith, *op. cit.*, II, 115.

[3] Clinton wrote at a later time that the rumor of the appointment of De Lancey as lieutenant governor gave "an unexpected turn" to this election. N. Y. Docs., VI, 523.

dian expedition in the following summer, it soon became known that the war was virtually ended and peace at hand. The critical attitude which the assembly exhibited toward Massachusetts showed that, had the expedition been undertaken, the former bickerings and obstructive tactics would probably have been repeated. Yet, with decent liberality, the house voted to provide for the repair of forts, for the supply of provisions for the garrison at Oswego, for the payment of scouts, for furnishing gunsmiths among the Indians and for finishing and furnishing the governor's house. The extra sum desired by Johnson was allowed. The accounts of the province were also called for and rendered by the various officials concerned. A bill which had failed of passage by the previous assembly, for the appointment of commissioners to examine and state the public accounts from the year 1713, now became law.[1] A letter from Newcastle elicited resolutions from council and assembly to build blockhouses and stockades at Schenectady and Albany and to make further provision for defence.[2] But the independent spirit of the assembly was shown by its resolution appointing Robert Charles agent for New York and authorizing the speaker to instruct him and correspond with him. Charles was appointed without Clinton's knowledge or consent and his salary was inserted in the bill which provided for the governor's salary, so that it was impossible for him to withhold his assent.[3] Charles was selected for the post on the advice of Sir Peter Warren. Clinton asked the board of trade not to permit the new agent to transact any business before them on behalf of the assembly without the governor's concurrence.[4] At midsummer Clinton and Shirley jointly held a conference with the Six Nations, and in a notable letter [5] which they sent to the lords of trade they condemned the Indian administration at Albany and insisted upon a wider coöperation among the colonies against the common enemy in terms which foreshadow the Albany Congress of six years later and the questions which were to come before it.

[1] Col. Laws, III, 692, 700, 717; N. Y. Docs., VI, 419.
[2] N. Y. Docs., VI, 683.
[3] Ass. J., II, 238; Smith, II, 143   [5] N. Y. Docs., VI, 420.
[4] *Ibid.*, 437. The subject of this letter will be treated more at length in another connection.

In Clinton's letter to the board of trade, of June 22, 1747, in which he sketched the origin of the De Lancey faction and of his connection with it and its founder, he stated that among the unwise courses of action which under De Lancey's advice he had adopted was that of accepting annual appropriations for his own salary and the support of the government in general.[1] De Lancey had told him that after he had gained the affections of the assembly and their constituents it would be much easier to recover any usurpations they had made on the prerogative than at that time. This and other courses of argument seemed plausible at the outset and Clinton confessed that he had unwarily yielded to them until he found that under the mask of friendship De Lancey was establishing his own interest and gratifying his own immoderate thirst for power till, by the alteration of the constitution, he put the administration absolutely in the hands of the faction of which he himself was the head. A move of the greatest importance in this game was the issue to De Lancey of a commission to the office of chief justice during good behavior by means of which he could hope to beat his rival, Colden, in the race for the succession to Clinton himself.

In the bills for the support of the government, continued Clinton in his letter of confession, " the salaries of the several officers were not affixed to the Offices but to the persons then in office. The view in this was not only to make the Officers entirely dependent on the Governing faction, and to deprive the King of that part of his prerogative of rewarding his own servants according to their merit, but in effect to deprive the King of the appointment of the Officers, for as the salary ceased as soon as any officer named in the bill should be removed, the officer afterwards appointed remained at the discretion of an Assembly whether they would allow him any salary, and in such a case persons at ease would not readily accept of an office subject to such a disgrace. Besides this, in all cases where his Majestie's prerogative might be in danger from the incroachments of Assemblies upon it the Officers must be deterred from doing their duty, when thereby they were in danger either of losing entirely or having their Salaries taken from them; . . . ; the Assembly not

[1] *Ibid.*, 352.

only made themselves the sole judges of the Salaries of the several Officers of the Government, for they will allow of no amendment from the Council to those Bills (which they call Money Bills), but likewise gave rewards for extraordinary services to be paid out of the Treasury, without any Warrant from me, and this has happened more than once, to persons openly in opposition to my Administration, and unless I had given my assent to this Bill, the whole support of this Government must have failed by the clauses directing those rewards being made part of the Act for the support of the Government." [1]

Clinton's excuse for thus consenting to the continuance of the system of annual appropriations, which Clarke had been compelled to accept, was that when he accepted office war was about to begin with France and, if possible, a conflict with the assembly should be avoided at such a crisis. But it was his determination and that of the British government, as soon as opportunity offered, to attempt the restoration of appropriations for five-year terms as they had been under many of the earlier governors. It was in his speech at the opening of the session of October, 1748,[2] when peace was virtually assured and it only remained to close up the accounts arising from the war, that Clinton, after consulting with Governor Shirley, told the assembly that he did not feel at liberty to give his assent to annual appropriation acts for the future.[3] In the same message he called their attention to a claim of Johnson for £2138, due him under an act of the last session for supplying the garrison at Oswego under the conditions of special peril which existed the previous year. This Clinton regarded as a debt of honor which the province was bound to discharge. Provision should also be made for paying the arrears due to the troops, the expense which arose from sending and receiving messengers and the exchange of prisoners.

As to the frontiers, the assembly thought that the three independent companies at Albany, which ought to consist of 100 men each, would be sufficient, and they of course would be

[1] *Ibid.*, 353.
[2] Ass. J., II, 243.
[3] N. Y. Docs., VI, 474. Shirley's very important letter of advice to Clinton is in *ibid.*, 432.

on the British establishment. They would provide for the small peace establishment at Oswego, and impliedly for no more. They advised that persons of higher rank and repute be sent to Canada to negotiate the exchange of prisoners, if he wished to succeed.[1] As peace had not yet been concluded, Clinton objected against such haste and completeness in the work of disbandment. Hostilities among the Indians might still be expected for some time, and danger from their skulking parties was one reason why it was difficult to find proper persons to send as emissaries to Canada. He also feared that his hopes of successfully concluding the negotiations would be defeated by the suspicion that the assembly would make no provision for the payment of the envoy.[2] Finally, when it became evident that the assembly would pay the forces only until November 1, Clinton agreed that they be disbanded.[3] One officer and about twenty-five men, the establishment of 1744, were left at Oswego.

On November 1, by order of the assembly, the treasurer submitted his accounts. Upon these and the petitions and accounts of the victuallers and various commissioners designated to execute the acts for supplying the forces, were based the resolves which were embodied in the revenue acts of this session. While engaged on this the assembly resolved that no accounts should be received unless they were sworn to and the time when they were rendered and the authority or order by which the services were performed were stated.[4] The governor was requested to conform to these rules in the accounts he should submit, and the accounts must be accompanied by a message recommending them in parliamentary form. The following day Clinton sent in Colonel Johnson's accounts, accompanied by a brief message.[5] But only partial provision for paying his claims was made. The only act for paying expenses of the war to which Clinton assented at the close of this session was one appropriating £3600 for the payment of the new levies which served under Schuyler. An act was also passed for supporting the garrison and trad-

[1] Captain Thomas Williams was employed on this service, and the Canadian officials declared themselves satisfied with his conduct. Ass. J., II, 248; N. Y. Docs., VI, 488, 490.

[2] Ass. J., II, 247, 248, 250.

[3] Ibid., 248, 250; Col. Laws, III, 367, 605, 736.

[4] Ass. J., II, 255.

[5] Ibid., 256, 264.

ing house at Oswego and to continue the duties levied for the support of the government for one year longer.[1] Two bills, one for the payment of continued charges and the other for the payment of salaries and services for one year to come, Clinton did not accept.[2]

During the session which thus closed, a discussion of the questions of annual and specific appropriations had been kept up between the governor and assembly and neither had swerved from the position each held at the outset.[3] The former dispute over the delivery of messages to the governor through members instead of the speaker was revived, and added spice to the proceedings. In the executive council De Lancey took advantage of a trifling incident to deliver both orally and in writing a most abusive attack on Colden, charging him with having " a most iniquitous, flagitious and wicked mind," [4] telling him he had a very mean opinion of him and going on in this strain at great length. It is to Colden's credit that his reply was a calm appeal to his public record as a sufficient answer to the charges of his enemies. Oliver De Lancey, the younger brother of the chief justice, tried to overawe supporters of the governor by the tactics of the bully.[5]

After the prorogation of the assembly, which was to continue until June, 1749, Clinton and Colden poured in to the authorities at home accounts of their sufferings at the hands of the opposing faction and of what seemed to be the almost hopeless condition of affairs.[6] During the interval until the next session the many creditors of the government were kept waiting for their pay. The governor in his opening speech [7] planted himself squarely on the requirements of his commission and instructions in reference to salaries and specific appropriations and the entire session was occupied with controversy over these subjects. Not a bill was passed or even introduced. After a session of more than two months, during

[1] Col. Laws, III, 732, 733, 736.
[2] The resolutions for this are in Ass. J., II, 256.
[3] Ass. J., II, 246 et seq.
[4] Ex. C. Min., Oct. 21 and Nov. 8, 1748.
[5] N. Y. Docs., VI, 413, 414, 471, 513–516, 692–694.
[6] Ibid., 458 et seq.
[7] Ass. J., II, 259.

which the deadlock was not broken, the assembly was prorogued and ultimately was dissolved.[1]

Clinton challenged the assembly to show wherein he had invaded any man's liberty or property or injured his reputation. He had never drawn, he said, the smallest sum of money from the treasury for any purpose except that for which it was granted. He also had searched the records for thirty years back and had failed to find evidence of any different line of conduct on the part of his predecessors.[2] There is no doubt of the substantial accuracy of this statement, and yet the assembly rode its hobby of "misapplication" as vigorously as ever, and drew the sharpest possible contrast between the king — whose interests they assumed to be necessarily the same as those of his subjects — and his needy governors, strangers to the people and thinking of nothing so much as ways and means for their own enrichment.[3] On the other hand, Clinton charged the assembly with having carried its control over the finances to such an extreme as to be guilty of "misapplications" themselves.[4] They had given money to private persons for services of which the executive was left in total ignorance, and by introducing these in their resolutions along with the regular expenditures had compelled the governor to assent to them. He might have referred to the appointment of an agent as a case in point, but instead he cited a large appropriation for the exchange of prisoners with the French islands, though the assembly asserted that in this case Clinton knew what was going to be done. The exchange of prisoners with Canada was certainly delayed for months by this state of affairs and the injury it was doing was repeatedly mentioned in the discussions.[5] The French also were availing themselves of the paralysis caused among the English by these conflicts to prepare for their advance into the Ohio valley, and the Indian allies were kept constantly irritated

[1] Ass. J., II, 274, 275.

[2] Ibid., 263, 273.

[3] Ibid., 267.

[4] Ibid., 264, 266. Clinton wrote to the board of trade that he had good reason to think that the speaker by order of the assembly drew considerable sums from the treasury for the secret service of the faction. N. Y. Docs., VI, 521.

[5] Ass. J., II, 263, 266, 268, 273; N. Y. Docs., VI, 515.

by the apparent weakness and vacillation of the English.

Taking the addresses of the house to be what they largely were — appeals to the people — one of these Clinton refused to receive. This opened again the question of privilege and it occupied a minor place in making the deadlock hopeless. The appeal which the governor took was as usual to the home government. He told the board of trade that the assembly had assumed in effect the executive power not only in the civil affairs, but in the military as well.[1] They directed officers as to places of rendezvous and times when they were to call their men together; they put the public stock of gunpowder into the custody of officers of their own naming, and the speaker ordered it out of the stores by his own warrant without the governor's knowledge and Clinton could not command one pound of the same. They tried to persuade the people that the king had no authority over the militia except what was granted by act of assembly. Clinton with the greatest justice reproached the home government for having in a measure allowed such conditions to prevail by failing to express its displeasure at them, though the efficacy of that was more than doubtful. He felt that if he had been effectively supported some who now appeared to act with the faction would have fallen away and it would have been impossible for the assembly to pass so many even apparently unanimous votes. But the controlling element in the existing situation was that Clinton had failed to govern New York and now was reduced to a condition of powerlessness. The report that a commission as lieutenant governor was intended for De Lancey would not down. If it should prove true, as it did, it would show that the " faction " had triumphed and Newcastle had struck hands with it as a compromise. Colden was already useless as a political factor, though he continued to be employed in many useful administrative capacities.[2] Being in need of some representative at home, Clinton sought the aid of Robert Hunter Morris, chief justice of New Jersey and son of its first governor, who was going to England on business connected with the boundary controversy between New York and New Jersey. But the only immediate result was the

[1] N. Y. Docs., VI, 522.
[2] Smith, *op. cit.*, II, 129 *et seq.*; Keys, *op. cit.*, 232 and context.

compiling by the board of trade for the use of the privy council of an elaborate digest of the events of Clinton's administration and of his controversy with the assembly, to which was appended no expression of opinion whatever.[1]

The remaining years of Clinton's administration passed without any important controversy to vary the monotony of routine business. With the close of 1750 he ceased to contend against the inevitable and thereby secured peace. An assembly was elected about the middle of 1750,[2] of which one session was held in the fall of that year, and two in 1751, one in the spring and one in the fall. This was the time of the French advance along the northern frontier and toward the Ohio valley. During the first session Governor Clinton submitted to the house a letter from Governor Hamilton of Pennsylvania, with an extract of one from Colonel Johnson which showed the necessity of conciliating and allaying the jealousies of the Indians.[3] Pennsylvania also desired the co-operation of New York in securing the fidelity of the Indians on the Ohio river. The assembly replied naturally that during the late war New York had in great measure defended its frontiers, which were also a protection to colonies further south, without their aid, and they now considered it reasonable that those colonies should secure the fidelity of their own Indians. But a conference with the Six Nations was considered.

[1] N. Y. Docs., VI, 614–703. [2] Ass. J., pp. 275–328. [3] *Ibid.*, 283 *et seq.*

CHAPTER XI

THE ADMINISTRATION OF ARTHUR DOBBS IN
NORTH CAROLINA

In January, 1753, Arthur Dobbs was appointed in England to succeed the late Gabriel Johnston in the governorship of North Carolina. Like Johnston himself, Glen of South Carolina and Ellis of Georgia, Dobbs was a man of scholarly tastes and attainments. He was from the north of Ireland, had served as high sheriff of Antrim, enquirer and surveyor general of Ireland and member of parliament from Carrickfergus. The extent of his knowledge of his native country and of the relations in which it stood to the commercial system of Great Britain was amply shown in his work on "The Trade and Improvement of Ireland." He had also shared in the efforts to discover the Northwest Passage and had written an account of the countries adjoining Hudson's Bay. As early as 1733 he had become interested in North Carolina and shortly after that date he had received three large grants of land, amounting in all to more than 200,000 acres. These grants were located mostly in the south-western part of the province, and upon them, by 1757, some 700 inhabitants are said to have been settled.[1] His interests in the province led him to join in the efforts to secure the recall of Johnston and naturally suggested his own appointment after Johnston's death. As Dobbs in his land speculations had been associated with McCulloh, it is reasonable to suppose that McCulloh's influence was used to secure him the governorship. Though at the time of his appointment Dobbs was already approaching seventy, his energy was still unabated and until near the close of an administration which lasted for ten years he retained the ability to discharge the duties of his office. During the first half or two-thirds of his administration, his speeches to the assembly, his letters to the

[1] Ashe, Hist. of North Carolina, I, 284. Saunders in introduction to N. C. Recs., V, XXXII.

board of trade and to other governors and his conduct of affairs in general gave him a place among the ablest and most intelligent governors of his time. His letters contain especially full expositions of policies and conditions in the province. His knowledge of his province became unusually thorough. His utterances upon the war reveal his almost fanatical Protestantism and in one notable speech to the assembly he also set forth at length and in elegant terms the orthodox British view of the French and of the deadly peril to which liberty in Europe and America was exposed by the growth of their power.

The drafting of the instructions for Dobbs furnished the occasion of a very thorough inquiry by Halifax and his associates upon the board of trade into the right which the inhabitants of the six northern counties claimed of sending five representatives to the general assembly, the rule which required the presence of a majority of its members to constitute a quorum of the assemby, and the manner in which the act of November, 1746, with its provisions for the return of only two representatives from each county and that fourteen members should form a quorum, was passed. This inquiry, which was carried back to the beginning of assemblies in the province, showed of course how the five-member counties and two-member counties had originated and how the system of unequal representation had been perpetuated after North Carolina became a royal province. The claim of the northern counties therefore appeared to rest upon a vested right; it seemed to have time in its favor, and with the ascertainment of this the board, as usual, rested its inquiry. The law officers refrained from giving a definite opinion, but were at a loss to find upon what the objection to the unequal representation of the counties was based. It was found that the requirement concerning the quorum dated back to the Fundamental Constitutions and had been perpetuated by the biennial act of 1715 and later practice. Upon this subject the law officers had a more definite opinion. They could not see that a majority of the members was necessary to a quorum, while the rule was very unusual, with likelihood of great inconvenience. When they came to the passage of the law of 1746 equalizing the representation of the counties, the law officers found, as they had done previously, that it had been secured " by management, precipitation and surprise, when only 14 members were present," that the governor ought not to have assented to it and that it should not be confirmed. The acts of that assembly, however, and those passed under its rule concerning the quorum should stand until repealed. In accordance with these opinions, the board recommended that a quorum of fifteen should be specified in the governor's instructions. In order to remedy the inequality of representation, it was recommended that thirteen acts erecting counties, townships and precincts and prescribing the number of members whom they should return to the assembly should be disallowed and that the governor should be instructed to confirm the rights of these counties and other jurisdictions by charters of incorporation. As the province grew, the governor should also create counties and towns by executive action, just and reasonable. This plan was approved by the committee of the council and embodied in the instructions which were given to Dobbs. It will be observed that by this shrewd action vested rights were conserved, while a way was opened toward conciliation between the hostile sections of the province by the development of a more equal system of representation. But the most important and immediate effect of the instructions, if they were obeyed, would be to transfer to the executive powers over the districting of the province and the organization of the assembly which in North Carolina and in the colonies generally had long been exercised by the legislature. It is in this connection that the conservative tactics of the British lawyers and officials became most evident and give to this incident its appropriate place in their general scheme of policy.

Another of Johnston's measures was brought under consideration at this time. This was the act for forming a rent roll and regulating the payment of quit rents. McCulloh's grants and the complaints which he had made of interference under Johnston's administration formed an important feature of this general subject. The history of instructions relating to land and of executive action under them in North Carolina was reviewed by the board, the numerous changes and the great irregularities and frauds being noted, of which Sir

Richard Everard especially and those who manipulated the blank patents after the purchase by the crown were guilty. Carelessness and irregularities also had not been lacking in Johnston's administration, as was indicated by the great reduction of revenue from quit rents after 1745 as compared with the four years preceding that date. Coming finally to the law of 1748, the board condemned it for various reasons. Its requirement for the registration of lands seemed to apply only to grants made under the proprietors; in a clause which declared that possession for twenty years should constitute a good title no exception was made of fraudulent or irregular patents; contrary to the royal instructions it provided that quit rents should be paid in commodities. For these reasons the board recommended that the act be disallowed and suggested a long list of regulations for guaranteeing the payment of quit rents and regularity in the issue of grants in the future. That a land speculator like Dobbs should be chosen to execute such a scheme of purification as this shows that the British government did not propose to interfere with the enormous grants which had already been made. As McCulloh had fallen short by far in establishing upon his grants the number of settlers who according to the terms of his patents should be there, it was recommended that the proportion of lands which were not settled should in such cases be surrendered to the crown. The disallowance of a long list of acts relating to land and kindred subjects, and passed at various dates beginning in 1715, was recommended. Included in this list was the act of 1749 to put in force a long list of English statutes including an omnibus clause declaring all the statutes of England, not mentioned, to be in force irrespective of their fitness for the conditions of the province. What especially condemned this act in the eyes of the board was the fact that none of the revenue laws of England or those by which provision was made for the court of exchequer and the other courts in which the rights of the king were pleadable were enumerated therein. This representation was duly approved and an order in council issued disallowing the acts in question. In the list also was included the act of 1746 fixing the seat of government at Newbern and providing also for the establishment of courts regulating their proceedings. Another decree was thus added to the considerable list of those by which the crown easily swept away the judicial system of a province or threw it back, as in this case, upon earlier and less adequate laws. The explanation which was given for this measure was that the act in question was passed by Johnston's assembly at Wilmington, as a result of " Management, precipitation and surprise " and, like the bill reducing the representation of the northern counties, should not have received the governor's assent.[1]

As a result of this inquiry and of the orders which were issued in accordance with it, which, taken together with special requirements affecting the amount of paper currency and its use, furnish an excellent example of the thoroughness with which the rights of the crown were guarded while Halifax was at the head of the board of trade, Dobbs took with him to North Carolina a notable list of new or revised instructions — no less than nineteen articles in all — for the reform of the land system of that province. Upon their successful enforcement depended largely the amount of salary he could hope to secure. The inquiries which these articles prescribed were to include all grants made since 1727, the patents for which must be submitted or new ones taken out, strict provision being made for the accuracy of surveys and the payment of quit rents. In the case of large grants, like those to McCulloh and Crymble and Huey, the tracts which after a period of ten years had not been settled as required in the patents should be declared forfeited to the crown. Strict regularity should also be enforced in all grants made and payments required under the new governor. Lord Granville's territory, of course, was especially exempted and no mention was made of the extent to which the territorial revenue of the province was reduced by that grant. With the social habits and administrative traditions which existed in North Carolina, it would have required extraordinary power to enforce conformity with the instructions concerning land which Dobbs took over with him.

One of the earliest acts of the new administration was the

[1] N. C. Col. Recs., V, 79–118, 1110, 1119, 1128–1134. The proceedings of the board of trade relating to these matters are printed on pp. 167–172.

dissolution of the "long assembly" and the election of a new one. By this means the northern counties recovered their representation of five members each and this "bone of contention" was removed. The legality of the new assembly no one could assail, and already, as was shown in the election of the speaker, the extension of settlement and formation of new counties had insured the transfer of the balance of power from the Albemarle region to the central and southern parts of the province. In response to his conciliatory speech and exhortation to turn immediately to the important task of legislative reform which lay ahead of them, both houses expressed their desire for harmony and their resolve to obliterate the remembrance of the former contests and their evil consequences.[1] The outbreak of war also made unity imperative and with the beginning of the new administration the contentions which had resulted from the first expansion of settlement were forgotten.

In order to avoid confusion, the governor postponed announcing the repeal of the laws affecting the election of members of the assembly and dissolving the courts of justice until the close of this session.[2] The necessity of securing an appropriation for the war also told imperatively in favor of this course. The result was that in the course of a harmonious session a satisfactory aid was voted and tonnage duty authorized. Laws were also passed facilitating the payment of quit rents, establishing anew the higher and county courts of the province and improving the jury system. In an act for strengthening the extremely weak parish and vestry organization within the province, Dobbs secured a measure which lay near to his official heart. A very detailed law regulating the production and exportation of tobacco completed the list of especially significant laws of this session.[3]

From an address presented by the lower house to the governor it appeared that great inconveniences would result from the repeal of the laws erecting towns and counties and providing for their reëstablishment by charters of incorporation.

---

[1] N. C. Recs., V, 217, 238.
[2] Ibid., 326.
[3] N. C. Recs., V, 3091; ibid., XXIII, 400. The most important of these laws are not in print and presumably are no longer extant.

If that were done it would be impossible to divide counties, as was often necessary, when the increase of population made desirable the subdivision of the large counties first erected. This and other evils which were sure to follow the enforcement of the order led the assembly to ask the governor to solicit through the board of trade the granting of permission to the assembly to pass new laws for the erection and remodeling of towns and counties as the interests of the province should dictate.[1] To this the board and privy council acceded, provided such new acts did not in any case authorize the towns or counties to send representatives to the assembly or ascertain the number of representatives to be sent, and that any acts conveying such right which in the meantime might have been passed should be repealed. The right of granting representation and determining its amount was to be reserved exclusively to the executive, the main idea underlying this probably being that in this way only the dangerous increase in the size of the lower house — a phenomenon which with the extension of settlement was becoming apparent in many colonies — could be held in check. An additional instruction embodying this modification of the original order and the concession accompanying it was accordingly issued to Dobbs. In 1756 the towns and counties referred to in the above mentioned order in council were reestablished by act of assembly, though with provisions for their representation in that body.[2]

The orders which Dobbs issued concerning land, quit rents and the related subject of currency met with the hearty approbation of the board of trade. Rutherford, the receiver general, was directed[3] not only to make out his account of receipts, payments and arrears of quit rents, but to prepare a rent roll, distinguishing grants by patent from those by warrant, and McCulloh, the deputy auditor, should coöperate in this work. Ultimately a complete survey of all the counties was contemplated and the board was asked to request Lord Granville to bear his proportion of the expense. The treasury was also to be asked to order that the cost of the

[1] N. C. Recs., V, 301–303, 340, 352, 364, 397, 404, 415, 482.
[2] Ibid., V, 445.
[3] Ibid., V, 145, 150.

survey should be met out of the quit rents. In order to encourage them in the collection of quit rents, the sheriffs were promised a proportional addition to their fees. Murray, the secretary, together with Rowan, the late president, were ordered to submit papers which would show what issues of currency had recently been made and what was the existing state of the circulation. This necessitated action on the part of the province treasurers, of whom there were two, one in the northern and the other in the southern district. They had not visited the governor at Newbern and none of the councillors resided there, seven living near Cape Fear, two at Edmonton and two being at present in England. "No meeting can be had of the Council," wrote Dobbs, "or public officers without sending expresses which travel very slow and at great expense, and no fund for contingencies to pay it." As to Rutherford Dobbs wrote that he had no doubt of his honesty, but believed him quite indolent and was told that he gave himself little trouble about collecting the quit rents. Before many months had passed evidence was also reaching Dobbs that James Murray and John Rutherford, who were councillors, were organizing a group in the assembly which threatened opposition and obstruction to the measures of the executive. With them, John Starkey, who was treasurer of the southern district, and was apparently a man of simple and democratic tastes, became associated.[1] Lord Granville, when approached upon the subject in England, refused to bear any of the expense of the proposed survey of the counties. Dobbs also wrote that it would be necessary to have an independent company to support the surveyors who were trying to locate overplus lands and seeking evidences of fraud, as one who was authorizing to enter a tract for the purpose of a resurvey had been shot by the planter. These circumstances indicated, each in its peculiar way, obstacles and forms of opposition which were sure to hinder if they did not totally defeat the governor's plan of reform in territorial affairs.

The extent to which reckless, if not fraudulent, land grants had been carried was brought home to the governor when he found that, except in the back settlements near the mountains, no compact areas of such quality as to be specially valuable

[1] N. C. Records, V, 945–960.

remained ungranted. Along the navigable streams all available sites had been taken up. Dobbs therefore asked that he might be instructed not to grant more than 640 acres in a single patent and especially referred to that as a grant of a size convenient for the purposes of the Scotch and German settlers from the north who were pouring into the up-country. The volume of that immigration was increased by the devastation of western Pennsylvania and Virginia by the Indians, which followed Braddock's defeat. By long journeys which he soon made not only along the coast but through the western districts when new counties were in process of formation, Dobbs was able to confirm his first impressions concerning the policy in reference to land which was apppropriate to the needs of the small proprietors who were settling the up-country. Assurance of title was what they most needed and this, at points remote from the offices of the registry, with very imperfect surveys, and among a people almost destitute of legal advice, of money and means of communication, was by no means easy to secure. Throughout the province, as elsewhere in the colonies, the settlers were averse to the payment of quit rents and to any recognition of the obligations of tenancy. Because of the fiscal and other elements involved, the government made the collection of quit rents, and especially of arrears of rent, one of the cardinal objects of its policy. But its aid was given to the colonist in all his reasonable efforts to secure valid title to his land. In no colony was this more important than in North Carolina at the period of which we are speaking. In 1755 a statute was passed making liberal provisions for the registry of lands and the recognition of claims based on quiet and peaceful occupancy, provided quit rents were paid.[1] Of such legislation as this the board of trade fully approved and in some points was disposed to be more liberal than the provisions of the colonial laws.

But the requirement that quit rents should be paid and the heavy accumulation of arrears raised a question upon which the colonists and the officials, with the British government behind them, were always at issue. Nowhere was the cause of the government in this matter more hopeless than in

[1] N. C. Recs., V, 270, 282.

North Carolina. Without an elaborate rent roll the ascertainment of the sums due was impossible. Rutherford, the receiver general, wrote in June, 1756, that the deputy auditor whose duty it was had not furnished him with a rent roll, but instead he had only certain accounts from the secretary's office which were so imperfect as to be of little value.[1] This, together with the obstinacy of the people, would account for the great disproportion between the sums due and those received. There was no court of exchequer in the province, and Rutherford vainly waited for the support of such a tribunal. The situation also was complicated by the failure to settle the boundary of Lord Granville's territory. The boundary dispute with South Carolina kept alive disorders in the south and had come near making trouble with the Catawba Indians. As McCulloh and his associates had failed to establish more than a small proportion of the settlers upon their grants which the terms of their patents required, after twenty years, that is about 1760, the unsettled areas lapsed back into the possession of the crown.[2] Surveyors were sent into the region by both McCulloh and the province authorities to lay out and readjust boundaries. These were often attacked by the settlers and occasionally lives were lost in the violent encounters which followed. Such were the frontier disorders which, added to the weak administrative system of the province, made it impossible to collect more than a small proportion of the quit rents and their arrears. One result of this was that McCulloh's salary as commissioner of the revenue, which was payable out of the quit rents, fell heavily into arrears. By 1752 nearly £10,000 sterling was due McCulloh. Notwithstanding what were said to have been his faithful efforts to discharge its duties, his office had proved a failure and he, an old man, had returned to England to petition the government for some form of remuneration. The treasury board gave him a warrant for two-thirds of his arrears of salary, but this McCulloh could not collect and consequently could not pay the quit rents which were steadily accumulating

[1] N. C. Recs., V, 587. The governor's criticisms of these statements, intended to show the neglect of the receiver, are on pp. 950–954.

[2] Their patents called for the settlement of one white person on every two hundred acres. The quit rent was at the customary rate in North Carolina, 4s. per hundred acres.

on his own lands. Finally £500 was granted him out of the 4½% duty and it was arranged that in 1760 the grants to McCulloh and his associates should be surrendered to the crown.[1] But, as has been noted, this agreement was not executed and the Revolution found the McCulloh claims and estates still unsettled.[2]

Out of these conditions developed, at the close of 1757, a quarrel in the council between the governor on the one side and Rutherford and Murray on the other. So inefficient was the administration of what should have been the land office and so futile were the efforts made to reduce the arrears of quit rents, that Dobbs charged Rutherford in particular with gross neglect of duty, combined with certain irregular transactions, and both men with efforts to form a cabal in the assembly for the purpose of thwarting the exercise of the governor's powers in several directions. Their last offense had been the issue of a quantity of private notes, some of them countersigned by Murray and others, without even that guaranty which the sheriffs were directed to receive in payment of quit rents. Only a moderate amount of bills of credit was in circulation in North Carolina, issued mainly to meet the expense of the war. The back districts were doubtless almost destitute of a medium of exchange. The device of Rutherford and Murray originated from an experience of this need, and, had the monetary history of the colonies been known to them, precedents for their scheme might have been found elsewhere. But it was an irregular proceeding and tended further to depreciate the currency and to add to the existing confusion. For these reasons the issue was raised by Dobbs in the council and the two offending members were suspended from their offices.[3] Starkey also came in for criticism at the hands of the governor, but respect for him

[1] N. C. Recs., V, 615–653, 987; VI, 569–578.

[2] Henry Eustace McCulloh was appointed his father's agent and in 1762 was sworn in as a member of the council of North Carolina, N. C. Recs., VI, 758.

[3] N. C. R., V, 821, 950–960, 987. In 1759, Dobbs, writing the board of trade, called Starkey a "republican "and said that he was always scheming to transfer power from the governor and council to the assembly. As he had been chosen treasurer without limitation, Dobbs urged that this act should be repealed and treasurers made appointive by the crown during pleasure and be made incapable of sitting in either house of the assembly.

throughout the province was strong and he continued to hold a prominent place in the assembly throughout this administration. The case of Rutherford and Murray was carried to England and the board of trade reported in favor of confirming their suspensions, stating that the case was similar to the removal of Wragg from the council of South Carolina which had recently been approved. The question of Rutherford's removal was referred to the treasury board and both he and Murray remained under suspension without further action by the authorities in England until after the accession of George III, when the instructions to Dobbs were revised. Then Rutherford's name was again inserted in the list of councillors and in 1762 Murray also was reinstated.[1] It was near the close of 1758 that the controversy between the governor and assembly which was growing out of these conditions began.

It had now become known that a certain sum, perhaps £15,000, was coming as a reimbursement to North Carolina for its expenditures in the war. Dobbs in particular was desirous of removing from Newbern and had proposed a site for a capital at Tower Hill, farther up the Neuse, or even that he should reside at Wilmington and hold sessions of the assembly, as was done in New Jersey, alternately there and at Edmonton. This, however, threatened to provoke the old sectional conflict again, and the assembly proposed to use a part of the reimbursement money for founding a new town. In characteristic fashion it was also planning to keep the money, when it came, under the control of itself and the treasurer of its choice, and also to designate James Abercromby as agent in England, to be corresponded with exclusively by a committee of the assembly. Dobbs told the council that his instructions concerning the share of the governor in the disposition of public money forbade his assenting to the bill for a new town and this resulted in the defeat of the obnoxious feature of the measure by the upper house. The assembly however secured its agent, for whose support and direction it made temporary provision.[2]   In the following spring another brief

---

[1] N. C. Records, VI, 45, 57, 217, 558.   In 1762 Rutherford was reappointed receiver general, *ibid.*, 755, 799.

[2] *Ibid.*, V, 998–1101; *ibid.*, VI, 1 *et seq.*

session was held for the purpose of securing, in response to an appeal from William Pitt, an appropriation for the war. But the aid bill which was then proposed by the assembly was rejected in the council because of the power which it gave the treasurers and the provision it contained respecting Abercromby, the agent.[1] The candidate of Dobbs and the council for this office was Smith, the governor's secretary. The board of trade, however, was not inclined to share the governor's aversion to these measures, because they agreed too fully with practices which the British government had long since been forced to recognize in the colonies.[2] The only criticism which it had to pass referred to matters of detail and to provision for disposing of a part of the reimbursement before the assembly was certain that parliament would grant it. The board would evidently have much preferred the appropriation even with the restrictions upon the provincial executive which would have accompanied it.

But if the board took a lenient view of the preferences of the assembly as shown in the aid bill, on its advice the privy council about the same time disallowed seven North Carolina statutes, some of long standing and great importance. Four of these were court acts, two providing for the establishment of a supreme court and another establishing and enlarging the jurisdiction of county courts. The chief justice and attorney general of the province, both of whom were Englishmen and as yet without experience in their offices, objected to these measures, to the former because of the large powers which it gave to the associate judges and to the latter on the familiar ground that the jurisdiction given to their untrained justices was far too large.[3] By this act of repeal the judicial system of North Carolina was again disorganized and the province in regard to these matters was thrown back upon the legislation of 1715 with its provisions that the courts should meet only at Edmonton. On the complaint of a number of British merchants the board of trade ordered Dobbs to secure the amendment of two acts for the issue of bills of credit, one passed in 1748 and the other in 1754, the objection to them being that the bills were declared legal tender and at rates considerably above their

---

[1] N. C. Records, VI, 32–40, 92, 99, 102, 110.   [2] Ibid., 55.   [3] Ibid., 26–29.

actual value in sterling.[1] When Dobbs received notice of the
disallowance of the court acts, he postponed the announcement of it until the effect upon the course of justice might be
as slight as possible. As to this "hasty repeal," though he
admitted that the acts were faulty, he did not put a high
estimate upon the wisdom of the non-resident officials who
had advised action in that form.

In the assembly at this time appear the names of men who
were to be prominent during the decades to come, John Her-
vey, Cornelius Harnett, Richard Caswell, George and Maurice
Moore, John Ashe.[2] As young men, many of them being lawyers, they were beginning to gain experience. Samuel Swann,
the speaker, and John Starkey had been longer in the service.
These men may be supposed to have given tone to the assembly, of which, according to Dobbs, Swann was the political leader. Child, the attorney general, is also said to
have struck hands with this group and to have added much
to its capacity for opposition.[3] They constituted what Dobbs
called the "junto" and were the body with which he and
the council were in conflict during the remaining years of
his administration. The assembly expressed its "sensible
concern" that so many of their laws, "well Calculated for
the advancement of Religion and distribution of Justice"
through "this large and extended province," and the quieting
of freeholders in their possessions, "had met with his Majesty's Royal Disallowance."[4] They were convinced, they
said, that if the province had had a duly authorized agent in
England, who could have shown to the ministers the importance and propriety of the acts, they might not have been
repealed. The assembly, however, addressed itself again to
the framing of judiciary legislation, the necessity for which
was shown by riots and disorders in various parts of the
province.

In its new judiciary bills, two of which were drafted during
the fall session of 1759, the assembly still insisted upon giving large jurisdiction to the county courts and declared that
it would address the king in support of the necessity of this
provision in a colony like North Carolina. Another feature

---

[1] N. C. Records, VI, 44, 56, 116, 172, 185. [3] Ibid., 244.
[2] Ibid., 132, 362. [4] Ibid., 139.

of their bills was that which prescribed for the judges a tenure during good behavior. This voiced a demand which was being made in a number of colonies, but was totally inconsistent with the policy of the British government and the governor's instructions.[1] The bills also required that appointees to the office of associate justice must have been in practice in the colonies as attorneys for seven years and have been residents for one year in North Carolina. These conditions the governor regarded as very seriously restricting his power of appointment. The house urged him to accept this measure before the aid bill was passed, but he refused, as in fact he was compelled to do by his instructions.

The fate of the court bill, moreover, in all its stages, was involved with that of appropriations for the defence of the colony. The very rudimentary forts at Cape Fear and Ocracook Inlet needed completion and something like adequate garrisons.[2] This was also the time of Governor Lyttleton's expedition to Keowee which resulted in a temporary peace with the Cherokees. Hugh Waddell, with a force of frontier militia, was sent to the assistance of South Carolina and, as the outbreak of war with the Cherokees approached, defence on the west became more necessary. The retention of at least two companies of militia in service in the east was also an evident necessity. Another equally desirable measure, and a favorite one with Dobbs, was the appropriation of a few thousand pounds for schools.[3] Closely connected with this was his desire for a vestry act and some provisions for glebes and churches which would give a few more indications of solidarity to the Anglican establishment in North Carolina. New counties were also being created by statute and they promptly applied to the governor for charters which would authorize them to choose representatives to the assembly. All these and other matters were dividing the attention of the assembly. The house desired to provide means for defence, not by laying a poll tax but, on the plea of the poverty of the people and the long time it would take to col-

---

[1] One of the best statements of the point of view of the assembly upon these subjects is in a memorial presented, in May, 1763, to the board of trade by Jouvencel, the colony agent. N. C. Recs., VI, 986.

[2] These were Forts Johnston and Granville.

[3] This was £6000, but was held up by a suspending clause. *Ibid.*, 477.

lect the tax, by borrowing from the sinking fund. This meant the putting out of more bills of credit, and this proposal the governor refused to accept because of the instruction which forbade him to assent to such issues when they were made legal tenor. But the decisive fault in the aid bill was this, that it contained a provision for an agent who should be under the control of the house. To this Dobbs and the council were opposed on principle, and aimed at an object which was not germane to the purpose of this bill. At the close of the session the governor dissolved the assembly and in a speech, a copy of which he did not leave with them, he sharply criticised their action.[1]

An election was soon held and, upon the receipt of another call from Pitt for aid against the enemy, the new assembly was called together in April, 1760.[2] The leaders of the former body were returned and Child, the attorney general, was added to its membership. It came together in an aggressive mood. A committee of grievances was created which, Dobbs said, met secretly. The house frequently resolved itself into committees of the whole and then discussed its resolutions and policies. In their reply to the governor's opening speech they defended with spirit the measures of the previous assembly and criticised the attitude of the executive.[3] They then adopted a series of resolutions declaring themselves strongly in favor of adequate provision for defence, a vestry act, a court act and the appointment of an agent.[4] They also claimed the right to model every appropriation act in such a way as would be most conducive to his majesty's service, and that the treasurers should account to the houses as had been customary and as was provided by law. Two court bills were then passed, but the governor refused to accept them until an aid bill was submitted and provision made for defence.[5] As the court bills referred only to the internal affairs of the colony, he considered them of inferior importance. To this the house replied by calling his attention to the disorders in the province. The governor denied that these were serious disorders which an ordinary commission

---

[1] N. C. Records, VI, 172–200, 226.
[2] Ibid., 345–438.
[3] Ibid., 370.
[4] Ibid., 380.
[5] Ibid., 400, 402, 403.

of oyer and terminer could not restrain, and charged the house with being controlled by " self-interested Gentlemen " who were trying to diminish the royal prerogative and involve him in the dilemma of betraying his trust to serve their selfish ends.[1] The aid bill must first be passed and then he would accept the court bill only if it were made temporary and the offensive clauses were omitted. In another long series of resolutions the house now attacked the governor and Spaight, his nephew and secretary, charging them with taking public money in fees and under other forms, contrary to law and without accounting for it, mentioning in particular exorbitant fees which were taken for the issue of charters to counties.[2] Various other abuses of the secretary's office were referred to and the fact that mob violence was widespread in the province was reaffirmed. This arraignment of the governor was followed by an equally strong address, one to the king and another to Dobbs himself in defence of their conduct.[3] With this the session was ended by a prorogation of three days, a number of acts receiving the governor's assent. Dobbs then wrote to the board of trade in no mild terms his version of the controversy and a character sketch of the " junto " which was running the assembly and plotting against the crown and the executive.[4] According to his view, Child was the chief plotter and had declared that countries had the right to send members without charters or the king's writ.

But the need of provision for defence was as imperative as was the need of courts, and both sides were ready for con- cession. The governor proposed that if the house would pass an aid bill and also a court bill with a clause limiting its duration to two years, he would accept it. The assembly fell in with his proposal and passed the court bill without change except as to its duration. This the governor accepted and for a decade the courts of North Carolina continued to exist under a series of temporary acts like this. When it came to the aid bill, the governor objected to some of its provisions but finally assented to it. The controversy over the agent also broke out again between the houses and in the end not

[1] N. C. Records, VI, 408.
[2] Ibid., 410.
[3] Ibid., 414, 418.
[4] Ibid., 243–251.

Abercromby but Anthony Bacon was appointed, by resolution of the assembly as its own agent and not the representative of the province.[1]

The relations between the assembly and the governor during the fall session of 1760 did not materially improve, though the exchange of controversial speeches and replies was not resumed.[2] The house, as had been its custom in previous sessions, insisted that the presence of a majority of its members was necessary before business could be transacted. This involved a recurrence to precedents of the proprietary period and of practice before Johnston tried to break the control of the northern counties over the province. The majority of the leaders in the assembly still came from Edmonton and its vicinity and Dobbs, who lived at Brunswick, still saw much evidence that the old sectional and dominating spirit in that region was not dead. The issue between the assembly and the governor upon the question of the aid and the designation of an agent was drawn the same in this session as previously and the aid bill failed to receive Dobbs' assent.[3] He also vetoed a bill designating a treasurer and one amending the statute regulating fees. At the close of the session the assembly was dissolved. As the Cherokee war was now in progress and the upper settlements were being ravaged, the lower house by resolution authorized the governor to raise and pay a company of militia for a year to come. The lords of trade, in commenting on the conduct of Dobbs and the assembly, approved the claim of the latter to the decisive voice in the choice of agents, though the method by which they sought his appointment as a part of the aid bill was irregular.[4] That, however, in its opinion, was too trivial a matter to be made the occasion of the defeat of the aid bill, depriving the province also of the advantage of the services of an agent at court. The attitude of the assembly on the subject of the quorum, as well as its method of passing public accounts, the board condemned. In the revised instructions which were now issued to Dobbs the earlier restrictions concerning the admission of new counties and towns to representation were modified into a brief order to him to issue

writs to those districts which were qualified to send representatives.[1]   In an important communication, which was
drawn out in part by events in New York, the board also
declared its irrevocable opposition to the permanent tenure
of judges in the colonies, and this view also, as well as its
dislike of the large jurisdiction given to county courts in the
assembly's bills, was repeated in a report to the king recommending that these acts be disallowed.[2]

The newly elected assembly of March, 1761, was called
to meet at Wilmington. This drew a protest from the members because of the expense which was imposed upon many
of them by the necessity of travelling to a part of the province so remote.[3]   The sectional struggle, however, was not
revived, for though the project of building a new town was
abandoned and Newbern was not especially acceptable to
any party, it was the most central place for a capital and the
government was soon settled there.[4]   Though the prospect
was that the Cherokee war would end before they would be
available, this session resulted in the passage of an aid bill
which made provision for 500 men.[5]   Such bills at this time
were regularly passed upon requisitions from the commander-
in-chief or direct from the secretary of state. Though it was
clear that such calls were not so imperative as in previous
years, Dobbs made them, together with the fact that the
appointment of the agent was temporary, his excuse for yielding to the assembly and accepting the bill.[6]   The board of
trade expressed the desire that, when the term of the new
agent should expire, Dobbs would not consent to the appointment of another unless provision for it was made in a
separate bill.

From the assembly of April, 1762, Dobbs was totally unable to secure an appropriation.[7]   Both Amherst and Lord

---

[1] N. C. Records, VI, 559.   [2] Ibid., 585–591.

[3] Ibid., 661–697.

[4] After a protest from the assembly of April, 1762, to the king against the
inconvenience of sessions at Wilmington, Dobbs called the next assembly together at Newbern and it addressed the king in favor of making that town
the capital; ibid., 834, 893, 933.

[5] It also carried with it the appointment of Jouvencel as an agent for the
period of two years.

[6] Ibid., 692, 695, 703, 748.   [7] Ibid., 800–837.

Egremont, the new secretary of state, had sent urgent calls for troops and these Dobbs enforced with his usual unction. But the French in Canada had now been conquered and, though Spain had come into the conflict, the war had drifted off to the West Indies and became purely a struggle for confirming the naval supremacy of Great Britain. This object did not strongly appeal to the members of the North Carolina assembly and they said so, duly emphasizing the poverty and debt of the province as an excuse for not complying. The governor tested them by several short prorogations, but with no result, and dissolved the body without securing any legislation.

The British government had actively continued its work of disallowing North Carolina laws. When the new assembly met in November, 1762, Dobbs announced that eight acts had met with this fate, triumphantly adding that they would gain nothing by opposing the king's just prerogative or disputing his instructions.[1] Of the acts disallowed, the most important were those for the establishment of courts. Two vestry acts were also included in the number, and measures of minor importance completed the list. Again the assembly bent itself to the task of drafting court acts, though with little hope that it would be able to satisfy the requirements of the British officials. The province was divided into five judicial districts and, in an act which was very detailed in its provisions concerning jurisdiction and procedure, authority was given for the holding of a superior court in each district.[2] In all except the Salisbury district in the extreme west these should be presided over by a justice and one associate. In the Salisbury district, in the absence of the chief justice, an assistant judge commissioned by the governor might preside. Provision was made in another law for inferior courts of pleas and quarter sessions in the counties with jurisdiction over cases involving £20 proclamation money. An act regulating the selection of jurors completed the legislation of this session on judicial subjects. There was bickering even between the houses over the court acts and the governor expressed his usual dissatisfaction, but as they

[1] N. C. Records, VI, 700–702, 707, 720–723, 748–754, 839, 893–971.
[2] Ibid., xxiii, 550.

were limited to a duration of two years he assented to them. In 1764 these laws were continued for another period of two years,[1] though no reference was made in them to the tenure of the judges, and thus the province was continued in the possession of a judicial system which satisfied its needs and escaped the confusion following persistent disallowance of its laws by the crown. In the session of 1762 a new vestry act was also passed, but it also gave to the vestries the power of filling vacancies in livings and by an act two years later vestrymen were only required by their oath not to oppose the doctrine, discipline and liturgy of the Church of England.[2] These were the features of the earlier act which had especially offended the bishop of London and had occasioned its disallowance, and Dobbs withheld his assent to the first bill pending further instructions. Among the other measures of this session was one dividing Anson county by a line drawn south from the boundary of Lord Granville's grant to the limits of South Carolina and erecting the region to the west of this line into Mecklenburg county. The contrast between the policy of North Carolina and that of its southern neighbor in the treatment of the up-country is marked and much to the advantage of the northern province.

[1] N. C. Records, VI, 632.   [2] *Ibid.*, 583, 601.

CHAPTER XII

IN Virginia between the retirement of Gooch in 1749 and
the arrival of Dinwiddie in 1752 almost complete quiet prevailed as to internal affairs. During that interval William
Lee officiated as president of the council until his death
in 1751. Lewis Burwell, as senior councillor, succeeded him.
Lee was already an old man and had been temporarily at the
head of the government before. Indian affairs, western settlement, and the questions of boundary which matters of this
origin brought to the front, always absorbed much of his attention. They formed the chief subject of the few letters
which passed between him and the board of trade and of his
correspondence with the executives of other colonies. Lee's
reports were also sent by the board to the secretary of state,
who at this time was the duke of Bedford.

These were the years when decisive steps were taken by
the French for the occupation of the Ohio region and they
directly threatened Pennsylvania and western Virginia. The
Ohio Company was trying to extend trade with the tribes to
the westward but they were so suspicious that Lee thought
a treaty and presents would be necessary. The erection of a
fort on the frontier would involve too great an expense for
the company, and the idea of Lee was that the boundaries of
Virginia westward to the Mississippi should be ascertained
and the government should manage relations on the frontier.
In the spring of 1750 Clinton, of New York, wrote to Lee,
inclosing a letter from William Johnson, in which the latter
told of plans of western Indians to destroy tribes along the
Ohio who were allies of the English. They had committed
themselves to the English cause during the late war and had
attacked the French Indians. Now they were threatened
and implored assistance, which Johnson was not in a position

to give them. This appeal had reached Virginia too late for aid to be sent that year, but it had induced the council to assent to expend £200 for guns and ammunition. With his letter to the board Lee sent an account of the scanty supply of guns and stores in Virginia, in the forts at Gloucester, York and the mouth of the James and stored in the governor's house and the magazine at Williamsburg.[1] In the following September, in answer to the usual queries from the board, Lee described the boundaries of Virginia and suggested a complete map of the province, showing especially the Ohio, Allegheny and other rivers which flowed into or toward the Mississippi and the location of the Great Lakes. He pointed out the fertility of the lands beyond the " great mountains," and the extent to which the natives there were inclined to the English. Lee desired the removal of the capital to some point west of Williamsburg as favorable to the important westward movement. He enlarged upon the strength of the neighboring Indians, from the Six Nations on the north to the Cherokees on the south, and upon his hope—in which he was disappointed —that by means of a conference at Fredericksburg he might bring to an end the feud between the Six Nations and the Catawbas. The northern Indians could not be induced to come so far for a conference. The forts throughout Virginia, said Lee, were quite out of repair, their guns were unfit for use and their stock of munitions was slight. A fierce storm had wrecked the principal fort of the province, near the mouth of the James River.

In 1751, the subject of Virginia's boundaries was brought more clearly to the front by Burwell's sending to the board a map of the province prepared by Joshua Fry and Peter Jefferson.[2] Fry had been a master and professor of mathematics in William and Mary College and later had removed into Albemarle county, where he became a justice and one of the commissioners for surveying the western limits of the Northern Neck and locating the head springs of the Potomac River. Jefferson was also a resident in the west and father of the future statesman. The map was praised by Burwell for its beauty. The statements concerning the claims of Virginia

[1] C. O. 5/1327, O. P. Va; July 12, 1750.
[2] *Ibid.*, Aug. 21, 1751; Dinwiddie Papers, I, 8, note.

accompanying it were said to have been taken in part from Stith's "History of Virginia," which had been published about four years before. In the explanations, going back to the charter granted by James I to the London Company and making allowance for the territory which had been taken away as the result of the Maryland, Pennsylvania and Carolina grants, the current bounds of Virginia were the sea coast on the east between Currituck inlet on the south and the boundary of Maryland as specified on the north; on the north the bounds were Maryland and Pennsylvania so far as they extended and thence — making use of the expression "north and northwest" in the charts of 1609 — a northwest line from a point of latitude 200 miles north of Point Comfort to the Pacific ocean. In this connection the importance to Virginia of determining the western limit of Pennsylvania was recognized. It was realized that probably both would abut on Lake Erie and together they might prevent that region from falling into the hands of the French. The southern boundary of Virginia would be the parallel of latitude extending due west across the continent from Currituck inlet. According to this interpretation, the settlements which had been established on the Mississippi as the result of La Salle's discoveries lay within Virginia, as did later French posts further east. Reference also was made to the enterprise of Thomas Walker and the Ohio Company west of the Alleghany ridge and to the claims of the English in the Mississippi Valley which had their origin in the conquests of the Iroquois and their transfer to his majesty. The security and possession of all those regions, it was seen, depended wholly on the proper management of the Indians. Therefore it was urged that the boundaries of the colonies be determined, that the Ohio Company be made to lay off its large grant and make settlements within it, that grants of smaller tracts be made with encouragements to settle, that a trading factory and fort be established among the Ohio Indians and all the colonies concerned unite in supporting it and maintaining alliance with the Indians.

Such was the English claim as stated from the standpoint of Virginia at the middle of the century. No challenge to the claims and plans of the French at that time could be more direct. The two rival nationalities were now facing each other along the line of the Alleghanies, and Virginia lay in the midst of the disputed territory with claims which traversed the entire middle section of French territory. This was the situation, with the French upon the aggressive, when Robert Dinwiddie was appointed lieutenant governor of Virginia.

Like Spotswood and so many others among appointees to official positions in the colonies, Dinwiddie was a Scotchman, a descendant of a merchant family in Glasgow.[1] Unlike most of these appointments in those days, his was a promotion from a lower place in the colonial service. He had first been collector of the southern ports of the continent of America, and later still inspector general of the customs of Barbados. While surveyor general he had been known in Virginia and elsewhere, as an *ex officio* member of the councils in the colonies where his duties lay. His record was that of an energetic, zealous and somewhat bustling servant of the crown. He brought to his new office the traditions of the treasury without the offensive legalism which had characterized Edward Randolph. As the great war broke out soon after he assumed office, and Virginia found herself at last in the midst of the conflict, Dinwiddie was forced to play a very active part in military affairs, a field in which his life of nearly sixty years had brought him no experience. As a civilian, his activities were necessarily confined to the raising of troops and procuring of supplies, and to dealings with the assembly upon the votes of which mainly depended the securing of means for carrying on the war. His lot was cast in a province the profound peace of which had scarcely ever been broken, certainly not for more than two generations and never by an invasion of French and Indians. No more pacific people than the Virginians existed in the colonies — save the Quakers — if the military qualities are to be measured by actual experience of war. As we know, in its aristocratic plantation system, with thousands of slaves, inhered certain regulations and qualities of leadership which might readily be developed into military achievement of rare excellence. But at the beginning of the last

[1] Brock, introd. to Dinwiddie Papers, Colls. of Va. Hist. Soc.

intercolonial war, so far as its militia laws were concerned, the training of its men, provision for their equipment and for coast and frontier defence, Virginia was acknowledged to be backward, even among a group of colonies whose military efficiency in general deserved little praise. Dinwiddie was suddenly called upon to overcome an inertia such as these conditions produced, and that solely by means known to a civilian, verbal and written exhortations, and such executive measures as the council and assembly and his orders from England enabled him to take. The account of what was accomplished must be given in another connection. At present we are concerned only with Virginia events and conditions which had their origin in the past, would have existed in any case, but now ran their course in the midst of the war.

One of these, an event which destroyed the harmony of the administration at the outset and seriously increased the governor's difficulties, was the controversy over the fee of the pistole. This was a sum, amounting to 16s. 8d., which the governor now began to levy on all patents which passed the great seal for the larger grants of land. Of these there were at the time nearly a thousand in the secretary's office ready to be issued and more than a thousand surveyor's certificates showing that, long since, all the preliminary steps had been taken which should have been followed by the issue of patents.[1] By this neglect Gooch or others had failed to enter about one million acres on the rent roll. Governors had taken such a fee in other colonies, though, except for a brief period, the Virginia executives had not collected it. Without this, wrote Dinwiddie to the board of trade, lands were not properly patented and were cultivated for some years without being brought into the rent roll. The collecting of the fee would make it the governor's business to see that this was done. When the policy was proposed the council assented, as also did the board of trade.[2] The order was not issued until after the close of Dinwiddie's first session with the bur-

[1] Bland, "A Fragment on the Pistole Fee claimed by the Governour of Virginia." Dinwiddie to B. T., Dec. 29, 1753; C. O. 5/1322, O. P. Va.; Dinwiddie Papers, I, 363.

[2] C. O. 5/1327, O. P. Va., Dinwiddie to Board, Oct. 6, 1752, June 16, 1753; C. O. 5/1367, E. B. Va., Jan. 17, 1753.

gesses, in the course of which they had made him a special gift of £400 and had named a county in his honor. A general protest against the imposition was raised throughout the province and petitions against it came before the assembly at its next session, one of these originating in Dinwiddie county. The subject was taken up by the house in committee of the whole and an address was sent to the governor requesting that he would acquaint them with the authority under which he made the demand. His reply was that he had done it in accordance with his instructions and with the unanimous consent of the council and was confident that he had not acted in an arbitrary manner.[1]

A longer address was now sent to the governor in which the practice of the colony from the beginning was traced with the result of showing that, except in the time of Lord Howard of Effingham, no fee for the use of the seal, in the issue of land patents, had been demanded.[2] In 1689 this temporary practice had been discontinued by William III and had never been revived. The collection of the pistole was not warranted by any known law and a long-continued practice, such as they described, could not be set aside by the advice of the council. Their conclusion therefore was that the demand of the pistole fee was a violation of a property right, of which according to the principles of English liberty, acknowledged since Magna Charta, they could not be deprived except by their own consent. Dinwiddie replied that the right which he was asserting related exclusively to the disposal of the king's land and lay outside the sphere of government; it therefore was not inconsistent with the privileges of the burgesses and he was determined in his adherence to it. The house then resolved that, as the demand was arbitrary and inconsistent with the charters of the province and with orders and instructions of earlier kings, they would address his majesty for relief from the fee as an illegal imposition and a public grievance. To a proposal of Dinwiddie that he would give up the pistole if the freeholders would pay the arrears of quit rent, they refused to assent. This address was drawn by a special committee, of which Bland, Randolph, Pendleton and others were mem-

[1] J. of Burgesses, 1752–1758, pp. 129, 136, 141.   *Ibid.*, 143.

bers.[1] It was also reported that a special agent of the burgesses should be appointed to support in England the rights and privileges of the people in this matter. They prepared also to resist any order which might be issued by the governor and council to collect the fee, and denounced any one who should pay it as a betrayer of the privileges of the people. This Dinwiddie considered to be "introductive of rebellion among the people." The council sent an address in support of the governor's contention. The burgesses appointed Peyton Randolph, the attorney general, as their agent, and when he applied to Dinwiddie for leave to go, it was refused and he was told that he had not acted up to his duty in failing to support the governor. But he went, nevertheless, and was held responsible for some of the sharp criticisms of the governor's policy in the press.

Their addresses the burgesses kept as secret as possible from the governor, but some time later a copy of the reasons they furnished Randolph in support of their contention fell into his hands.[2] He then wrote to Abercromby, the agent of the province, and pronounced them inconsistent with the truth. The extraordinary sum of £2500 which they appropriated for Randolph's support on his mission also came in for criticism at the hands of the governor, in view of the plea of poverty which was always made when appropriations were demanded for defence. As was to be expected, the board of trade approved of the fee as legal and reasonable in amount, citing the fact that the taking of fees in such cases was common in the colonies.[3] The address of the house was rejected by the king, but the board was directed to caution the governor in reference to the enforcement of his right that he should not collect the fee upon grants of less than 100 acres or upon those which were proportional to the number of persons imported by the applicant or to the number of his family. They were also of the opinion that, in order to avoid unnecessary obstacles to settlement, the fee should not be collected upon grants west of the mountains and also that they should be exempt from quit rents for a

---

[1] J. of Burgesses, 154, 155, 168.

[2] Dinwiddie Papers, I, 71.

[3] C. O. 5/1367, E. B. Va. B. T. to Dinwiddie, Jan. 17, 1753, July 3, 1754.

period of ten years. All those who had got orders for grants or had lodged certificates for them before April 22, 1752, should also be exempt from the fee. The board also took occasion to desire the governor to issue no more patents in excess of 1000 acres for any one person, and to urge him to avail himself of every legal means to enforce the payment of quit rents and obedience to the conditions of cultivation. As to Randolph, because he had left the province without his majesty's permission, his office was declared vacant, but Dinwiddie was left at liberty to reinstate him if, on his return, he should behave in a decent manner. This was what actually occurred and application was duly made to the king for his reappointment.[1]

After this controversy had been in progress for some time Dinwiddie wrote to Abercromby that, if he had known that it would have caused so much uneasiness to himself and trouble to his friends, he would not have taken the fees, " but when it was established by the Council here and approved by the Lords of Trade, I could not in honor to the Board, submit to the urgent clamours of our House of Burgesses, who by the opinion of Sir Dudley Ryder had no Cognizance of it." [2] By the collection of the fee Dinwiddie also had in mind not only an increase of his perquisites but the correction of an abuse by forcing the taking out of patents and the settlement and payment of quit rents upon vast tracts of land which were being monopolized in the most unproductive way possible. As this was an innovation in Virginia and was bound deeply to affect the territorial policy of the colony and the pockets of many freeholders, the burgesses could not avoid taking it up. But in order to bring this question under the traditional British doctrine of the right of the subject to consent to all taxes upon his property, they had to confound a fee with a tax. Neither party understood or would admit the justice in the other's contention and neither conceived in advance what the reaction of the other to his proposal would be or into what complications they would be led. In all these respects the controversy over the pistole was exactly typical of the struggle between pre-

[1] Dinwiddie Papers, I, 363, 492, 506, II, 2, 91.
[2] Ibid., I, 137.

rogative and popular rights which was going on in all the provinces.

When the question of the payment of Randolph's salary as agent came up, the affair of the pistole reacted upon the more imperative interests of defence. It was after Washington had capitulated at Fort Necessity in July, 1754, that the assembly was called together for its fourth session. In response to the earnest appeal of Dinwiddie, the burgesses voted to raise £20,000 by a poll tax, but added as a rider to this bill a clause for the payment out of this fund of the £2500 which previously had been voted to Randolph. This provision it was impossible that either the council or Dinwiddie would accept, though the governor promised that he would sign a separate bill for the payment of the salary provided it contained the usual suspending clause. To this the burgesses refused to agree and the session closed without any appropriation for the war being made.[1]

At this stage of the affair the decision of the British government in reference to the fee was not known and Dinwiddie made use of that, though in vain, as an argument to induce the burgesses to refrain from insisting in the way they did upon the payment of Randolph's salary. But before the next session was called, in October, this decision, with the slight concessions which it involved to the colonial point of view, had become known. This, with the evidence now furnished that the home government stood ready to assist the colonies in the war, made the assembly more conciliatory and an appropriation of £20,000 was obtained. Robinson, the speaker, also apologized to Dinwiddie for the ill manners which the house had exhibited toward him and after this yielding to the influence of authority peaceful relations seem to have been restored.[2] In May, 1755, Randolph, who had now returned, made his report and received the public thanks of the house, but no reference appears to any provision for the payment of his salary.[3]

Though the war was the most pressing business in Virginia during the next half-dozen years, the usual degree of

---

[1] J. of Burgesses, 1752–1758, pp. 202, 204–205; Dinwiddie Papers, I, 303, 306, 312, 324, 328.

[2] *Ibid.*, 376.   [3] J. of B., 1752–1758, 250–251.

activity seems to have been continued in other directions. Sessions of the assembly were held oftener than in time of peace and in some of these almost nothing was done except what concerned the war. But on other occasions — and these were the longer sessions — much business was done along accustomed and traditional lines. As elsewhere, the war, of course, occasioned a resort to all the usual fiscal resources of the province. A land tax, a poll tax, duties on imports, inclusive of slaves, a duty on wheel carriages and on licenses for keeping ordinaries, and a lottery were utilized, in addition to the old standing export duty on tobacco. Interest-bearing treasury notes were issued and also, after opposition by the council and a dissolution in November, 1755, by the governor, bills of credit in limited quantities.[1] Committees or commissioners were usually appointed by the house to examine all accounts and thus practically to control expenditures. An appropriation act, however, of 1757 provided that the commissioners should examine only such accounts as were turned over to them by the governor, they assisting him in that work. Except in rare cases the burgesses made use of their regular standing committees — on elections, claims, and propositions and grievances, in later years committees on courts of justice and on trade being added — and much business was transacted by means of them. The three first-named committees continued active throughout the war and each in its respective line furnished a medium, in addition to individual members, through which local and special demands could find a hearing at Williamsburg. They contributed much toward suggesting or preventing legislation, as the case might be, and formed avenues of connection between the counties and the assembly. With the exception of the controversy over the pistole, a long time had passed since the two houses or the executive and the burgesses had been involved in conflict. During this long interval of peace the house of burgesses, increasing steadily in size and representing the various interests of a large province, had imperceptibly attained a firmer lead in affairs, the council rarely making opposition. Councillors and burgesses ceased

[1] J. of B., 328, 330, 332; Dinwiddie Papers, II, 266, 269, 355; Hening, VI, 454, 461, 471, 521; VII, 926. J. of B. *loc. cit.*, introd., xxviii.

to have divergent interests and since Spotswood's time comparatively few questions had become controversial. Thus the lead of the burgesses in most matters of decisive import was quietly acquiesced in.

On the general body of legislation and on subjects which came up for debate in the houses, the division of counties and parishes or the creation of new local jurisdictions appear with their customary frequency during the war. These were occasioned by the shifting of population and especially by its advance into the upper and relatively unoccupied parts of the colony. Owing to disputes or illegal practices, several parishes also were dissolved and petitions were presented, though not granted, for the dissolution of not a few others. This phenomenon was in many cases connected with the growth of dissenters in the northern and western parts of the province.

An act, which was passed in 1749 and later revised, for the relief of insolvent debtors was the subject of much discussion and of opposition by British merchants and the government. The reason for this was that it contained a clause respecting the recovery of English debts and bills of exchange which provided that current money should be rated at 25% below sterling. Previously this had not been regulated, and sheriffs when they levied executions fixed rates of exchange as they thought just. The rate now designated by law was regarded as unjust to creditors because current money usually circulated at much lower rates than this.[1] For some reason this act escaped disallowance when first submitted, but later the merchants, especially of Bristol and Liverpool, petitioned against it, and an additional instruction was prepared directing the governor to secure, if possible, the passage of another act without the objectionable clause. In 1755 a bill was passed leaving it to the judge to fix the rates of exchange,[2] but the original law having received the king's assent stood, and until this was repealed the assent could not be obtained for the new measure.[3] But

[1] C. O. 5/1327, O. P. Va., Din. to board, June 5, 1752, June 16, 1753, Mar. 1754; C. O. 5/1367, E. B. Va., B. T. to Din., June 27, 1754, also Aug. 6, 1754.

[2] Hening, VI, 478 et seq.

[3] See addresses of the burgesses, 1763, printed in introduction to J. of B. 1761–1765, p. xxx et seq.; C. O. 5/1330, O. P. Va., June 1, 1763.

the Virginia courts meantime enforced the new law and fixed rates of exchange as they thought just.   Meanwhile, especially during the years 1757 to 1759, considerable quantities of treasury notes, or bills of credit, were issued to meet the demands of the war, defence against the Cherokees, support of Forbes' expedition against Fort Duquesne and aid to operations further north.   By the beginning of 1762 these issues amounted to £412,962, the first experience of Virginia with paper money.   Provision, however, was made for the levy of taxes which should retire all or nearly all of these notes by 1768 or a little later.[1]   But exchange in the meantime fluctuated and sank lower than had been customary. Creditors lost correspondingly on their long debts and British and Virginia merchants again began to complain.

Dinwiddie was in office when the first two issues were passed and he consented to them because all its gold and silver had been taken from the province for the payment of the troops in service, and had it not been for the new currency it would have been necessary to disband them and give up the frontier.   But the merchants complained that, as the result of these issues, debts which were due in sterling of a certain fixed value were being discharged in paper notes of a local, uncertain and fluctuating value, without provision for the difference of exchange at the time of making payment. The board of trade noted the fact that this was a new phenomenon in Virginia, where, because of its staple commodity, paper currency must be less necessary than elsewhere. But as the acts had already been carried into execution and disallowance might cause great inconvenience, upon the suggestion of Dinwiddie — who had now returned to England after the close of his term — Fauquier, his successor, was specially instructed to procure an amendment of the acts providing that all debts due before their passage should be discharged in sterling money only and that those contracted later should be paid in accordance with the actual difference of exchange, between paper and sterling at the time of payment.[2]   On receiving the instruction, Fauquier replied that

[1] See financial statement appended to the address of the burgesses.
[2] C. O. 5/1367, E. B. Va., B. T. to King, July 12, 1758, and Jan. 31, 1759; C. O. 5/1329, O. P. Va. Feb. 2, 1759, Fauquier to B. T., July 14, 1759; J. of B, Nov. 18 and 20, 1759.

he would recommend obedience to it by the assembly, though he was sure the colony's intention was just and that the merchants, if they had reflected, would have seen that they were secured even by the law as it stood. This sentiment was also embodied in the most definite form in a resolution by the burgesses, and a bill which was sent down from the council better to preserve the credit of the paper currency was summarily rejected. Provision also was made for additional issues under the customary regulations, and Fauquier both spoke and wrote in a tone of general satisfaction with the way in which the assembly was dealing with the finances of the war. The sum which had been allotted by parliament to Virginia in reimbursement for its services was also being utilized, not directly for the retirement of the bills but in general to strengthen the resources of the province.

On this question, as well as most others, the governor stood well with the burgesses, the majority of the councillors supporting the merchants, charging Fauquier with subserviency.[1] The unfavorable effect of the depreciated currency, which every one had to use, upon the net revenue from quit rents was noted by Richard Corbin, the deputy receiver general.[2] The Virginia merchants sent a remonstrance to the board of trade relating to their debts and the currency, and because of their feeling that Fauquier was not with them they kept it, so far as possible, from becoming known to him. Fauquier, on his part attributed their attitude and the difficulties of the situation to causes different from those which they assigned. Their opposition to further issues he attributed to a desire to procure the disbandment of the regiment the continuance of which in service was made possible solely by the emissions. The unfavorable condition of the exchanges can also be explained by the fact that the volume of imports had so increased that the crops of tobacco would not pay for them and this in turn was due to the large expenditures of the Virginia planters and merchants for luxuries.[3] The appeal of the merchants to the home govern-

[1] Ludwell to Dinwiddie, Mar. 22, 1759.

[2] C. O. 5/1330, O. P. Va., Feb. 24, and Dec. 16, 1762. See protest of the Council, inclosed in Fauquier's letter of July 10, 1762, to the board.

[3] Fauquier to B. T., July 10 and Nov. 3, 1762. The essential material for this subject in its later phase is printed in the introduction to the volume of J. of B. for 1761–1765.

ment, without previously consulting it, increased the irritation of the assembly and it became even more persistent in its chosen line of policy.

The board of trade, to which the British as well as the Virginia merchants continued their appeals and complaints, condemned the attitude not only of the burgesses but of the governor.[1] They declared such amendments of the law as had been made to be inadequate and censured Fauquier for the manner in which he had communicated to them the king's additional instructions. Though he had pretended, they said, to obey this, he had destroyed its effectiveness by expressing doubt of the existence of the evil. By the later acts of issue the periods of redemption had been prolonged and the instruction had been systematically disregarded. The mild protests which Fauquier addressed to the burgesses and the arguments which he used, as stated in his letters home, prove that the statement of the board was essentially true. On one occasion he contented himself with telling them that they were showing a preference for debtors over creditors. Later, he confined his attack to the legal tender quality of the bills, but of course with the result of convincing very few.[2] He contended that had he not yielded he would have secured no men for the war and this was doubtless true. The burgesses, though freely admitting that their currency was inferior to the exchequer bills and notes of the Bank of England, maintained that it was the best which was possible for them under the conditions, while Fauquier admitted that the taxes appeared to be sufficient for the redemption of the bills. The British merchants, however, continued to demand that being sterling creditors, their debts should be paid in sterling. To this it was impossible for Virginia or any colony to conform, because they had not the specie. But, in 1764, the burgesses expressed a willingness so to revise the laws as to provide for the payment of such debts in amounts of currency which would be equivalent to the original sterling value. To this the British government assented and in this way, aided by the redemption of its bills, currency ceased to be a subject of dispute in Virginia. But an act relating to bankruptcy and the relief of insolvent debtors continued

[1] C. O. 5/1367, E. B. Va. B. T. to Fauquier, Feb. 7, 1763.
[2] J. of B., 1761–1765, introd., p. xxxiv.

to be the object of severe attack by British merchants, because of its favoritism as compared with British laws, toward debtors and toward creditors resident in Virginia.[1]

The heavy cost which had attended the despatch of an agent to England when the case of the pistole fee was under discussion, as well as the alleged failure of Abercromby, the accredited agent of the province, properly to support later contentions of the burgesses, led to the passage of an act in 1759 for the appointment of another agent, the governor, and so far as possible the council, being ignored in the new arrangement. Edward Montague, of the Middle Temple, was named for the office in the act and a committee consisting of members of both houses — eight burgesses and four councillors — was named to correspond with him. The amount of his salary was also designated in the act and the appointee was left virtually under the control of the burgesses. At first Fauquier refused to assent to this measure without the leave of the king, but was persuaded by Peter Randolph and other leaders to yield. When the act came before the privy council, it ordered the governor to inform the assembly that it would not be approved unless amended. This led to an amendment providing, not for any change in the case of Montague, who was to hold for seven years, but that when his successor should be named he should be approved by the governor and hold only till the next meeting of the assembly.[2]

Since 1738 John Robinson had held the two offices of colony treasurer and speaker of the assembly. As treasurer — an office which since 1691 had been named by the burgesses — he had administrative control over all the provincial revenue except the quit rents and the income from the ten shillings export duty on tobacco. As speaker he was leader of the house and thus of the opposition to the executive in the province and in England. His long incumbency of these offices testifies to his ability and influence, a fact to which strong testimony is borne by Fauquier. Dinwiddie had considered Robinson as perhaps his most dangerous opponent upon the question of the pistole. Therefore — as

---

[1] C. O. 5/1336, O. P. Va., June, 1763.

[2] C. O. 5/1329, O. P. Va., Nov. 1759; J. of B., 1758–1761, introduction, xvii.

Fauquier thought — he had procured the issue of an instruction to the latter to bring about a separation of the offices. The existing practice the board of trade pronounced irregular and unconstitutional, one which should not be tolerated unless it was evident that the service of the crown would suffer from the change. Fauquier understood, however, that he had some latitude in the matter and after looking into the situation and seeing how valuable Robinson's services were in procuring support for the war, as well as in many other ways, concluded that he could not fulfil the purpose of the board without setting the province in a flame. He therefore allowed the existing arrangement to continue. The board sharply reproved him for this and refused to admit that it could not be set aside. But so strong was the opinion of the governor to the contrary that the board was forced to yield so far as to allow Fauquier to fix the time when he would seriously attack the question.[1] In discussing this subject, Fauquier wrote, " The people of Virginia are so jealous of their liberty and so reluctant to give up any point, that though they daily see the ill consequences of their conduct, they cannot be persuaded on to give any power even to those in whom they must confide."

[1] C. O. 5/1329, O. P. Va., Fauquier to B. T., Apr. 10, 1759; C. O. 5/1367. E. B. Va., B. T. to Fauquier, Jan. 18 and Nov. 20, 1759.

CHAPTER XIII

DURING the decade of the fifties two important changes occurred in the conditions affecting the colonies along the southern and southwestern frontier. One of these directly affected Georgia alone; the other concerned the whole tier of provinces on the west, but was perhaps better exemplified in the Carolinas than elsewhere. In Georgia occurred the transition from proprietary to royal government, a change which brought that province fully into line with the routine of British administration. In the Carolinas and along the western frontier generally the most important matter of the time was the occupation of the up-country, the piedmont region above the middle course of the rivers, by Scotch Irish and German immigrants from the north and the entrance of that section as a social and political factor into the history of the seaboard colonies. The course of that migration in general has already been traced and the present task is to explain its effect upon the internal development, as shown in its early stage, upon the colonies concerned and especially upon South Carolina.

Since the founding of the colony that region had been traversed by the hunter and the Indian trader. Until now it had belonged to the native tribesmen and from it, as from the country beyond the mountains, had come the skins and furs which formed so large a bulk of the exports from Charlestown. Herds of deer and buffalo roamed over the region and it was only by the long-continued assaults of both Indian and white men, aided by the firearms which the latter had brought, that the numbers of these animals were so reduced that at last they disappeared from the country east of the mountains. Indian trails, used also by English hunters and traders, traversed this district and indicated in general the routes which became roads and even railroads from the east when the time came for their building.

But these subjects have been dwelt upon sufficiently in connection with Indian relations. We are now concerned with the advent of the permanent white settlers. They came in families and groups, less organized even than were the primitive Germans when they overran central Europe. They became squatters upon the soil, with no enemy to fear except the Indian. A heterogeneous array of settlements with frontier cabins and small farms was the result. As the up-country was far more open and less heavily wooded than the low country, it was easier to settle by a people who were unaided and possessed little capital. It was also a highland country to which they came, with abundance of pure water and air, and its temperature not intolerably hot in summer. The land was fertile and suited to agriculture. The frontiersman building his cabin, opening up his clearing and developing it into a small farm, was typical of the settlers of the up-country. They were the first genuine frontiersmen who appear in American history. They were not tenants, did not bring with them indented servants or slaves, were not planters upon large estates devoted to the production of staples for the European market. They were not simply an extension of Europe but, so far as was possible in those times, were emancipated from its influence and especially from its control. For the time they were a primitive independent democracy, individualistic to the verge of anarchy, subject to no government except that which they evolved among themselves. They were located some three hundred miles from the seacoast, with only the crudest means of communication and were isolated as communities well could be. The more adventurous among them did not care for long to touch elbows with anyone, but as the country began to fill up moved on across the mountains, desiring to keep in the van of the westward exodus. It was by a population of this type, largely Scotch Irish, that the up-country of the Carolinas and Georgia was settled. In South Carolina this belt of territory extended from the Lancaster district on the northwest across to the Edgefield and Abbeville districts above Hamburg on the southwest and thence westward to the mountains.

The industry which first developed here on such a scale as to lead to export and in this way to bring about some connection again with the outside world was stock raising. Large herds of cattle were reared and something like western ranch life developed.[1] The stock driver with his cow-pen succeeded the hunter and the Indian trader as the representative of the economic life of the region. It was about 1740 when stock raising began and the cow-pen made its appearance here and there and became the germ out of which permanent settlements in the future often developed. The cow-pen was the herding place for the cattle, where they were brought together preparatory to being driven to market or for any other purpose. It was officered by a superintendent and a corps of assistants, all of whom were woodsmen, skilful on horseback and with the rifle. Cabins were built at these places and large fenced enclosures for the stock. Cleared land lay near by for the raising of corn. It was necessary that a supply of water should be accessible. If the supply of grass gave out or settlements encroached, it was necessary to move to another region. Individual settlers also had their own herds of stock, some of which they had driven from the north. The horse, usually of Spanish and Indian breed, played a large part in this economy. The stock was driven hundreds of miles to the towns on the seaboard and there slaughtered for market.

The fur trade reached its maximum in South Carolina about 1743 and then began to decline, the movement in this direction becoming rapid after the beginning of the Cherokee War in 1755. Contemporaneously with this decline came the develpment of cattle-raising and the export of beef, pork, hides, tallow and dairy products. This constituted the next phase in the economic development of the up-country, its contribution, along with rice, indigo, and naval stores from the middle and low country, to the total productions and export trade of South Carolina. In Georgia a similar process was going on, though it developed somewhat later and less perfectly than in the older provinces, and in both it continued until the Revolution. The export of provisions

[1] Logan, History of Upper South Carolina.

and breadstuffs from these two colonies, both to northern ports and to the West Indies, was large. In the labor system of the up-country slavery bore almost no part and white servants were not numerous. Farms commonly varied in size from 50 to 300 acres. It was a system of small proprietors, as distinct from the economic arrangements of the low country as could well be imagined.

At the beginning and for a considerable time thereafter no provision was made for local government in the up-country. It had neither courts nor officials and there was no thought of giving it representation in the assembly. The division of the two provinces into counties and parishes included only the seaboard and the middle region and in South Carolina it was made before the up-country was settled at all. Now that it had been settled, there was no disposition on the part of the politically privileged of the low country to extend the advantages of government to the frontier settlements. Disorders arose, robberies and other outrages were committed, but the only redress, if there was any at all, was in self-defence or through the courts at Charlestown or Savannah. The latter were beyond reach, and, indeed, without officials to execute their decrees would have been powerless. The Cherokee War came on and Indian outrages were added to the other disorders of the frontier. Thus affairs continued until after the close of the period which we are now considering. So unlike were the two sections of these provinces — especially in the case of the two Carolinas — in economic and social structure that there existed conditions out of which prolonged sectional struggles were almost sure to develop. Such was the up-country and from the sketch which has been given of it, as contrasted with the province in its original form and extent, may be seen the deep significance of the up-country for the internal history of the colonies.

It is now necessary to consider at some length the other change which came about in political conditions in the extreme south, the establishment of royal government in Georgia, and after that we shall return to South Carolina and follow its development until the close of its decisive struggle with the Cherokees, which was so nearly contemporaneous with the collapse of French power in America.

Compared with South Carolina, Georgia was a weak colony

and its people were several decades behind their neighbors in political experience. Until 1732 South Carolina had been the border province and stood without a rival on the southern frontier. In a military sense it had been temporarily somewhat overshadowed by Oglethorpe, but with his disappearance the leadership which was due to its position and superior resources naturally reasserted itself. With this was mingled some of the superciliousness which so often mars the relations of older toward younger communities even though the difference is measured by only a few decades. This appeared especially in connection with the controversy over the disposition of the territory south of the Altamaha, while some insisted that Georgia ought to be incorporated with South Carolina. So far as negro slavery was concerned, South Carolina had become much more deeply involved than Georgia and for a time the latter could at most be only an imitator of her neighbor. In soil, climate and industries the two colonies were fitted to become an economic unit. The local systems, particularly as to the size of estates, were very similar. Rice, indigo, the fur and skin trade, lumber, live stock and provisions were their staple products in common, and the general course of their oversea traffic was the same. Their location necessitated that they should develop into the nucleus of the southern section of the colonial area, a fact which in the long run was only slightly obscured by their separate political organizations.

On April 25, 1751, more than two years before the date when the grant of powers of government made to the Georgia trustees would expire, their common council appointed a committee, with the earl of Shaftesbury at its head, " to adjust with the Administration the proper means for supporting and settling the Colony for the future." [1] In a memorial which this committee submitted to the king brief reference was made to what had been accomplished under the royal charter, with the assistance of the grants — amounting to £130,000 — which had been made by parliament. But the province, of course, had not become self-supporting, the last grant had been expended and no means were left with which to meet the expenses of government. They found that general confusion in Georgia would follow and that all which had been accomplished, including the favorite silk culture which they were striving to galvanize into prosperity, would be ruined or lost. Therefore they asked that the government might be put on a surer basis, and before the end of the year declared themselves ready to make an absolute surrender of all their rights and trusts under the charter, recommending the inhabitants and their privileges to the king's protection. The guaranties which they asked for Georgia and its inhabitants were that the efforts of South Carolina to bring about the incorporation of Georgia with herself should be brought finally to an end by an express declaration that it should be a separate and independent province, that its inhabitants should be confirmed in their property rights, that existing arrears of quit rents should be remitted and the rate for the future be reduced from four to two shillings per hundred acres. They also requested that Benjamin Martyn, who had served the trustees so acceptably as secretary and was so well informed concerning the province, should be recommended for appointment as its agent.

The business was taken up in due form by the British executive,[1] the committee of the privy council considering the memorial and also reports from the treasury board and board of trade upon the financial and other aspects of the question. The parliament also made an additional appropriation, sufficient to carry the province through to the following midsummer. As the trustees had proposed action before the term of the grant had expired, it was the opinion of the law officers, Ryder and Murray, following precedent, that they should execute under their common seal a deed of surrender, including land as government, and subject to the vested rights of the colonists.[2] This was done and a proclamation was accordingly issued authorizing the existing magistrates in the colony to retain their offices until a new form of government should be settled. The trustees proceeded to close out their transactions and on June 23, 1752, their seal was defaced and the last entry made in their records. The taking of the steps in England necessary to the institution of a new government in

---

[1] Acts P. C. Col., 1745–1766, pp. 123–128.
[2] The eighth granted to Lord Carteret was included with the rest.

the province was delayed for a year longer and it was not until August, 1754, that the first royal governor was appointed.

During the months which passed between the surrender of the charter and the arrival of the royal governor, affairs in the province were administered by the president and his four assistants, they being directly responsible to the crown. In September Patrick Graham succeeded Henry Parker in the presidency.[1] From time to time communications were received by the board of trade from this body direct and also from James Habersham, one of its members, who from this time was to play an increasingly important part in Georgia affairs. Edmund Gray, a man said to be of Quaker antecedents, and a newcomer from Virginia, also laid his views concerning Georgia before the board. The accounts given of the province were to the general effect that colonists were coming or ready to come in from South Carolina or elsewhere to the north, or from Europe, but the uncertainty concerning the government and the validity of land titles under grants made by the president and assistants operated as a hindrance.[2] Of special importance was the migration from Dorchester in South Carolina of a congregation of independents who had originally come from Massachusetts and who now found their permanent abiding place in the Midway district which was to become St. John's parish. The silk culture was also imperilled by the doubt whether parliament would continue the subsidies by which it had hitherto been supported and which were necessary to keep it going. The people who produced the cocoons and brought them to the public filatures were now in doubt whether they would be paid any longer for this service. The colony also was poor and weak, containing probably fewer than 4000 whites and perhaps 1800 blacks. The defences at Frederica were in ruins and those at other posts in the province in scarcely better condition. Since the disbandment of its troops near the close of the last war the colony had been nearly destitute of arms or of anything that could be called an effective militia. Its government hitherto

[1] Ga. Recs., VI, 375.

[2] See board of trade to president and assistants, July 12, 1753, in which they were told that such grants as they made could only be considered allotments, as the crown alone could make effectual grants. Ga. Recs. Ms., XXXIII, p. 604.

had been a very crude affair. The body of colonists had received no training in self-government and had thus far shown only a certain capacity for ineffective quarreling and complaints. By the introduction of negroes the labor power of the colony in its lowest form had been increased and hence its capacity to produce rice and indigo. But the economic capacity of the great body of whites had been forever stunted by the change, as was coming to be the result in all the slave-holding colonies. The persistent efforts of the trustees during twenty years had made a beginning, but settlement had scarcely advanced beyond the unhealthier coast region and Georgia was certainly too weak to avail much as a border province for defence against a serious attack from the Indians or from its nearby European rivals. It was weaker even than New Hampshire on the northern frontier and much less inured to conflict. Neither was it supported by colonies with the strength of Massachusetts and Connecticut in the rear. In general the chances of coöperation and successful defence on the southern frontier were decidedly less than they were in the north, the security of the south lying in the weakness and remoteness of their enemies.

But the imminence of another war with France and of conflicts which it was likely to bring with the Indians, taken in connection with other elements of the problem, finally moved the British government to act. The board of trade, under an order from the committee of the council, submitted the familiar plan for the government of a royal province, with a council of twelve members, an assembly, a secretary, register and surveyor, provost marshal, an admiralty court, customs officers, and provision for an Anglican clergyman and schoolmaster.[1] This was approved and duly formulated in a governor's commission and instructions. John Reynolds, an officer in the navy, was selected to be governor and sent to Savannah, where he arrived in October, 1754. Government under the crown was duly instituted, James Habersham being sworn in as secretary and clerk of the council, Alexander Kellet as provost marshal. William Clifton came from Eng-

---

[1] C. O. 5/6644, O. P. Ga., July, 1752– July, 1754; Ga. Ms. Recs., XXXIII fol. 598 et seq.; Acts P. C. Col., 1745–1766, pp. 176–180; Jones, Hist. of Ga., I, 450 et seq.

land under appointment as attorney general. The appointment of two surveyors general, one of whom was William de Brahm, indicated that the business of granting land and at least ascertaining the quit rents that were due was to be carried on more systematically than under the trustees.[1] Sir Patrick Houstoun also was appointed register of grants. As usual, several of these officials were made members of the council.

A proclamation was issued continuing minor officials in their places, and after consideration by the attorney general of the governor's instructions on that subject, a judicial system similar to that of other royal provinces was created, with a general court, meeting four times each year, courts of oyer and terminer and common pleas, a court of chancery with the governor as chancellor and a court of admiralty. A table of fees for the services of all administrative and judicial officers thus created was also prepared. General orders for all these changes were issued by the governor and council.[2] But the sense of dignity of the board and the feeling that they might be doing something important must have been a little shocked when, during one of their early sessions, the chimney and one end of the building in which they were sitting fell with a crash and the magistrates came near being buried in the ruins. This was one of the earliest occurrences which Reynolds had to report to the board of trade, and one does not wonder at the somewhat contemptuous references which he made to the type of colonial architecture which he found at Savannah. Because of the neglected state of most colonial prisons, we are glad to learn that the repairs which naturally followed this accident were made to include the prison as well. After royal government had been set going the time of the executive council was to a large extent taken up with land grants, inquiries into the origin and justice of applications and claims and approving or disapproving of the proposed cessions. Many of the grants which were now made were on the Ogeechee and in the Midway region, between Savannah and the Altamaha.

[1] Ga. Recs., VII, Minutes of Gov. and Council.
[2] Ibid., 18–88. See Stokes, View of the Constitution of the British Colonies in America, 1783, for an excellent description of government in Georgia after it had become fully developed as typical of that of the royal provinces.

It was to this region, as we have seen, that the Dorchester settlers came, and later in the next administration the town of Hardwicke, named from the lord chancellor, and for a time all effort was made to remove the capital from Savannah to this place. At the same time settlers under the lead of Edmund Gray, were establishing themselves south of the Altamaha, on territory which lay outside of proprietary Georgia, was still claimed by South Carolina and was also in dispute between the English and the Spanish. As these people were a rough set, commonly deemed outlaws, since they had neither authority nor government over them, they were considered a source of danger. The Indians, too, had not yet surrendered their claims to land above the flow of the tide in the rivers and the Bosomworth case had still to receive much attention before it was brought to a settlement. Frequent conferences, though on a small scale, were held with Indians of the various neighboring tribes, Augusta maintaining its leading place as a centre of trade in skins, furs and other Indian commodities. Jealousies and rivalries between Indian traders from Georgia and South Carolina still continued. These were some of the questions which the reorganized government of Georgia now had to meet.

On January 7, 1755, the assembly took its place as a permanent institution of Georgia. Its members were elected from the towns and districts of the province and subject to a property qualification which was prescribed in the governor's instructions but extended in certain details by order of the governor in council.[1] The lower house, if all the districts were fully represented, should consist of nineteen members; but the election of two of these was found to be undue. Trouble began at once, taking the form of the secession of six of the members.[2] These were led by Edmund Gray, who now made his entrance into Georgia politics by securing election from the Augusta district on the pretence that he had great influence in England and could dominate the government of the province and monopolize the Indian trade. He and the five members whom he induced to withdraw with him issued a letter calling upon the freeholders of the prov-

---

[1] Ga. Recs., VII, 26; XIII, 7 *et seq.*
[2] *Ibid.*, 23 *et seq.*; Ga. Recs., VII, 94–100.

ince to come at once to Savannah to defend their liberties and secure those blessings which alone could render the colony flourishing and happy. Because of this seditious utterance, which met with no response from the settlers, its six signers were expelled from the assembly and new elections were held to fill their places. A proclamation was also issued for keeping the peace. It was after this that Gray repaired to the region south of the Altamaha and entered upon the disorderly life to which reference has already been made.[1]

What was certainly a real grievance was then taken up by the assembly with a view to securing redress. This was a requirement which in pursuance, as he claimed, of his instructions, Reynolds had set forth in a proclamation, that all settlers should clear and cultivate at the rate of five acres per year of every one hundred acres contained in their grants. Considering the small labor power which planters on the average could command and the fact that Georgia lands, especially those near the coast, were very heavily wooded, this must have been a very excessive requirement, surpassing conditions which were imposed elsewhere. In the case of those who had received their grants from the trustees, comprising nearly the whole body of freeholders, this also imposed a new condition in violation of the original contract. The two houses, therefore, drew up a remonstrance to the king on this subject, which was accepted by the governor and forwarded.[2] It drew from the board of trade a representation upon which was based an order in council changing the regulation and directing that a new instruction should be prepared. As the officials of the trustees had kept a register of land grants only since 1741, it was necessary for Reynolds to require that all who held land in the province should submit their deeds for examination and confirmation. Many did so, and, to avoid expense, were content with a warrant from the new governor confirming their title instead of a new grant.

Addresses were also sent to the king asking that the regu-

---

[1] Jones, I, 486; Ga. Recs., XIII, 24, 39, 68, 77.

[2] *Ibid.*, 31–36, 273, 291, 295, 299, 337; C. O. 5/644, O. P. Ga., July 23, and Sept. 8, 1755; Ga. Ms. Recs., XXXIV, fol. 162, B. T. to Reynolds, May 5, 1754.

lation of fees and also the fixing of qualifications for electors, as well as for representatives in the assembly, should be left to the legislature and not settled by orders of the governor and council, as had recently been done. These elicited an unfavorable response in England and several years passed before further action was taken.[1]

In September, 1755, a controversy of much warmth developed between Reynolds and the council[2] and as an incident of it Clement Martin, one of its members, was suspended. The board of trade supported the council in the opinion that the chief blame for this rested upon the governor, and it appears that his difficulties were greatly increased by the activities of William Little. Little was one of those factotums, such as appeared in many of the provinces, who was brought in as the governor's private secretary and appointed to a whole group of offices which gave him control over the records, and therefore to an extent over the business of the legislature and courts. He was also justice of the peace and commissary of Indian affairs. The council in a memorial to the governor charged Little with remissness, arrogance and nearly all the faults of which an official could be guilty, short of dishonesty in financial relations. Little defended himself in a detailed reply, which the governor, to the " surprise and concern " of the council, ordered to be spread upon their minutes. They charged that his defence consisted of palliations and gross misstatements and that he was systematically undermining the confidence of the governor in the council. Reynolds, on the other hand, in his defence stated that Little rendered more service for his majesty and the province than did any other person there. His income from all his offices is also said to have been only £80 per annum, which was a very moderate return for such services as he was said to have rendered.

The councillors also complained that Reynolds had acted on many occasions without taking their advice, and he in reply insisted that they were trying to reduce him to the position of being merely their president. The spirit of the

[1] Ga. Recs., XIII, 72–76, 92.
[2] Ga. Recs., VII, 252 *et seq.* Answer of Reynolds to the charges against him, C. O. 5/645, Apr. 18, 1758.

naval officer came out when he told them that the word " you "
in his instructions did not always include the council and
that in certain contingencies he proposed to act without their
advice.[1] " I expect," he continued, " that no member of this
Board will presume again to tell me in Council, that he
thinks I ought to lay all the Public Letters I write, before
the Council for their Approbation before I send them to
England, or that I ought to give a copy of all my Instructions to the Council." The council in reply [2] reminded the
governor that out of eight proclamations which he had issued,
four had been published without their advice or consent. They
acknowledged that the royal commission and instructions
were the basis of their government, but firmly insisted that
the concurrence of a majority of their number, preceded by
" a decent Freedom of Speech and Debate," was necessary in
all the important business of the executive. There the dispute in this form ended and Little was not removed from
his offices.

The presents which had been solicited for the Indians arrived on the 30th of September. The governor arranged for
a conference at Augusta as soon as they should reach that
place, but made no communication to the council on that
subject until November 7, when he requested that body to
appoint a committee to accompany him to Augusta for the
distribution of the presents. A committee of three was appointed. The governor stayed at the conference about ten
days and then, in order to attend to the needs of a considerable body of Acadian exiles who had just arrived in the
province, returned to Savannah. Little was left to make
the speeches to the Indians and distribute the goods, the
councillors not being consulted at all in reference to the business.[3] The Bosomworths, however, were permitted to be
present and thus to keep alive their claim to act as media-
tors between the Indians and the English. The management
of this conference, it was thought, had therefore left relations
with the Creeks in an unsatisfactory condition and that at
a time when careful management was specially needed. The

[1] Ga. Records, VII, 267.
[2] Ibid., 271.
[3] Rep. of board of trade on state of colony of Georgia, July 29, 1756. Ga.
Ms. Recs., XXXIV, fol. 171 et seq.

complaint was also made that in the matter of the Acadians, Reynolds had not properly followed the policy urged by the council.

The assembly met for its second session at the beginning of February, 1756, only ten of the nineteen members being in attendance. As only very small appropriations had been made at the previous session, Reynolds now asked specially that provision be made for the expense of holding the courts of oyer and terminer. The members expressed a sense of the importance of this, but fell back on the "present circumstances" of the colonists as making the levy of even a small tax extremely difficult.[1] The governor presently took the offensive by sharply criticising the house for proceeding to business without admitting those who had been elected under his writs to fill its vacancies, thus robbing constituents of their rights and showing contempt of the king's authority. No election law as yet existed in Georgia and Reynolds and his secretary were giving a liberal interpretation to their powers in this matter, as the governor had in his dealings with the council. The house, however, replied that writs were never issued in such cases as the governor referred to except on the request of the assembly concerned, and that could not be made during a recess; but, in spite of that, they were doing their best through their committee to determine the rights of contestants in the premises.

At the very session when this reply was voted the fact was very clearly brought out that the governor and Little, who was clerk of the house by executive appointment, were working together to seat the men whom they had chosen for the vacancies. Little refused to enter anything on the minutes until the "members returned duly elected and who were now in Town, were admitted; the governor having declared that he will not look upon anything done as valid till they are admitted." The immediate reply of the house to this bold attempt to coerce it was an order to Little to withdraw and the appointment of another to take his place. An address to the governor was then adopted and sent and his reply to it was almost in the very words which Little had used. When this was followed by another message from

[1] Ga. Recs., XIII, 81 *et seq.*

him adjourning them for a week, the members by force prevented the speaker from reading it. In spite of the protests of the speaker the session was continued, another address to the governor adopted and other business done. The speaker was forced to assent to all this, though he at the time and afterwards in the most formal way protested against it as illegal. When the time came for the house to reassemble Reynolds dissolved it.

It also appears that prior to this affair in the house Little at the instance of the council had been brought under investigation before the governor, but accurate records of the evidence were not kept. Little was charged with malversation in all his offices and with secreting two bills which had passed both houses in order that they might not receive the governor's assent. As Reynolds had hushed up the inquiry as much as possible and retained him in most of his offices, it was charged that the dissolution of the assembly was directed in order to prevent it from inquiring into the secretary's conduct.[2] However, the controversy was now transferred to England. The board of trade, on the strength of such information as they gathered from various quarters, made a representation which was unfavorable to Reynolds, charging him among other things with failing to keep them properly informed as to his doings. They therefore recommended that he be called home to report and that Henry Ellis be sent over as lieutenant governor. The order for this was very promptly issued through Henry Fox, who was then secretary of state.[3]

During the interval before the arrival of Ellis, Reynolds met a new assembly. Of this body Little was chosen speaker and one of the Bosomworths was among its members. Naturally the governor's relations with this house were friendly. The danger that the province would become involved in the war, as especially revealed by correspondence which was sent by the governor of South Carolina, caused the assembly to engage in a long and anxious inquiry into the condition

[1] Ga. Rec., XIII, 95–102.
[2] This Reynolds denied in his defence.
[3] Ga. Ms. Recs., XXXIV, fol. 171 *et seq.* B. J. July 29, 1756; C. O. 5/645, O. P. Ga. Letters of Reynolds, Kellet and Bryan during 1756.

of the province. In prosecuting this it searched through the available records of the trustees and blamed them chiefly for the present weak and defenceless condition of the colony.[1]

The report of the committee closed with an arraignment of the influence still exerted by the former trustees, and especially by Benjamin Martyn in misrepresenting the present officials of the province and helping to set up and maintain an unfair system of election districts for the assembly. Martyn, they declared, was not properly an agent of the province, as he had not been chosen by the assembly, and they deprecated the influence he was exerting.

Little remained some time longer in Georgia, but Reynolds, as he had been summoned to do, returned promptly to England. The attitude assumed by his last assembly showed that he had not entirely lost influence in the colony. He also presented to the board of trade an elaborate defence of his conduct, and of that of Little, from the reading of which one derives the impression that an important reason for the controversy was the lack of definition in Georgia, either by custom or legislation, of relations between the governor and council and especially of relations between the executive and the assembly. Reynolds' training in the navy predisposed him to direct and imperious methods. Little, his civilian adviser, doubtless furnished him with many addtional incitements to this. In this connection the fact should be borne in mind that the office of governor had never existed in Georgia before the appointment of Reynolds. The same was substantially true in the case of the assembly. All parties concerned were inexperienced and except for the governor's instructions had to be guided chiefly by general impressions of practice in England and in other colonies. Under the conditions, all that could be done in England was to restore Reynolds to his place in the navy and in 1758, after the qualifications of Ellis for the position had been proven by a short trial, to promote him to the full rank of governor as Reynolds' successor.

Henry Ellis[2] was apparently a man of a very different type from Reynolds. Though to an extent he had followed

[1] Ga. Recs., XIII, 128, 147, 152.
[2] Dict. of National Biography.

a seafaring life, he was more a traveller and a scientific observer than a seaman. He was much interested in Arctic discovery and in 1746 and 1747 had gone as hydrographer, surveyor and mineralogist on an expedition to Hudson's Bay. On the strength of the account of this voyage, which he had published, he was elected a member of the Royal Society. Later he published a more general work on the advantages which would come from the discovery of the Northwest Passage and also contributions to the Philosophical Transactions. Ellis was therefore a man of some culture, of scientific and literary tastes, who had travelled widely in Europe, but who had had no experience in government or administration. He appears also to have been a man of even temper and good judgment, who was interested in the varied natural and social phenomena which the new world presented to his attention. Before leaving England, Ellis had induced the government to send to Georgia a quantity of rather unfit arms and ammunition, and the arrival of them added to the heartiness of his welcome.[1] But irrespective of such aid, Ellis from the first proved personally and officially agreeable to the colonists. He reached Savannah in February, 1757, and returned to England near the close of 1760. During his administration of nearly four years nothing of importance occurred to mar the internal peace of the province. Such was the satisfaction of the British government with his conduct that, after about two years, he was raised to the full rank of governor.[2]

The first assembly which Ellis met was the one which, in the last year of Reynolds, had been dominated to such an extent by Little. At first Little and his supporters, specially Patrick Mackay, tried similar tactics again, but Ellis by certain judicious removals, broke up the faction and had no more trouble.[3] Little soon left the province and thereafter public business seems to have proceeded without

---

[1] Acts P. C. Col., 1745–1766, p. 345.

[2] Ellis took the oaths as governor Feb. 26, 1759, J. of Ex. C., Ga. Recs., VII, 909.

[3] C. O. 5/645, Ellis to B. T., July 8, 1757; letter to Ass., June 25, 1757; C. O. 5/646; Ellis to B. T., Feb. 10, 1759. The full account of the last stage of the opposition, given in this letter, was drawn out by a proposal of the board to appoint Mackay and James Reid to the Council.

a jar. Certain reasons why this assembly came to view Ellis with such favor became apparent when among the acts which it passed, with the governor's sanction, is found one for the issue of a small sum in bills of credit and another making the province an asylum for insolvent debtors. Of this latter act the board of trade disapproved as inconsistent with good policy and sound justice, and it deprecated the governor's yielding to the demand for paper money, as Reynolds had begun to do, on the plea that there was scarcely any other medium of exchange in the province. Ellis, however, expressed himself strongly in favor of the advantage of paper especially when it was issued, as in Georgia, simply as a loan and would surely be redeemed in a very short time. If it were not for currency, he said, the people would be able to trade only with South Carolina and its currency, which was on a far less substantial basis, would come into general use in Georgia. So limited was the currency legislation of Georgia that it was allowed to stand.

But before this as well as later assemblies the chief business was the strengthening of the province against its enemies, taxation, and the passage of measures of internal regulation and police about which there could be little or no controversy.[1] One of the most noticeable acts of the administration was one dividing the province into parishes, which now became the election districts, and providing for Anglican worship. This drew a mild protest from the Salzburgers, but nothing more. Laws also were passed confirming titles to land, forbidding trade with the enemy and also unlicensed trade with the Indians, regulating affairs in the town of Savannah, repairing the lighthouse at Tybee, providing for the support and enlargement of the courts, and for the setting up of forts at the important settlements of the province. The work of constructive legislation which was begun under Reynolds was steadily continued by the assemblies under Ellis, and by the close of his administration Georgia had a substantial body of laws which had been approved by the crown. It was with the help of Ellis that the Bosomworth claim was finally adjusted by the compromise to which ref-

[1] C. O. 5/646, Ellis to B. T., Aug. 1, 1857, Apr. 24, 1759; Ga. Ms. Recs. XXXIV, B. T. to Ellis, Apr. 21, 1758.

erence has already been made.[1] The way was thus opened
to a more peaceful assertion of the claims of the English
as settlement advanced beyond the flow of the tides toward
the interior of the province.

Frequent conferences with the Indians, especially with
the Creeks, were held. Presents were regularly sent from
England and a policy of conciliation successfully pursued.
So long as that tribe was divided in its preferences as between
the French and English, Ellis considered that peace was
tolerably secure. Negotiations were held between Georgia
and South Carolina both concerning Indian relations and
the common interests of defence. The Carolinas thought
that in the conduct of Indian affairs the first place belonged
to them, and Ellis was content that it should be so. They
were better able to entertain the visiting tribesmen than was
Georgia and it was arranged that generally they should
go first to Charlestown and then visit Savannah. It was not
until near the close of the administration of Ellis that hostilities with the Indians began, and then the peace was broken
by the Cherokees in what proved to be the preliminaries of
their great war.

Gray's settlement of so-called outlaws at New Hanover,
south of the Altamaha, was the object of much attention at
this time. The relations of Georgia and South Carolina
to this tract, especially now that Georgia was a royal province, were uncertain and likely to become conflicting. The
presence of a settlement so far south might provoke hostilities with the Spanish in Florida. It was from this standpoint in particular that Pitt interested himself in the matter.
On June 10, 1758, he wrote to Governors Lyttleton and
Ellis [2] to order the settlers to remove and to see to it that no
settlements were made without royal authority. The governors appointed commissioners to see that this order was
executed, and early in the following year it was reported
that the settlement had been abandoned. As to relations
with the Spaniards in general, Ellis was disposed to be very

[1] J. of Ec. C. Ga. Recs., VIII, 85–87, 323. The settlement was reached in
July, 1759.

[2] Corresp. of Pitt with Col. Govs., I, 269; II, 38–41, 77; Ga. Ms. Recs.,
XXXIV. B. T. to Ellis, Apr. 21, 1758; B. T. to Pitt, Nov. 24, 1758; C. O.
5/645, Ellis to B. T. Nov. 28, 1759; report of Powell, Jan. 23, 1759.

friendly, holding among other things that it would be good policy to encourage trade with them, to be carried on even in Spanish vessels, in order to obtain by exchange more of their coin, bullion and dyestuffs,[1] and also to secure some of the profits which were going to the French at New Orleans. For various reasons he had no fear of the power of the Spanish in Florida ever being dangerous. His solution for the question of Gray's settlement was to extend the bounds of Georgia at once to the northern limits of Florida and in this way take New Hanover, as well as Cumberland island, under control. This was statesmanlike and in harmony with the purposes of Oglethorpe, but hardly possible under the circumstances of war which then existed.

The administration of Ellis was contemporaneous with the ascendancy of Pitt in England. To the urgent demands of that minister for coöperation in aggressive campaigns against the French in the north, Georgia, like the other remote southern colonies, could not respond. The same attitude had had to be maintained toward the earlier appeals of Loudon. Reynolds had undertaken to raise three troops of rangers as a defence against the Indians, but only forty men had been levied and provision had not been made for their pay. Ellis continued them, but had to subsist them on their own credit, while a small detachment of an independent company was obtained from South Carolina. Forts were decayed and there was no guardship service off the coast. Therefore, as Georgia was a barrier province, it needed assistance and protection and pleaded its weakness and need in answer to the demands for help. The only response of this kind which was obtained from Loudon was an order upon the deputy paymaster at New York for money to the amount of £850, to maintain the rangers until further orders. James Abercromby had wholly failed to reply to the appeals which had been sent to him,[2] and after the small sum which Loudon had ordered was expended Ellis had to shift for himself.

After the beginning of the great Cherokee War, in 1760, the attention of Georgia was largely occupied with efforts

[1] C. O. 5/646, Ellis to B. T., Oct. 22, 1757. For an instance of this trade and export of cattle, 1760, see J. of Ex. C., Ga. Recs., VIII, 347.

[2] Pitt Corresp., I, 376; C. O. 5/646 Ellis to B. T. Oct. 25, 1758, Jan. 28, 1759.

to keep the Creeks from joining their Indian neighbors. Edmund Atkin, the royal agent among the Indians, was charged by some of the Creeks with harsh treatment of them. They said that he unjustly called them allies of the French and repelled their offers of friendship. It was incumbent upon Ellis to remove so far as possible the effect of this unwise conduct. During 1759 and 1760, many conferences were held with visitors from the Creeks and other tribes. They refrained in the main from outrages upon the English and at the beginning joined in hostilities against the Cherokees. This attitude Ellis did all he could to encourage, but the Indians soon ceased from intertribal attacks. As South Carolina withdrew troops from the neighborhood of Augusta, it became necessary for Georgia to call out her forces for the defence of her outlying settlements, but she escaped with no serious breaches of the peace.[1] The brief hostilities with Spain, with which the Seven Years' War closed, also caused some anxiety. But by that time Ellis had been relieved from his duties on the plea of ill-health, and James Wright had taken his place.

Wright was a native of South Carolina and a son of its former chief justice. He had held for years the office of attorney general of that province, and was to prove perhaps an even better governor of Georgia than Ellis had been, both of these men being wise and tactful and equally diligent correspondents with their superiors at home. Before Wright had been long in office it became known that South Carolina, under the lead of Lieutenant Governor Boone, was making grants of extensive tracts of land south of the Altamaha river. These were made without adequate surveys and no steps were taken by the grantees for settling the territory. Also, some of Gray's people had returned to the region.

These events raised the question anew and in a form which not only threatened claims which the Creeks had to a large part of that country, and therefore increased the difficulty of keeping the peace with them, but imperilled the inde-

[1] Ga. Recs., VIII, 5, 162–175, 226–228, 284, 308–334, 381, 414 *et seq.*, 515; *ibid.*, XVI. J. of U. H., 393, 399, 435, 440, 498–502; Jones, Hist. of Ga., II, 29 *et seq.*

pendence of Georgia itself. It was intolerable to that province to see itself in danger of being hemmed in on both the north and south by its rival neighbor. Therefore Wright not only filed a protest with Boone, but filled his letters with accounts of what was going on and arguments against it.[1] The Carolinas were acting on the strength of the territorial extension of their province under its original proprietary charter. But, the Georgians in effect argued, those claims were extinguished by the Act of 1729, and the ungranted land of Carolina became royal domain. The part which had not been included in the grant to the Georgia trustees still remained such. Now it was insisted that the plans of Oglethorpe should be carried out by the extension of the boundary of Georgia so as to include all of the original English territory which lay south of the Altamaha.

The Georgia assembly passed an act requiring that claimants of land in the disputed region should make proof within six months before the governor and council of that province that they had settled their grants, as required by law, and have their deeds fully registered. The board of trade supported the position taken by Georgia and reported the above law to the king for approval. The treaty of Paris, by which Florida was transferred to England, helped to decide the question, and soon, therefore, the bounds of Georgia, which was no longer a border province, were extended to the river St. Mary's by the famous royal proclamation of October 7, 1763.[2]

Returning now to the consideration of South Carolina, we are brought immediately into connection with the problem of defence. At the period of which we are speaking, one war had recently closed and another was soon to begin. Relations were dominated largely by these conditions and the necessities of defence, Indian relations and the frontier. Though Georgia and South Carolina had each its distinct regulations, activities and policy in reference to these matters, they related to the same coast, the same line of frontier and the same enemies. When a report was spread that a French squadron was in the West Indies and that it might descend

[1] Ga. Recs., VIII, 585.
[2] Brigham, Royal Proclamations, Trans. Am. Antiq. Soc., XII, 213.

upon the coast of the continent, Savannah and Charlestown, with the smaller settlements adjacent, were affected in much the same way. The steps which were taken for their protection were much the same, even in their ineffectiveness, though at Charlestown the greater show of bastions, sea walls and the like was made. The bar, however, at the entrance of its harbor, was more effective as a defence than all the works which were laboriously erected on shore. In 1752 Charlestown was visited by a hurricane which destroyed its fortifications and in this and its consequences the experience of that town was unique. But the French made no descents, during the last two intercolonial wars, upon the southern coast of the continent, while in the last war the Spanish did not become involved until the very close. Therefore on the south and east Georgia, during the last war, was as little menaced as South Carolina.

For these colonies the problem of defence centered on the west. The Indian tribes, with the French of Louisiana beyond, whose influence upon the Indians was the subject of much rumor and discussion, raised the sole effective issues along the southern section of the frontier during the last, and the greatest, of the colonial wars. That war, so far as it furnished an exhibition in America of European sea power and land power was fought in the Caribbean and about the gulf and river St. Lawrence. The continental coast line which lay between was not affected. Owing to events on land along the frontier the colonies from the Cape Fear river northward became involved in varying degrees, not only in conflicts with the Indians but with the French as well. South of that region the English and French did not come directly to blows, and therefore with them the war was simply a continuation of the Indian relations which had borne so prominent a part in their policy from the first. Though each of the two provinces had its distinct relations, commercial and political, with the tribes of the region and their allies — Georgia more with the Creeks, South Carolina with Cherokees quite as much as with the Creeks — the two were bound together by common interests of this kind and the problem the two had to deal with was much the same.

James Glen, who held the office of governor in South Carolina until 1775, retained an ardent interest in Indian affairs throughout his administration. As was natural, his attention and that of his government, was chiefly directed to the Cherokees and through their country to the Chickasaws and Choctaws beyond and to the French, with whom these tribes were in close relations. Through the Catawbas also and their feud with the Iroquois attention was directed northward and to the possibility of negotiations at Albany for the termination of the raids which had so long disturbed the western frontier. A large correspondence was carried on with the traders in the Indian country and on their visits to Charlestown reports of what they heard and did were made.[1] Letters upon Indian relations were interchanged with the magistrates of other colonies, especially those of Virginia, New York and Georgia. From time to time Indian emissaries, in larger or smaller numbers, appeared at Charlestown or at points along the frontier and conferences were held. A commissary of Indian affairs, John Dart and later William Pinckney, was continuously active. The volume of business which was done in this way — and it was steadily increasing — passed under the eyes of the executive council and the most important parts of it came before the assembly, which had among its standing committees one on Indian Affairs. It seems that during the later years of the proprietary period special journals of the commissioners of Indian trade had been kept. Whatever intermediate governors had done, Glen at any rate revived this practice and during the middle and later years of his governorship special Indian books, so-called, were kept, in which the executive proceedings relating to Indian affairs were recorded and correspondence upon this subject was copied.[2]

With the advance of settlement, the increasing efforts of both French and English to attract the neighboring tribes into their alliance and the recognition by the Indians of the advantage which came to them from this situation, the vol-

[1] See references to these in Logan's Hist. of Upper S. C. and many references to them in the ms. records of the time. A part of these volumes still exist at Columbia.

[2] C. O. 5/402, B. T. E. B. B. T. to Glen, Dec. 20, 1748.

ume of Indian business steadily increased. The judgment with which Glen acted did not always satisfy the board of trade, though no criticism of him seems to have come from the secretaries of state. But though his sanguine temper sometimes exposed him to deception by Indian traders, there can be no doubt of his diligence and the wide connections which he kept up in this department of administration. The voluminous records conclusively prove this fact.

None of the southern provinces had a town suitable for conferences and for the distribution of presents which was so accessible to the Indian country as was Albany. Charlestown in particular was remote from the village of the Creeks and especially from those of the Cherokees, while, as the result of the earlier wars, Indians had been mostly cleared out of the intervening country in South Carolina. In Georgia this process had been carried by no means so far, and the Creeks still lived much nearer the settlements of the whites. The board of trade in the late forties had insisted that Glen should hold conferences in Charlestown rather than at some intermediate place or places in the up-country. But Glen argued against this policy and enlarged upon the difficulties and perils of such long journeys, of several hundred miles, for the Indians. They were exposed to attack on the way, some fell sick, the experience gave rise to rumors that they were called so far in order to be sacrificed. Because of the evident unwillingness of the Indians to come farther, it was insisted that Fort Monroe or some other place near the frontier would be more suitable for conferences. As we know, there were abundant precedents for this course in the conferences of Nicholson, Cuming and Oglethorpe, while the location of Albany with reference to the New York frontier was similar to that of an up-country settlement rather than to Charlestown. In 1750 the board gave a grudging assent to the proposal.[1]

The expenditures for presents to the Indians was steadily on the increase and, unfortunately, goods which were sent were in many cases unfitted for this use. It was said that the French were following the same course and must be

---

[1] *Ibid.*, B. T. to Glen, Nov. 15, 1750; C. O. 5/373 O. P. S. C. Glen to B. T., Dec. 25, 1751.

beaten at their own game. The Indians of course played their cards adroitly, and the traders on both sides encouraged the process as tending to keep business good. The course of development was the same in the south as in the north, the provinces and the British sharing the cost. The assembly complained, but yielded to necessity. When, in 1749, presents to the value of £3000 were granted by the home government for the Indians of Georgia and South Carolina, it was announced that such grants would be made annually in the future. The payment of Indian agents, interpreters and special messengers, and the support of Indians at conferences, it was claimed, cost even more than the presents and these miscellaneous expenditures the province had to meet. An important part of the business of the agents for South Carolina and Georgia in England — Fury, Crokatt, Wright and Verelet — was the soliciting of grants for Indian presents. Presents, of which ammunition formed a most important part, were sent even to the Choctaws. As the French at this time became involved in a war with this tribe, their former allies, one McNair, a trader who had carried the presents, took great credit for this result, and a long controversy ensued over his claims for reward.[1] The famous James Adair, also an Indian trader, took a hand in the discussion as a critic of the governor and for certain of his utterances was threatened with prosecution. South Carolina was not disposed to honor applications from Georgia for grants on behalf of the Lower Creeks, thinking that its southern neighbor should provide for these with the help of the presents received from England. In general the assembly was skeptical toward the stories told by traders of their influence with the Indians and the claims of reward which were based upon them. The board of trade on the other hand, thought McNair's claim a good one and that £1000 should be given him.[2]

Early in 1750 hostilities began between the Creeks and Cherokees. Of such an event as this two views might be

---

[1] Much material on this appears in the papers; see especially a long report of Committee on Indian Affairs in U. H. J., May 23, 1750. This is unfavorable to McNair.

[2] C. O. 5/402, E. B. C. B. T. to Holder, Mar. 19, 1752.

taken. It might be said that if these two peoples should weaken each other, they would be less dangerous to the English. But the more general view was that it would be safer to keep the two friendly and united as a common barrier against the French. The outbreak of hostilities of course imperiled the settlers on the frontier. The opinion of a joint committee of the two houses was that the trouble had been occasioned by the Iroquois stirring the Cherokees up against the Creeks,[1] though the French were always regarded as originally responsible for this mischief. The building of a fort in the lower Cherokee country had been proposed some time before the board of trade expressed itself as favorable, but nothing had been done. Now the joint committee reported that a fort ought to be built. Representations, they thought, should also be made to the governors of Maryland, Pennsylvania and New York covering the conduct of the Iroquois and the extent to which they disturbed the peace by raids against the Catawbas. With the headmen of the Cherokees traders should be urged to hold meetings and "talks" should be sent to them urging peace. A fort also should be built in the upper Cherokee country, where the Iroquois and other northern Indians usually came, in order to protect the trade and encourage the Cherokees to an independent attitude toward the Iroquois. Finally it was found necessary to send several troops of rangers to the frontier.

Meanwhile attacks upon the Catawbas continued and northern Indians appeared within a few miles of Charlestown. Ammunition was sent to the Catawbas and Cape Fear Indians, but the raids were so serious that settlers in the south threatened to leave the colony. The governor wrote to the northern colonies about the disturbed conditions and there was talk of holding a conference at Fredericksburg in Virginia, at which the Catawbas and their enemies should be brought together. But the northern Indians could not be induced to come so far, and William Johnson in a letter insisted that Albany was the proper place. Glen remarked that the Catawbas were a proud people; they might be induced to go as far as Virginia but

[1] U. H. J., May 31, 1750.

not to Albany to conclude peace. A conference had been called for July, 1751, at Albany, which was to be attended by commissioners from Massachusetts and Connecticut as well as New York. About the middle of May Glen informed the assembly that an interpreter had brought the chief and seven men of the Catawbas to Charlestown, who were willing to go to New York to conclude peace. The joint committee reported in favor of sending them at once by sea. The house agreed and also that, if the cost could not be defrayed from the money granted by the crown for Indian expenses, it would make the provision therefor. So it was arranged and William Bull was appointed commissioner to accompany the Indians.[1] He took with him a talk from Glen, to which was attached the seal of South Carolina, urging that peace be concluded and a chain of friendship formed between the tribesmen concerned, one end of which should be kept by the governor of New York and the other by the governor of South Carolina. To this Bull added a persuasive address, duly emphasizing the fact that they had come a long distance. The Catawbas, coming from their quarters, then lighted the calumet and placed it in the mouths of the chief sachems of the Six Nations, expressing at the same time the desire for peace. At the next meeting the chiefs of the Six Nations proudly accepted the proffer, but only as a truce till the Catawbas should return a year later with the Iroquois whom they held as prisoners.[2] Though complaints of Iroquois raids ceased for a time in South Carolina, when the conference of 1753 was held Clinton reproached the Six Nations because they were again taking scalps and prisoners from the Catawbas.[3] We have no proof that the Catawbas had returned all their prisoners, though the South Carolina authorities took steps to bring it about and some prisoners at least were returned. The feud continued until it was utterly obscured by the larger events which were soon to occur.[4]

Hostilities between the Creeks and Cherokees continued

[1] U. H. J., May 17, 1751.
[2] N. Y. Col. Docs., VI, 721–726.
[3] *Ibid.*, 812. S. C. L. H. J., Apr. 1753.
[4] L. H. J., Aug. 1751; C. O. 5/374, G. C. O. P. Glen to B. T., Dec. 16, 1752; Glen to B. T., June 25, 1753; S. C. Gazette, Apr. 11, 1753. These last references concern later raids from the north.

until the summer of 1753. They kept the frontier in a turmoil which threatened to involve the English on the one side or the other. At one time Glen wanted to intervene on the side of the Cherokees, but the assembly considered that tribe to be the more dangerous. When Glen urged the building of a frontier fort, the assembly reminded him of the ruinous condition of the fortifications of Charlestown and elsewhere. In September, 1752, occurred the great hurricane which utterly wrecked the defences of Charlestown. Upon the repair of the damage thus wrought attention was centered for months. Thus affairs drifted on until the summer of 1753, when Glen succeeded in bringing first the head men of the Cherokees and later those of the Creeks to Charlestown. Peace was concluded between the Indians and as a result the frontier for a time became quiet.[1] The Creeks complained that one occasion of their troubles was the encroachment of settlers in Georgia on their lands, especially when the original understanding had been that the Indians had granted them only the temporary use of the land. These complaints it was believed were the result of the influence of the Bosomworths while the trader McGillivray was furnishing Reynolds, the new governor of Georgia,[2] evidence that the French at Mobile were constantly stirring up the Indians against the English. The low prices paid for skins and furs was another grievance and it was with difficulty and by the aid of presents that Glen in this matter was able to maintain the existing ratio except in the case of flints and ammunition. These had to be lowered. For the conduct of Georgia Glen of course could disclaim responsibility. It was the Cherokees, however, who had insulted the English and committed the chief outrages upon them and Glen with the South Carolina government has been blamed for not taking occasion at this time to punish them for their treachery. If it was an error, the whites were soon to suffer for it, when the two Indian peoples, Creeks and Cherokees, united to overrun the English frontier. The uncertain value of the peace which had been concluded is indicated by the

[1] C. O. 5/374, O. P. S. C. July 1, 1753. Logan *op. cit.*, 451 *et seq.*; McCrady, Royal Govt., 305.

[2] C. O. 5/644 O. P. Ga., Reynolds to B. T., Dec. 1754.

fact that the Cherokee chieftain Attakullakulla, soon to become so famous under the designation of Little Carpenter, made his advent as a diplomatist and leader of his people at this time. As a young man he had gone with Cuming's Cherokee embassy to England and there had been impressed with the power of the great king. But later he had fallen under French influence and thus in true Indian fashion had come to balance between the two interests, on the whole with a leaning toward the English which was probably the result of a shrewd estimate of future possibilities.

The conclusion of these treaties, together with a reasonable provision for the defence of other parts of the province, cleared the way for the building of the fort in the lower Cherokee country. Nearly twenty years had passed since such a plan as this had first been proposed. The board of trade had always supported the project, as it usually did in such cases. But the obstacle had been financial. But now the pressure of conditions on the frontier had become so strong that it had induced the assembly to appropriate £3000 in currency for the fort. On the advice of the council the governor himself now visited the upper country in the fall of 1753 [1] and the site for Fort Prince George was selected at Keowee, a Cherokee village in the northwestern part of the province, about 170 miles above Fort Moore. The land on which the structure was built was bought from the Indians and a tract of the width of the fort and extending westward to Long Canes was expressly included in the purchase. But the English acted on the supposition that a large tract, including the later counties of Abbeville, Edgefield, Laurens, Union, Spartanburg, Newberry, Chester, Fairfield and Richland, had been included in the grant. Glen even stated, in his report to the assembly, that many thousand acres of the best land in America had been bought. This was not the truth; like so many other claims of the kind, it provoked much trouble in the future.

Events soon began to move more rapidly and to show that the building of the fort had come too late, if it was intended to bring peace on the frontier. In 1754, sixteen

[1] C. O. 5/374 O. P. S. C. Glen to B. T., Oct. 25, 1753, Aug. 26, 1754; Logan, Upper S. C. 494; McCrady, *op. cit.*, 306; U. H. J., Nov. 7, 1754.

members of a party of recent immigrants from Pennsylvania were massacred by French Indians near Buffalo Creek in that very region. Governor Dinwiddie, of Virginia, was already calling for the aid of the colonies generally against the threatened occupation of the Ohio valley and invasion of his province by the French and Indians. The British government was supporting this demand, and Charles Pinckney of the council of South Carolina, but now in London as a spokesman for the governor, memorialized the board of trade in a report that the French designed to build a fort in the upper Cherokee country. At present, he said, the Cherokees were rejecting the overtures of the French, but they might not do so if the French got possession of the Ohio; and, if the French got a footing among the over-hills Cherokees, they would soon be masters of the whole nation. Then South Carolina and Georgia, with only two independent companies available and about 6200 men at call, would be seriously imperilled.[1] Glen held another conference with Cherokee leaders at Saluda Old Town, which, if Glen's statements are to be trusted, was the most important he had yet held. It was largely attended by head men of the tribe, and goods to the value of £600 were distributed among them. In return a surrender of their territory to the English was alleged to have been made, a story being at the same time told by Ludwick Grant, an aged Indian trader, that no surrender had been made in Cuming's time.[2] Glen used these accounts to bolster up his reputation after his recall and the only possible conclusion is that both transactions were in a legal sense worthless and that by Glen's time the Cherokees had been so corrupted by both French and English bribes that rival factions or groups among them could be brought together who would promise anything. Though the efforts of Glen may have staved off the effects of Braddock's defeat for the time, it could hardly be for long. The change of executives, which was now imminent, made this all the more

[1] C. O. 5/374, O. P. S. C., June, 1754. B. T. in a representation to the king, Dec. 24, 1756, put the number in Georgia at 750 and in South Carolina at 5500, C. O. 5/403. E. B. S. C.

[2] C. O. 5/375, O. P. S. C. Glen to B. T., Apr. 14, 1756, inclosing a variety of papers, among them being Ludwick Grant's Relation of facts delivered to Glen.

certain.   William Henry Lyttleton was already appointed in England as Glen's successor, though he did not arrive and assume office until a year later.

By that time, under the pressure of French competition and with the coöperation of Virginia the project had been launched of building another fort, this time west of the mountains in the upper Cherokee country near the head-waters of the Tennessee. Though South Carolinians were jealous of interference by Virginia in Cherokee affairs, which they thought their peculiar province,[1] Glen and Dinwiddie corresponded at length upon this matter and their letters were in due course laid before the assembly at Charlestown. It was the opinion of the governors that, as indicated in the letters from the secretary of state concerning the expenses of the war, the cost of this fort would be paid, at least in part, from the royal exchequer. In March, 1755, while the subject of defence in general was under consideration, a conference committee reported its inference from the correspondence that the entire cost of the fort was to be borne by the crown, but that if that was not true all the colonies from Virginia to Georgia should be called upon to contribute toward it.[2]   It would be a presumption to expect South Carolina to build the fort alone, though she would advance her share.   Relations with the Creeks meantime became delicate, because of their demand for cheaper goods and the control which the French and Spanish were steadily securing over their trade. It was therefore necessary to consider the dispatch of an agent to them and finally to bring their head man to Charlestown for a conference.[3]   The Acadian refugees had recently arrived in the province and must be provided for, while, as we shall see, a controversy was in progress between the council and house. The question of the fort therefore drifted on until the beginning of 1756. Glen now brought it up again and stated that it would probably cost about £5000 [4] toward which Dinwiddie had contributed

[1] See journals of the session of Sept. 1754, report of joint committee on grant of aid to Virginia.

[2] L. H. J. Mar., 11, 1755.

[3] *Ibid.*, Sess. of Sept. 1755; L. H. J., Jan. 1756.

[4] James Wright, as agent of South Carolina, stated in a memorial to the king, in 1757, that it cost £7000; C. O. 5/375, O. P. S. C., Nov. 24, 1757.

£1000. Glen told the assembly that he had promised the Indians that the fort should be built and Little Carpenter represented that they were impatient that the promise should be kept. The house responded fully to the governor's desire and was ready to appropriate £1000 sterling, but because of its controversy with the council this failed. Glen, however, took the matter into his own hands and sent a force to coöperate with the hundred men dispatched from Virginia under orders from the earl of Loudon. In this way the fort which was named after the earl, was built in 1756, and the Indians were restrained from an outbreak for a little longer. Captain Raymond Demeré, in whom on several occasions Glen had shown his confidence, was placed in command of this post.[1]

Relations with the Cherokees did not essentially change until 1759. They sent parties to the assistance of General Forbes in his expedition against Fort Duquesne. Little Carpenter went among them, but deserted with nine warriors, all of whom were arrested by order of the general and disarmed. Another party later deserted and on their way home committed murders in North Carolina. Still another band, who were returning after the close of the expedition, quarrelled with Virginians on the frontier about some horses. The young warriors now escaped, as usual, from the control of the older men and began to commit outrages on the Carolina frontier. A few of the leading chiefs after an interview with Captain Demeré went to Keowee for ammunition and, being refused it there, proceeded to Charlestown. They were without authority from their people, but appeared to be sincere in their desire for peace. Governor Ellis, of Georgia, had also been asked by the chiefs of the nations to use his good offices in the same direction. But Lyttleton treated the Indians who now visited him, one of whom stood very high in their council, with great haughtiness, and at the end of prolonged conferences took them with him, practically as prisoners, to Fort Prince George, whither he now went at the head of a military force to secure peace on the frontier. Little Carpenter was summoned and a conference

---

[1] On one occasion Demeré had been sent to St. Augustine to negotiate in reference to the return of fugitive slaves.

was held, in December, 1759. Here the governor continued his haughty and boastful tone and demanded that twenty Indians should be delivered up for punishment in reprisal for the murders they had committed. Though a treaty was signed and chiefs were left in the fort as hostages till the murderers should be punished, at the end the Indians were more enraged than ever.[1] The governor and his force returned to Charlestown without any cost to the colony except a considerable sum of money.

But at once outrages were resumed on the frontier and one of the first victims was the commander of Fort Prince George himself; enraged at his fate the garrison murdered all the hostages. The flame of war now spread through the entire region and, just as the conflict was beginning, Lyttleton, the man whose conduct certainly had contributed much toward precipitating it, was transferred to the governorship of Jamaica " as a fresh mark of his majesty's favor." [2]   Lieutenant Governor Bull, who had not approved of the course followed by Lyttleton, was left to help guide the colony through the crisis. Thomas Pownall, who had been governor of Massachusetts, was appointed with the full rank of governor as Lyttleton's successor, but he did not come to the province and it was not until the close of 1761 that Thomas Boone was transferred from New Jersey and superseded Bull during a brief administration.

The military conditions which had been established in America during the fourth intercolonial war — now approaching its close — were such as to revolutionize the conditions of Indian warfare. Their effects first became apparent in the present conflict with the Cherokees. General Amherst could spare an abundance of regulars for the service and, though they were pretty sure in the end to make thorough work of the savages, they came and went under the orders of a distant commander and the local governor, for all his patrol rangers, troops and other forces of militia, was left in a decidedly subordinate position. In April, 1760, 1200

---

[1] C. O. 5/403, E. B. S. C. B. T. to Pitt, Feb. 21, 1760, and C. O. 5/376, O. P. S. C.   The letters of Lyttleton, Bull and others concerning this war are in these volumes.

[2] C. O. 5/403, E. B. S. C. B. T. to Lyttleton, Nov. 14, 1759.

men were first sent from New York under Colonel Montgomery, these including a Highland regiment which was to remain as a garrison in Charlestown. With the exception of Oglethorpe's regiment this was the only considerable body of British regulars which had ever appeared in South Carolina or Georgia.[1] They marched promptly into the country of the Lower Cherokees, destroying their villages and destroying their crops east of the mountains from the region of Keowee to beyond the limits of North Carolina. Then, as ordered by his chief, Montgomery returned to New York as quickly as he had come. This sealed the fate of Fort Loudon. Before militia from Virginia who had been levied for the purpose could come to its relief, it was starved into surrender. On the following day, in revenge for the hostages who had been killed at Fort Prince George, Demeré and 26 others were slain. At the instance of Little Carpenter, the life of Captain Stuart, the second in command, was saved in order that he might aid them, with the supply of cannon and powder which they now had, to capture Fort Prince George.

By Stuart, Bull was informed of the fate of Fort Loudon and the peril of Fort Prince George. Another appeal was sent to Amherst for aid and Colonel James Grant was sent to take command of the Highlanders at Charlestown, while Bull raised a militia regiment which was led by Thomas Middleton. Under Middleton served Laurens, Moultrie, Marion, Huger, and Pickens of later Revolutionary fame. In the early summer of 1761 this force relieved Fort Prince George and ravaged the middle Cherokee country till all its towns were destroyed and its inhabitants slain or driven across the mountains. The Creeks had not come, as was found, to the assistance of their neighbors and for the time the Cherokees were thoroughly humbled. Little Carpenter, after the troops had retired, sued for peace at Charlestown, and it was granted him by Bull in a kindly spirit.

The spirit of independence which was characteristic of South Carolina and the disposition of the assembly to give a broad interpretation to its power were much in evidence and were stimulated by the activities of the time. In 1748

---

[1] For the independent companies, see Smith, S. C. as a Royal Prov., 192.

Governor Glen,[1] in a letter to the board of trade, described with his usual eloquence the extent to which the assembly by its encroachments upon the executive had drawn to itself the powers of government in the province. The list of officials, including the treasurer, commissary, Indian commissioner, powder receiver, controller of duties, who were chosen by the assembly, and commissioners of the market, workhouse, pilots, fortifications and the like, with executive functionaries which they appointed, bore unmistakable testimony to the truth of what he said. Ecclesiastical preferments were disposed of by the people and the governor was not even prayed for in the churches though the assembly had prayers constantly offered up for itself during sessions. The assembly, in short, attempted to direct everything. The council might correct this, but, as many of its members lived at a great distance from the capital, it was divorced too much from the governor and now he was excluded from any share in its legislative sessions. The conservative and loyalist spirit of the governor reached its fullest expression when he came to denounce the ballot, used in the colonies, as " a vile Venetian juggle " which tended " to destroy that noble generous openness that is characteristic of an Englishman." The requirement of so large a number as nineteen members to constitute a quorum often proved a hindrance to business, and was a minor evil which should be removed. And yet, notwithstanding these loud complaints, which the reader must believe, in Glen's case, were intended in part to strengthen him with officials at Westminster, who had been severely criticising him, he maintained on the whole very friendly relations with the assembly throughout a long administration.

Somewhat heated controversies, however, occurred in the course of Glen's governorship, but they were chiefly between the two houses. These began over the appointment of an agent. Peregrine Fury had held this position under successive appointments since 1731.[2] In 1747, perhaps because he failed to secure the approval by the crown of the paper money act of the previous year, the assembly passed a bill

[1] C. O. 5/372, O. P. S. C. Glen to B. T., Oct. 10, 1748.
[2] Smith, op. cit., 164 et seq.

for the appointment of John Sharpe as agent. The council amended by substituting the name of Fury, and on the report of a joint committee in favor of Fury the house acquiesced. But the next year James Crokatt, who had been a merchant in Charlestown but had now gone into business in London, was chosen in Fury's place. This appointment seems to have been viewed with disfavor by Glen,[1] who considered Crokatt as a possible opponent of himself. In 1753 Charles Pinckney, having been displaced from the chief justiceship in order to make room for Peter Leigh, removed with his family to England.[2] The appointment of Leigh, who had been high bailiff of Westminster and returning officer in one of the hotly contested elections of that borough, was one of the famous political deals of that period. Whether or not Pinckney was elected for the agency when he went to England, soon after his arrival there Crokatt wrote asking to be relieved on the ground that his duties as agent interfered with his private business, and suggested that Pinckney should be appointed. The council voted to accept Crokatt's resignation, but the assembly undertook to retain him. Glen desired to have Fury reappointed.

Somewhat later Crokatt wrote that he was willing to continue as agent. A violent dispute now arose between the houses over the payment of his salary. The assembly attempted by means of its control over money bills to provide for Crokatt's salary under the designation of writing, printing and other services for the public, without mentioning him by name and without his formal reëlection. Against this sharp practice the council protested and insisted that they should have the particulars of his services. Such an appointment also should be made jointly by governor, council, and assembly. The assembly now fell back upon its claims of exclusive right as representative of the people and declared " That no Account, Petition, or other Paper that shall be laid before the House for the future, of, for or concerning any claim or demand whatever for any matter or thing done or to be done for the service of the Public shall be sent to the council for their Inspection." This was made

---

[1] Journals of L. H. and U. H., June, 1747, May, 1749.
[2] McCrady, op. cit., 279; Ravenel, Life of Eliza Pinckney.

a standing rule of the house. The council angrily denied that Crokatt had any standing as agent without an election and insisted that he should not correspond with either house separately. Two tax bills were defeated as the result of this dispute and when, in May, 1755, the third one was brought forward, amid the clamor of public creditors for their money, the council yielded.[1] The house, having won this skirmish in its general battle for exclusive control of appropriations, agreed to the choice of another agent in the place of Crokatt. James Wright was selected and served until 1760, when, as we have seen, he was appointed governor of Georgia. Charles Garth then succeeded to the agency and held it until relations were broken off with England in 1775.

In the spring of 1756, when provisions for defence and the Acadians were especially needed, the houses again fell out over the tax bill. The council demanded vouchers and accounts on which the estimates were based. The house, in accordance with earlier resolutions, refused to send them. Glen pleaded for harmony, in order that provision might be made for building the fort in the Cherokee country. The house in reply declared that, if it could be shown that since the English Revolution accounts and vouchers had been sent to the house of lords, they would abandon their claim. To this impossible condition no response, of course, could be made and a short recess was taken. After business was resumed Glen, in a long address, took the ground, that though the council could not demand the accounts and vouchers as a right, they had previously had them and it had not caused much inconvenience, and the practice might be continued without injury to the right of the people. The house, in a remonstrance in which they flattered the governor on his knowledge of the British constitution, stated that the trouble had begun with objections on the part of the council to the disbursements of Crokatt, the agent, and this had been followed by their holding up for amendment a succession of appropriation bills. In view of the fact that the council was an appointed body, removable at pleasure, the blame rested upon it, and the governor was urged to procure the

---

[1] See Smith, *op. cit.*, and the Journals of the two houses for 1754 and till May, 1755.

removal of those who were responsible and their replacement by others, but if the assembly was wrong they wished he would dissolve it. By this adroit communication Glen was won over, and in his final reply to the house admitted that they had done right and the attitude of the council had been wrong, for this was not the time to dispute about rights; the council should have suspended their claims until a more suitable juncture, though without abandoning them. But he acknowledged the right of the council to reject many bills and saw no reason for suspending any of its members. If Glen really felt much sorrow over the encroachments of the assembly, as his previous letters to the board of trade indicated, it is difficult to see how he could have expressed himself in this way. One sees that he had been piqued by his exclusion from the legislative council and probably also by criticism on the part of the board of trade and, like Keith of Pennsylvania, was ready for a certain coöperation with the assembly, with which he had always been on reasonably good terms. With Glen's consent the remonstrance of the assembly was published, but no appropriation was secured.

With this Glen's administration closed. When the assembly was called together again, soon after the arrival of Lyttleton, a deadlock was again threatened, but on the advice of the new governor the council gave way and the appropriation bill was passed. A separate schedule of amendments was sent down by the council, but this the house refused to read.[1] Among the publications in the "Gazette" which were occasioned by this controversy was a notable argument, supposed to be from the pen of Thomas Wright, son of the former chief justice and brother of the future governor of Georgia. The purpose of this was to prove that since the failure of the attempt of the proprietors to create a nobility, the legislature consisted solely of the governor as the representative of the crown and the assembly as representative of the people. The council was not like a house of peers, but simply a body of advisers to the governor, their existence and powers were derived solely from the governor's instructions, they held during pleasure, were not

[1] Smith, *op. cit.*, 321–325; L. H. J. and U. H. J. for April, May and June, 1756, S. C. Gazette, May 6, 13 and 22, 1756.

summoned by writ, and were represented by those members of the assembly whom they helped to elect. Therefore the writer denied that the council was legally an upper house and enlarged upon the inconsistencies involved in its assuming at times to act in that capacity while it was really only a part of the colonial executive. An upper house could be created only by act of parliament and not by royal instructions. Instructions, the writer continued, were binding only on the executive, being enforced by means of removals, but they were not binding on the people, else there would be no need of assemblies and laws could be passed and taxes levied by instruction. Many instructions had certainly not been executed, because laws had not been passed for the purpose. And, whether the council was an upper house or not, it was absurd for it to demand the accounts when it could neither increase nor lessen the sums named in the tax bill. This stands among the earlier, as it does among the most excellent, statements of what the colonists were beginning to become conscious of as their point of view respecting the important questions involved. But, like all such statements, it set forth an ideal, toward which political and social conditions in the colonies were slowly tending, rather than the actual law or facts of the case. The pointing out of inconsistencies, especially in a British constitution or practice under it, could never serve by itself as a disproof of the facts of the case. Under the flexible constitution which existed in the colonies as in Great Britain, there could be no doubt that the council had held substantially the position which their defenders now claimed for them. It was the keystone of the arch of provincial government and on its being kept in place or thrust aside depended largely the perseverance of that structure. Around it, in many colonies, some of the hottest battles were waged. Before the statements of the writer could be accepted as in harmony with the facts the councils must be entirely shorn of their legislative powers and circumstances so weakened that by instructions the crown could not influence or control legislation. That situation certainly had not yet been reached and it is doubtful if it could be reached without undermining the power of the British executive over the colonies. Since the struggle for supremacy of the assembly in South Carolina as a royal province had begun, about 1725, great strides had been made by that body. As everywhere else, advantage was taken of financial needs to wrest from the council its right to amend money bills or to have any knowledge of the nature of the items of which they were composed. As incidents of the struggle executive functions were assumed by the assembly and appointments made that were unwelcome to the executive. As a result of the whole, the balance of political power was readily being transferred to the lower house, and the governor, as we have seen, was fully conscious of the fact.

But, so far as South Carolina was concerned, the process stopped for a time at the close of Glen's administration. During that of Lyttleton and those which immediately followed controversy was silenced by the necessities of war and discussion of constitutional questions remained in abeyance until after the end of our period.

CHAPTER XIV

WESTWARD EXPANSION AND THE ALBANY CONGRESS
OF 1754

As was customary after the close of the colonial wars, bickering between the Canadian authorities and officials especially of New York and Massachusetts continued for about two years after 1748 over the exchange of prisoners. Many letters upon the subject were exchanged between La Galissonière and his British rivals, but he had returned to France and had been succeeded by La Jonquière before a settlement was reached.[1] A few white men and Indians were held as prisoners on both sides. Those who were held by the British were partly in Boston or vicinity, and partly in Albany or among the Mohawks. Some of the French had been captured at sea and, being brought into New York, numbers of them were sent to the West Indies for exchange. So far as those captured on the northern frontier were concerned, exchanges were made piecemeal, a few at a time, others being retained on various pretexts, this course of conduct furnishing an excuse for mutual reproaches and charges of bad faith. The French complained because part of their prisoners in New York were allowed to remain in the custody of the Mohawks, while it was claimed that all British prisoners were under the immediate care of the French themselves. The exchange of prisoners was made a pretext for attempts, especially on the part of the French, to lure the Iroquois to Canada for negotiations and trade. This was opposed by the English on the ground that they were subjects. This claim the French of course denied and insisted that in the recent war the Iroquois as a whole had been at peace with them and hostile relations had existed only with the Mohawks. Indians who were held in jail in Canada sent urgent messages to their friends to come there and by negotiation

---

[1] N. Y. Col. Docs., VI, 452, 488 et seq.; X, 185–199, 209–216.

secure their release. Johnson worked actively to prevent such a course as this and succeeded.[1] Early in 1750 royal orders were issued in Europe for a general exchange of prisoners.[2] But after that occurred negotiations continued about some Abenakis said to be still in New England, as well as certain prisoners which New York and Canada had not exchanged [3] and midsummer, 1750, had arrived before Clinton could write to the duke of Bedford, the secretary of state, that the exchange had been made. The British in New York had received twenty-four and the Canadians thirteen, but the latter had persuaded thirteen to change their religion and remain in Canada.

In the process of colonization, expansion, or empire building, by whatever name it is described, land and trade are the two impersonal objects sought, while increase in the number of the populations involved, with their physical and spiritual improvement, and that of the world at large, is the only justifiable and ultimate goal of the effort. A treatment of the subject which throws any one of these three elements into the foreground, to the neglect or undue obscuring of the others, is one-sided and inadequate. In tracing the development of the Anglo-American colonies during the eighteenth century we have now reached a point where the influence resulting from the slow but steady expansion of more than a century began to make itself decisively felt upon the question of the balance between the French and the British on the continent. The colonies of both nations had been expanding, but in different ways, and by virtue of this the character of the two movements had been made apparent. The expansion of the French had been the result of exploration and trade, following the river and lake systems of the St. Lawrence and Mississippi and extending through vast spaces in the interior of the continent. It had started from the lower St. Lawrence and extended westward through the region of the Great Lakes and thence down the Ohio and Mississippi to the Gulf of Mexico. There the province of Louisiana had been founded, and from Mobile

[1] N. Y. Col. Docs., VI, 512, 517, 520, 525; Stone's Johnson, I, 371, 374.
[2] N. Y. Col. Docs., VI, 544.   [3] Ibid., 562 et seq., 578.

and New Orleans as centres a reflex movement up the Mississippi and northeastward toward the Carolinas had been started. The two had met in the Illinois country and as the result a chain of trading posts had been established connecting Canada and Louisiana. The process had been a quiet and a rapid one and its effect seemed to be to block the westward advance of the British and to preëmpt the interior of the continent for the French. Such was the hope of the French when, by the middle of the century, this stage in the process had been reached. It was also the fear of the leaders among the British when, at the same time, they awoke to a sense of what had been accomplished.

Viewed superficially, the achievement of the French was brilliant and impressive. It had been carried to success by means of the fur trade with the Indian tribes of the Great Lakes and upper Mississippi. With an irresistible passion for the wild and lawless life of the forest, the most active and adventurous part of the male population of Canada rushed into the fur trade and spread themselves in small and widely detached bodies throughout the interior of the continent.[1] Neither the restraints of the Church or the government, nor the monopoly of trading companies, could control or regulate their action. Wherever they went they spread among the natives the blighting influence of French brandy and lust, and with a total disregard of the conditions of the market coöperated with the savages in the rapid reduction or exhaustion of the stock of fur-bearing animals throughout large sections of the west. A few priests and soldiers followed in the wake of the *coureurs de bois* and a chain of trading posts, located at strategic centres, was established. In this way, and by means of such treaties and alliances with the Indians as accompanied the process, the claims of the French were extended over vast areas, but such occupation of the soil or spread of population as to give a firm support to the claims was not effected. The agriculturists, the substantial part of the Canadian population, were confined to the lower

---

[1] The classic description of this phenomenon is in Chap. 17 of Parkman's "Old Régime in Canada." The significance of the fur trade in American history has been incisively discussed by McIlwain in the Introduction to his edition of Wraxall's "Abridgement of the Indian Affairs." Harvard Hist. Studies, XXI See his references to the literature of the subject.

St. Lawrence valley and there they remained. Scarcely any foreign trade developed, furs and certain minor products being exported to France. The population never even reached a hundred thousand in number and their rate of increase, rapid though it was, was never such as to enable them to spread far into the interior. Above Montreal settlements were very scattering. The European French have never been a migrating people and, after the Huguenots had been excluded from New France, there was no longer a chance for a large influx of people from the Old World. The portals of New France were even more closely barred against the victims of old world persecution than were those of New England, and it was from this class that America received its largest and most valuable reinforcement. It therefore follows that French colonization in North America, romantic, daring, bold in conception and execution though it was, favored also by certain great natural advantages, as a political and social fabric was weak and unsubstantial. The government of the French possessed the military strength which results from autocracy; such strength as comes from perfect unity and the exclusion or repression of all dissent belonged to its religion. But notwithstanding these, Canada found its chief protection in its inaccessibility, in the frigid cold of its long winters, and in the almost impregnable strength of the citadel at Quebec. Louisiana and the Illinois country did not seriously count. For military purposes their imposing array of Indian allies, though necessary, were quite as much a source of weakness as of strength. When it came to the final test, the chief contribution of the west was the *coureurs de bois* who came back to fight for the lilies of France.

The propriety, reason or necessity for the long struggle between the French and British for supremacy in Europe and in the world outside has been touched upon elsewhere and need not detain us here. What concerns us now is the position of the British colonies on the North American continent as compared with the dependencies of France. The word "type" has been borrowed from the natural sciences to indicate what is characteristic in social and political organization. So far as that term is applicable, it may be used here, though in a very general sense, briefly and upon a subject the general nature of which is well known. No fact is more familiar than this, that in all important respects the British colonies were the opposite of the French. They were situated along the Atlantic seaboard, within a temperate region as to climate, exposed to approach from abroad and dominated by no single river system. They had been settled at a variety of different centres along a coast a thousand miles in length, and by colonists who were moved by a variety of motives. A multiple system of colonies, instead of a single province, had resulted. The settlers became mainly agriculturists on a large or small scale. Certain trade centres developed, through which an active commerce not only with Great Britain but with other parts of the world was carried on. The fur trade was also prosecuted in various degrees in all the colonies.

From those regions which lay adjacent to the frontier large numbers of fur traders were continuously sent into the wilderness, and the morals which they exhibited and the methods which they pursued were not essentially different from those of the French, except that they usually failed to conceal in any manner their brutality or dishonesty by the *bonhommie* which made the Gaul so attractive. The grossness of the Englishman or Dutchman was not usually relieved by a show of wit or manners. With the British, as with the French, Indian relations were closely connected with the fur trade, especially so far as they affected the remoter tribes. The alliance with the Iroquois also rested to a large extent on this trade. But in the case of nearly all the colonies the extension of settlement and pressure of population, steadily encroaching on the hunting grounds of the natives, constituted the most important element in the problem. The British advanced slowly but steadily, like an organized army, toward the west, and only now and then planted a trading post, like Oswego, some distance in advance of the main line of settlement. Until a late period they had little knowledge of the interior, and showed little curiosity concerning it. They were not bold explorers, but rested their claims on the original sea to sea charters rather than on expeditions along the water ways of the west and the planting of trading posts at remote points.

To a certain extent the principles on which their government rested were autocratic, but these as time went on were more and more obscured by the influence of the representative assemblies and the policies of self government which in all the colonies emanated from them. Though the English, Scotch and Scotch Irish, with other components which made up the mass of the colonists, were combative by nature, made so by their religion and their inherited ideas and qualities in general, they were also strongly individualistic and frugal. They had not been reared under the military monarchies of the continent of Europe and, unlike the French, were not accustomed to move at the word of command. Their assemblies controlled the purse and in the great majority of cases, where the assemblies did not control the government, strained relations existed between them and the colonial executives. The pressure exerted by the imperial government in support of its executives was weak and ineffective. Therefore the forces which tended toward military efficiency were not strong, and the crude militia systems which were established when the colonies were founded continued essentially unchanged. The particularism of the different colonies, as directly expressed through the assemblies, made it very difficult, if not impossible, for them to unite in joint measures of offence or even of defence, unless they were directly imperilled. No machinery for securing joint action among them had yet been devised, and in time of need the only resort was to exhortations by the British government, requisitions in the form of quotas, and occasionally direct military assistance from the same quarter. In no respect was the difference between the French and the British in North America greater than in the adaptability of their political systems to the effective prosecution of war. So far inferior were the British to the French in this respect that, though in natural combativeness the two peoples were not unlike, it went far to counteract a superiority on the part of the British in population of about fifteen to one.

As the middle of the eighteenth century approached, the expansion of these two peoples had reached a point where they became fully conscious of each other's presence. As they believed themselves to be natural enemies, and that, as it were, by divine decree fitly reflected in the terrestrial order, the only natural relation between them was one of hostile rivalry, and each began to protect itself according to the approved methods of the time against its opponent. This method involved rapid and decisive advance or aggression at pivotal points or along lines where frontiers approached most closely. The object of this was to seize desirable territory, confirm the hold on trade routes, favorably influence the Indian tribes and thus confirm and extend trade relations and treaties of alliance with them. All this was done with about equal rapidity by both the British and French during the years which immediately followed the treaty of Aix la Chapelle. While commissioners at Paris were vainly trying to find an adjustment of boundaries which might be permanent, soldiers and traders under authority from their governments were pushing forward and upsetting previous arrangements. As events rapidly succeeded one another, it became evident that, though the last war had been sluggish, the peace which concluded it was likely to be only a brief truce, and the slow gathering of forces in the wilderness and along the frontier, as well as in Europe, was preparing for a more decisive struggle than any which had preceded. The place of Indian relations in this crisis, including those of trade and territory combined, together with the move toward colonial union which they helped to induce, it is now our duty to trace.

The stream of immigrants which for more than a quarter of a century had been pouring into Pennsylvania and thence spreading westward and southward, had now carried the line of the British frontier well up to the Appalachians. In the region of Pennsylvania and Virginia, this was a fact of great and immediate significance, because just opposite on the west lay the valley of the Ohio, the central line of approach to the Illinois country and the Mississippi. Into that region, as scouts despatched on ahead of the main line, British fur traders were being sent in unusually large numbers. The Indian tribes of the Ohio region, among whom these traders now sought an increasing influence, were Delawares, Shawnees and Wyandots. Among them were also fragments of other tribes from Canada. West of them, on the Miami and Wabash, lived the confederacy of the Miami or Twightwees, and still further west the Illinois, left after their defeat by the Iroquois. The native population of this region was of mixed origin, tribes and fragments of tribes which had been brought together by wars and recent migrations. The Shawnees in particular were newcomers after extended and somewhat mysterious wanderings up and down the interior of the continent. Over the Ohio region and its peoples the Iroquois claimed, by virtue of their earlier conquests, a vague right of control, and this the British insisted had been transferred to them by the treaties of 1701 and later. The long and bloody feud between the Illinois and the Iroquois, however, had proved indecisive and the former confederacy still retained considerable strength.[1] Traders from Pennsylvania and Virginia, however, were now crowding into this region, and it was these colonies, rather than New York, which were forcing the question of the Ohio country and its Indians to the front.[2] The plans which Spotswood had suggested, when he wrote about building a fort on Lake Erie and thus giving life to the claim of Virginia to a vast extension northwestward, were now beginning to come to fruition. Among the Indians of the Ohio the one who was most devoted to the British interest was Old Britain, called by the French La Demoiselle, the head of the Miami confederacy, whose town on Loramie Creek was called by the English Pickawillany. This was fortified with a stockade in 1750 and became the centre of the British trading interest for the entire region.[3] The pushing of English trade interests in this region irritated the French, who came down from Detroit, and murders were not infrequently committed by both parties in the brutal fashion of attack and reprisal familiar to the wilderness. In 1748 Pennsylvania sent George Croghan with presents to the Twightwees and those Indians in turn sent deputies to Lancaster, where they agreed to have nothing more to do with the French. Later in the year Weiser visited Logstown, about eighteen miles below the fork of the Ohio, where a

[1] Goodman, The Journal of Captain William Trent; Fernow, in The Ohio Valley in Colonial Days, traces the relations of the Iroquois to this region.

[2] Goodman, op. cit., p. 42, gives a long list of traders licensed by Pennsylvania about this time to go into the western country.

[3] Goodman, 43.

general treaty on behalf of Pennsylvania and Virginia was
held with the various tribes of the Ohio region.[1] As a result
of this treaty it was hoped that the trade of those tribes
had been secured for the British and that Pennsylvania
would reap the chief benefit from it.

In 1747 and 1748, moved perhaps by the activity of Pennsylvania, a number of prominent Virginians took what was
intended to be a decisive step toward opening up the Ohio
valley for settlement, by forming a partnership and applying
to the crown for a large grant of land west of the mountains.[2]
The application was made through Governor Gooch, not
long before the end of his administration, and among the
petitioners were John Hanbury, a London merchant, and
Thomas Lee, Thomas Nelson, Colonel Cresap, William
Thornton, John Carlisle, Lawrence and Augustine Washington, and George Fairfax. George Mason subsequently became an active member. The board of trade reported
favorably upon the plan, and the committee of the council
ordered that the governor of Virginia be instructed to issue
the grant as desired. It was to be located on both sides of
the Ohio river between the Monongahela and the Kanawha.
A tract of 200,000 acres was to be first surveyed on condition
that, within seven years, one hundred families be settled upon
it and a fort built, all at the expense of the company, and
that the usual conditions as to quit rents be observed.
When these terms should be complied with, 300,000 acres
additional should be granted, making a total of 500,000 acres.
This was the origin of the famous Ohio Company. In applying for its grant express reference was made to the concession
made by the Indians of that territory at Lancaster in 1744,
and in the grant the promotion of trade with the western
tribes was mentioned as a leading object, as well as settlement and defence.

The first important step taken by the Ohio Company was

[1] Watson, Life of Weiser, 186–194.
[2] Fernow, *op. cit.*, p. 240 *et seq.* Darlington in his edition of the Journals
of Christopher Gist, 220–240, prints the chief documents relating to the Ohio
Company. See also a contemporary pamphlet, written in defence of Newcastle and his government at the beginning of the war — "The Conduct of
the Ministry impartially Examined in a Letter to the Merchants of London,"
1756.

to employ Christopher Gist, in September, 1750, a frontiersman of English descent who lived in western North Carolina, to make a tour of exploration as far as the falls of the Ohio. Dinwiddie had then become governor of Virginia and a member of the company, and by him Gist's instructions were issued. Gist was to note the passes through the mountains, observe the courses of the rivers and report in particular upon tracts of fertile and accessible land which should be large enough for a settlement. In successive journeys during the next two years, of which he kept brief journals,[1] Gist explored large parts of the present states of Ohio, Kentucky and West Virginia, with parts also of western Maryland and southwestern Pennsylvania.

In the course of his first and most important journey Gist traversed the route from Colonel Thomas Cresap's, at Old Town on the Potomac river in western Maryland, by the way of Indian paths and the Juniata river to Shannopin's Town, later Pittsburg, at the junction of the Allegheny and Monongahela rivers. At Logstown he met a parcel of traders from Pennsylvania whom he found "reprobate" and too inquisitive about his business in that region. Gist quieted them by referring to himself as the bearer of a message from the king and by inquiring for the half-breed Andrew Montour who, with George Croghan, was busily employed as agent of Pennsylvania in that region. Passing westward through what is now southern Ohio, he came to an important town of the Wyandots near the Muskingum, where Croghan had a trading house. There Gist met both Croghan and Montour and learned of recent captures of English traders by the French and of the building of a fort to the northward. A Protestant service was held and by presents and speeches an effort was made to promote friendly relations with the natives. Croghan and Montour accompanied Gist westward, and on the Scioto further conferences were held, with Delawares and Shawnees. At Pickawillany the most important series of councils were held by Gist and his companions, and treaties of friendship concluded. But the harmony was interrupted by the arrival of four Ottawas with a French flag, a gift

---

[1] His journals are reprinted by Darlington, with abundant topographical comment.

of brandy and tobacco and an invitation to the Indians to visit Detroit. But the French envoys were at once dismissed by the chief with a message of defiance, and festivities in honor of the British were continued with the special feature of an Indian feather dance. But owing to fear of the French Indians to the westward, Gist did not continue as far as the falls of the Ohio, but turned southward and crossed to the southern bank of the river, whence he returned through the rugged and mountainous region of what is now West Virginia and submitted his report to Dinwiddie and his fellow partners.

The company had now imported goods from England [1] and had built a trading house on the south bank of the Potomac, opposite the mouth of Wills Creek, on which is located the present city of Cumberland in Maryland. In 1751 Gist was sent from this point on another journey through the region to the south of the Ohio and as far as the Big Kanawha. This lasted into the following year and was accompanied with invitations to a conference at Logstown, which it was intended to hold in 1752. It was also the intention of the company to construct a road from Wills Creek to the fork of the Monongahela, and to build a fort in the neighborhood of its western terminus as an outpost for defence and a centre for Indian trade. A town, it was expected, would grow up around it. Thus it was proposed, by means of a private company organized directly under the authority of the British government, to extend the territory of Virginia and the crown and plant the British flag permanently beyond the Alleghanies — a method of expansion so effectively used by the English, to say nothing of other nations, in all quarters of the globe. The object of the conference at Logstown, which was held in May, 1753, by Joshua Fry and two other Virginians, and attended by Gist, Croghan and Montour, was to secure from the Indians a confirmation of the grant of western territory made to Virginia in the treaty of Lancaster in 1744. Since that date the concession had been disowned, but now in a private conference with Half King and other chiefs of the Six Nations its validity was

---

[1] C. O. 5/1326, O. P. Va., Lee to B. T., Oct. 18, 1749.

acknowledged.[1] All of these proceedings had the support of the board of trade and apparently also of the privy council, including an application for a number of small cannon for the company's projected fort on the Ohio.[2]

After the conclusion of the conference at Logstown, Fry, Lomax and Patten, as commissioners of Virginia, accompanied by Captain William Trent, left for the country of the Miamis to deliver to them the present which, at the instance of Governor Dinwiddie, was to be made to them also in the name of the king further to bind them in friendship to the English. When Trent and his companions reached the Miami country they learned that a body of French and Indians under Langlade had just surprised and destroyed the post at Pickawillany, killing Old Britain, one Englishman and a few Indians and carrying off others as prisoners.[3] This attack not only led to more urgent solicitation of the Indians for their support, but hastened the decision of the British to build a fort at the fork of the Ohio and also revealed more clearly the need of opening a road from Wills Creek to that point and building other posts on the way thither. These measures, as yet, lay within the sphere of Indian relations and the fur trade.

Before referring to the action of the other British colonies which were most directly concerned in these events, it is necessary to describe more clearly how the French who were most closely in touch with affairs viewed the crisis that was approaching. Among them, as well as the British, there was a question as to the relative value of their island colonies in the tropics and Canada and Louisiana, both so remote and inaccessible not only from Europe but from one another, and one of them hermetically sealed by snow and ice during half the year. But men like La Galissonière, La Jon-

---

[1] *Ibid.*, Burwell to B. T., Aug. 21, 1751. Darlington, *op. cit.*, 221, 234. An account of the treaty at Logstown was sent by Dinwiddie to the B. T. as an enclosure with his letter of Dec. 10, 1752. C. O. 5/1326. It was at this time that Virginia perfected on paper her claim to territory west and northwest to the Pacific. The map of Fry and Jefferson was sent in confirmation of it. C. O. 5/1356, Dec. 9, 1751, Apr. 14, 1752.

[2] C. O. 5/1367, May 10, 1753. Report of Committee of the Council on a report of the Ordnance Board concerning cannon. Darlington, *op. cit.*, 236.

[3] Goodman, The Journal of Capt. Trent, Pa. Col. Recs., V, 599.

quière and Duquesne, who during the next decade were at the head of affairs in Canada, had no doubt of the value of the colonies on the continent and of the necessity of preserving and extending them. La Galissonière, in a notable memorial written in 1750,[1] threw into the foreground the strategical considerations involved in the maintenance of Canada, the Illinois country as a connecting link between it and Louisiana, and Louisbourg as a bulwark of Canada toward the sea. Canada, because of its fertility, he considered as the centre of the system, from which chiefly must come the man power necessary to hold the British in check. Though it was likely long to be a burden to France, it must be maintained, he thought, as the strongest barrier against the British in war and trade. Notwithstanding the naval superiority of Great Britain, he did not think she would be able to conquer Canada except as the result of a rare combination of circumstances. In order to protect it from a land attack and promote the extension of French power in the interior, its outlying settlements and defences toward the west should be strengthened. The immediate objective which the writer had in view was the Ohio valley, which had been discovered by the French and now lay ready for their occupation. This should at once be undertaken as the necessary means for strengthening the system of Indian alliances and trade and obstructing the progress of the English. Niagara, Detroit and the other western posts should also be strengthened and the effect of all this on the attitude of the Iroquois could be awaited with confidence. One of the foundations upon which this argument rested was the French interpretation of the treaty of Utrecht, according to which it only bound them not to attack the Iroquois. The argument used was simply an expansion of that employed to justify the occupation of Niagara and all the earlier extensions of the French sphere of influence, and if the plan could be successfully executed the effect of the settlement of Oswego would be more than nullified. The news of the expedition of the previous year under Céleron de Bienville,[2] for the purpose of

[1] N. Y. Col. Docs., X, 220.

[2] The most thorough study of this is in the Historical Writings of Orsamus H. Marshall.

burying lead plates at points along the Ohio and displaying other signs of French occupation, had circulated most widely among the Indians, and all Europeans concerned noticed that the plan was already in process of execution. This was the first reply of the French to the creation of the Ohio Company, and its influence may be seen in all which the British subsequently did.

The building of Fort Rouillé at Toronto on the northern shore of Lake Ontario and the establishment of La Présentation, the mission to the Iroquois, at the site of the later city of Ogdensburg on the St. Lawrence, were further steps of importance in the advance of the French.[1] Father Piquet, the founder of the last named settlement, combined the zeal of the early French missionaries with the military and commercial instincts of the fur traders and the commandants of the western posts. He coöperated well with the younger Joncaire in ceaseless labors to win and hold the central and western cantons of the Iroquois to the French alliance. As an agent he served the aggressive policy of the later governors of Canada. The site which was chosen for Piquet and his mission was the one suggested years before by Clerambaut d'Aigremont. It was situated above the rapids of the St. Lawrence, whence communication was open to the Great Lakes beyond and from which it was to be hoped that trade could be diverted from Oswego. It was at the mouth of the Oswegatchie, in the midst of a rich and level agricultural region and accessible to the Iroquois country on the south. After the first stockade had been burned by the Indians, another fortified post was quickly built, furnished with a chapel, storehouse, barn, stable, ovens and a saw mill. Fields were planted with corn and beans, and partially converted Iroquois were attracted thither in numbers sufficient to stock three villages. An officer and garrison of soldiers with a few small cannon were furnished for the protection of the mission. La Présentation thus took its place beside Caughnawaga as a station where it was hoped that inroads might be made upon the fidelity of the Iroquois toward the English. As Conrad Weiser learned at

[1] N. Y. Col. Docs., X, 201, 203; Doc. Hist. of N. Y., I, 423 et seq.; Parkman, Montcalm and Wolfe, I.

Onondaga, Iroquois converts — of whom Piquet was said to have made a hundred at that place alone — were dressed in fine clothes, adorned with gold and silver lace, and taken to Montreal to be introduced to the governor and to be given presents.

In the summer of 1751 Piquet, accompanied by a number of his Indian converts, made a voyage around Lake Ontario. They visited Fort Frontenac which, under the destructive competition of Oswego, had ceased to be frequented by Indians for trade. The place was now far on in decline. Skirting the northern shore of the lake, the party visited the new post at Toronto and found a prosperous trade there and conditions good. By keeping there an ample supply of goods and brandy, Indians from the north and west were being drawn thither for trade and kept away from Oswego. Passing on to Niagara, Piquet met Joncaire and numbers of Senecas, by whom he was joyously received, won converts for his mission, viewed the falls and noted the advantages of the post for trade and the purposes of French dominion. On his return the falls of the Genesee were visited and the flotilla passed within sight of Chouaguen, the hated Oswego. Piquet did not land there, but passed near enough in his canoe to observe carefully its topography and strength as a defensive work. In his report Piquet dwelt upon the extent to which Oswego facilitated communication between the English and the western tribes, and on the superior cheapness of English goods at that market as compared with what the French were forced to charge. French liquor was preferred to the English, but that did not prevent the Indians going to Oswego. The place, in his opinion, should be destroyed and a French post built at Sodus bay, the entire southern shore of Lake Ontario being thus secured to the French. With exultant praise of La Présentation, the " key of the colony," which in two years without aid from the government he had founded and peopled with four hundred savages, Father Piquet closed his report.

Virginians were making their push into the Ohio valley and the French were meeting this with counter moves, partly military and partly commercial. New York and Pennsylvania were directly affected, while Massachusetts, especially when Shirley was present and at the head of the government, was watching developments from its standpoint as the colony which was chiefly responsible for the defence of the New England frontier. As the crisis became more acute, both parties redoubled their efforts to maintain and extend their Indian alliances, and the Six Nations, as always, occupied the centre of the stage. Owing to the vague overlordship which the Six Nations claimed over the various tribes north of the Ohio, as well as by the conflicting claims of the two competing European nations to that region, the Indians of the Ohio were inevitably drawn into the conflict. The old standing feud between the Iroquois and the Catawbas drew South Carolina within the fringe of these relations, and that fact, as well as the interests of the French on the lower Mississippi, revealed the possibility of joint, or at least contemporary, action along the entire frontier line. At a score of centres throughout this vast territory, and in Europe as well, the subtle web of frontier diplomacy was now being woven on a larger design and with greater speed than ever before. The weavers were not only Europeans of Gallic and British stock, but native Americans of many tribes, all working instinctively upon a pattern which, at the beginning, was faint in outline, but grew in distinctness as it developed under their hands. The material of which it was composed was the interests and claims, territorial, commercial and military, which they all had in the region involved, and the belief they all fondly cherished, that the type of society which each embodied was of the greatest value at least to themselves. The European also was in one form or another a crusader and had embarked on an endless campaign of world conquest. Assumptions of this kind, as well as equally exaggerated and unsubstantial territorial claims, were used by both these peoples as the flowers and other decorative figures wrought into the parts of the fabric of policy which they were weaving. Largely destitute of substantial truth they all were. Some were mere figments of the imagination, even more gigantic falsehoods than were usually palmed off by diplomatists in Europe. But they furnished material for the imagination, tickled national conceit and therefore furnished the chief interest of the game to the minds of those who set the rules and chiefly managed the play.

Maryland took but little interest, but we have seen Pennsylvania, since 1740 or earlier, taking a more and more prominent part in negotiations with the Indians, and her position, combined with the activities of her Indian agents seemed to indicate that she might take a leading share in the development of British interests along the Ohio. Her traders were active there. Weiser, by virtue of his long connection with both the Six Nations and the Pennsylvania Indians, seemed to be in a position to mediate among the tribes and perhaps to secure something like united action. As compared with Johnson, who was just rising to prominence in New York, Weiser was a veteran in the service and no one understood Indian character better than he. At first he was somewhat contemptuous toward Johnson, but relations which were at least outwardly friendly were always maintained between them. When, in June, 1749, letters and papers concerning Céleron de Bienville's expedition reached Philadelphia from New York, Croghan was ordered to go to Allegheny and send a trusty messenger to the lakes or eastward to discover what the French were doing and to put the Indians on their guard.[1] Governor James Hamilton, like the governors of New York and Virginia, instituted inquiries and gathered information respecting the extent of French claims and the danger they involved, and sent them early in 1750 to the board of trade. Thomas Penn thought that the governor, council and assembly should do something at once, as, for example, securing the privilege of settlement in the disputed region and building and garrisoning a fort there; the proprietors, he said, would contribute handsomely toward its cost and maintenance.[2] Croghan also gave encouraging reports concerning the attitude of the Indians in the Ohio region, though both thought Weiser and Johnson at times expressed fear lest the British interest among them was being wholly undermined and the French were winning them and the western Iroquois over to their alliance. But whatever truth there might be in these impressions, when Hamilton turned to the Quaker assembly, he found it willing, as had always been the case in the past, to appropriate money for presents

[1] Pa. Col. Recs., V, 387; Pa. Arch., II, 60–63.
[2] T. P. to Hamilton, Feb. 12, 1749/50. P. L. B., II, 295; Hamilton to T. P., Feb. 3, 1750/51. Off. Corr., V, 129.

and to meet the cost of negotiations with the Indians. Pennsylvania is said to have expended more upon presents to the Indians than any other colony. But when it came to the building or garrisoning of forts, the Quakers would contribute nothing.

During the winter session of 1750–51, the governor had several private conferences with Speaker Norris and leading members of the house and hoped that they could be induced to join with the proprietors in an appropriation for a fort or blockhouse in the Ohio country. But the members were extremely averse to it, and so no overtures on the subject could be made to the Indians.[1] In April, as news came of further advance of the French southward from Lake Erie, Croghan urged the need of at least building a trading house west of the mountains, and Weiser was planning a trip to the Ohio or to Onondaga or both. Hamilton approved of all this, but saw no hope of inducing the assembly to vote money for a fort. Asking the privilege and then failing to build would expose the English to the contempt of the Indians.[2] Hamilton wrote to Penn that he had talked again with Norris and Pemberton, the two leading members, and urged the creation of a fort to save the Indian trade, but had received only trifling and evasive answers. As to the proposal of Clinton to hold a joint conference as a prelude to united action, if it was intended to support the Indians by force of arms when attacked by the French, Pennsylvania would not meddle with it. If it meant the furnishing a constant supply of money for the support of Indian trade and negotiations, the assembly would be cautious how they entrusted its expenditure to any who were not accountable to themselves.[3] Hamilton, however, doubted the advisability of making a joint representation to the crown on the unfortunate attitude of the assembly, lest it might cause parliament to regulate colonial affairs. Yet something must be done, or the Indians would be forced into the French interest. When, in the following month, the governor reminded the assembly of this prospect, it re-

[1] Col. Recs., V, 514.
[2] Croghan to Hamilton, Apr. 11, 1751. Off. Corr., V. 133; Hamilton to Weiser, Apr. 27, 1751, Peters Papers, II.
[3] Hamilton to T. P., Apr. 30, 1751. Off. Corr., V, 135.

plied that no material change appeared in the state of affairs and they hoped that the presents already sent to the Ohio would be accepted as a proof of friendship. They did not consider it necessary to join in the conference at Albany, but directed that Weiser should attend with a small present and a message of condolence on the death of Canassetego.[1] On this occasion the assembly leaders did not deny that the proposal to build a fort was reasonable, but argued against it on religious grounds, while Norris and Pemberton thought that the money for it should be provided by the proprietors and the traders.

At the next session, in August, Hamilton laid before the house the journal of the important conference which Croghan had held with the western tribes in May at Logstown, and also the report of Weiser's visit to Onondaga. Joncaire, the French agent, had also attended and spoken at Logstown in no uncertain terms about the plans of his government. They were to induce the Indians to drive the English traders out of the Ohio country and to discontinue all further dealings with them, on pain of the displeasure of the French. Hamilton did not believe that the Indians would do this unless forced to it, but that the French were ready to use force if solicitation failed. So apprehensive were the Indians, that they had requested Pennsylvania to build a fortified trading house on the Ohio. The assembly, in reply, expressed scepticism as to the danger involved in the threats of Joncaire and reaffirmed its confidence in upright dealings with the Indians and friendly treatment of them on all occasions, relieving their necessities by suitable presents, as the best means of securing their friendship. The financial burden occasioned by Indian relations was also growing heavier, and the proprietors had been asked to share more fully in bearing this. Their reply was now received, to the effect that they were maintaining Weiser, the interpreter, and were providing his son with a tutor in the Indian languages; they also purchased the land from the Indians and paid for it and bore general costs for the province both in America and England. Therefore they did not consider themselves under

[1] Col. Recs., V, 522, 524, 526; Hamilton to T. P., June 27, 1751. Off. Corr., V, 157.

obligation to contribute to other Indian expenses,[1] especially as for years no taxes at all had been levied in the province. This led the assembly to appoint a committee to search the records and report on the cost of Indian treaties in the past. The general conclusion reached from the evidence was that the cost of treaties had been shared about equally between the assembly and the proprietors. After the beginning of the late war, in order to prove that they were not induced by mercenary motives to refuse joining in military preparations, the assembly had on several occasions contributed more largely than before. During the past four years they had contributed nearly £5000, and now the danger of introducing such precedents was shown by the attempt which the proprietors were making to fix the whole charge on the public.[2] After considering the report of this committee the house resolved that, though formal taxes had not recently been levied, the excise was really a tax; that the proprietors, being lords of the soil as well as governors, were more nearly interested in the prosperity of the colony than were any other governors in America not so circumstanced; that the purchase of land from the natives was for the sole benefit of the proprietors and therefore they ought to bear the whole expense of such treaties; and, as the maintenance of peace with the natives was of great importance to province and proprietors alike, the latter should willingly submit, as did the assembly, to bearing a proportional share of the cost of treaties which had this as their object. It was to this interesting result, which foreshadowed the rise of the question of the taxation of proprietary estates, that the agitation respecting the erection of a fort on the Ohio led in Pennsylvania. When, in 1752 and 1753, reports came of the actual advance of the French southward from Lake Erie, the assembly did not resort to measures other than a grant of £600 for distribution among their Indian allies.[3] So far as measures looking to the occupation of the Ohio valley by force were concerned, Pennsylvania had to retire into the back-

[1] Toward the building of a fortified trading post on the Ohio the proprietors later offered to give £400, and £100 a year for its maintenance. Col. Recs., V, 632.

[2] Col. Recs., V, 528–541; Votes, IV, 190, 194, 195.

[3] Pa. Col. Recs., V, 607, 614, 617.

ground and leave to other provinces the taking of the initiative in that matter.

Of the provinces along the western frontier those, if any, which must lead in preparing for active defence against the French must be Virginia and New York. Of the intense factional conflict which was still in progress in New York, incapacitating it for vigorous aggressive measures, an account has elsewhere been given. It grew out of conditions which were present in all the provinces, but which were intensified by personal and party rivalries that were peculiar to New York. Though it reacted upon the conduct of Indian relations, as upon everything else, the executive was still left with the means of making a show of activity in that department. Clinton could still correspond with neighboring governors, send agents among the Six Nations, hold conferences at Albany, plan joint conferences at which a semblance of united action on the part of the English could be exhibited before the Indians. All this he did and had the efficient aid of Johnson throughout. But for the time the most valuable support of English interest among the savages lay in the advantages of their trade. They could undersell the French and furnish a better class of goods in exchange for the furs which the Indians brought than could the French. Their alliance with the Iroquois also continued, though the French were making serious inroads on the fidelity of the western tribes. Oswego was an outpost of great value and, as long as it remained in British hands, it was clear that active trade between Albany and the far Indians through the Iroquois country would be continued, and that insured the permanence of the alliance. The Iroquois had always coquetted with the French and would continue to do so, but English rum and woolens were a stronger attraction than French brandy. And yet the English were steadily encroaching on the lands of the Mohawks; and in the last war, it had been observed, they had made a woefully poor showing in all their military ventures along the frontier.

The way in which the growing activity of English traders in the Indian country impressed the French is well shown in a letter of La Jonquière, a copy of which was forwarded to Clinton:[1] "I must not conceal from Your Excellency my great surprise, that a party of English Traders are scattering themselves all over the territory belonging to my government, who distribute their goods at a low price in all the Indian villages of the Upper Country within the limits of the King of France. This so seriously injures the trade of this Colony that I cannot avoid reporting the matter to the King my Master. It is not very difficult to divine the views which the English entertain in anticipating all the wants of the Indians. It is, I shall be answered, to attract them to themselves, and that is not forbidden, since the Nations are not dependent on any Crown. But all the world knows that the King of France is Master of his territory as much as the King of England is over his, and that consequently I would be wholly justified in expelling those who will take it into their heads to establish a trade there contrary to the King's Interest, and in confiscating their goods. Ought I not to do it unhesitatingly, since, independent of motives of interest, the English are endeavoring to debauch the Indians and inspire them with feelings of hatred toward the French? . . . I have the proof in my possession of what I advance and, in order to support it, feel no difficulty in transmitting, annexed hereto, a copy of the message the English of Chouaguen [Oswego] have sent among all the Nations. The English taking advantage of the abundance they cause do not hesitate to tell these Indians above board and to exhort them warmly to make use of the Tomahawk which I gave them against me and my French; they accompany these messages with Belts of Wampum painted red, the calumet, English flags, etc. The whole has been sent to me. I showed it to Mr. Stoddart,[2] and cannot think without shuddering that malignity has been pushed to the length of meditating the destruction of the French."

It was the knowledge among both nationalities, or the exaggerated belief, that a spirit like this existed, which led to the forcible expulsion of both English[3] and French traders

---

[1] N. Y. Col. Docs., VI, 565.

[2] Benjamin Stoddard, who was employed by Clinton as an envoy in the negotiation concerning the exchange of prisoners.

[3] See for example, N. Y. Col. Docs., VI, 599, 600, 706. Also a letter of La Jonquière to Clinton, Aug. 10, 1751, Pa. Col. Recs., V, 554–558, and N. Y. Col. Docs., VI, 731.

from the Indian country, to their imprisonment, to assaults and murders committed by the Indians or by mixed bodies of whites and Indians. In this fashion trade and war were combined in the wilderness in a way which was very likely to lead to a crisis in which trade would be wholly merged in war. The Indians also were sensitive to these conditions and became more so as the whites advanced further into their country and their predominance became more threatening. As in previous wars, so now, panics arose among them. Wild rumors were again circulated that the French or the English, or both combined, as the case might be, were plotting the extermination of the red man; that attacks and wholesale massacres of them might at any time be expected. Against fears of this kind Johnson had to contend, and the lethargy and weakness shown by the English in the recent war made it difficult for him to induce the natives to believe that their British allies would afford them any protection against a French attack. In August, 1750, Johnson wrote to Clinton concerning a recent visit of Hendrick, the Mohawk sachem, and other Indians and of their insolent conduct.[1] " I asked them what they meant by such behaviour, they answered they had sufficient Reason: saying your Excellency, Myself etc. were all French and had endeavoured all in our power to bring the French Governor into our Plot, which was to fall upon all the Indians on both sides and destroy them, that they were all assured of it, it being told to Nichus [2] by all in Canada, and further says that the Governor of Canada, in full meeting of Indians, produced a very large Belt of Wampum he had from Your Excellency desiring him to join you in said Scheme. . . . This and a great many other things they said, not worth mentioning now, which I assure your Excellency gave me three days hard work to get the better of, but at last convinced them it was French Policy to stir up the Indians against us and make a division among the five Nations, which could they accomplish they would set one half to kill the other, so that at last there would not be one of them left, which is what they aim at." Johnson also was informed from all sides that the French were doing

---

[1] N. Y. Col. Docs., VI, 589.

[2] Nichus was a sachem who had been long a prisoner in Canada.

all they could to break down his influence with the Indians, as he also was doubtless doing toward Joncaire and all similar French agents. He had also just learned of the revival of another plan of the French, which was to induce the Indians to allow them to build a fort at Onondaga, where they would amply supply the savages with ammunition and clothing.[1]

In an interview which Johnson had with a Cayuga sachem, in December, 1750,[2] he expressed, from the British standpoint, the opinion which both contestants pretended to hold as to each other, whether they were fighting in Europe or America. Of course the conduct of nations at war, and of individuals engaged in the conflict, is often such as to give a semblance of truth to such statements, but taken literally and in the large they are always the grossest of falsehoods and are uttered simply for effect. Johnson told this sachem that the French were the greatest enemies of the Indians, that they had never had their welfare at heart, and that now, as was shown by the claim set forth on one of Céleron's leaden plates, they were planning to seize all the lands and best hunting grounds of the red men and to cut them off entirely from their true friends, the British. Governor Glen, of South Carolina,[3] also gave one of his comprehensive statements concerning the situation, to the effect that the French were trying along the entire border to rouse the Indians to inter-tribal war, with the purpose of destroying in this way the chief barrier which served as a defence of the English, thus leaving their frontier exposed to successful attack. This interpretation was based on the wars between the Creeks, Cherokees and other tribes of the south and southwest, and, if it was to fit conditions in the north, would have to be so modified as to imply an effort to win over from their English alliances as many tribes as possible, but without any plan to stir up inter-tribal wars. As to Johnson's statement, the Indians were soon to find, if they were not already aware of the fact, that the English were really their most dangerous enemies, and that the triumph of the English meant their certain annihilation. Their only hope of the perpetuation of

[1] See N. Y. Col. Docs., VI, 599, 602, 609, etc. for further statements by Johnson and Clinton about the plans and doings of the French.
[2] Ibid., 609.   [3] Ibid., 709.

their race characteristics, by the mingling of their blood with
that of white men, lay in the establishment of the Romance
nations in control of America. Everything in French colonization up to that time showed that they were friends of the
Indian, and that their occupation of the wilderness meant
that the two races were to coexist indefinitely side by side.
It was the feeling that this was true which made the successes of French diplomacy and trade so easy and far reaching, and made it so hard for the stolid and slowly aggressive
British to hold any number of the Indians in their alliance.
Alongside of the French and even the Spanish the Indian
flourished, but when brought into real contact with the
British he sank into helpless misery and soon vanished from
the earth. But it was by means of such one sided and er-
roneous views as have been cited, supported on both sides by
acts of aggression, that animosity between the two nations
was stimulated and moves and counter moves of frontier
diplomacy proceeded, as the conflict between the French and
English over spheres of influence became more intense.
Newspapers had attained but slight vogue among the British and were non-existent among the French, but, had the
press in this form been developed, it would doubtless have
accelerated the processes of hostility and added greatly to
the literature of national recrimination.

Oswego now proved a specially valuable outpost for the
British, from which to watch the moves of the French. Early
in 1751 a report reached Clinton from there, that the French
were strengthening their post at Niagara and were already
sending or about to send an expedition to the Ohio country
for the purpose of building a fort in that region, and that
Joncaire was their advance agent in this business. Because
of the immediate bearing of this on Indian alliances, Clinton
resolved to call a joint conference of the colonists with the
Six Nations and the tribes dependent on them at Albany for
the following June. Invitations to join in this were sent
to all the colonies from New Hampshire to South Carolina.[1]
The governors were all in favor of the plan, but, except in
Massachusetts, Connecticut and South Carolina, it was found
impossible either to call the assemblies together or, if called,

[1] N. Y. Col. Docs., VI, 703 *et seq.*, 714, 717.

to procure appropriations for the dispatch of commissioners. Though, since 1746, the assembly of New York had neglected to make the usual annual grants for the management of Indian affairs, it now made a small sum available, so that it was possible to hold the conference.

But another circumstance, which contributed even more toward defeating the purpose of the conference, was the absence of Johnson. It is true that he appeared before the cessions closed and was sworn in as a member of the New York council, but he took no part in the proceedings and had previously announced his retirement from the management of Indian affairs. His reason for this was the failure of the assembly, now for three years and more, to provide for the payment of a sum which in the total aggregated over £7000, that he had advanced out of his own pocket for the Indian department and the supply of the garrison at Oswego.[1] A part of this sum had been paid, but a large arrear remained. Johnson, because of his close connection with Clinton, was an object of dislike to the De Lancey faction. His rapid rise in the management of Indian relations had provoked the jealousy of the commissioners at Albany, and their close affiliation with the majority in the legislature insured the combination of the two in opposition to Johnson. Therefore he felt that the only course for him was to retire before he became more involved financially. The Indians had been informed of this by a belt which Johnson had sent to the tribesmen and, before the conference began, through Hendrick, the Mohawk, and in a private interview with Clinton and the members of the council who were with him at Albany, they protested against his retirement. Clinton sympathized with them, but could do nothing to remove the difficulty because Johnson, when he arrived, persisted in his refusal to serve any longer.[2] In the public conference which followed Clinton and William Bull, the commissioner from South Carolina,[3] were the only Englishmen who spoke. Bull had brought six Catawba chiefs with him, and after he had

[1] Stone, Life of Johnson, I, 383, 393–396.
[2] Ms. Min. of the Ex. Council of N. Y.; N. Y. Col. Docs., VI, 739.
[3] The commissioners from Massachusetts were Jacob Wendell, Joseph Dwight and Oliver Partridge, and, from Connecticut, William Pitkin and John Chester.

spoken they appeared and the calumet was smoked. Words of peace were spoken between the two hereditary foes, but no prisoners were exchanged. The burden of the message from South Carolina was that inter-tribal wars should cease and a united front be presented to the common foe. But nothing that occurred had insured such a result, even so far as the Six Nations and the Catawbas were concerned. Clinton also exhorted the Iroquois to draw the neighboring tribes into a strict alliance,[1] securing a general liberty of trade, and to send a sufficient number of men to Niagara to stop the building operations of the French at that place.

This was the last Indian conference held by Clinton, and it naturally contributed nothing toward the removal of the difficulties ahead. During the year and more which followed, equally futile conferences were held with Ohio Indians at Carlisle [2] in Pennsylvania and elsewhere; the Indian agents were kept busy collecting information and a correspondence, steadily increasing in volume, was carried on between the governors of the frontier provinces. Reports kept coming in from Oswego and from points beyond the mountains of the movement of bodies of French troops to points south of Lake Erie, and that they were building one or more forts there.[3] This was in exact accordance with what Colden had written in his able memorial to Governor Clinton on Indian relations: [4] " The English only complain and expostulate. . . . The French give amusing or evasive answers, but still go on with their works, and in pursuing their great design, till they shall have brought their work to such perfection that they can without fear avow their Intention." Among the remedies which Colden urged for the perilous situation in Indian affairs was the bringing of them under the control of a single superintendent, who should not be allowed to carry on trade, for in New York in particular many of the existing evils had arisen from the extent to which the commissioners at

[1] N. Y. Col. Docs., VI, 714.
[2] Pa. Col. Recs., V, 665. At this conference the Indians asked that the English withdraw their traders from all the Ohio country except three trading posts — at Logstown, the mouth of the Monongahela and the mouth of the Great Kanawha.
[3] E.g., N. Y. Col. Docs., VI, 779.
[4] Ibid., VI, 738–747.

Albany had allowed their interests as traders to paralyze efforts to promote common British interests against the French. This reform was made a few years later, but Indian relations and the military situation combined had now brought about a crisis which demanded more than the palliatives which Colden had become accustomed to value in comparatively peaceful times.

On the night of April 20, 1753, Johnson was awakened at his residence by the frightful whooping of many Mohawks who had come to inform him, though for nearly two years he had had no official connection with Indian affairs, that some of their young hunters two days before had seen below Cataraqui a large body of French Indians — probably belonging to Martin's expedition — in warlike array.[1] So afraid were the Mohawks of a French attack, that they would not be satisfied until Johnson had dispatched a messenger with the news to Albany. This feeling of panic was due to distrust in the minds of the Indians of the New York assembly and of the Dutch commissioners at Albany, and to the exhibition of weakness which the English had made in the late war. They were also irritated by recent encroachments of settlers on their lands, and by the general practice of including in the surveys and deeds larger tracts than the Indians understood that they had sold.

In June following the night alarm at Johnson Hall, seventeen Mohawks appeared at Fort George, in New York City, and there met in conference[2] not only the governor and certain members of the council, as was always the case at Albany, but members of the assembly and citizens as well. Hendrick, the leader and spokesman, told his hearers with brutal frankness that the council and assembly did not care what became of the Indians and were leaving Albany defenceless; that if their grievances were not promptly redressed all the paths between the English and the Six Nations would be stopped. At the next session Hendrick took up the wrongs which they had suffered in connection with land grants. He mentioned by name several who had appropriated more land than they had bought, and stated that in one case Colden had been the surveyor, though the Indians did

---

[1] *Ibid.*, 778.　　　　　　　[2] *Ibid.*, 781 *et seq.*

not blame him for the error. After such examination of deeds as was possible, Clinton replied that the records, except in the case of Conradt Gunterman, seemed to support the claims of the purchasers, but, looking toward a final adjustment, that all the disputed cases should be referred to the Indian commissioners at Albany. To the minds of Hendrick and his associates this seemed equivalent to the loss of their suits at the outset and to a perpetuation of the frauds. "You tell us," exclaimed Hendrick, "that we shall be redressed at Albany, but we know them so well we will not trust to them, for they are no people but Devills. So we rather desire that you'l say, 'Nothing shall be done for us.'" Therefore the conference was ended with the declaration that, so far as they were concerned, the covenant chain was broken. All the cantons would be informed by a belt to that effect. "So, Brother, you are not to expect to hear of me any more, and, Brother, we desire to hear no more of you." Though this conference was with only a small company of Mohawks and related in part to personal or local issues, it well illustrated the *impasse* to which Indian relations in New York had well nigh come. When the affair became known to the board of trade, it considered it very serious and saw that it might be attended with very bad consequences.[1] Therefore, as Clinton had just retired from office and his successor, Sir Danvers Osborne, had been appointed, the board wrote specially recommending that, as soon as possible, he should hold a conference with the Six Nations; and the governors of the other provinces, from Virginia to New Hampshire, were also to be asked to send commissioners.[2] A circular letter was sent to the governors concerned desiring them to urge their councils and assemblies to make proper provision for the expense, and that in appointng commissioners men of ability and integrity and acquainted with Indian affairs be selected.

Meantime the facts bearing on the military situation, which are stated elsewhere, were having their influence on this same problem of joint colonial action. On August 28, 1753, the earl of Holdernesse, the secretary of state, in a circular letter

---

[1] N. Y. Col. Docs., VI, 799, 800, 802.

[2] Royal letters were not dispatched to Connecticut and Rhode Island, but they were not omitted from the invitation as finally sent from New York.

to the governors warned them to be on their guard against hostile expeditions of Indians, supported by European regulars, into British territory. They should prepare to resist force by force, and to that end should keep up an active correspondence with one another and call their assemblies together and secure appropriations adequate to meet the need. Osborne, upon whom as the newly appointed governor of New York reposed the obligation of summoning a congress and leading in such joint action as might be decided on, as the result of private grief committed suicide almost as soon as he had taken the oaths of office. The active duties of lieutenant governor then devolved on James De Lancey, who for a long time had been the leader of the faction which had so tied the hands of Clinton as effectually to block all measures of defence. The instructions and letters which had been intended for Osborne now came into the hands of De Lancey, and he undertook the execution of the measures which the crisis demanded. He was a man of ability and large experience, a native of New York, and since by his accession to the chief executive office the factional conflict which had been waged with such bitterness for nearly a decade was brought to an end, De Lancey was more favorably situated for meeting the crisis than Clinton could ever have been. A first important step in this direction had been taken before Clinton's retirement, in view of the pressing necessity of appeasing the anger which had been shown by Hendrick and his companions. Clinton proposed to the assembly that commissioners should be appointed to meet the Indians during the summer, and the two houses in a joint address, signed by De Lancey and David Jones, the speaker, asked that Colonel Johnson, as the fittest man,[1] be appointed to meet the Six Nations at Onondaga. Other steps were also taken to settle the local disputes about land which had so irritated the Indians.[2] At Onondaga Johnson by tactful speeches,[3] in which he combined a sufficient degree of domineering self confidence with choice imitations of Indian eloquence, gratified the taste of the savages, and the chiefs in their joy at welcoming him back forgot their grievances for the time and were intent only on brightening the covenant chain anew. These senti-

[1] N. Y. Ass. J., II, 350.   [2] N. Y. Docs., VI, 818.   [3] Ibid., 808 et seq.

ments were expressed even by Hendrick, whom Johnson also employed as the interpreter through whom he made his chief speech to the Indians.

In making the early preparations for the conference at Albany, the predominant idea was that it should result in an unusually inclusive and important treaty with the Indians. It was to be the outgrowth of Indian relations as just described, and was to have as its outcome a general alliance between the British colonies and the Indian tribes south of the Great Lakes, bringing to an end inter-tribal wars, convincing them that common opposition to the advance of the French was necessary to the proper interests of the Indian trade, and that to promote this general movement concerted measures should be taken by the English for building forts at certain points in the Indian country.[1] It was a counter stroke to the French, a plan of the same kind as theirs, only as yet with less emphasis on the military as a compelling force, and was to be carried into execution by the joint action of a pseudo-confederation of colonies rather than by the prompt initiative of a single autocratic government. When the governors of the provinces along the western frontier brought the subject under discussion before their councils and assemblies, this aspect of it was the one predominantly considered. Virginia, as Dinwiddie wrote De Lancey in January, 1754, could not participate because of the expense she was incurring for the defence of the frontier, and because of a meeting with the southern Indians and the Six Nations which they had planned to hold at Winchester on May thirtieth.[2] From the Maryland assembly Governor Sharpe with difficulty secured an appropriation of £3000 for the support of the neighboring colonies against any hostile troops which should attack or invade his majesty's continental territories.[3] The Pennsylvania assembly made the necessary appropriation for the sending of commissioners,[4] but its attention was greatly occupied with the claim of Connecticut to the Wyoming country, with the Virginia

---

[1] See De Lancey to B. T., Apr. 22, 1754, N. Y. Docs., VI, 833.
[2] *Ibid.*, 828.
[3] Md. Arch., Sharpe Corresp., I, 69.
[4] Votes, IV, 303; Col. Recs., V, 755, 756.

boundary question, which seemed connected with every event
in the Ohio region, and with the demand for further issues
of bills of credit. New Jersey was still divided by its internal disputes over land titles; the relations between the
assembly and Governor Belcher were strained; while the
boundary dispute with New York was at its height. Like
Maryland, New Jersey had no exposed frontier and had
never shared in treaties with the Indians. Therefore no commissioners were appointed and only a vague resolution was
passed by the assembly, that they were ready to assist the
neighboring colonies according to their ability against the
French in any well concerted scheme for that purpose,[1] whenever it should be laid before them. This resolution was
passed on the day when the congress was appointed to meet.
In December, 1753, the New York assembly voted unanimously that the next year, as soon as the weather should
permit, the governor should meet the Indians and renew the
" antient Treaty " with them, and upwards of £1000 was appropriated for presents.[2] In New Hampshire the question of
paper money affected, but did not prevent, action.[3] Connecticut passed a resolution which referred both to Indian
relations and the adoption of proper measures for general
defence and safety.[4] In the instructions to its delegates it
laid stress on the large sums in excess of the meagre support
from the southern colonies which it had spent on defence,
while they received great benefit from the Indian trade and
Connecticut nothing. Therefore it was a limited and temporary support which this colony proposed to give, while it
looked with disfavor on the proposal of making presents to
the Indians. If troops were to be raised, they desired that
those of Connecticut should be joined with the eastern and
not the western troops, while it was to be understood that
nothing agreed to at Albany should be binding on the colony
until approved of by its assembly.

It is when we turn to the correspondence of Governor
Shirley and to the instructions which were given to the commissioners of Massachusetts, that we see the idea of colonial

---

[1] N. J. Arch., XVI, 463.
[2] Journal of N. Y. Ass., II, 368, 375.
[3] N. H. Prov. Papers, VI, 245, 249, 251, 282, 285–287, 295.
[4] Conn. Recs., X, 268.

union brought into the foreground. Shirley corresponded widely with other governors on the subject of the Albany Conference and hoped that a defensive league might be established. Massachusetts carried on no trade with the Six Nations or with the remote tribes, but she had long felt the pressure of the wars with the French and the difficulty of securing joint colonial action. Therefore its assembly shared the views of Shirley, and declared that it had long desired a union of the several colonies for their mutual defence and the annoyance of the enemy. In the instructions to the commissioners, three of whom the assembly insisted should be taken from its own number, they were directed to take " joint action in regard to Indian affairs and in addition, acting in concert with Commissioners from all or any of the said Governments, to enter into Articles of Agreement and Confederation, as well offensive as defensive, for their general Safety and Interest." [1] As usual, Shirley's mind was already busy with the actual difficulties which those who undertook to form a confederation would have to face. In a letter to Holdernesse, under date of January 7, 1754, he called attention to the unfairness of the existing quotas, which had not been changed since the reign of William III. The growth of Pennsylvania and Connecticut in particular made their quotas too small as compared with Massachusetts and other colonies. The commissioners from Massachusetts, Rhode Island and Connecticut were designated by the assemblies of those colonies and commissioned by their governors.[2] Those from the other colonies were appointed by the governors, and the only share taken by the assemblies in the proceeding was that of providing for the expense of their mission.[3] In the very brief instructions which were given by the governors of all the colonies except Massachusetts and Connecticut, reference was made only to Indian relations and especially to the alliance with the Six Nations, while everything else was left obscure or, in the case of Maryland, positively discouraged.

But so general was the recognition of the seriousness of the crisis that more widely extended action had been secured than on any previous occasion and a larger representation

---

[1] Shirley Corresp., II, 47; Acts and Recs. of Mass., Apr. 10 and 19, 1754.
[2] N. J. Arch., VIII, 194.   [3] Pa. Arch., II, 137–143.

of men was brought together who were prominent in their respective colonies. Among them were, besides lieutenant governor De Lancey, together with Joseph Murray, William Johnson and William Smith of New York, Theodore Atkinson of New Hampshire, Thomas Hutchinson of Massachusetts, William Pitkin and Roger Wolcott of Connecticut, Stephen Hopkins of Rhode Island, Benjamin Tasker of Maryland and John Penn, Richard Peters, Isaac Norris and Benjamin Franklin of Pennsylvania.[1] They were in nearly all cases members of the councils of their respective colonies. Pennsylvania and New York, the two colonies which were most conveniently located and whose interests were most directly involved in what was supposed to be the chief business of the conference, sent the ablest body of delegates. Though the jealous exclusiveness with which New York had hitherto asserted her control over conferences with the Indians at Albany was not shown on this occasion, she, under authority from the British government, had called the conference and her governor presided. But, to avoid disputes over precedence, it was agreed that the colonies should be named in the minutes in the order of their situation from north to south. Four of the five delegates from New York were lawyers of high reputation, while Richard Peters of Pennsylvania, that unusual combination of clergyman and politician, not only took an active part in the business of the conference, but on the first Sunday after it met preached so acceptable a sermon before it that he received the thanks of its members, and unanimous consent was given that it should be printed. Peter Wraxall, secretary of the commissioners of Indian affairs at Albany, was chosen secretary of the conference.

At the opening session, in addition to the submission of the credentials of the members, and the reading of a letter from the board of trade to the late governor, Sir Danvers Osborne, enforcing the necessity of a joint treaty with the Six Nations which should result in a renewal of the alliance with them and the redress of all their grievances, the minutes of the two meetings of the Indian commissioners were also

---

[1] See the Journal of the Congress as printed in N. Y. Col. Docs., VI, 853–892. Also printed in Pa. Col. Recs., VI. See also R. I. Tracts, IX.

read in which they suggested that the tribesmen should be urged to live more compactly together and that the British should build two forts, one at Onondaga and another in the country of the Senecas. A protest from the traders to Oswego was also read, which furnished evidence of the ill will with which they were regarded by the Mohawks. A general speech to the Indians was drafted by a committee and approved after extended debate by the whole conference. The speech was delivered by De Lancey, and was accompanied by the giving of a chain belt which signified that the colonies were acting jointly in the name of the king with the entire body of the Six Nations, together with such other tribes as could be brought into the general alliance. The question of their attitude toward French encroachments was the all important one submitted to them. Before the Indians made answer to the general speech, very frank talks were held by the Mohawks with the New York delegates,[1] at which the chiefs aired again the grievances of the previous year, and expressed their liking for Johnson and their feeling that in recent years the New York government had turned its back upon them. The fraudulent land patents, among them the great Kayadarosseras patent along the Hudson above Half Moon, came in for sharp criticism.

When the reply of the Indians to the general speech was made, the orators were chosen from the Mohawks, and Hendrick again held the chief place. His proud, though impotent, contempt for the British again found full expression. " You ask us," he said, " why we live so dispersed. The reason is, your neglecting us these three years past [then taking a stick and throwing it behind his back]; you have thus thrown us behind your back and disregarded us, whereas the French are a subtle and vigilant people, ever using their utmost endeavors to seduce and bring our people over to them." The Indians could not find that they had sold land to the French for any of the posts they had built, but they had simply taken it without consent. The same course had been followed by the English; Virginia and Pennsylvania had " made paths through our Country to Trade and built houses without acquainting us with it." Virginia and Canada were " quarrelling

[1] N. Y. Docs., **VI**, 865–868.

about lands which belong to us, and such a quarrel as this may end in our destruction." Referring sarcastically to the Indian commissioners, Hendrick declared that the Six Nations had never been invited to smoke with them, but for the sake of their beaver the Canadian Indians were frequently invited to conference. "Look about you and see all these houses full of Beaver, and the money is all gone to Canada; likewise powder, lead and guns, which the French now make use of at Ohio. The goods which go from thence to Oswego, go from thence to Ohio, which further enables the French to carry on their designs at the Ohio." Turning from land and trade to defence, Hendrick told the commissioners that it was the fault of the English that Crown Point had not been taken. "When we were ready to go and take it, we were told it was too late, that the ice would not bear us. . . . But instead, you burnt your own forts at Sarayhtoga and run away from it, which was a shame and a scandal to you. Look about your Country and see, you have no Fortifications about you, no, not even to this City; 'tis but one step from Canada hither, and the French may easily come and turn you out of your doors. . . . We are ashamed to say it, you are all like women." Another chief concluded the talk with a demand that Colonel Johnson be reinstated in the management of Indian affairs, for they had lived happily under him and knew that he was their good and trusty friend. He desired that the Indian commissioners would duly observe what he said.

The reply which the commissioners made to the charge that the English frontiers were open and defenceless was contained in the articles of union, of which nothing in detail was said to the Indians. Conrad Weiser was brought in to reply to the charge that Virginia and Pennsylvania had been unwarrantably invading Indian territory, and he reviewed at length the course of trade and negotiations since, thirty years before, Delawares and Shawnees had removed into the Ohio country. He showed that no hostile steps had been taken against the Indians and only now, as the result of French encroachment, had Virginia begun to build a house at the mouth of the Monongahela, from which they had just been driven by the enemy. As to Johnson, De Lancey told the Indians that he would make trial of commissioners for another year, and if they did not give satisfaction, effectual means would be taken to secure it. By the release of certain claims which the Livingstons had to lands about Canajoharie and a promise of better regulation of the rum trade some steps were taken toward quieting the complaints of the Indians concerning local evils. But as to the defenceless state of the frontier, the Indians at the close of the conference were as emphatic as ever, and begged that some improvement might be resolved upon speedily. In this was revealed their abject fear of French attack and their instinctive reliance on Johnson as the only Englishman who they thought could bring them protection. The River Indians, of whom a few still remained, were also included in the conference and in the pious exhortations to peace and friendship with which it closed.

While the talks with the Indians had been in progress, a committee had drafted a representation on the present state of the colonies, which was debated and adopted by the conference.[1] This set forth the territorial claims of the British in North America, especially as stated in the treaty of Utrecht, and denounced the encroachments which since the time of that treaty the French had been making. It then went on to indicate, in terms really as strong as the Indians had used, the divided and defenceless condition of the British colonies, the unjustifiable neglect of the affairs of the Iroquois, the evils of the rum traffic and the fraudulent grants and surveys of land. These evils, so far as they directly affected the Indians, it was resolved should be checked and, to this end, that reliable persons should be appointed to reside with each tribe and report to the superintendents all complaints and questions which needed adjustments; forts should be built in the Indian country and trade and the granting of land should be regulated in the public interest. The western boundaries of existing colonies should be limited by the Appalachian mountains, and from time to time inland colonies should be settled west of those mountains. And, finally, there should be a union of the several British colonies on the continent, so that their counsels, treasure and strength might be employed in due proportion against the common enemy.

It was the devotion of a large share of the attention of the

[1] N. Y. Col. Docs., VI. 885.

commissioners to the line of policy indicated in the last sentence which made this assembly more than a mere Indian conference, large and important though it was in that connection, and gave to it its chief fame as a Congress of the American Continental Colonies, the first which in any large sense is entitled to that designation. We have seen that Shirley had urged that a plan of union be worked out. Franklin's mind was already working on the same problem. In his "Gazette," under date of May 9, he had drawn from the capture by the French of Captain Trent's party, who were building a fort at the fork of the Ohio, the moral that the colonies must unite in order to resist successfully the French aggression, and had enforced it by the famous picture of the snake divided into thirteen parts, with the motto at the bottom "Join or Die."[1] He drew up some "Short Hints towards Uniting the Northern Colonies," and on his way to Albany showed them to James Alexander, Archibald Kennedy and Cadwallader Colden for their criticism. When the commissioners had met at Albany, private discussion of this subject at once began among them and, in view of the well known political weakness of the colonies, it was generally agreed that a union was absolutely necessary to their security and defence. On June 24, the subject was first brought forward, probably by Franklin, in the conference and a resolution embodying the above sentiment was unanimously passed. A proposal of De Lancey to build two forts in the Indian country was postponed until some method of effecting colonial union had been considered. Each colony then chose one of its own commissioners to make up a committee to formulate and report a plan, De Lancey being asked to designate one of the council of New York to a place on the committee. Its members, as thus chosen, were Thomas Hutchinson, Theodore Atkinson, William Pitkin, Stephen Hopkins, William Smith, Benjamin Franklin and Benjamin Tasker. The representation on the state of the colonies was also drafted by this committee. On July 2 the board passed the decisive vote to form a plan of union, to be established by act of parliament. Aside from the fact that the inauguration of a scheme of colonial union without authority from the

[1] Sparks, Writings of Franklin, III, 22 *et seq.*

imperial government would be an almost revolutionary innovation, it was considered that only by act of parliament could the union be made permanent and colonies be prevented from withdrawing at pleasure.[1] The Connecticut commissioners were opposed to the plan and did not vote for it. De Lancey and Murray, of New York, also refused to vote for the plan.[2] Some dissatisfaction was also expressed with the plan as already drafted, and Franklin was asked to prepare a new draft. This he did, and on the tenth of July, the day after the representation on the state of the colonies had been accepted, this also was approved and the members were desired to lay it before their constituents for consideration, while the secretary was ordered to send a copy to the governor of each of the colonies which were not represented in the Congress. It was then voted that a fort ought to be built at Irondequoit, in the Seneca country, and papers on French and Indian relations, submitted by Johnson and John Pownall, were accepted with thanks.

The Plan of Union, as drafted, was a statesmanlike document, and by his connection with it Franklin laid the foundation of his intercolonial reputation; but, as events soon proved, it struck a note to which as yet there was no favorable response either in the colonies or Great Britain. It was the first impression of the constitution-making instinct, which was to become so active both in Europe and America before the close of the century. Had it been put into operation, not only would a federation of the colonies have been established, but a long step would have been taken toward freeing them from the maze of ill defined or undefined relations in which they existed under the charters and royal instructions. The new constitution was to be established by act of parliament, each colony retaining its existing government except so far as it might be changed by the said act.

The executive power was vested in a president general, to be appointed and supported by the crown. The legislative power was vested in a grand council, to be chosen triennially by the representatives of the people in the assemblies of the respective colonies. The provision which was made for the

[1] Sparks, Franklin, III, 33.
[2] Colls. of Mass. Hist. Soc., VII, 213; Smith, Hist. of New York, II, 185.

support of the executive was the only one that opened a way of escape from the conflicts over salaries which had done so much to pervert and nullify government in the colonies. It was also expected that the quit rents of crown lands in the colonies would soon be sufficient for the purpose indicated. The powers assigned to the president general were: to call special meetings of the grand council on the written consent of seven members to such call; to assent to all acts of the grand council and to see them carried into execution; with the advice of the council to hold or direct all treaties with the Indians in which the general interests of the colonies might be concerned, and to make peace or declare war with the Indian nations; to nominate military officers subject to the approval of the council before they received their commissions, while all civil officers were to be nominated by the council but receive the approval of the president general before they could officiate. Vacancies by death or removal could be temporarily filled by the governors of provinces where they occurred till the pleasure of the president general and council should be known.

The legislative powers, which must be exercised subject to the assent or veto of the president general, related to Indian affairs, the making of new settlements, the raising and equipping of soldiers and guardships for the coasts, lakes and rivers, and the raising and expenditure of the revenue which was necessary. These were the issues of the day, the questions which were uppermost in the Albany Congress, on which united colonial action had been seen to be so necessary. They were questions primarily of the frontier, and the prominence which was given them in this proposed constitution shows how naturally it was evolved from conditions which had occupied the attention of the commissioners in their capacity as an Indian conference. Not only were the president and grand council to make all general treaties with the Indians, but to make such laws as were necessary for regulating trade with the Indians, to make all purchases from them of lands not within the bounds of particular colonies, meaning chiefly lands beyond the Appalachians, to make new settlements by granting lands in the king's name and reserving quit rents for the general treasury, to make laws for governing such settlements until the crown should organize them as distinct colonies; to make laws also and levy equal and just taxes upon the people of the colonies, for the purpose of the federation, they appointing a general treasurer and a particular treasurer in each colony, all money to be issued upon joint orders of the president and council except in cases where the former should be empowered to act alone. The general accounts should be annually settled and reported to the assemblies of the several colonies. The laws passed should be as near as might be agreeable to those of England, and should be transmitted to England as soon as might be after their passage, in order to their submission to the king in council; and, if not disapproved within three years, they should remain in force. Had the plan ever been put in operation, Indians relations and the interests of the frontier would have been taken out of the hands of the individual colonies.

It was provided that the grand council should consist of forty-eight members, distributed among the colonies in proportion not to population but to the proportion they contributed to the general treasury. The largest colony should not have more than seven members, nor the smallest colony less than two. From time to time the proportion of numbers assigned to each colony should be changed to correspond with changes in their relative contributions to the general fund. Regular wages during sessions, with travelling expenses to and from the place of meeting, were to be paid to members of the council. Philadelphia was designated as the first place of meeting. The council should neither be dissolved, nor prorogued, nor continued sitting longer than six weeks at one time, without its own consent or the special order of the crown. The quorum empowered to act was twenty-five, among whom there must be one or more from a majority of the colonies. The council was to be presided over by a speaker of its own choice, and on the death of the president he should succeed, with the same powers as the president, until the king's pleasure should be known. In exercising its military powers the general government was forbidden to draft soldiers within any colony without the consent of the legislature of that colony. Every colony should retain its existing constitution and military and civil establishment and might defend itself and lay the accounts of the expense thus incurred before the president and council, who should allow the payment of the same so far as they found them just and reasonable.

Though the control of the crown over legislation by this general government was assured in the usual way and a certain independence was insured to the executive by the provision for his salary, his influence over the council was limited in the ways that had long been provided for in those colonies which possessed the largest powers of self government. Though the acts of the council were subject to two vetoes, through its control over the purse and its share in all appointments it could to a certainty determine the policy of the confederation. Therefore the scheme embodied the principles for which the colonists stood and, had it been put into operation, must have strengthened the tendencies among them to self government. Though the members of the council were not chosen directly by the electors of the lower houses in the colonies, in the long run those electors must have determined such choices and so the policy of the federation, so far as they were permitted to do so by the crown. But they could not so easily bring affairs to a deadlock and thus enable the council to take over executive functions as often occurred in the provinces. The councils of the separate colonies would have no share in the new government and therefore another blow would have been dealt to these unpopular bodies. It was owing to a realization of this fact that the delegates from New York, all of whom were or had been councillors, thought that the governors and councils of the colonies should be given a share in the choice of the grand council.

The unanimity with which the Plan of Union was either ignored or rejected by all on both sides of the ocean whom it was supposed to concern, shows how little diffused was the real feeling of danger from the French and how indifferent or positively averse the great mass of the colonists were to the erection of a second superior body which, in addition to the imperial government, might restrict their liberties. The two corporate colonies, Rhode Island and Connecticut, were especially outspoken in opposition to it, on the ground that it tended to infringe on the privileges which they enjoyed by charter. In Rhode Island the fact that Hopkins had shared in drafting the plan and had submitted it to the legislature, was made the subject of a bitter attack on him.[1] By the assemblies of these two colonies, and especially by that of Connecticut, strong opposition to the plan was expressed and both of them instructed their agents to oppose it in England.[2] The only response made by a colony which failed to send commissioners was from the provincial council of New Jersey, in the form of a resolution that union was necessary but the colonial councils should be given a place in the federal legislature.[3] The assemblies and executives either took no notice whatever of the plan or, like Dinwiddie, waited to see how it was received in England. A report of the proceedings of the congress, together with its journal and Plan of Union, was sent by Governor De Lancey to the board of trade, but this was not accompanied by an address, and no attempt was made either in the colonies or in England to promote the acceptance of the plan.[4]

Shirley, who had so strongly advocated the Congress, now opposed the plan with all his might, both in America and England. To his mind it too much resembled the " Charter form of Government," and as that was " unfit for ruling a particular Colony," it was much " more improper for establishing a General Government and Imperium over all the Colonies." " The Prerogative is so much relaxed in the Albany Plan, that it doth not appear well calculated to strengthen the dependency of the Colonies upon the Crown, which seems a very important Article in the consideration of this Affair."[5] So he wrote to Secretary Robinson, and to Governor Morris, of Pennsylvania, he wrote that he was supporting with all his strength a plan of union to be concerted in England and put into force by act of parliament.

---

[1] Stephen Hopkins, A true Representation of the Plan formed at Albany, etc., reprinted in R. I. Tracts, No. 9.

[2] R. I. Recs., V, 393, 424; Conn. Recs., X, 292; R. I. Tracts, No. 9, p. 59–61.

[3] N. J. Arch., XVI, 488.

[4] N. J. Col. Docs., VI, 851; R. I. Tracts, No. 9, p. 42.

[5] Shirley Corresp., II, 96; N. Y. Col. Docs., VI, 930.

In the correspondence which passed between Shirley and Franklin, the Massachusetts governor indicated his preference for a plan of union which should include a provision for the taxation of the colonies by parliament, as well as the exclusion of the colonists from all share in the choice of members of the grand council.[1] The result would have been a scheme embodying the principle of parliamentary autocracy in an extreme form. To these propositions Franklin wrote an answer in which were set forth the principles of English liberty for which the great body of the colonists stood, containing substantially the platform upon which the American Revolution was subsequently fought. The inference from this is that, in his views concerning colonial policy, Shirley stood substantially with such men as Halifax, Charles Townshend and George Grenville and, had he been active a decade later and maintained a consistent attitude, would have given them his sympathetic support.

At the time of the Albany Congress the subject of Indian relations and of joint colonial defence was being as actively discussed by the statesmen of England as it was in America. But while the American plan laid the emphasis on colonial initiative, the ideas of the imperial officials centered upon the crown and the colonial executives, upon the steps which would but secure the means, financial and military, for joint offensive action against the French. What they aimed at was such an improvement upon the methods used in the earlier wars as would secure adequate quotas from the colonies. In April, 1754, Halifax, the president of the board of trade, in an important memorial to the secretary of state,[2] proposed that the English should build forts at all the important disputed points along the frontier; that the governors of the colonies in which these were to be built should be instructed to build and partially garrison them and that the seven independent companies then in the colonies should be used as part of the garrisons. These forts should also be made to serve in some cases as warehouses for Indian goods and trade; while two general commissioners of Indian affairs should be appointed, like the surveyors general of the cus-

[1] Sparks, Writings of Franklin, III, 57–68.
[2] C. O. 5/6, Halifax to Robinson, Apr. 30, 1754.

toms, each with a separate district, whose duties it should be to control their deputies and their accounts, visit the forts, make presents to the Indians and hold conferences. To support this establishment, it was urged that the imperial revenues, now annually and occasionally raised in the colonies, be consolidated by act of parliament and applied to this service under direction of the crown.

On June 14 the king, in consideration of the state of affairs in America, ordered the board of trade to prepare a plan of concert to be entered into by the continental colonies for their common defence.[1] That this subject was discussed at considerable length, is certain. During the last half of June, James Walpole, then auditor general of the plantations, wrote repeatedly to Newcastle[2] on the financial aspects of colonial defence. As the trade of the colonies, said he, was the chief source of England's riches and strength, to allow their defence to be neglected would raise an outcry which no government could withstand. On the other hand, landed proprietors in England would be terribly alarmed if they were to be taxed on all occasions for the defence of the colonies. As in any plan of joint defence it would be necessary to establish a scheme of proportional contributions from the colonies, their resources and strength should be ascertained as soon as possible from the board of trade, the governors, colonial agents and other well informed persons. Owing to neglect since Blathwayt's death, the office of auditor general did not possess accounts of the revenue voted by the colonial assemblies. He wondered whether the quit rents of Virginia, or the revenue from its export duty on tobacco, had been used for defence. After the heads of articles of union had been substituted by the board of trade, Walpole continued his correspondence with Newcastle and learned that Lord Willoughby had been thought of as lord commissioner, but he had declined, and after him Colonel Cornwallis was next approved, if he would accept.

The articles or plan of concert, as drafted by the board of trade, consisted of three parts. The first two had as their object provision for the forts and garrisons referred to in the

---

[1] N. Y. Col. Docs., VI, 844, 901, 903.
[2] Newcastle Papers, Addit. Mss., 32, 735.

letter of Halifax already quoted, and for the appointment by the crown of a commander-in-chief over all the forces serving in America. The steps to be taken to secure these objects were, to procure from the colonial councils and assemblies the appointment of commissioners to meet and deliberate on the number of forts to be established, the regular forces necessary to garrison them, the cost of these and also of the presents and other charges necessary to the management of Indian affairs. When these estimates had been settled, the commissioners should agree upon the quota of money to be contributed by each colony, regard being had to their population, trade, revenue and wealth. Extraordinary expenses arising from sudden invasions and the like should be met in a similar way. The colonies should be notified of the appointment of the commander-in-chief. The commissioners should meet from time to time and agree upon quotas, and the commander and commissary for Indian affairs should call on the leading finance officials of the colonies for the payment of the sums due from them. Provision was also made for a system of annual accounting to each colony, and also to the royal exchequer, by the commander for all his disbursements. In case any colony should neglect to appoint commissioners, or if such appointees should neglect to attend, the rest should proceed without them. These commissioners should draft a general convention from the foregoing points, submit the same to the governors and legislatures of the colonies for amendment and, after its terms had been agreed upon, the document should be submitted to the king for his approval.[1]

In passing on the Albany Plan of Union to the king, the board of trade made no comment except to note,[1] as a serious defect, that no provision had been made for the management of Indian affairs or the strengthening of the frontiers until after the plan had been considered by the colonial assemblies and parliament. The board again took occasion to urge that the control of Indian affairs be taken out of the hands of the separate colonies and brought under commissioners, and in particular that Johnson be given command over the Six Nations. It is needless to say that, before the

[1] N. Y. Col. Docs., VI, 901–906.   [2] Ibid., 917.

preliminary stages in the execution of this scheme were
reached, the outbreak of war diverted attention to more
immediate issues and the only feature of it which was adopted
was the appointment by the crown of a commander-in-chief
and of two commissioners of Indian affairs.

For some weeks, however, after its submission to the king
the plan prepared by the board of trade was discussed by
Halifax, Newcastle, Hardwicke, Charles Townshend and
others in their correspondence.[1] Halifax, of course, defended
it as his own product, and wrote that the board had tried
to adapt it to the constitution of the colonies and to make it
as perfect as the nature of the thing would admit. Hardwicke
criticised it as too complicated in its provisions for raising
money. He thought the power of decision should rest with
the executive of the colony attacked and that all the rest
should be obliged to contribute quotas. He also objected to
the many steps required to put the plan into execution.

The criticisms of Townshend were much more detailed,
though to the same general effect as those of the chancellor.
They reveal at this early date his wide acquaintance with
colonial conditions as viewed from the imperialistic standpoint. So extensive would be the duties of the commissioners,
he said, that none could be found in America who had knowledge enough of colonial resources to decide on the proportional
quotas of men and money. The poorer and more exposed
colonies would probably have to bear an undue burden,
while the richer and more protected, like Pennsylvania, Maryland and Rhode Island, would escape too easily. He also
believed that the commissioners would be so under the influence of local prejudices that they would never be able to
reach such broad conclusions as the plan contemplated, and
the assemblies back of them would be still less liable to do
so. His idea of the place where the power of decision should
be located was indicated by the statement that the board of
trade had better information as to the relative abilities of
the colonies than any body of men in America could get.

"It is well known," continued Townshend in terms which
indicated a still broader generalization with which the reader
of the utterances of the board of trade could hardly fail to

[1] Newcastle Papers, Addit. Mss., 32, 736.

be familiar,[1] " to those who have attended to the affairs of America that the provinces have been for many years engaged in a skillful design of drawing to themselves the ancient and established prerogatives wisely preserved in the crown as the only means of continuing the superintendency of the mother country and their manner of doing this has been by their annual bills of supply, in which they have appointed all the officers of the crown by name to be employed in the exchequer, substituted warrants for drawing out public money in the place of the governors' and in one word dispossessed the crown of almost every degree of executive power ever lodged in it. It is as certain that whenever the Bill of Supply to follow this Scheme of a general Concert is past, the same provinces will insert into it the same scheme of Encroachments, & then the Crown will be reduced either to purchase this security to the colonies by sacrificing our only security for their dependence upon us, or to have a partial supply in consequence of a general Fund to be settled, or to drop the whole design of an Union upon this Plan.[2] I am supported in this Opinion by the History of America for fifty years past, where New York has gone for several years without force or legal administration of justice and suffered itself to be exposed to a powerful enemy rather than relinquish the usurpations she began upon the Crown in the manner of raising and appropriating the public Supply. Every one of the points of Civil Government which has of late years been the subject of Debates and Contest in New York cannot but be revived again when that Province shall sit to raise her proportion of Supply, for it is not probable so favourable an Opportunity of Establishing what they have so long aimed at will be passed over, and I should imagine no consideration will induce His Majesty to consent to their raising even a perpetual Fund at the expense of his own just power and Legal prerogative, so necessary to be preserved to preserve the colony." Townshend added that he

[1] A recent one to this general effect was its elaborate abstract of the experience of New York in Clinton's time. A reference by Townshend further on shows that he had this clearly in mind.

[2] See N. Y. Docs., VI, 998, for similar opinions from Governor Shirley, but in milder language. He thought in 1755 that the colonies would submit to a plan of union proceeding from parliament.

could support what he said by a vast collection of proofs from what he had observed in the history of America. All the provinces might be overrun while the ceremonials of this plan were performing. What must be the state of a country, he exclaimed, whose last resource in danger could not be recurred to until thirteen commissioners had met from thirteen provinces, resolved upon the degree of danger and force of the enemy, reported their opinion to the provinces, and until these thirteen provinces had summoned their assemblies and they had passed their acts of supply. It was known how American assemblies acted in such cases and one might easily foresee how likely they would be to agree under this plan.

The way in which Townshend would have tried to solve the problem was indicated by his reference, at the beginning of the letter, to the bill that was designed to have been introduced into parliament in 1710 for raising a permanent revenue in America. He said that he cited it only as precedent showing what the administration had then resolved to do if New York had not been induced by fear of such an act to provide for public security in the way the crown approved. Though the exports which it was then proposed to tax were ill chosen — for it was bad policy to encumber with duties what extended the trade of Great Britain in America — the principle of the bill was right, as it professed to regulate a disordered colony and to compel them by the authority of the mother country to provide for their own safety and for British interests in it.

Thus spoke reinvigorated officialdom in England, and it was quite time that the policy to which it referred was tried, if the imperial system as conceived by the board of trade was ever to be put in operation. Early in October William Murray, the attorney general, wrote from Bath agreeing with Townshend,[1] " in all he says and proposes, for his own Reasons and many more that might be given." He also promised to send Newcastle the ideas of a West Indian who had a large estate in Carolina and was reported to be speaker of the assembly, about the proper way in which to put the continent of America in a posture of defence and to secure means

[1] *Ibid.*

of defraying the expense. But already news had reached the
ministers of Washington's defeat at Fort Necessity, and they
began to exchange views on the immediate needs not only of
frontier defence but of relations in Europe, and attention
was diverted from plans of union. Murray thought that some
officer from Ireland should be sent to America, with an engineer and arms for 20,000 men, and that a military man
should be appointed governor of New York, especially as it
was reported that De Lancey was not a friend of the British
government

CHAPTER XV

WHILE as yet the frontiers of the French and English in
North America were separated by scores of miles of wilderness, through which roads other than the natural waterways
had not been constructed, the prosecution of war between
them was a difficult matter.   The fur trade and the exchange
of such limited stocks of general merchandise as accompanied
this trade with the natives could be carried on through
Indian trails and by such paths as nature provided.   But
for the transport of troops and their supplies roads were
necessary where natural waterways were lacking.   During
the earlier wars the resources of the colonies had been limited,
their aggressive force too weak, to construct roads of any
length.   Hence the impossibility of attack by bodies of troops
more numerous than a few companies supported by their
Indian allies.   If larger bodies of troops ever reached the
enemy's works, it must be after transportation by sea.   For
this reason among others British forces which were sent up
the Hudson had never reached their destination.   The French
had sent out only war parties or pushed garrisons and trading posts forward to the frontier and maintained rather precarious communication with them.   So far as the southern
frontier of Canada was concerned, French settlements made
little progress and such outposts as were established were not
supported by a vigorous growth of population in the rear.
The situation among the British, as we have seen, was quite
different.

So gradual had been the process of expansion that after a
century and a half the frontiers of the British and French
had approached within comfortable striking distance of one
another at only one point.   That was on the extreme east,
in Nova Scotia.   In New England the frontiers remained as

they had been left by Râle's War and a broad and almost impassable wilderness lay between them. Though the French had planted Crown Point well up toward the head of Lake Champlain, the approaches to it from Albany were as difficult as they had been at any time since the century began. The British had established a weak trading post at Oswego, but if a garrison of any strength was to be maintained there and it was to be assured of adequate and continuous supplies, a road to it must be opened from the Mohawk valley. This would be made doubly necessary if through Oswego as a centre an attempt should be made to strike the posts of the French at Niagara and Fort Frontenac on Lake Ontario. Finally, in consequence of the advance of both English and French toward the forks of the Ohio, that point had become a centre of absorbing interest, but approach to it in a military sense, whether from the north or the east, involved engineering problems of the greatest difficulty for the slender resources, material and scientific, of those times. So far as frontier communications in the remoter south were concerned, conditions were still more primitive. Though the two nationalities which had been taught by European conditions to believe themselves natural enemies desired ever so passionately to fight one another, nature still presented almost insuperable obstacles to actual encounters.

The last and greatest of the colonial wars began in the Ohio region as the result of the convergence at that point of the almost simultaneous advance of the French from the north and the British from the east. In appearance the French were the aggressors, because they had done more conscious planning. Their resources were very limited but, with their superior unity and military efficiency, they were able to put their plans into more prompt execution. But, on the other hand, plans had long been preparing for an advance of the British into the Ohio valley, and the growth of population and expansion of settlement in their colonies made such an advance about this time quite inevitable. But the way in which this was done, supported by the bland assumption of the sea-to-sea charters and of sovereignty over the Iroquois with influence over all the territory which these tribesmen claimed to have conquered, enabled the British honestly to think themselves exemplars of regularity and victims of unscrupulous aggression. The historian, however, cannot dismiss the case of the French without a long and sympathethic look at what was implied in their hitherto undisputed control of the two great river systems of the continent and the vast inland seas between, together with the bold conceptions, followed by heroic execution on the part of their explorers, traders and colonists, which had given them their hold upon these regions. Interests were involved in this which demanded and merited a bold stroke to perpetuate, and this was the occupation of the valley of the Ohio. The French were aware that, because of the advance of the English, this step could be no longer postponed. In that lay their only aggression and under the rules by which international relations had hitherto been conducted, history will justify them for taking the step, though they had to bear the consequences of a risky act. For some years, however, the course of events seemed to justify their move and to promise it success.

The reports of the French advance reached the British of New York from observers at Oswego and at other points on the northern frontier. They were transmitted from New York to Pennsylvania and the other colonies. But Pennsylvania and Virginia had their own traders and interpreters in the Ohio region and they reported directly to their superiors the approach of the French. At the close of April, 1753, Johnson reported to the council at New York that Indians out hunting had seen a French force going toward the Ohio. A month later was recorded the report of Lieutenant Holland from Oswego to similar effect. Captain Benjamin Stoddard, in command at Oswego, also reported the passage of " 30 odd French Canoes," part of a much larger force on its way toward the Ohio.[1]

The force whose advance was thus reported consisted of about 250 men, under Captain Pierre Paul Marin, the advance guard of a larger body numbering 480 militia, 40 regulars and 45 Indians, which set out later under Captain Michel Péan. To this considerable additions, especially of Indians, were made at points west of Montreal. The ex-

[1] Ex. C. Min., Apr. 30 and May 30, 1753; N. Y. Col. Docs., VI, 779–781, 825; 2 Pa. Arch., VI, 138 *et seq.*

pedition had been fitted out by the Marquis Duquesne, after his arrival as governor general of Canada, with authority to build such forts as were necessary on the Ohio. Corruption now flourished in Canadian politics and the governor was reputed to be concerned with the intendant, the disreputable Bigot, in plans of profit from contracts for this and other public enterprises. Another notorious phase of Bigot's conduct was the illicit connection alleged to exist between him and the wife of Péan, the report being that the husband was appointed to the command of the expedition to the Ohio in order to get him out of the way. The ability, however, and social standing of Péan were such as to entitle him to the command even if scandal, true or false, had played no part in procuring it for him.

The purpose of the expedition was to cross from Lake Erie to the headwaters of the Ohio, build forts and storehouses, gain the friendship of the Indians and warn off or arrest any English traders who might be encountered.[1] The region to which claim had been expressly made by the expedition of Céleron, four years before, was now to be occupied, and as originally planned the return of a part of the force through the Illinois Country, Detroit and Sandusky was intended. But the difficulties which were encountered rendered this quite impossible. Le Mercier, an engineer of the advance force, hit upon the harbor of Presque Isle, now the site of Erie, Pennsylvania, as the most available starting point for the overland march from Lake Erie southward. The advance of the main body of the expedition, with its outfit of many needless supplies, was delayed by the heavy labor involved in crossing the Niagara portage. Meantime a log fort was built at Presque Isle, and Le Mercier planned the building of another similar post on Le Bœuf or French Creek, now Waterford, Pennsylvania, fifteen miles south of Lake Erie. But the completion of these posts and the opening of the difficult road between the two could not be accomplished till after the arrival of the main body. That did not occur until September, and by that time the fatigues of the Niagara portage and the heavy task of road building in un-

[1] Severance, An Old Frontier of France, II. To this careful and original work I am much indebted for the French side of these events.

favorable weather between Presque Isle and Le Bœuf had necessitated the sending of hundreds of the sick to the rear. Such work as this was not what the Indians desired and they gradually and silently disappeared. Marin and Péan, the two commanders, labored valiantly, but the former succumbed to dysentery and died at the close of October. The approach of winter made it necessary to suspend serious operations before the Ohio had been reached. But the building of a third fort at the junction of Le Bœuf and Allegheny had been planned. There John Fraser, a Pennsylvanian, had a trading post which he abandoned on the approach of the French. At the beginning of December Captain Joncaire, brother of the famous Chabert, and two other officers took possession of this and raised the French flag. Venango was the name of the place, on the site of the modern city of Franklin, Pennsylvania. The effect of this bold advance on the Indian tribes of the region had been to spread wild rumors among them of the strength of the French and to induce them to make submission or offer aid. The Miamis abandoned their English allies, and a movement had been started which threatened to cause a general defection if steps were not taken to check it.

Meantime through Governor Dinwiddie reports had reached England of the French advance, and on August 28 the earl of Holdernesse, who two years before had succeeded Bedford as secretary of state, wrote to the governors directing them to learn how far the report was well grounded, to put their colonies in a condition to resist all hostile attempts, and to require the French, if found to be making encroachments, forthwith to desist.[1] If they should still persist, while the king did not intend to be the aggressor, the governors were instructed to use within territories which were undoubtedly English the armed force under their command to repel the enemy. The governor of Virginia was especially authorized to build forts on the Ohio and, if necessary, to drive the French from the limits of Virginia by force of arms.

Governor Dinwiddie had long been watching the movements of the French and since the beginning of 1753 had been corresponding about this with neighboring governors.

[1] N. Y. Col. Docs., VI, 794.

He now promptly took action by writing a letter to the French commander expressing his surprise that they were building forts on land "so notoriously known to be the property of the Crown of Great Britain." He demanded the authority under which they made the invasion and required their speedy and peaceable departure.[1] George Washington, then twenty-one years of age and recently in the employ of Lord Fairfax as a surveyor of western lands, was intrusted with the delivery of this letter. In November he set out, accompanied by Christopher Gist as guide, by a French and an Indian interpreter and by four servants. They passed by Wills Creek to the forks of the Ohio and thence to Logstown. From that point, accompanied by the Iroquois Scarrooyady, or Half King, a well known friend of the English, and eight other Indians, they struck northward. At Venango they found Joncaire and his companions, and the young Virginian officer was unexpectedly confronted by one of the most experienced French and Indian negotiators. In order to communicate they had to depend on interpreters. But the wine of which the French officers freely partook at supper,[2] unloosed their tongues and with oaths they revealed their determination to take possession of the Ohio. Though they realized that the English could raise two men to their one, they relied on the slowness of their movements to prevent decisive action on their part. But Legardeur de St. Pierre at Fort Le Bœuf was the commander and Washington was referred to him. When the Virginians reached that post a council was called and three days taken in which to consider the English demand. Washington was then told that his message would be referred to the Marquis Duquesne and until by that official he was ordered to retire St. Pierre should remain at his post. With this soldierly reply Washington retraced his painful journey to Virginia and reported to the governor about the middle of January. As soon as spring opened, Joncaire-Chabert, under orders procured from the Canadian government, built a defensive work at Venango which was named Fort Machault. These steps had been taken and were known to the English when the

---

[1] N. Y. Col. Docs., X, 258.
[2] Washington's Journal, in Sparks, Washington, II, Appendix.

congress met at Albany and are to be reckoned with in estimating the forces which led to it and which forced it to
action.

At the time when he sent Washington across the mountains to meet the French Dinwiddie summoned the burgesses
to meet at Williamsburg and laid before them the chief peril
of the hour.[1] But as in New York the factional conflicts
and in Pennsylvania the pacifism of the Quakers, taking
refuge in part behind the questions of instructions and the
taxation of proprietary estates, prevented aggressive action
in those provinces, so it was the dispute over the fee of the
pistole [2] which prevented the assembly from responding to
the governor's demand for aid. The session passed with the
transaction only of routine business and an exchange of messages upon the subject of the pistole. At the middle of
December the governor prorogued the assembly until
April, warning them that they had neglected the most pressing interests of the British in America in order to dispute
the rights of the crown over the disposal of its own lands.

Though Dinwiddie had not been furnished, as he desired,
with money enough to pay a regiment of volunteers, he
commissioned Washington as major to raise one hundred
men from Augusta and Frederick counties, and William
Trent as captain to raise an equal number and, with John
Carlisle as commissary, ordered them westward to build a
fort at the forks of the Ohio. They were also to drive away
or destroy any not subjects of Great Britain who should
try to settle in that region. This the governor did with the
advice of the council and by virtue of his powers as commander-in-chief.[3] At the same time he wrote to the governors of nearly all the colonies stating what he had done
and the reasons, and urging them to coöperate by sending
troops to Wills Creek as the place of rendezvous for the
expedition. He also sent messengers to the Catawbas, Cherokees, Chickasaws and the Iroquois in the Ohio region inviting them to take up the hatchet against the French.[4] Such
cannon and military supplies as he was able to procure were

<hr/>

[1] Dinwiddie Papers, I, 39–48; Journal of Va. Burgesses.
[2] See above, Chap. XII.
[3] Dinwiddie Papers, I, 49–59.   [4] Ibid., 58–71.

collected at Alexandria, where Washington was ordered to train his company.

So anxious was Dinwiddie to rouse the province to action that he called the burgesses together again in February and pictured to them the horrors of a French and Indian invasion.[1] By whatever influence they were moved, £10,000 in Virginia currency was appropriated, to be expended under the control of a committee of the house.[2] Dinwiddie used this for the purpose of raising six more companies and wrote again to the nearby colonies asking for their coöperation.[3] Under the king's orders two independent companies from New York and one from South Carolina were also sent. The assembly of New York voted £1000 toward the support of the two companies sent from that province, £456 for strengthening the garrison at Oswego and £800 for presents to the Indians,[4] but naturally it could not be induced to send any militia or vote additional supplies. A clause was introduced into the bill making several allowances payable on receipts or vouchers and not on the governor's warrants. This form of appropriation had been insisted on during the long controversy between Clinton and the assembly, but had been forbidden by royal instruction. Therefore the council rejected the bill and the governor prorogued the assembly, the plan for the coöperation of New York in the general service thus being defeated.

In Pennsylvania Hamilton had to contend not only with the deeply rooted scruples of the Quakers against war, but with the feelings which had been aroused by the controversy over bills of credit and the jealousy of Virginia growing out of the uncertainty respecting the western boundary of the two provinces. The assembly of New York fell back on the assertion, which very likely was true, that they possessed no evidence which made it appear that the occupation of French Creek was an invasion of any of the British colonies. With the same aggravating agnosticism the Pennsylvania assembly declared that it would be presumptuous for it to attempt to judge the limits of his majesty's dominions or to fix boundaries.[5] To proofs, as submitted by the gov-

[1] Dinwiddie Papers, I, 73 et seq.   [3] Dinwiddie Papers, I, 79 et seq.
[2] Hening, VI, 417.   [4] N. Y. Col. Docs., VI, 834, 838.
[5] Pa. Col. Recs., V, 748 et seq.

ernor, that the region attacked lay within Pennsylvania the assembly closed its eyes. It also tried to discredit the royal instruction to arm and said it would wait for the other colonies, meaning especially Virginia, to act. When, in April, after Virginia had made its first appropriation, Hamilton called his assembly again, it replied that it could not make an appropriation at that time and adjourned until May. Hamilton wrote to Dinwiddie that it was altogether uncertain whether anything would be done at the next session which would contribute to the success of the expedition. In reply he was assured that, if any money was voted, it might be used for the purchase of supplies. Belcher's appeals to the New Jersey assembly were equally vain.[1] Those of Sharpe to the Maryland assembly elicited the offer of a small appropriation for a present to the Indians, but this was prevented from becoming law by a clause which appropriated the money arising from the licenses to hawkers, peddlers and keepers of ordinaries, all or most of which the proprietor still claimed as his own. The Maryland assembly also echoed the sentiment of New York and Pennsylvania to the effect that, so far as they could see, no " invasion or hostile attempt has been made against this or any other of his Majesty's colonies." [2]   North Carolina voted £12,000 and hoped to enlist 750 men. Thirty cannon and some military stores had arrived from England.

Apart from independent companies which were on their way from New York and South Carolina, Dinwiddie must rely on a so-called regiment of 300 raw recruits which had been enlisted in Virginia. Of these Joshua Fry was appointed commander and Washington colonel, with the second place in command. This was the first time that Virginia had seriously felt the pressure of the colonial wars, and of the equipment and quality of her men Washington wrote,[3] " We find the generality of those who are to be enlisted are of those loose idle persons who are quite destitute of house and home and, I may truly say, many of them of clothes. . . . There is many of them without shoes and not a few that

[1] Din. Papers, I, 82, 87; N. J. Arch., VIII, 25.
[2] Mereness, Maryland as a Proprietary Province, 318, 319; Md. Arch., Sharpe Corresp., I, 33, 38–39.
[3] Din. Corresp., I, 92, 96.

have scarcely a coat or waistcoat to their backs; in short they are as illy provided as can well be conceived." Both the soldiers and Washington asked that they might be supplied with clothes and the cost deducted from their pay. These men were encouraged to enlist by offers of land west of the Alleghanies, where, according to a proclamation which the governor issued, 200,000 acres would be granted, on which it was hoped to make the soldiers permanent settlers.

In February Captain Trent was sent across the mountains with a band of backwoodsmen to build the projected fort at the forks of the Ohio. As soon as spring opened Washington was sent after him with one-half of the troops.[1] Fry followed later, it being conceived that the special task of this force would be to escort the cannon and supplies with which it was planned to stock the fort. Though over much of the distance of 150 miles beyond Wills Creek a road for cannon and baggage would have to be constructed, it was hoped that Washington might be able to join Trent in due time to make the fort secure against the French. But while Dinwiddie had been striving to secure troops in the face of such obstacles, Duquesne and the French, as soon as the weather permitted, had pushed forward their plan of the previous year toward completion. By arduous labor a way was opened through the Chautauqua portage, so that men and a considerable body of supplies could be pushed forward by that route as well as by Presque Isle.[2] By that means the French succeeded in reaching the forks of the Ohio with a strong armed force before Trent had completed his fort and occupied it without firing a gun. Contrecœur, the commander of the French to whom Trent surrendered, permitted him and his men to retire over the mountains, where he met Washington and his little force. Fort Duquesne was at once constructed by the French, and a part of their force began advancing eastward in order to drive any English who might appear across the mountains. The efforts of the Virginians and the regulars from South Carolina to check this advance were doomed from the beginning to defeat. The stand made by Washington at Great Meadows, brave though it was and made famous by the later reputation of its leader, need not

[1] Din. Corresp., I, 106, 109.   [2] Severance, *op. cit.*, Chap. 22.

detain us here. Fry meantime had died and Washington as commander, with the troops who surrendered to Villiers at Fort Necessity, was treated as Trent had been and allowed to retire across the Alleghanies. The French were left masters of the Ohio country and a most important initial move in the game had been lost by the English.

Under the influence of these events the Maryland assembly, in July, voted £6000, to be expended as Governor Sharpe in his discretion saw fit. A small company was raised, armed and clothed, placed under the command of John Dagworthy, who had held a captaincy of New Jersey troops in the late war, and sent to Wills Creek. There were gathered also the independent companies from New York and South Carolina, and by these troops the stockade known as Fort Cumberland was built. But endless difficulties had to be encountered, for the soldiers of the independent companies demanded higher rates of pay than were given to the colonials. So high were the wages voted by North Carolina for its men that the appropriation was soon exhausted and the 400 men who came to the rendezvous at Wills Creek deserted in a body.[1] Though Dinwiddie desired a fall campaign, because of obstacles both military and financial it had to be abandoned. But meantime, as the result of advice given to Newcastle in England by John Hanbury of the Ohio Company, by Sharpe's two brothers, John and William, and by Lord Baltimore, the Maryland governor, though wholly without military experience, was appointed commander of all the king's forces in America. In regard to the performance of the duties thus imposed he was to consult Dinwiddie. His commission was brought over by Arthur Dobbs, the newly appointed governor of North Carolina, and it reached Sharpe early in October.[2] Dobbs also brought £10,000 in specie for the use of Virginia. Sharpe was a clearer headed man and more efficient administrator than Dinwiddie. One evil, however, which followed his appointment was the placing of new officers over the heads of the Virginians who were

[1] A comprehensive account of these early levies is in a letter of the board of trade to Pitt, Jan. 21, 1757. C. O. 5/7.

[2] Sharpe Corresp., I, 139, 184 and many other references, Md. Arch., XXXI, p. 52. Walpole's Memoirs of the last Ten Years of George II, I, 347; Schlesinger in Md. Hist. Mag., June and Sept., 1912.

already in service, and this led to the temporary retirement of Washington in disgust. But when Sharpe visited Wills Creek and saw the disorganized condition of the 340 privates and officers who were gathered there, many of them without proper clothing, all without adequate food, quarrelling among themselves and totally unfitted for service, he devoted himself with such means and ability as he possessed to the task of improving on Dinwiddie's mistakes. Though in January, 1755, Sharpe received notice from England that he had been superseded by an officer, as yet unnamed, who would be sent at the head of two regiments destined for America, he continued his work until spring. In coöperation with Dinwiddie he was thus able to accumulate a valuable store of provisions and to raise and discipline additional recruits to fill the ranks of the regiments expected from Europe. This was the service rendered during the brief period of Sharpe's command, and it proved of decided value when the work of the next campaign had to be directly undertaken.

When the news of the defeat of Washington at Fort Necessity reached England, in September, 1754, the recently formed Newcastle ministry, as we have seen, dropped the discussion of its plan of concert for the colonies and took up the question of immediate defence. But in doing this such steps were taken for military purposes only as to lead to an important advance in organization beyond what had been attained in the earlier wars. In July Dinwiddie, in giving an account of the defeat, had asked that troops be sent from Europe.[1] On the receipt of this Newcastle suggested that they be selected from the Scotch Highlanders. The duke of Cumberland, the commander-in-chief, was consulted, but nothing was decided except that Sharpe would be superseded by the new appointee. Though it was the holiday season, in response to the urgent requests of Newcastle the inner committee of the cabinet was brought together.[2] It appeared that both Hardwicke and the duke were opposed to the sending of Highlanders because their loyalty was so much a matter of doubt. The duke suggested Edward Braddock as the properest man for the American command, and that two regiments from the Irish establishment which had served

---

[1] Din. Papers, I, 239 et seq.   [2] Newcastle Papers.

with him at Culloden had better be sent. These regiments now numbered only 500 men each and should be filled up by quotas from the colonies. The duke also thought that operations should be undertaken not only on the Ohio but in Nova Scotia and at Crown Point. The king was pleased with this advice and had a good opinion also of Braddock, as well as of Colonel Dunbar, who was mentioned as a possible second in command. When the cabinet meeting was held, attended by Hardwicke, Granville, Robinson, Holdernesse, Lord Anson, Newcastle and the duke, the plan in general as above stated was adopted. It was a meagre proposition at best and even as such was imperilled by the indecision of the prime minister, his indifference concerning America and superior interest in European issues.

When the items of cost came to be considered, Newcastle tried to hedge on the subject of expenditure in Nova Scotia. He wrote to Hardwicke that he thought that operations should at first be confined to the Ohio and Crown Point and the other left until they could deliberate further. Hence Robinson postponed writing to Shirley and Pepperell and giving orders to the ordnance board for supplies for that expedition. But on talking with Anson and William Pitt, the latter of whom was paymaster of the forces, he had found that both were in favor of utilizing the regiments of Shirley and Pepperell for service in Nova Scotia and possibly also against Crown Point. Three years before Pitt had warned Newcastle of dangerous encroachments by the French in Nova Scotia and now, piqued and discouraged by exclusion from the king's counsels, he at first refused to express an opinion. But on being pressed he declared that the duke's plan was a good one so far as it went, but that it did not go near far enough.[1] The proposal for artillery was infinitely too short. He was in favor not only of sending regiments but of raising some thousands of troops in America. He was in favor of making an end of the business with the French, but it could not be done by Europeans alone, though some should be sent to countenance the Americans. This advice caused Newcastle to let the orders pass for raising the regiments of Shirley and Pepperell and for providing the necessary artillery and

---

[1] Basil Williams, Life of Pitt, I, 182, 253; Newcastle Papers.

that the two Irish regiments should be raised up to the English establishment before they embarked. Henry Fox, the secretary at war, acting in concert with the duke and perhaps with Pitt and without consulting Newcastle, procured the signature of the king to the warrants appointing officers for the troops to be raised in America and arranged with the treasury and admiralty for transports and pay.[1] The aversion of Newcastle and Hardwicke to prompt action at this crisis was almost as difficult to overcome as was the particularism of the colonies, but the irritation of Fox — attributed to his love of power — supported by the great name of the duke, carried the business through.

Had Braddock been a genius in generalship, in engineering and diplomacy, and had he been furnished with ten times the troops he took with him and also been well acquainted with the American colonists and their frontier, in perhaps two campaigns he might have accomplished what was implied as expected of him in his instructions.[2] Sir John St. Clair as deputy quartermaster general and James Pitcher as commissary of musters had been sent in advance to prepare what was necessary for the troops when they came to be marshalled for the expedition. Halket's and Dunbar's regiments, which Braddock took with him, were raised to 700 men each. Shirley's and Pepperell's regiments were to number 1000 each, and, if possible, 3000 colonial militia should be raised and put under Braddock's command. Augustus Keppel was to command the squadron on the American station. Braddock was to apply to the governors for fresh provisions, quarters and transportation for his troops. He was to find out what the governors were doing and give them all the advice he could respecting a common fund for the support of the service. He should correspond with them, visit their provinces and aid them in raising and improving their levies. He should cultivate friendship with the Indians, employing Johnson in the north and also sending some fit person to the southern Indians. He should take all possible steps to prevent illegal

[1] See letters of Fox of October 6 and 7 in Newcastle Papers and other dates, and War Office, 26/22, Miscellany Books.

[2] The law officers stated that these instructions were based on the act for punishing mutiny and desertion and on a standing clause in the commissions given to royal governors.

trade between the English and the French. In all matters Braddock was to use his own judgment, calling to his aid a council of war consisting of himself, the commanders of the ships in the American squadron, together with such governors and field officers as were within reach. He was also told that Dinwiddie had been given permission to draw £10,000 in addition to the sum already sent, while Braddock himself was permitted, if he found the provision made by the colonists inadequate, to draw upon money deposited with the paymaster of North America so much as he found it absolutely necessary in order to raise and pay the number of troops intended. In secret instructions the plan of campaign was outlined. This included the capture of the French fort on the Ohio, and seeing that a good and sufficient fort was built there and strongly garrisoned; dislodging the French from Niagara and fortifying that post, also if he found it necessary, building vessels on Lake Ontario, using Shirley's and Pepperell's regiments and aid from New York and New England in that service; but if they should not be ready in time, Braddock should take his own force to Niagara. In that case the two American regiments might be used against Crown Point. As to operations in Nova Scotia, no positive instructions were given, but Braddock was ordered to correspond with Lawrence, who was in command there. If he could reduce Fort Beauséjour, it should be done, but if not that task must be undertaken after the other expeditions were completed.[1] These furnish a good illustration of the passion of the duke, Fox and the law officers for thoroughness, but show little understanding of the difficulties attending military operations in America when carried on according to European methods.

The question had necessarily arisen, whether or not the rules of discipline of the British regulars should be extended to the colonial militia. The law officers stated that Braddock's commission, in which no distinction was made as to discipline and martial law between the two bodies of troops, was based on the act for punishing mutiny and desertion and on a standing clause in the commissions given to royal gov-

[1] C. O. 5/6, N. Y. Docs., X. Sargent, Braddock's Expedition, Memoirs Pa. Hist. Soc., V.

ernors. But they were in doubt as to the legality of this, for if the colonials were a sort of country militia and not in the king's pay, they could not be subjected in time of peace to the articles of war applicable to regulars. Every colony had governed its troops by its own articles and acts of assembly and such power could not be given to a commander merely by an instruction or article [1] in his commission. This could be done only by a declaratory clause in the mutiny act. To remedy this difficulty a clause was introduced into the mutiny act of 1754, providing that colonial troops when acting in conjunction with regulars should be subject to British martial law and discipline.[2]

The earl of Halifax is said to have recommended that the force which was to undertake the expedition should consist chiefly of provincials, with enough British regulars to enforce discipline. In this way a body of troops which was accustomed to frontier life and methods would have been secured and, if within it could have been developed a tolerable spirit of discipline, it was believed that the best practicable results would be attained. The capture of Louisbourg, the only successful operation of the previous war, would seem to have taught a lesson like this. But the duke of Cumberland, a purely European soldier of the bull-dog type, believed that the best results could be obtained by British infantry of the line and his views were accepted out of hand. Therefore the Irish regiments were selected to constitute the bulk of the force, and a veteran in the Coldstream Guards was appointed to command, a man who was versed in the routine of fighting in Flanders and who knew and cared for little else. Edward Braddock [3] was a brave and well trained soldier of the Anglo-German school, obstinate and passionate and with scarcely a gleam of originality. Ruined in fortune, he accepted this American appointment, though at the same time he acknowledged it as probable that he and his command would never return. He regarded the colonists generally with contempt and it must be confessed that their military arrange-

---

[1] S. P. Dom. Military.

[2] Parl. Hist., XV, 375.

[3] Though the home of the Braddock family had long been in Ireland, it was of Teuton and not Celtic extraction; Sargent, Braddock's Expedition, Memoirs of Pa. Hist. Soc., V.

ments, so far as he observed them, seemed to merit an opinion of that kind. Except for outbursts of impotent rage, he was tolerably courteous and fair in his treatment of the leaders among them, though of course he was unable to allow for the variety of causes which made the colonies so unlike the plains of Flanders as a stage upon which to carry on systematic warfare. Young John Shirley, Washington and Franklin, with all of whom Braddock had rather intimate dealings, agreed in an unfavorable judgment of the general. They all were of opinion that, though he had good qualities, they were not such as to fit him for the task which lay ahead of him. With the force of more than 2000 men which Braddock was able to bring together, the capture of the little French fort on the Ohio would be an easy matter if he could only reach it. But between it and tidewater lay a stretch of wilderness 150 miles broad, most of it mountainous, through which a road must be made, at least twelve feet wide, over which the army could march with its artillery and baggage train. As the troops crept slowly along through the latter half of their journey they might at almost any point fall into an ambush of French and Indians. The construction of the road was the engineering problem of the expedition; the conflict with the enemy, under whatever conditions he might be met, was its strictly military problem. Both of these involved experiences entirely novel to Braddock and his men, and they also greatly transcended the capacity of the colonists for joint effort, at least as it was commonly exhibited.

Robinson, the secretary of state, had informed the governors that a fund should be raised by the assemblies to meet expenditures for recruiting, provisions and other general purposes.[1] This was to be provisional for the service of North America, "until such time as a plan of general union of his Majesty's Northern Colonies for their common defence can be perfected." Supplies of arms and ordnance were sent from Great Britain. Dinwiddie was tireless in efforts to procure appropriations from his own assembly and in the expenditure of the money which had come from England in the purchase of pork, salt and other provisions. He

[1] C. O. 5/7; N. Y. Docs., VI, 915–934.

appointed two commissaries and set them at work in the country along the Potomac. He wrote to Shirley for a supply of salt fish. He called urgently upon Pennsylvania for flour, but Morris was able to obtain nothing except a resolve, passed without his knowledge, empowering a committee to borrow £5000, which they finally decided to expend for flour.[1] Upon the insistent demand of Braddock, however, a road from Shippensburg in Pennsylvania to Great Crossing or vicinity was begun with the hope of facilitating the transport of flour and other supplies,[2] but it was not completed in time to be of use to the expedition. In February an effort of Sharpe to procure a grant from the Maryland assembly was defeated by a recurrence of the same dispute which had arisen at the last session. So impatient was the bustling Virginia executive with the apathy of the colonists and with reports that they were supplying the enemy with provisions at Louisbourg, that he repeatedly urged upon the ministers in London that an embargo should be laid upon exports from America and that parliament should tax the colonies. St. Clair had arrived in time to coöperate with Dinwiddie, and in February Braddock with his regiments reached Virginia. It was decided that the troops should land at Alexandria, and there with a council of governors, originally called to meet at Annapolis, the general discussed his plan of campaign.

The council was attended by Braddock and Keppel and by the governors of Massachusetts, New York, Pennsylvania, Maryland and Virginia. Colonel Johnson was also present.[3] This meeting, which was held under a tent at Alexandria on April 14, marks the nearest approach which was ever made to the realization in practice of a British plan of concerted action for the American colonies. Only one brief session was held and it consisted of approval by the governors of the

---

[1] Din. Papers, I, 439, 447, 473, *etc.*, *etc.*; Pa. Col. Recs., VI, 295, 298, 301, 308, 352–354, 386.

[2] Pa. Col. Recs., VI, 380, 396, 406, 415, 425, 436, 475, 476, 500. A dispute over the amount expended on this arose between Morris and the assembly, the latter alleging that the original estimate was £800 and that the cost far exceeded this. Votes, IV, 486; Pa. Col. Recs., VI, 620, 629.

[3] See Orme's Journal, in Sargent, *op. cit.*, 300. Keppel's account is in Admiralty In-letters, 480; Keppel to Cleveland, Sec. of Admiralty, Apr. 30, 1755. The minutes of the council are in the Doc. Hist. of N. Y., II, and Pa. Col. Recs., VI, 365.

plan of campaign, of the policy, as Braddock stated it, which should be followed toward the Indian allies, and of his designation of Johnson as the man best fitted not only to administer Indian affairs in the north but to command the expedition against Crown Point. Shirley was put in charge of the expedition against Niagara and for the strengthening of Oswego. He was also to superintend the building of two small armed vessels for service on Lake Ontario.[1] Braddock dispatched a courier to Lieutenant Colonel Robert Monckton directing him to command the attack upon Fort Beauséjour in Nova Scotia. The governors had to inform the general that all their efforts to induce the assemblies to establish a general fund had failed and that they were of opinion that such a fund could never be established without the aid of parliament. They therefore all agreed that some method should be found of compelling them to contribute in due proportion to the support of the war. As things were, though the governors would continue to do all in their power, they thought that operations would be at a stand unless the general made use of his credit at home to defray the expenses which they involved.

An initial error of serious importance had been made in planning Braddock's part of the campaign before he left England. It consisted in the decision that he should land in Virginia and proceed thence toward Fort Duquesne. The distance by that route was much greater, more rugged and less settled than the one which would have been followed if the expedition had started from Philadelphia. The choice of the Virginia route was said to have been due to the advice of Hanbury and to have been made in the interest of the Ohio Company. It also fell in with the natural preference of British officials for acting with their own appointees in the royal colonies rather than with the chartered colonies, especially if they were governed by Quakers. A long and difficult march was necessary before Fort Cumberland, the base of supplies and situated at the foot of the Blue Ridge, could be reached. To this point a part of the force pro-

[1] See Keppel's account of the council. and Severance, *op. cit.*, 169. Thomas Pownall had suggested the building of such vessels in the paper which he had submitted to the Albany Congress.

ceeded by the way of Frederick in Maryland, and the rest crossed into Virginia and over a part of the distance followed the Winchester road south of the Potomac. Those who went by the Maryland route had to cut a new road for thirty miles over the mountains and through the forests to Little Meadows, where it was planned to build a fortified camp. The labor involved in this, some of it useless because of the lack of a previous survey, was enormous, and so slow was the advance that it took from the 30th of May to the 18th of June to reach Little Meadows. There the two divisions, each containing one of the regiments and the militia accompanying it, formed a junction.

By the time this point was reached most of the difficulties of the undertaking had revealed themselves. They were an inadequate supply of provisions, quantities of provisions delivered found to be spoiled and unfit for use, and above all a lack of wagons and horses for the transport of the stores. So indifferent did the people of the region appear to the fate of the expedition that Braddock and St. Clair were intensely irritated and denounced them in unmeasured terms. At Frederick Benjamin Franklin was a witness of this administrative chaos and of the helpless rage of the British officers. In response to a request of Braddock he undertook to procure 150 wagons and a large number of horses. This he could do for the British government without aiding the proprietors and it would help to redeem the military fame of Pennsylvania. So tactful and persuasive was the proclamation which he issued that the farmers brought in their horses and wagons in such numbers that the march could really be begun. This was almost the only bright spot which relieved the hard and discouraging conditions under which this expedition was prosecuted.[1] In the early stages of the march it became necessary to leave behind considerable quantities of baggage, and as the column

---

[1] Franklin described it in a letter to Shirley in telling phrase; "I did not reach home till the 12th Instant, from the Journey, in which I had the Honor to accompany your Excy. as far as Annapolis. In my way I have had the good Fortune to do an acceptable Piece of Service to the Forces under General Braddock. I found them stuck fast, and unable to move for want of Horses and Carriages; all their Dependencies for the Articles having failed. They are now supplied with both as well as with 6000 Bushels of Oats and Indian Corn which were much wanted but scarce expected." Shirley Corresp., II, 173.

advanced the horses of many of the officers had to be taken for draught purposes. Exposure, exhausting labor, poor and inadequate food, the use of little except salt provisions, all of them combined caused much sickness among the men and not a few deaths. The wastage of horses, wagons and tools was correspondingly great. With the slow progress, more trying than battle, the soldiers became discouraged and the prevention of straggling became more difficult. As the force advanced, however, this straggling became more dangerous, because such Indians as were ranging the woods were mostly on the French side. At the beginning Braddock had made a great point of gaining Indian allies and a few natives had joined the force. But the success of the general and his aids in conciliating them was slight and they gradually disappeared, so that what might have been their valuable service as scouts was lost and in the final encounter Indians took practically no share on the British side. This was one of the chief causes of the disaster which followed.

When the force was ready to start from Little Meadows, Washington advised that the heavy baggage be left with a rear division and that a chosen body push on more rapidly toward the fort. This advice was accepted by the general and Colonel Dunbar was left in charge of this camp, while Braddock with 1200 men, thought to be more than adequate for the capture of the fort, advanced at a more rapid rate toward the fords of the Monongahela. That point was reached on July 8. Meantime the French had gathered a force of several hundred regulars and Canadian militia and about a thousand Indians. As was to be the practice during the rest of the war, the latter had come from the widely extended tribes along the entire course of the St. Lawrence, the Great Lakes and the Ohio, who were in alliance with the French. Their numbers had just been increased by the Delawares and Shawnees, whose defection from the Six Nations and the British had seriously affected the balance of power and was now bringing peril to the frontier of the middle colonies. With Contrecœur at Fort Duquesne were associated the able captains, Beaujeu, Dumas and Ligneris.

The British force was so superior to the French that, should it reach the fort, the speedy capture of the French post would be inevitable. It was determined, then, not to allow them to reach it, but to prevent this by an ambush. A force of about 900 was called out, of which about 650 were Indians,[1] to perform this task. Though, owing to delays, the ambush was not formed, the effect upon the British of the firing of the Indians and a part of the French — for many of the Canadians fled at the first onset — from behind the trees of the densely wooded field was similar to that of an ambush. Though the British at first recoiled, they recovered themselves and were permanently rallied by the arrival of Braddock from the rear. When the attack was made the British also were advancing with every precaution against surprise, as they were within only six or seven miles of the fort. The fatal mistake in their tactics, in which the general fully shared, was that they kept their close formation and did not, like the French, distribute themselves behind the trees. In close rank,[2] firing volley after volley and at first making the futile effort to use artillery, they stood or huddled together, their bright red uniforms a splendid target for the marksmen of the enemy. So the British regulars stood for three hours until a large majority of the privates and 63 out of 86 officers had been killed or disabled. Braddock was among those fatally wounded. A retreat was then ordered and it immediately broke into a rout, everything being abandoned in a wild flight which could not be checked until Dunbar's camp was reached.

Even then the defeat might have been retrieved and the purpose of the expedition have been finally attained. The road need not have been abandoned and a post on the line of the mountains could have been held until reinforcements could be hurried up from the colonies. The regulars who survived would thus have formed the nucleus of a force which surely was needed to protect the border settlements against Indian raids. But none of this was done and, as Braddock was dying, Dunbar ordered or permitted a disorderly retreat which did not stop until they reached Fort Cumberland. Cannon, ammunition, provisions and wagons

---

[1] As to what happened among the French, see the material cited by Parkman, Montcalm and Wolfe, II, App. E.

[2] Orme's Journal, Pa. Col. Recs., VI, 488, 501, 517–519.

by the wholesale were destroyed. In this consisted the disgraceful feature of the campaign.[1] In June, while Braddock was in the later stages of his westward advance, Morris told the Pennsylvania assembly that they, together with Maryland and Virginia, were expected promptly to send forward under convoys sufficient cannon, military supplies and provisions for the garrison of the fort on the Ohio when it should be taken, for Braddock could spare none of these for such a purpose.[2] It was also believed that the French and Indians would immediately attack the back settlements. In fact isolated attacks of this character were already beginning, as reports from John Harris and others proved. Morris therefore urged his assembly to pass a militia law and provide adequately for the defence of the frontier. The governors of the three provinces were also corresponding in reference to this subject. But under the pretext of the old dispute over paper money the assembly of Pennsylvania adjourned without responding to this demand. A similar cause defeated the effort of Sharpe to procure an appropriation from the Maryland assembly.[3] Dinwiddie, as usual, was tireless in promoting this service, urging it upon all the nearby provinces and keeping the Virginia assembly in session until he got from it an appropriation of £10,000.[4] He also kept in view the necessity of strengthening Fort Cumberland, where Colonel Inness was in command. The arrival of reports from Lord Fairfax of the beginning of outrages on the frontier redoubled his activity. The militia officers of the border counties were ordered to call out companies of rangers and send them in search of the enemy. At the middle of July, as soon as he heard of the disaster on the Monongahela, he ordered the militia of nine upper counties under arms and that a reinforcement should be sent to Fort Cumberland. Pennsylvania was even more directly menaced than Virginia. Morris at once called its assembly and it voted a tax on all real and personal estate which was estimated to yield £50,000.

[1] Pa. Col. Recs., VI, 517.
[2] Ibid., VI, 413, 453, 455, 457.
[3] Sharpe Corresp., I, 232; II, 316; Md. Arch., VI, 457; Mereness, op. cit., 325.
[4] Din. Papers, II, 51, 59, 60, 67, 80, 83–98; Pa. Col. Recs., VI, 461, 465.

In order, if possible, to secure the frontier independently of the assembly, Morris briefly entertained the idea of obtaining defenders by grants of land west of the mountains.[1] As the assembly had brought squarely forward in its bill the issue of the taxation of the proprietary estates, the bill failed to receive the governor's assent.[2] All hope that the remnant of Braddock's force which was still fit for service could be used in another effort against Fort Duquesne was dissipated by a statement from Dunbar and his officers that the troops were so destitute of clothing, camp equipage, artillery and Indian allies that it was impossible. As Shirley, who had now succeeded to the American command, thought that the three middle colonies were able to defend themselves and desired such help as Dunbar's force could render in the north,[3] they marched to Philadelphia to recuperate and then departed northward. The assembly adjourned until September without a favorable response to any of the governor's demands for a militia law or other provision for defence and he sent an arraignment of his conduct to the secretary of state.[4] Reports that the French and Indians were harrying the frontier from Augusta county in Virginia to the Delaware river and had advanced nearly or quite to the Susquehanna forced Morris to call the assembly together twice during the fall, but without result so far as an appropriation was con-concerned. Urgent representations of principal inhabitants and of tribesmen of the Six Nations, together with harrowing accounts from the border, all showing that the Delawares and Shawnees had gone over to the French, failed to move the assembly to grant money until the proprietors began to yield in the matter of taxation.[5]

But the pressure during the November session led the assembly to pass a militia law, the nature of which is indicated by its title — " a bill for the better ordering and regulating such as are desirous to be united for Military purposes." It exempted Quakers. It was left to the option of all others to form themselves into companies, each com-

---

[1] To this the proprietors subsequently agreed. Pa. Col. Recs., VI, 732.

[2] *Ibid.*, 485, 492, 502–525, 546, 588; Votes, IV, 417.

[3] Pa. Col. Recs., VI, 559, 563, 565, 593.

[4] *Ibid.*, 590, 591, 599.

[5] *Ibid.*, VI, 645, 662, 670, 676, 678, 684, 688, 700; Votes, IV, 496, 502, 530.

pany to elect officers by ballot. The officers of the companies might then choose the regimental officers. These last, with the governor, might frame articles of war, to which no officer or private should be subject unless after three days' consideration he subscribed them in the presence of a justice of the peace and declared his willingness to be bound by them.[1] It is said that Franklin, who was now the leader of the assembly, drew this bill in the expectation that Morris would incur increased odium by refusing to accept it. But the governor by this time was ready to accept almost anything and gave his assent even to this quakerized bill, though shortly afterwards the concession of the proprietors arrived which made it possible for him to accept the bill appropriating £60,000, thus enabling him to make some further provision for the defence of Pennsylvania. Four forts were built beyond the Susquehanna and the Blue Ridge at distances of fifteen or twenty miles from one another and located upon the trails or passes which led westward. These and four other posts east of the Susquehanna were garrisoned with small bodies of militia, but not under regular military discipline.[2]

Meanwhile in Virginia Dinwiddie condemned Dunbar's conduct in unmeasured terms to all his many correspondents, arraigning him in letters to the secretary of state and Lord Halifax and denouncing his monstrous and unprecedented conduct in abandoning the defence of the frontier and marching to Philadelphia for winter quarters in midsummer.[3] Governor Glen of South Carolina was another object of his dislike because of his alleged neglect to rouse the Cherokees and Catawbas to coöperation against the French on the Ohio and because of the peculiar method he took in forwarding the money granted by his province toward the expense of the expedition. These criticisms, however justifiable, were now futile, but Dinwiddie was equally prolific in measures of defence. The assembly was called and promptly responded with a grant of £40,000. With this the governor at once proceeded to increase the number of militia companies

[1] Pa. Stats. at Large, Col. Recs., VI, 724.
[2] Shirley Corresp., II. 388; Pa. Arch., II, 569, 415.
[3] Din. Papers, II, 118 *et seq.*

called under arms in Virginia to sixteen, ordered them formed into a regiment and appointed Washington its colonel. Though Dinwiddie would probably have preferred Inness, this step was taken in recognition of the distinguished service which the young Virginia officer had rendered on Braddock's field.[1] Washington was ordered to establish his headquarters at Winchester and from this as a centre he and his men were expected to hold the French and Indians in check and reassure the panic-stricken inhabitants along the frontier hundreds of miles in extent. In this region now developed a warfare of the New England type, which lasted through much of 1756, carrying massacre and ruin far into the interior of Virginia and Pennsylvania. Dinwiddie was incessantly active, driven not only by the tales of horror from the frontier but by dismal forebodings of what might happen if the French, following Braddock's road, should make a systematic attack on the middle colonies.

The details of this part of the struggle it is impossible here to relate, but the criticisms to which Washington gave utterance concerning the Virginia militia and the military arrangements of the province in general are too suggestive to be passed over.[2] "If we talk of obliging men to serve their country," he wrote to Landon Carter, "we are sure to hear a fellow mumble over the words liberty and property a thousand times." The officers often showed a similar spirit. "I see," wrote Washington, "the growing insolence of the soldiers, the indolence and inactivity of the officers . . ." "Most of the new appointed officers have been extremely deficient in their duties in not repairing to the rendezvouses according to appointment."[3] He complained loudly of the

---

[1] *Ibid.*, 171, 184. The board of trade stated in its letter to Pitt of Jan. 21, 1757 (see reference above), that after Braddock's defeat, by authority of an act of assembly, the Virginia force was increased to 1000 men, but that by the following February not one-half that number had been raised. A year later than that the number in pay did not exceed 600. Through the influence of Dobbs, North Carolina had sent 100 men to the assistance of Virginia and had raised 50 for the defence of their own frontier. Later three more companies were sent to the aid of the colonies further north, that is, to New York. The board severely criticised the conduct of Virginia and considered North Carolina the more generous of the two.

[2] Ford, Washington's Writings, II.

[3] Din. Papers, II, 237, 241.

delays in recruiting. " There has been such total negligence among the recruiting officers in general," he wrote Colonel Stephen in November, " such disregard of the service they were employed in and such ill proceedings, that I am determined to send out none till we all meet, when each officer shall have his own men and have only this alternative, either to complete his number or lose his commission. Several officers have been out six weeks or two months without getting a man, spending their time in all the gaiety of pleasurable mirth with their relatives and friends; not attempting nor having a possible chance to recruit any but those who out of their inclination to the service will proffer themselves."

In his attempts to enforce discipline Washington's hands were tied. As the military spirit, though for different reasons, was little stronger in Virginia than it was in Pennsylvania, so both colonies were alike destitute of a militia act. In a letter of October 11 to the governor for the third time he urged the imperative necessity of such a law and threatened to resign his command unless it was passed. Without it, he said, " we shall become an unsupportable charge to our country and never answer any one expectation of the Assembly." He expressed surprise " that we alone should be so tenacious of liberty as not to invest a power where interest and politics so unanswerably demand it." Washington found that the people were harboring deserters and assisting them " with every necessary means to make their escape." His command also was in want of supplies of all sorts. On October 18 he wrote to Dinwiddie, " We are at a loss for the want of almost everything necessary; tents, kettles, arms, ammunition and cartridge paper." There was a commissary, but Washington himself was obliged to purchase supplies and have them forwarded. " I am sorry to say Mr. Dick has been of no use, but disservice, to me, in neglecting my orders and leaving this place (Winchester) without flour and Fredericksburg without any provisions for the recruits, though there was timely notice given." Let the present commissary act or a new one be appointed. Though Dinwiddie provided as far as he was able for the men, complaints respecting these matters continued as long as Washington was in command. He could not induce the people in the neighborhood to contribute supplies, if they had them, or means of transportation. "In all things," he writes, "I meet with the greatest opposition. No orders are obeyed but what a party of soldiers or my own drawn sword enforces. Without this a single horse for the most urgent occasion cannot be had, to such a pitch has the insolence of these people arrived by having every point hitherto submitted to them."

The Virginia assembly at its October session passed an act for the government of the militia.[1] Under this a reward was offered for those who should apprehend deserters, and those who aided desertion in any way were to be severely punished. Now authority was given to act, but recruiting proceeded very slowly and supplies were always behind the need. The result was that Washington was forced to view the desolation of the frontier, and his correspondence abounds in descriptions of it, without the power of greatly aiding the sufferers. He had to go into winter quarters, knowing that the number of his men must be greatly increased before he could take the offensive. At the close of December the governor wrote to the secretary of state that not one-half of the thousand men ordered had been enlisted. It was during the winter that Washington's quarrel with Dagworthy, the Maryland captain at Fort Cumberland, occurred, which led the Virginia colonel to make the journey to Boston in order to get his commission direct from Shirley.[2]

When one turns from the remote western frontier to events in Nova Scotia and the northwest connection is at once established with operations of the British and French fleets and so with naval, military and diplomatic moves in Europe. It was the desire of both the British and French governments that the everlasting boundary disputes and conflicting rights of trade in America might be settled by negotiation. It was also held that hostilities growing out of these might proceed some lengths in America without leading to a general European war. In this light the Newcastle ministry desired that the operations of 1755 in the colonies should be regarded — a pushing of the French back from territory upon which they had encroached without involving Europe in the struggle. The conflict in America would thus be isolated and a war

[1] Din. Papers, II, 237.   [2] Shirley Corresp., II, 412.

in which the resources of the contestants and their allies throughout the world must be put to the test would be avoided. This was the idea of the limited war and it was the one upon which Newcastle and his inner cabinet worked until, largely through the connection with Hanover, circumstances became too strong for them and a general world conflagration resulted.[1] France was equally unprepared for another general war and was drawn into it mainly as the indirect result of the ambitious plans of Frederick of Prussia and the general readjustment of alliances which followed in consequence of them.[2] The expedition of Braddock and the plan of campaign of 1755 in America, taken as a whole, was not regarded as necessarily involving a breach of the world's peace. But it was a dangerous game.

During the spring and early summer of 1755 the British and French cabinets were playing a furtive game of mutual aggression under the disguise of national and colonial defence. It was one of the usual diplomatic masquerades used to conceal a play for position. Each party was trying to prove the other to be the aggressor, while in fact both were out for all the territory they could get. In March parliament met and the forces by sea and land were augmented to maintain peace. France proposed an armistice, which was rejected by England. Mirepoix, the French ambassador at London, then began to warn his government that war was inevitable. A squadron of fifteen ships of the line at Brest was understood to be preparing to sail for America. In order to offset this, the British cabinet ordered a strong squadron to Plymouth, and about a week later Admiral Boscawen was put in command of ten ships of the line and a frigate, with instructions to cruise off Louisbourg and to capture, if possible, any ships of war or other vessels having on board troops or warlike stores and which were bound for Nova Scotia, Cape Breton or Quebec. Granville and Robinson tried to calm the fears of Mirepoix by telling him the diplomatic lie that orders for offensive action had not been given to Boscawen, and Mirepoix so informed his government.

Meantime, on May 3, the French squadron sailed, having

[1] Corbett, England in the Seven Years War, I.
[2] Waddington, Le Renversement des Alliances.

on board 3336 men in six battalions of the best troops of France,[1] under the command of Baron Dieskau, a Saxon by birth and a veteran of the armies of the Marshal de Saxe. As soon as news of this reached the cabinet, Admiral Holbourne was sent, with six ships of the line, to reinforce Boscawen and was ordered, if he met a superior force, to avoid action, but if he was insulted or attacked he should do his best. Hawke, with the Channel fleet, was ordered to put to sea for training but not till later was he instructed to attack the French fleet or seize merchantmen. The rule of Anson which Boscawen, it was held, should have followed was, " all or not at all," that is, not to attack unless he could intercept the entire French force and prevent their landing. But what he did among the fogs of Cape Race was to capture two French vessels, the *Lis* and *Alcide,* while all the rest escaped, the major part through the Straits of Belleisle to Quebec and the rest into Louisbourg. Boscawen, a good officer, thought he had done well; but the tight-rope performers in the cabinet were disappointed, for their plan of defensive offence had been unmasked. War now seemed inevitable and the French had been able to send the needed reinforcements to Canada. The further diplomatic moves, with the accompanying evolutions of the fleets and armies which led to the opening of this great war in Europe, it is not necessary here to relate. But the capture of the *Lis* and *Alcide* helped to kindle the flame.

Along the New England frontier and eastward, a region which was directly affected by action at sea, the thread of events was taken up where it had been dropped at the close of the previous war. Shirley in Massachusetts and Lawrence in Nova Scotia, both incessant in their activity and relentless in their purposes as imperialists, were now working together in the interest of Great Britain. The temper of the New England people — even those of Rhode Island — was sufficiently aggressive to respond to such leadership, while the British in Nova Scotia had at last got adequate backing at Halifax, with all which that implied as a station for the fleet. Opposed to these really formidable resources, as in the time

---

[1] The battalions of La Reine, Bourgogne, Languedoc, Guienne, Artois and Béarn.

of Râle's War, were the weak and scattered Indian tribes of the interior, much weaker than they had been in earlier times, with such support as might possibly be given by war parties from Canada. In Nova Scotia the Indians were inspired chiefly by the priest Le Loutre and supported by a garrison of 160 regulars and by the doubtful aid of several hundred Acadians whom the priests had partly cajoled and partly forced into the service. As often, the conduct of the priests was violent and oppressive, and the outrages which they incited the Indians and French to commit from time to time on the British were most irritating. The real danger to the British in that region came not from these petty intrigues and attacks but from what larger forces by sea and land from Louisbourg might accomplish in order to recover Nova Scotia and possibly a port of New England, thus opening much freer communication between Canada and the sea.

Before Braddock's expedition was planned Shirley wrote to the board of trade,[1] and still earlier to the earl of Holdernesse, about the anxiety which was felt in New England because of the news which kept coming in of the activity of the French on the isthmus near Bay Verte, their possessing themselves of St. John's river and the trade they were carrying on upon the Bay of Fundy. Their encroachments at Crown Point in the other direction were an equal source of fear. At the close of March, 1754, Shirley told the general court of Massachusetts that he had information of the establishment of French posts on the carrying place between the headwaters of the Kennebec and Chaudière rivers;[2] also that the St. Francis Indians and the Penobscot tribe were growing restless and beginning hostile demonstrations, so that he had already ordered the strengthening of the frontier garrisons in Maine. Shirley insisted that a fort should be built near the head of the Kennebec and the French forced to retire. In June, following his return from Alexandria, Shirley with a strong escort, and accompanied by members of the Massachusetts legislature and commissioners from New Hampshire, visited the eastern posts and at Falmouth held a conference with the Indians.[3] This was the most important meeting since the close of Râle's War, and Shirley could easily assume

---

[1] Shirley Corresp., II, 31, Jan. 1754. [2] Ibid., 33, 52. [3] Ibid., 69, 71–83.

the firm tone with the result that the Maine Indians ratified
Dummer's treaties while the St. Francis Indians, on the
Canadian border, did not appear. Their position was similar
to that of the Caughnawagas as related to the New York
Indians. If an attack was now made on Fort Beauséjour,
the French could expect no diversion in the form of attacks
on the New England settlements by the Indians of Maine.
In the struggle which was now beginning the *petite guerre*
of past times played little part on the northern frontier.
The line of frontier posts was extended through to the Hudson
and such raids as occurred were in that western section.

In the fall of 1750 Lawrence, with about 700 men, had
landed and established a fortified post at Beaubassin opposite
that of the French at Beauséjour, and it was named from
himself Fort Lawrence. In May, 1754, Shirley wrote to
Robinson, the secretary of state, as to the practicability of
the capture of Beauséjour with the aid of, say, 1000 men from
New England, and this it was hoped would put an end to
threatened French encroachments in that quarter.[1] The reply
of Robinson was such as to give full authority for concerted
action to this end by the governments of Nova Scotia and
New England.[2] Lawrence and Shirley were at the same
time corresponding with the same purpose in view. Preparations were therefore made in Massachusetts as a result of
which 2000 volunteers were enlisted and the necessary transportation secured for taking them to Nova Scotia.[3] This plan
was well under way when Braddock arrived and it was incorporated as part of the campaign of 1755. Since in Nova
Scotia the two frontiers touched and the two opposing works
lay within sight of one another, the principal force could be
transported by sea over an accustomed route and no delay
was caused by the necessity of opening a road through a
difficult country, this part of the campaign could be quickly
completed. The vast superiority of the British was at once
shown and after a short siege Beauséjour surrendered at the

---

[1] Shirley Corresp., II, 62.

[2] Robinson to Shirley, July 5, 1754; quoted by Parkman, Montcalm and
Wolfe, I, 240.

[3] For details as to the enlistment of these troops for one year and the subsequent failure of efforts to induce them to serve longer or submit to incorporation
into the king's regiments, see Shirley Corresp., II. 464.

middle of June, followed by the occupation of two other small forts further east on the frontier. So far as fighting was concerned, it was an affair of small magnitude, even for colonial wars, but it removed a thorn from the side of the English and gave them an important strategic advantage. Immediately afterwards they clinched it by the cruel and unnecessary expulsion of the Acadians. The only obstacle which now lay in the path of the British in their efforts to secure pretty complete control of the fisheries was Louisbourg.

The death of Braddock left Shirley in command in America. This was Shirley's own interpretation of the situation, and the lords justices in England soon ordered that he should hold his position until the pleasure of the king was further signified.[1] Though this was never regarded as more than a temporary arrangement, Braddock's defeat had administered a severe blow to the duke's idea of the superiority of regulars for the American service and opened the way, at least as a possibility, for greater reliance on colonial troops and leadership. Though a civilian, Shirley was undoubtedly the only man in the colonies who was in any way fitted for such a responsibility as this. Such reputation as the exploit at Louisbourg had given him had not been forgotten. He had recently returned from Europe fresh from the studies of British claims in America which his position as commissioner to France had imposed, and they had helped to make him more familiar with the frontier, even in its strategic bearings, than any other man. He had anticipated the general plan of operations which the British government had adopted, and this in fact was only an extension of that for the execution of which he had labored in the closing years of the last war.[2] His letters contain the ablest theoretical expositions of the time concerning the objective points toward which the British should direct their advance, Niagara being in his opinion the key to the French position as a whole. If that could be seized and held, the main artery of communication between Canada and the Ohio and Mississippi valleys would be cut

[1] Shirley Corresp., II, 216, 218, 241; Newcastle Papers, Addit. Mss., 32, 858.

[2] See the Letters from the Governors in America to the Secretaries of State, where much of Shirley's correspondence after his return from Europe is to be found. C. O. 5/14-17.

and Canada would be impoverished by the loss of the fur trade. To the great importance of Oswego in this connection he was keenly alive, and this was chosen as the base from which Shirley in person should launch the attack on Niagara. Its relation to his career in this war was to be analogous to that of Nova Scotia and Louisbourg in the previous war.[1] His position in New England, as well as his activities in the previous war, insured adequate attention on his part to the importance in any plan of offence and defence of Crown Point and the line of the Hudson and Lake Champlain.

The close of July had arrived before the news of Braddock's defeat and death had been circulated through the colonies and the new commander had notified his subordinates of the continuance of the campaign under his general management. Except for a momentary resolve that Dunbar and his men should be sent back to the Pennsylvania frontier, which was soon changed to a definitive order that they should march northward, Shirley attempted in no way to influence the course of events on the Ohio front. So far as his activities went, they were now confined to New York and to the projected expeditions against Crown Point and Niagara. Since early spring Shirley had been in what seemed to be friendly communication with Johnson and other New York officials concerning these enterprises.[2] He had early called for enlistments in all the New England colonies for the Crown Point expedition. An appropriation was secured from the assembly of Massachusetts for a share of the expense of Johnson's work in securing the coöperation of the Six Nations. Steps were taken for raising a regiment from Massachusetts to join in the Crown Point expedition and quotas from the other New England colonies. Stirred by Shirley's appeals, De Lancey had called the New York assembly and promoted action in the council which resulted in a vote to raise 800 men.[3] All of this was done before Braddock's arrival and the conference at Alexandria. At the time of that conference and by virtue of authority given him by the Massachusetts legislature to appoint a commander, Shirley commissioned Johnson as

[1] Shirley Corresp., II, 147, 180, 196.
[2] *Ibid.*, 152 *et seq.*
[3] N. Y. Col. Docs., VI, 946, 950.

major general and commander of the New England forces which were to go against Crown Point.[1] De Lancey issued a similar commission not only for the New England forces, but for the Indian and New York troops as well, the whole proceeding having the approval of Braddock. Finally all the colonies whose troops served under him granted him commissions. Johnson modestly confessed that his slight experience in military affairs made his claim upon the honor less than that of many New Englanders,[2] but he was aware that his appointment was due to his influence with the Indians, though he would have labored as hard to insure their aid had some other person been selected to command. Soon, however, the question of his emolument was brought forward, and the value of the business interests which he was being obliged to surrender was widely urged by Johnson in appeals for appropriations to the various colonies concerned.

The three thousand French regulars who had crossed upon the squadron from Brest, reached Canada in June, in time for the opening of the campaign. At about the same time the Marquis de Vaudreuil, son of the previous governor general of the same name and the first man of Canadian birth to be appointed to this office, was designated to succeed Duquesne. The intention at the beginning was that the force under Dieskau should attack Oswego, but the arrival of news after a part of them had started up the St. Lawrence on this errand that the British were advancing against Crown Point caused the diversion of the attack to the region of the upper Hudson. This shows that, whichever course the French took, it was quite time for the British to be defending their frontier or assailing the French outposts. The action of the New England assemblies and executives, supported by volunteering on a considerable scale among the farmers and mechanics of the region, showed that the spirit of coöperation there was adequate and gave an earnest of what was to be the spirit of New England throughout the war. The feeling toward Shirley was quite different from what it had been toward Dudley at an earlier time, and the New Englanders had grown up to a

[1] N. Y. Col. Docs., VI, 956; Doc. Hist. of N. Y., II, 651-654.

[2] Johnson to Shirley, Braddock and Pepperell, March 17, 1755; Johnson Mss.; N. Y. Col. Docs., VI, 946, Johnson to De Lancey and Shirley, May 16, 1755, Johnson Mss.

certain feeling of strength and maturity which, with the expected aid from Great Britain, carried with it a growing conviction that at last the time had come when they could rid themselves forever of the horrors of French and Indian massacres. Massachusetts voted 4500 men; New Hampshire, 500; Rhode Island, 400; Connecticut, 1200; to which New York added 800, making altogether a force of more than 7000. But the actual levies never equalled the numbers voted and they reached camp slowly, many never appearing there at all. So the force which actually mustered under Johnson never exceeded about 3600 men, all of whom except a few hundred were untrained rustics, though of better fighting quality than those with whom Washington had to deal on the Virginia frontier. Phineas Lyman, the second in command, was a brave and able officer. With great difficulty Johnson got together about 300 Indians, mostly Mohawks. The force which was advancing from Canada numbered about 3600, French regulars of excellent quality, Canadians and Indians, the last mentioned under the command of Legardeur de Saint Pierre. A force from New Hampshire which had struck directly across toward Lake Champlain, was diverted southward and thus saved from falling into the hands of the French.

Johnson and his men had some of the difficulties to encounter which had confronted Braddock, but far less in extent and degree. The troops, with their artillery, military supplies and provisions had to be taken up the Hudson on bateaux and beyond on wagons. Though the government of New York had ample warning of the need of bateaux and men to propel them, and wagons and horses, the supply of these was inadequate.[1] At the Great Carrying Place a fort was built, called first Fort Lyman and finally Fort Edward.[2] From that point the way divided and the first resolve to advance by the way of the so-called " drowned lands " to the head of Lake Champlain, with a difficult road to be built all the way, was abandoned. At the instance of Johnson a road fourteen miles long, extending due north through the forest from Fort Edward to

[1] Shirley Corresp., II, 435.
[2] Because of the location there of the house of the well known John Henry Lydius, among the French the fort often went by his name.

the head of Lake St. Sacrament, was built. Johnson re-christened this beautiful sheet of water with the prosaic name of Lake George, and at its head built a stockaded and earth fort, which he named William Henry. Johnson's affection for the royal family was shown by the names which he gave on these occasions.

Meantime the French had advanced southward from Crown Point, or Fort Frederic, and begun what was to be the permanent occupation of the rocky promontory at Ticonderoga as a fortified position. With a picked force Dieskau then undertook a rapid advance up Lake Champlain to South Bay, with the view of capturing Fort Edward. But the Iroquois who were with Dieskau refused to face the guns which they thought were mounted on this fort. Finding, at the same time, that Johnson was encamped at the head of Lake George, they passed around the southern end of French Mountain and, on September 7th and 8th, started north toward the camp of the English. A detachment that was sent under Colonel Ephraim Williams and Lieutenant Colonel Whiting to meet them, fell into an ambush and was saved from the fate of Braddock by the fact that the survivors had a much larger force to fall back upon. It was in this initial conflict that Williams and Hendrick, the chief who had so often voiced Mohawk discontent, were slain. The French pursued and at Johnson's camp was fought the battle of Lake George. As the Canadian militia and Indians rendered little valuable service, this was an encounter chiefly between French regulars as the assailants and the British, who fought from behind an improvised breastwork of wagons and logs. The commanders on both sides were wounded, Dieskau very seriously. The place of Johnson was taken by Lyman, who was leading the troops when the day was won. The British provincials stood their ground well and lost as heavily as did the enemy, the conflict being decided by a rush of the Americans forward from their position as they saw the enemy begin to weaken. A rout of the French followed, which the stubborn resistance of the 200 French regulars was powerless to prevent.[1] The Canadians and Indians who escaped retreated northward to positions at Ticonderoga and Crown Point. The affair at

[1] N. Y. Col. Docs., X, 316–337.

Lake George was the counterpart of that at Louisbourg in the late war. In the case of the latter the victory was won wholly by New Englanders, while at Lake George it was chiefly their work. So it had been throughout the colonial wars and was to continue to be till their close. Such crude military efficiency as existed in the colonies had its habitat chiefly in New England, and that for very good reasons which the origin and history of that section made perfectly evident.

The Crown Point expedition, however, has been well described as " a failure disguised under an incidental success." The Mohawks immediately went home to mourn their dead, but recruits from Massachusetts and Connecticut came in large numbers after the battle. Though undisciplined and thinly clad, they were ready for an advance, and this was strongly the desire of the colonies which sent them, as was clearly shown when Oliver Partridge came to the camp as a commissioner from Massachusetts. Shirley from Oswego urged Johnson to push on. But the general's flesh wound and inflamed eyes kept him in his tent, while he complained of the lack of wagons and the impossibility of maintaining discipline over a horde of rustics who elected their own officers. As weeks passed and the weather grew cold, disgust among the soldiers increased. Governor Sir Charles Hardy came up to Albany, where he was met by Peter Wraxall, Johnson's efficient secretary, and it was decided not to consult the New England governments more fully about the conduct of the expedition. Councils of war meantime were held at Lake George, over which, because of the illness of Johnson, Lyman presided. After protracted debates the officers decided that the condition of the army was such that, with the insufficient supply of wagons and especially of provisions, an advance would be impossible the present season.[1] It was the idea of Johnson that the completion of the forts south of Lake George

---

[1] As authority for these statements see the correspondence, during the months of September and October, in the Ms. Johnson Papers at Albany. The decisive reason was probably stated in a minute of the council of war of October 20th, to the effect that Johnson's army had never been possessed of two weeks, provisions in advance, except meat. It was owing to this that they did not dare to attempt the reduction of Crown Point. This is to be found among a mass of material relating to the controversy between Loudon and Shirley, in the Hardwicke Papers, B. M. Addit. Mss. 35909.

would furnish an adequate conclusion to the campaign. And
so it was decided, though this course was criticised by officials
at Albany. Johnson resigned his command, and took as
rewards a baronetcy from the king, a grant of £5000 from
parliament and the applause of Europe. Wraxall and his New
York friends saw to it that this was gained for their favorite,
while Lyman, who won the battle, so far as any officer did it,
was not even mentioned in the general's report.[1]

Prior to the summer and autumn of 1755 both Niagara and
Oswego, in a military sense, were very weak and neglected
posts. The regular garrison at Niagara numbered only about
thirty men and the fort was in the usual state of decay. But
after Braddock's defeat a number of troops came there temporarily from Fort Duquesne, and also a force of regulars
was sent thither after their arrival from France. Under the
direction of the engineer, Pouchot, the works were much
strengthened. But owing to the difficulty of supporting a
large garrison at a point so remote, it was reduced to about
300 men for the winter of 1756. For his projected expedition against Niagara Shirley had about 1500 men — his own
regiment and that of Pepperell and 500 men from New Jersey.[2] Two companies under Bradstreet were sent ahead in
April to build the vessels which had been ordered for use on
Lake Ontario. The main body was sent on in detachments
during the early summer, Shirley himself not leaving Schenectady till near the end of July. The troops with their provisions and equipment were transported in bateaux up the
Mohawk river to the modern Rome and thence over the long
portage to Wood Creek and Oneida Lake and down the
Oswego to the fort. The distance was long, much of it was
difficult and the transport of troops and their supplies, especially over the portage, was subject to many and long delays.
The shallows in the Mohawk were also likely to make its
navigation slow and arduous. The difficulties of this march
were not so great as those which confronted Braddock, but
they far exceeded those of a similar nature which were sur-
mounted by Johnson.

[1] Shirley suggested in a letter to Johnson that Lyman or Ruggles be ordered
to go on and seize Ticonderoga and hold it as a good point from which to begin
another year's campaign. Shirley to Johnson, Sept. 25, 1755, Johnson Mss.

[2] The latest detailed account is by Severance, An Old Frontier of France, II.

As was always the case, Shirley by his profuse letter writing and elaboration of plans advertised this expedition far and wide. After his return from Alexandria, as his mind became more fixed upon it, he began mildly to disparage the Crown Point enterprise as of inferior importance in comparison. He desired to divert some troops from Johnson's to his own force. He also insisted, and rightly, that he needed a body of Indians as guides and helpers, and sought them among the Iroquois whom Johnson had just entertained in large numbers and at great expense in order to induce them to march to Crown Point. Johnson and his friends insisted that the protection of Indians was not needed on a march through the country of friendly tribes, like the Six Nations. But Shirley got the help of Colonel Lydius of Albany, who was personally and politically offensive to Johnson, in making his appeals to the Indians. As he passed through their country he held conferences and spoke to them at length. But the New Englanders had no command of Indian rhetoric, in which Johnson was a master, and Shirley's appeals did not move the sachems. He got very little aid from them, but he did secure the help of some young men from Albany. He also provoked the wrath of Johnson to the boiling point. New York officials were naturally jealous of interference with the Six Nations, especially by New Englanders. Johnson was especially sensitive on the subject of his exclusive control in this department and declared that Shirley was throwing his arrangements into utter confusion.[1] Wraxall and Banyar echoed and still further exaggerated his complaints. Even old Hendrick had a hand in the affair. John Pownall, who was active in the colonies as a general agent and in-

---

[1] See in particular Shirley Corresp., II, 243. Shirley's statements are in *ibid.*, 233, 355 and in the pamphlet entitled "The Conduct of Major General Shirley," issued in his defence. The merciless exposé by the author or authors of the "Review of the Military Operations in North America," of the spirit and doings of the New York clique in this connection, especially as it bears upon De Lancey and Johnson, is of great interest and value. Although this is a thoroughgoing defence of Shirley and is written in the style of an acute controversialist, characteristic of William Livingston, it contains one of the most valuable discussions extant of New York politics in the eighteenth century. Wraxall's, "Some Thoughts etc.," in N. Y. Docs., VII, 15–31, gives the Johnson view concerning Indian relations. It is also enforced in many letters of Johnson, to be found in the N. Y. Docs., Doc. Hist. of N. Y., and in the Johnson Mss. See Stone's Life of Johnson for the authoritative defence of him.

spector, ready to do or accept whatever came to hand, offered to be bearer of charges against Shirley to England.
Governor Hardy and Lieutenant Governor De Lancey threw
their influence on the same side, and the positive recommendation of Hardy [1] that the exclusive control of the affairs of the Six Nations should be continued in the governor
to be exercised through Johnson would have sufficed to continue in his place, even had it not been for the support of
others and Johnson's vehement protests against the interference by Shirley and his agents.

It was a sordid, but characteristic, sectional and political
quarrel, and as one reads Shirley's letters and the record, so
far as it is available, of what he and his agents actually did
in the Indian country, the conviction grows that it was too
slight to have been the real cause of so much intrigue and
bitter feeling. And yet one can see that, if Shirley had
remained in command during another campaign and had
succeeded in his Niagara enterprise, he would have tried
to make Oswego the centre of Indian trade and thus
would have drawn it away from Albany and from Johnson's
control.[2] He would also have introduced the New England
method of establishing truck houses in the Indian country.
In that way he hoped to break the connection with Canada
through the Caughnawagas and move the trade further west,
where he thought it now properly belonged. But though
this sweeping plan was not known to Johnson at the time,
the bland self-assurance with which Shirley tried to put his
clear cut New England ideas into operation in New York
could not help being offensive. If the New Yorkers could
have read his letters to Sir Thomas Robinson and others,
with their elaborate plans for a decisive victory the next
year in a campaign of which he hoped to be the leader, they
would have been still more disturbed.

But the actual achievement of Shirley was less than that
which went by the name of Johnson and much less dramatic.
His last detachment reached Oswego at the beginning of
September, and began the construction of a fort on the east
bank of the river, soon known as Fort Ontario. This proved

[1] N. Y. Col. Docs., VII, 3.
[2] Shirley Corresp., II, 373–377.

to be the only work there which was properly situated for the defence of the place. Shirley had at that time 1400 men fit for duty.[1] A sloop and schooner of 60 tons each and two row-galleys of 20 tons each, all armed with small guns, and 8 whale boats had been provided. The bateaux which had been used on the march, with the addition of such as were needed, together with canoes, were to be used for transporting the supplies and most of the men. It was estimated that 600 regulars would be needed for the expedition against Niagara, the rest of the troops being left to protect and work on the defences of Oswego. The force was to skirt the southern shore of Lake Ontario on their voyage of four or five days westward to Niagara. Assurance of the weakness of that post had been obtained, but not such information about Fort Frontenac as to convince the council of officers that an attack could also be made on that post. On the arrival from Fort Duquesne[2] of large reinforcements at the end of summer and also of detachments from the regiments of Béarn and Guienne Shirley was also not adequately informed. Moreover, if one-half of his men were taken to Niagara while the French held Fort Frontenac with a considerable force they might easily cross the lake and capture Oswego, thus entirely cutting off Shirley's communications. In such a case his men at best would be exposed to starvation, as the procuring of sufficient provisions even at Oswego was one of the most difficult problems. After the council of war, however, had voted to take the risk, the weather became bad and for thirteen days[3] rain and strong winds prevailed on the lake, making navigation impossible. It was now the close of September and, when the officers were again brought together in council, it was decided that the season was too advanced to admit of the attack on Niagara. It was now decided to devote the rest of the autumn to the strengthening of the works at Oswego and the accumulation of provisions and equipment there, so that early the next summer the expedition could be resumed with good prospect of success. Two

---

[1] Shirley Corresp., II, 248, 261 et seq.

[2] The troops from the south brought with them the artillery which had been captured from Braddock. Fort Niagara during the following autumn and spring was largely rebuilt and greatly strengthened.

[3] Ibid., 289–292.

small fortified posts, Fort Williams and Fort Bull had been built to guard the Great Carrying Place and as storehouses for supplies on the way to Oswego. A month after the attack on Niagara had been abandoned Shirley returned to Albany and thence to New York, leaving some of the independent companies and his own and Pepperell's regiment at Oswego.

Prior to his arrival in New York, Shirley had invited several of the governors to meet him there in conference over plans for the coming year. He issued to Johnson a new commission, from which all reference to him as sole superintendent of Indian affairs was omitted.[1] This was followed by instructions about holding a general conference at Onondaga, a step for which Johnson on his own initiative and that of the New York government was already preparing. These measures which indicated a determination on Shirley's part to take a controlling hand in Indian affairs along the entire frontier, Johnson had for the time to accept with a show of meekness. But when he came to hold a series of conferences with the Indians,[2] continued at intervals from December to March, he met with so hearty a reception as to prove that he was still their favorite and that in comparison with Johnson Shirley had no standing in their affections. The flow of Indian rhetoric and the tiresome negotiations were resumed, with the purpose not only of rousing the Six Nations to greater military activity but also of inducing them to labor with the Delawares and Shawnees to persuade them to cease attacks on Pennsylvania and Virginia and return to friendship with their former masters. By taking the petticoats off the Delawares and, with the assent of the Six Nations, welcoming them again as men, Johnson did contribute something toward the restoration of quiet along the western frontier. The board of trade also interested itself in an effort to induce the assembly of New York to quash the Kayaderosseras patent and other land grants which were specially offensive to the Six Nations, as a means of conciliation.[3] Upon these matters Johnson worked hard and congratulated himself on the progress he was making.

Shirley's council of war which met at New York in De-

---

[1] *Ibid.*, 336–340, 362, 364.   [2] N. Y. Col. Docs., VII, 44–74.   [3] *Ibid.*, 77.

cember,[1] was attended only by the governors of Connecticut, New York, Pennsylvania and Maryland. Under the lead of Shirley, it was dominated by the idea that the main strength of the next campaign should be directed to the conquest of Lake Ontario, that is, to the capture of Niagara, Toronto, Fort Frontenac and La Gallette or Fort Présentation, with such a strengthening of certain of these places as to isolate lower Canada and make the control of the British over the Great Lakes and the interior definitive. This was accompanied by projects for securing aid from the Indians on a large scale.[2] Crown Point, it was planned, should be attacked by a force of 10,000 men. Shirley's dispatches containing these details were intrusted to Captain Roger Morris for safer conveyance across the ocean.[3]

The campaign of 1755 had now come definitely to a close. Colonial troops under colonial leaders had not met with so dramatic a defeat as Braddock had suffered, but they had won no victories. War was now actually declared between France and Great Britain and the conflict raged on three continents. The British naturally resumed the policy with which they had started and upon a larger scale, by sending regular troops under European commanders, relying upon the coöperation of the fleet and formulating plans for wide reaching operations by land and sea.

[1] N. H. Prov. Papers, VI, 463–467; Shirley Corresp., II, 344, 371; Severance, *op. cit.*, II, 142.

[2] Shirley Corresp., II, 367, 373, 402, 433.   [3] *Ibid.*, 368.

CHAPTER XVI

THE FOURTH INTERCOLONIAL WAR. SUCCESS OF THE
FRENCH DURING THE YEARS 1756–1758

So far as the American campaigns and the external events of the war are concerned, the honors for the years 1756 and 1757 belonged to the French. This was not owing to the dispatch of especially large reinforcements from France, for throughout the war, now beginning in earnest, the masses of her soldiery were employed in central Europe " to fight the battles of Austria." Only two battalions, one belonging to the regiment of La Sarre and the other to that of Royal Roussillon, could be spared for service in Canada. These numbered 1050 men.[1] This force, after a prosperous voyage, reached Quebec in May, 1756. The change which was to follow their arrival was due not so much to the troops or their equipment as to the ability of their commander, the Marquis de Montcalm, and the group of talented officers who accompanied him. The new commander was of noble lineage from Provence, high minded, cultured and a veteran in the service, to which he was ardently devoted, and in which his ancestors for generations had borne an honorable part. On receiving his appointment to the Canadian service he was raised to the rank of major general. Associated with him as second and third in command were the Chevalier de Lévis and the Chevalier de Bourlamaque. His first aide-de-camp was Bougainville, a man trained in the law, learned and possessed of literary gifts of a high order, but who had abandoned these callings to enter the army. Montcalm, after his unexpected appointment, had sought to prepare himself for his task by reading Charlevoix, and the scholarly tastes which he shared in common with Bougainville fitted them for intimate companionship. It was this group of officers, with

[1] For an exact statement of the military strength of the French in Canada at this time, see Chapais in Doughty, Siege of Quebec, I, 156.

certain engineers and others of similar spirit, and the regulars (*troupes de terre*) who were brought from France during this and the preceding year, that were mainly instrumental in winning the victories which temporarily checked what seemed likely to be an irresistible advance of the British.

Though Montcalm was a major general and the officers and regular troops in Canada were placed under his command, his commission from the king placed him in turn under the command of the governor general, and his instructions on this point were very explicit.[1] The incumbent of the office at this time was Pierre Rigoud, marquis de Vaudreuil, a native of Canada and son of Philippe de Vaudreuil, who had been governor general early in the century. The present Vaudreuil, who was the successor of Dusquesne, was the first Canadian who had attained the dignity of a governor general. Directly under his command were the colony regulars (*troupes de la marine*) and the Canadian militia. The former were troops originally sent from France but who, with their successors in the organization, had been so long in the province as to lose in a measure their original discipline and, like the independent companies in the English colonies, to approximate in character to the militia, which was made up of Canadian *habitants*.[2] Vaudreuil was a man of average ability and honesty and was tireless in his activity and devotion to the interests of Canada, as he understood them. But he exhibited the petty jealousies to which men of narrow calibre are subject. It was therefore almost inevitable that the sensitive pride of the colonist should appear as one of his leading characteristics. By virtue of his office he was commander of all the troops which might at any time be serving in the colony. His word therefore must be decisive as to plans of campaign and, so incessant was his activity, that his influence was likely to be felt in the arrangement of most details. Vaudreuil was anxious to retain the management of the war in Canada in his own hands, and Bigot, the intendant, who controlled the finances of the colony fully enjoyed the

[1] N. Y. Col. Docs., X, 394. Chapais, Le Marquis de Montcalm, decidedly the most thorough and satisfactory work on the general.

[2] These troops now numbered nearly 2000 and their discipline had recently been improved by Duquesne.

confidence of the governor general. Moreover, in October, 1755, after the defeat of Dieskau, Vaudreuil had written to the home government that it was not necessary to have a general sent over to command the regulars. "War in this country," he wrote,[1] "is very different from wars in Europe. . . . However brave the commander of those troops may be, he could not be acquainted with the country, nor perhaps be ready to receive the advice subalterns may offer; would rely on himself or on ill-enlightened counsels and would not succeed though he should sacrifice himself." His influence over the Indians was also likely to be less than that of a native.

With such a man and under such conditions Montcalm was indeed likely to find it difficult to coöperate on easy terms. One source of the difficulty was that Vaudreuil was ambitious to pose as a military man. Not only did he desire to manage the civil affairs of the colony but its military policy as well, and in the latter sphere he had much less experience and was apparently a less able man than Shirley. The experience of both these men in war was simply administrative, in a sense little better than secretarial, while in the actual conduct of campaigns and battles and the management of men under arms both were tyros. Because among the British there were so many colonies and no single governor could pretend that he was entitled to general command, such a condition of jealousy as developed on the part of Vaudreuil toward Montcalm could not exist. The inefficiency of most of the British commanders during the war and the domineering attitude assumed by some of them might very properly have justified severe criticism and opposition but the conditions under which this could assert itself did not exist. In Canada, however, the conditions were favorable to it, and had not Montcalm been an officer of such high character and ability, and had not such marked success attended his earlier operations, Vaudreuil might easily have defeated his efforts and procured his recall. But at first relations were friendly and the campaign of 1756 started off with an inspiring French victory.

Though an expedition against Oswego had been planned the

[1] N. Y. Col. Docs., X, 375.

year before by Vaudreuil and abandoned when the report came that Johnson was advancing toward Crown Point, when the time now came to undertake it, he had misgivings concerning its success. Montcalm had previously visited Ticonderoga and, being convinced that the British would not seriously threaten that post for the present, under orders from Vaudreuil he left it in charge of Lévis and returned to Montreal. Whenever operations directed toward the lakes on the south and the west were in progress, that town rather than Quebec was the military capital of the province. When points on or beyond Lake Ontario were to be attacked, Fort Frontenac became the immediate base of operations, the place where most of the force, with its artillery and supplies, was collected and whence the expedition was launched. Thither the battalions of Guienne and La Sarre now came from the east and that of Béarn from Niagara. Rigoud, a brother of the governor general, was sent on in advance with the chief body of Canadians and encamped at Niaouré bay, now Sackett's Harbor, on the south-eastern shore of Lake Ontario. On the fourth of August Montcalm embarked and joined Rigoud. The force numbered about 3200 men, with 51 cannon, and from Sackett's Harbor they skirted the shore to a point where, with some difficulty, they landed within less than two miles of Fort Ontario. The landing was effected at midnight on the tenth. So thorough had been Montcalm's preparations that the plan had succeeded at every point and the enemy did not discover the presence of the French till the morning after they had landed.

It is now time to review the events which had been taking place on the British side. Early in the spring of 1756 Vaudreuil had sent an expedition under de Léry, by the way of La Présentation (Ogdensburg), to cut the communications, if possible, between the Mohawk river and Oswego. Their objective was the two forts which had been built by the British, one at the head of navigation on the Mohawk (site of the present city of Rome) and the other at Wood Creek, the western end of the portage. The latter of these posts, Fort Bull, de Léry attacked and destroyed, with nearly all of its garrison. Other attempts were made later to harass the garrison at Oswego. But the line of communication was kept open and Shirley hired 2000 boatmen, drawn from eastern New England and from all available intermediate points, whom he armed and divided into companies of fifty.[1] These he put under the command of Lieutenant Colonel John Bradstreet, a veteran of the previous war. This force, according to his plan, while they propelled the bateaux, loaded with supplies, up the Mohawk and traversed the portages and streams beyond, would be able to defend themselves and so would need no escort. To this plan Shirley resorted after all efforts to secure protection from the Indians or in other ways had failed. One convoy of provisions and supplies had thus been taken by Bradstreet successfully to Oswego when, early in July, on his return up the Onondaga river, he was suddenly attacked by a force of several hundred French under Coulon de Villiers. A bloody fight followed, in which Bradstreet's men lost rather heavily, but with the aid of reinforcements were finally able to drive the French off. The affair, however, was reported throughout Canada as being a great French success.

During the winter Shirley did what he could by correspondence with the governors of the middle provinces to rouse them to joint action. But when recruiting was begun in Maryland and Pennsylvania old protests against the enlistment of servants were renewed and no help was obtained from provinces south of New Jersey for the campaign on the northern frontier. Massachusetts, on the other hand, heartened by a promise of at least partial reimbursement of her war expenditures by Great Britain, had increased the number of troops which she was prepared to raise to 3500, or more than double her quota. The other northern colonies also increased their grants, New Hampshire and Rhode Island to 500 men each, Connecticut to 2500, New York to 1700, and some with improved equipment.[2] But several months must pass before these men could be raised, equipped and marched to the frontier.

Near the close of May Shirley held his last council of war at Albany.[3] It was composed only of military officers, neither Johnson nor any of the governors being present. Shirley's

---

[1] Shirley Correspondence, II, 442 et seq.
[2] Ibid., 386 et seq., 433.   [3] Ibid., 453-459.

plan of campaign was again expounded, as well as the present strength and location of all the forces. The reorganized regiments of Braddock, together with the provincials of New England and New York — something over 6000 — must be reserved, he said, for service on the Lake Champlain front, but for the present they had better be kept within a comfortable distance of Albany. As to the campaign for the control of Lake Ontario, about 550 men in four small detachments, together with four companies of rangers which Shirley proposed to raise, were estimated to be sufficient for keeping open communication between Schenectady and Oswego. But only 2000 men, including the garrison of some 1400 already at Oswego, were available, for the Ontario enterprise. Such recruits of inferior quality as Shirley could gather during the early summer were sent thither, but this availed nothing. As it had been estimated at the council of war the previous December that at least 6000 troops were necessary for the Ontario enterprise, its execution during the present year was now seen to be impossible.

Shirley's anxieties were soon increased by the reports which were received of the deplorable condition of the garrison and defences of Oswego itself. Vicars, a captain of Shirley's regiment, who reached Albany an invalid after passing the winter in the garrison, told how several times they had been on the point of abandoning the place because of their sufferings from hunger and disease. Of his regiment more than half had died, and so weak had the garrison become from exposure, lack of food, and filth diseases that they were seldom able to mount a guard of more than sixteen or eighteen men and that many of these were so weak that they could not stand without the support of a stick. Pepperell's regiment, which had been lodged in Fort Ontario and better protected, had not suffered so much. Both regiments, however, complained that they had received no pay for eight months. The letters of Mercer,[1] the commander, to Williams, who was commissary at the Oneida Carrying Place, threw much additional light upon the situation. They revealed an experience which was perhaps more horrible than that to

[1] These letters were sent as inclosures by Loudon to England and are among the Hardwicke Papers, B. M. Addit. Mss. 35, 909.

which any other colonial garrison had ever been subjected, a veritable Valley Forge of the colonial wars. He wrote that in 1755 Shirley brought no provisions with him though he and his secretary gave out that ample supplies were coming. All through the winter the garrison was on three-fourths allowance and no attention was paid to Mercer's representations. His last letters were sent unsealed, so that officers on the way might send some provisions. Many soldiers were sent away on furlough to keep them from starving, and starvation was used as the plea to excuse desertion. All that saved the garrison was the open winter and small supplies sent by Williams. Near the close of March Mercer was on the point of abandoning the place, as they had only three days' provision left. On April 28 another supply found the garrison with provisions for only five days. If many had not died, there would not have been enough to subsist them. In the spring they had not more than 140 men fit for duty in the two regiments.

The account given by Vicars and also by Mackellar, the engineer, of the state of the defences of Oswego, showed that the situation regarded from that point of view was equally desperate. The old Fort Oswego, on the west side of the river, was only a block house, built originally as a trading post, and surrounded by a wall of dry rubble pointed up with mortar. Three small cannon were mounted, but the garrison feared to fire them lest the shock might bring down the wall. Fort Ontario on the height above the east bank, was a more pretentious structure, but Mackellar thought it badly located and planned and at best it was only a timbered stockade. The garrison did not expect a siege, and so weak and ill disciplined were they that scalping parties of Indians could seize or tomahawk the unwary almost under the walls of the forts.[1] Bradstreet brought relief in the spring, not only in food but in the form of artillery and military supplies, and the condition of the garrison greatly improved. A considerable body of men was then put to work on Fort Ontario and by August it had been pushed toward completion. But at best it could not stand before artillery.

[1] Mackellar to Montresser, May 26 and July 2, 1756, C. O. 5/46. Military Corresp. to Sec. of State; Mercer to Shirley, July 2, 1756, W. O. 1/4; Parkman, Montcalm and Wolfe, I.

As both the French and the English were contending for the control of the lakes, and especially of Lake Ontario, they could not be ignorant of the necessity of having armed vessels on that sheet of water The French had long possessed a few such craft on the lake, which had been used in convoying men and supplies on their many excursions between Fort Frontenac and Niagara. From the early part of 1755 Shirley had been alive to the necessity of providing such vessels on the British side. This formed an important part of his plan for the control of Lake Ontario. In that connection, as we have seen, he caused the building of a few vessels in 1755 and the matter was discussed in his councils of war. Captain Housman Broadley [1] was in charge of this work, and early in 1756 he was sent back to Oswego with a number of ship carpenters and seamen under orders to build two brigantines and another armed sloop. The capture of Fort Bull by the French delayed and imperilled their journey, but they passed through in safety. When, however, they reached Oswego and the work of cutting timber for their use was undertaken, Indian scalping parties made the task very dangerous and costly. And yet additional seamen came up with Bradstreet and the improving of the older vessels and the building of one or two new ones was prosecuted. Cruises also were made on the lake and on one occasion an encounter was just escaped with a superior French force which was conveying the Béarn regiment from Niagara to Fort Frontenac. By midsummer the British are estimated to have had, in the form of armed schooners, sloops, brigantines and whale boats, a force which was superior in men, number of guns and weight of metal, to that of the French. But in comparison with the French the British were inexperienced in the navigation of the lake, its winds, shoals, currents and the topography of its shores, and in Broadley's attempts at navigation he met with mishaps. The British also were more occupied in building a fleet and other defences than in watching for the approach of the enemy, which was not wholly unexpected. Therefore, not only was Montcalm able to convey his men by water to their destination

[1] See article by W. L. Grant, in Transactions of Royal Soc. of Canada, 1914; everance, Old Frontier of France, II, 161–167, 176 et seq.

without discovery or loss, but Broadley, while the attack was in progress, was not able to give any assistance to the garrison or to save his vessels and men from falling wholly into the hands of the enemy.

It is certain that the continuance of Shirley in command could not have saved Oswego from capture by the French. The remoteness of the place, the natural difficulties attendant upon overland communication with it, the inability of Shirley to arouse to the slightest extent the spirit of co-operation with him on the part either of the Indians or of the clique which governed New York, these causes alone were sufficient to defeat his efforts. The animosity of Johnson toward Shirley knew no bounds and he expressed it without the slightest restraint on all occasions. In this attitude he was supported with all the subtler arts of James De Lancey, whose natural gifts as a politician had been matured and made doubly effective by an experience of more than twenty years amid the factional conflicts of New York. These men hated Shirley as an intruder from New England, as a colonial, a civilian, who, largely by accident, had attained high command and who now, by his skill in devising plans and his incessant activity in executing them, by his insinuating manners and quiet assumption of superiority, even in the sphere of Indian relations which was always so jealously guarded by New York, appeared to be striving to rise above all competitors. It was a situation which could hardly fail to arouse sectional and personal jealousies. The support of Governor Hardy and the council of New York was secured for this view and it insured that Shirley's opponents would be fully heard in England.[1]

And it did not follow, because Louisbourg had been captured in accordance with a plan which he had led in promoting, that in the much wider and more exacting problems which he was now facing he had not ventured beyond his depth. He had certainly overlooked the difficulties of supplying his garrison at Oswego with provisions. No magazine was established for supplying that post. Colonial resources

[1] For the full exposition of this aspect of the case, though with a strong bias against the New York clique and in favor of Shirley, see the "Review of the Military Operations in North America from 1753 to 1756," attributed chiefly to William Livingston, 1 Mass. Hist. Colls., VII.

were soon exhausted and means of communication were so poor that camps must be kept near the settlements. Evidence was also produced later that Shirley issued warrants for the expenditure of large sums in the gross without itemized accounts, and that a number of lower officials and agents who were concerned in these transactions were allowed their "rake-offs" of 5 per cent to 10 per cent each. Profits on army contracts were said to have been shared by men who stood by Shirley, though no one showed that the general himself was corruptly concerned; but he should at least have known and prevented it.

While he was in the midst of preparation for the campaign of 1756 the British government came to its inevitable resolve that Shirley's temporary command should cease, and that the war in America should again be placed in charge of officers of the regular army. But the way in which the change was made furnishes a classic example of the absurdities of which the Newcastle ministry was capable. The intention was that the earl of Loudon should have permanent command, but Shirley was immediately superseded by Colonel Daniel Webb and he by General James Abercromby, who in turn was to hand the office over to Loudon. This meant that before the actual commander should arrive and be ready to begin operations months of delay and indecision would pass and the best part of the year for military operations be wasted. At this time also a commission direct from the crown was issued to Johnson, making him sole superintendent of the affairs of the northern Indians, with an annual salary of £600.[1] Though Shirley's highest hopes were crushed by this event and his critics and enemies were given the apparent support of the highest authority in what were sure to be their efforts to blacken his reputation, he continued work along the accustomed lines to the last without sign of impatience. He showed himself throughout to be not only a loyal official but a gentleman. He treated his fate as a incident in the operation of the system the perfecting of which he had advocated less than two years before and made no complaint except what was implied in the defence of his case and in efforts to obtain a proper hearing in England.

[1] N. Y. Col. Docs., VII, 75, 76 ; Shirley Corresp., II, 425, 428.

Under Shirley, Livingston and Morris had been the favored contractors for army supplies. But Loudon, very likely with good reason, at once insisted that a new contract, for victualling 12,000 men for a year, should be drawn in England. This was awarded to Baker and Kilby, a firm which, it was said, had sufficient resources to make it safe.[1] Loudon was specially desirous of having their contract so drawn as to remove the danger that the troops should suffer from lack of provisions, as had always been the condition in the past. But, according to Shirley and his friends, after Webb and Abercrombie had arrived at Albany and the business was being transferred to the new contractors, fatal delays occurred in the shipment of supplies, and such troops as the 44th regiment for Oswego.[2] This, they said, occurred when it was known that the capture of that post by the French was imminent and the hurrying forward of aid in every form was a pressing necessity. The embarkation of the troops was delayed owing to this cause, from about July 11 to August 12, or thirteen days after Loudon arrived at Albany. Two days later Oswego surrendered. Possibly at no time after the beginning of July could its fall have been prevented, but it was typical of what had always been going on in British-American relations, that this humiliating event should occur just when the men who had been designated to prevent such occurrences were engaged in a sordid quarrel, and when Webb, the officer who was first on the ground, was too sluggish or too intent upon humiliating a rival to act.

Whatever were the actual or possible conditions in Canada, the exploit of Montcalm was a clear cut, unqualified success. Not a mistake was made. The only real chances of failure had been avoided when his troops were landed on the shore near Fort Ontario. After the French had planted their cannon and fired upon that work but a single day, the garrison abandoned it and crossed the river to the other defences.

---

[1] See minutes of treasury board on this, under dates of February and March, 1756, in Hardwicke Papers as above. The contractors had previously been concerned in furnishing supplies in Nova Scotia.

[2] See "The Conduct of General Shirley"; also a "State of the Dispute about the provisons for the transporting the 44th Regiment to Oswego and the true Cause of the Delay of its Imbarkation," W. O. 1/4, C. O. 5/46. Much correspondence full of charges and counter charges, passed back and forth on this subject. See Shirley Corresp., II, 521, 536, 542, 575-580.

Montcalm then took possession of Fort Ontario and from the height on which it stood opened fire on the weak defences across the river. The British briskly replied, but soon Mercer was slain. A force of Canadians and Indians were seen crossing the river above and a complete investment, with the prospect of a massacre, seemed to be impending. Further resistance was seen to be futile and surrender was resolved upon. The officers who were chiefly concerned in this were Lieutenant Colonel Littlehales, who had succeeded to the command on the death of Mercer, and Captain Peter Schuyler. Soldiers, mechanics and laborers to the number of about 1600 thus surrendered to a French force of about 3000. Less than fifty were killed on the English side, while the casualties among the French were still fewer. The forts and vessels were burned and all the supplies which the captors could not carry away were destroyed. Oswego was left in ruins and the French were encouraged to believe that the Six Nations would now come over wholly to their alliance. Though the numbers who fought at Oswego were small, its capture was an important event. Montcalm had administered a severe blow to British prestige throughout the north. Iroquois from the western cantons, as usual, were supporting the French and now it might be expected that both they and other tribesmen who hitherto had nominally been neutral would flock to that side.[1]

As Loudon looked into the doings of Shirley during the later months of his command, he became more and more disgusted with the confusion which, as he observed it, everywhere prevailed. Of course he held Shirley responsible for the loss of Oswego, though since the opening of spring the garrison had been well fed and somewhat strengthened. There was evidently no denying that the defences of the place were inadequate, but could anyone since the beginning of the war have built a stone fort there which could withstand artillery? Loudon not only charged Shirley and his friends with a certain amount of graft, but Shirley in particular with attempting, after he had been superseded, to put through a number of appointments and promotions, ante-

[1] In the Doc. Hist. of New York, I, is some important contemporary material relating to the fall of Oswego, most of it, however, procurable elsewhere.

dating some of them for this purpose.[1] Against these charges Shirley defended himself in England with vigor, asserting that he had always made appointments promptly and had reported them to the war office. As to his muster rolls and accounts in general, they had been audited by a committee of prominent New York merchants appointed by Sir Charles Hardy. "I have always tried my best," he wrote to the treasury board, " to carry on the service in the most economical manner that was for its good, consulting the proper officers on expence in their several departments and ordering money expended in such proportions as appeared necessary to my best judgment. I had discretion and have not abused it, as the accounts will show."

Another subject which increased the suspicions of Loudon and officials, especially Halifax, in England, was certain intercepted letters addressed by some one in the colonies to the duke de Mirepoix and suggesting efforts which were being made by large levies among French, Germans and others in Pennsylvania and elsewhere to aid the cause of France.[2] Webb and Loudon were ordered to discover the guilty party, if possible, but his identity has remained a mystery till the present time. Neither did they succeed in discovering evidence of any accomplices of any movement such as the writer said was on foot. But it gave Halifax an occasion to express a dislike for Shirley very much like that which Loudon felt. Yet the suspicions and charges were not so grave as to lead to a trial or even to an inquiry,[3] though Shirley repeatedly demanded that an opportunity be given him to clear his reputation. After Pitt came into office the matter appears to have been shelved and forgotten.

It is not surprising that John Campbell, earl of Loudon, was filled with lofty contempt for much that he saw and experienced in the colonies, because it was hard to make their inhabitants all go the same way. They were as independent

---

[1] Loudon to Barrington, Aug. 20, 1756 and Aug. 22, 1757. W. O. 1/1; Loudon to Pitt, Nov. 22, 1756, Sec. of State, Military C. O. 5/48.

[2] These are printed in Reports of Am. Hist. Assoc., 1896, Vol. I. The originals are in C. O. 5/51, with the letter of Fox to Loudon, under date of May 7, 1756, transmitting them.

[3] The documents relating to this are in War Office Papers, spring of 1757. A reference to certain accounts is in Corresp. of Pitt with Col. Govs., I, 21.

and hard to drive as his own native Highlanders. Loudon seems to have been a sort of combination of Andros and Nicholson, though built upon a somewhat larger plan than either of them. He was a routine military officer like the former and irascible like the latter. His correspondence upon purely military affairs is abundant and he presumably talked freely on occasion to his fellow officers about the faults of the provincials. He certainly intended to improve on poor Braddock, though, so far as appears, his desire was to conduct operations from the rear and at a safe distance from the firing line. Whether or not he was greatly influenced by the New York clique, Shirley at once became for him the embodiment of most that was evil in the conduct of the war in the colonies. Though a civilian, he had ventured to enter the sacred precincts of the military profession. He always referred to Shirley with contempt and took no pains to conceal this feeling even in the personal correspondence which he had with him. He absurdly insisted that the charge which he preferred against Shirley of responsibility for the loss of Oswego should be laid before the general court of Massachusetts. Indirectly this was accomplished, but the process drew from Shirley such calm and detailed exposition of the points involved as made his lordship's anger uncontrollable. He now ordered Shirley out of the country, much as one would kick a troublesome dog out of the back door. But even that did not disturb Shirley's equanimity, for he argued this point as much in detail as any. The governor's career, however, was ended. He had been led to expect a transfer to the governorship of Jamaica, but in the end he was forced to content himself with that of the Bahama Islands, the most insignificant of the British American colonies. His regiment and that of Pepperell, which had surrendered to the French at Oswego were now ordered broken up and Shirley himself disappeared from view with the Newcastle régime of which he had formed a part.[1]

Two infantry regiments accompanied Abercromby and Loudon to America, and by act of parliament authority was

[1] On the incorporation of these men by Loudon with the Royal American, and the forces serving in Nova Scotia, see Corresp. of Pitt with Col. G overnors I, 17.

also given to enlist in the colonies four battalions of Royal Americans, as they were called, consisting largely of foreign Protestants, but commanded by a British colonel. As this force was to be recruited largely in Pennsylvania, it has been thought that the move was in part designed to counteract plans of the French to recruit in the colonies, which had been suggested in the intercepted letters. With the advent of the new British commanders in America came also an order respecting the rank of general and field officers of the provincials in the forces which were henceforth to operate jointly against the enemy. It was that when regulars and provincials were serving together none of the officers of the latter should hold rank above that of senior captains. The effect of this would be that the entire provincial army might be put under the command of any British major. As the only organized body of troops at that time was on the front adjacent to Lake Champlain, the force which New England chiefly had been raising for the capture of Ticonderoga and Crown Point, the outburst of protest against the new order was raised chiefly in that quarter. After debate in camp the officers came unanimously to the conclusion that the army was an organized body and that they had been made, by the governments from which the troops were raised, executors of a trust which they could not resign.[1] And, even if the officers should obey the order, it would result in a dissolution of the army, as the privates held it to be a part of the terms on which they enlisted that they were to be commanded by their own officers, and this was a principle so strongly held that it was not in the power of man to remove it. This resolution was adopted near the close of July, when the army in its slow advance northward had reached Fort Edward. The action which was taken and the method of it reminds one of the proceedings of the Agitators in the Cromwellian army in their camps at Saffron Walden or Putney. Both were citizen soldiery, not mercenaries or conscripts, and the colonials, following the New England tradition, virtually declared themselves a corporate body and proposed to stand together in their assertion of military equality. John Winslow, whom Shirley had appointed, was their general and Lyman was

[1] Shirley Corresp., II, 492, 497 et seq.

second in command. When Shirley himself learned of their intentions he protested against it with all his might, as rash and mutinous in character and almost sure to end in the defeat of the British forces. After a meeting of provincial officers with Loudon at Albany and a long discussion, to avoid mutiny they promised obedience to the order, but at the same time they practically negatived it by compelling Loudon to permit them to act independently. As no effective action whatever followed, even that contingency was avoided.

The dissatisfaction of the commander-in-chief was further increased by opposition in New York to quartering the regular troops,[1] by the difficulty he found in procuring wagons and other facilities for moving his troops northward from Fort Edward, and from reports which his officers made of the wretched condition both of the defences and the camp at Fort William Henry. By August about 2500 provincials were established in camp at this place, and Lieutenant Colonel Burton, who was sent by Loudon to inspect it, reported that it was filthier than any thing he could have conceived, the outhouses, kitchens, graves and places for slaughtering cattle all mixed through the encampment. The result was that about 500 of the men were sick and most of the remainder "what they call poorly." They buried from five to eight daily. The men were indolent and dirty, and there was great waste of provisions. Neither pickets nor scouting parties were properly kept up. Not enough ground had been cleared about the fort, and the bateaux which they were building, with whaleboats and a few small craft, seemed to be so poorly protected that the enemy might be able to seize them. The fort itself was unfinished and from the description given by the engineer seems to have been as poorly located and even less defensible than the forts at Oswego. The camp at Fort Edward, which was under the command of Lyman, was re-

[1] The public houses in the colonies usually were small, many of them having only the one room available, in which liquor was sold. Loudon requested that a clause be inserted in the mutiny act extending the right of quartering troops in the colonies. He wrote that he could only quarter 50 men in the public houses of Albany, whereas in private houses he could provide for 1400 or more. But the opposition to billeting in private houses of course was general. Loudon to Pitt, March 10, 1757. W. O. Papers ; Corresp. of Pitt with Col. Govs., I, 20.

ported to be in much better condition.[1] But Loudon wrote
that he had not yet seen a fort in America that could command a river, lake or pass which was not itself commanded,
the same criticism which was passed upon the location of
Fort Cumberland, in Maryland, at the beginning of the war.
These were typical colonial conditions which his lordship had
to face. In addition he was told that the road to Lake
George was very rough and that a force passing over it
might easily be ambushed, as had occurred the previous year.
This was the condition on the lake front when the news of
the fall of Oswego was resounding through the colonies.
Webb, who was advancing for its relief, on the rumor that
a large French force was coming southward, burned the
forts at the Great Carrying Place, filled up Wood Creek again
with logs and returned to German Flats. Loudon had about
10,000 men under him, but he concluded that discretion was
the better part of valor and ordered that the intended advance
on Ticonderoga should be abandoned for that season.

In November, 1756, William Pitt was appointed secretary
of state for the southern department and Newcastle for a few
months was driven from office. With him also disappeared
Hardwicke, Fox and Anson, the cleanest sweep since the
rout of the Tories in 1714.[2] At about the same time William
Murray who, with Fox, had been one of Pitt's chief rivals in
the oratorical contests of the commons, sought more con-
genial surroundings as chief justice of king's bench, with a
seat in the house of lords. This change was forced by the
great reversal of alliances on the continent of Europe and
by the defeats which British arms had suffered at sea and in
America. In consequence of the fault of the admiralty and
of Byng, the admiral in command, who paid for it with his
life, the island of Minorca had reverted to its natural owners,
the Bourbon powers, and what at that time was considered a

[1] The originals of these reports are in C. O. 5/47. Burton's report is quoted
at length by Parkman, as well as the contents of certain diaries which confirm
the account.

[2] The negotiations leading up to this may be followed in great detail in the
Newcastle Papers, Addit. Mss. 32866, 32867, 32868, and in many well known
printed sources. Basil Williams, Life of Pitt, I, 284 et seq. For an elaborate
and well balanced discussion of Pitt's career in all its phases, see Von Ruville's
William Pitt, Graf von Chatham, 3 vols. The second volume deals with the
Seven Years' War.

valuable link in the chain of ports which was forging for the control of the Mediterranean on the plea of the protection of British trade was lost. Corsica also was soon occupied by the French. Under the sting of this and of the defeats in America, with the possibilities of what might follow from the Hanoverian connection, the pride and fighting spirit of the nation was aroused and the demand for Pitt, the one man who could lead it, became general and was echoed by the Tories, country gentry and clergy even, as well as by the merchants. The country began to fear a French triumph and even an attempt to invade Great Britain, so that a general invigorating of the militia became a prominent issue.

With Walpole and Pitt we enter upon the golden age of British statesmen who have risen to power as the result of their commanding ability as orators, combined with skill in the management especially of the house of commons, the whole crowned and made effective by energy and success in the conduct of business in the public departments. Pitt, though seriously, almost fatally, handicapped by illness on many critical occasions, proved himself during the war which we are now considering to be one of the greatest of administrators. He was also an orator of the first rank, but that was rather the flowering of his genius than the substance which gave it an enduring value and effect. As to his position in parliament and among contemporary statesmen in general, he was not a manipulator like Walpole, Newcastle or Henry Fox, but he compelled recognition by the force of his personality. In the house he cowed his opponents by the power of his sarcasm and denunciation. As a colleague or in conference with his rivals he was often dictatorial and scorned all the usual arts of management. He was also very much an actor and poseur, dramatic to the finger tips, a man whose imagination often outran the limits of sound judgment. For ultimate decisions he appealed over the heads of all politicians to the nation at large, and his greatest distinction lies in the fact that he was the first British statesman to do this. It was on questions of war, foreign relations and the empire, and not upon issues arising distinctively within the realm, that he made his appeal. Therefore he was a British imperialist, the greatest of them all, and with him the empire in its earlier form reached its culmination. Though he was a thoroughgoing mercantilist, yet under his touch many of the badges of inferiority which the colonists had worn fell away, and for a brief period, till success against the French was won, the realm and the dominions seemed to be one. The supreme evidence of his greatness, recluse and invalid though he was, appears in the fact that he was able to inspire this feeling even for a short time. This was the secret of his popularity and fame then and for all time to come. Embodied in him and his life the old empire seemed to take form as an ideal, exalted above the infinite petty jealousies and failures which constituted so much of the substance of its history. Among the great statesmen of the nation which Pitt was fighting, Richelieu appears as the one with whom he best compared, though of course with the greatest contrasts in the background and details of the pictures.

The wars which hitherto had been waged between Great Britain and France were limited in character. This means that neither of the adversaries had sought by every possible exertion of its strength to destroy either the naval or land power of the other. This purpose does not appear even in the campaigns of Marlborough, while the efforts of Louis XIV were directed chiefly toward conquests among the smaller states of the continent. But at the time we have reached and as it took form in the resolution of Pitt, the war, so far as was possible under the conditions which then existed, became unlimited in its purpose and intensity. Pitt resolved, if possible, to destroy the naval power of France and to deprive her of all her over-sea possessions. To this end he sought to have the complete control of war by sea and land and of diplomacy centered in his hands. The premiership he could not and did not at this period obtain, but though he was only secretary of state for the southern department, he insisted that his influence in these matters should be predominant. This position he finally attained and for four years wielded with tireless energy the entire power of the British empire for the purpose of defeating France. Such spirit was infused into the service, followed presently by such triumphant results, that the world has adjudged him to have been one of the greatest war ministers who ever lived.

Pitt's first period in office continued for little more than four months, until April, 1757. Though he was able to hold very few cabinet meetings and appeared but rarely in the house, his letters and orders abounded and reached every quarter and every department of the service which could be concerned in the common task.[1] The duke of Devonshire, by whose name the ministry went, was only nominally the premier, while the fact that Temple was first lord of the admiralty and Holdernesse held the northern province insured as a result that Pitt should have his own way.[2] Great activity was at once developed in strengthening the military forces of the crown and especially the navy. The building of many more ships was ordered and this process was continued till the end of the war, the navy then numbering 412 ships of all classes. A corresponding increase was made in the provision for seamen. The most significant and popular measure of Pitt connected with the army was his incorporation with it of Highland regiments, two battalions of which were at once sent to America. The army in general was considerably increased, to make up for the Hessian and Hanoverian troops which were sent back to the continent. The point upon which Pitt was compelled most directly to reverse himself was the provision for an army of observation in Hanover; but that had been made necessary by treaty as a means of protecting Prussia, the new ally, from French attack.

But in point of time, as well as of importance, the first place was given to measures for winning the war in America. Immediately preparation was made for sending 8000 men and seventeen ships of the line and five frigates on that service. Holburne was selected to command this squadron, while Loudon, with such force as he could bring from New York, was to join Holburne at Halifax. A joint land and sea attack was then to be made on Louisbourg. Another part of the operation as planned, was so to blockade the French ports of Toulon and Brest as to prevent squadrons sailing thence for the reinforcement of Louisbourg.[3] This failed,

---

[1] Williams, I, 314.

[2] The office of secretary of war, held by Lord Barrington, was only an adjunct to that of secretary of state.

[3] Corbett, England in the Seven Years' War, I, 159 *et seq.* Memoranda in the Chatham Papers (Bundle 95) indicates that Pitt, in sending out his first

for Revest got away with five sail from Toulon and De Bauffremont with five others from Brest, carrying needed relief to the French West Indies and fortunately reaching Louisbourg unharmed after this long cruise. Finally, Du Bois de la Moth, with a still larger force of nine ships of the line and three frigates, also escaped from Brest and reached the same destination. Holburne was not ready to sail until April 16 and the lateness of his departure enabled the French successfully to carry through their plan of concentrating forces to oppose him.

Meantime Loudon had formed a plan which supplemented that of Pitt.[1] It was that with about 5300 men, made up chiefly of regulars and coöperating with a force from Great Britain, he would attack Louisbourg early in the spring. If that enterprise succeeded, an effort should be made to reach Quebec before the end of the summer. In order to accomplish this it would be necessary to remove from the northern frontier in the region of Lake George all its defenders except the provincial troops and about three battalions of the line. Moreover, for escorting the transports which should convey his troops and the siege material which must accompany them, from New York to Halifax, only one fifty-gun ship and four small cruisers were available. Of this insufficient force — should any of the French squadrons which were converging on Louisbourg be met on the way — Sir Charles Hardy, who had been a post-captain before he was appointed two years before to the governorship of New York, was made commander. In the light of conditions as they existed in America it was a risky undertaking. Not only was there the chance that the force might be captured on the way, but the even more probable eventuality that the French would avail themselves of the removal of troops from the northern frontier in order to make a raid there which might seriously theaten Albany. Then, too, there were the manifold uncertainties attending the enterprise on its European side.

---

circular letters to the governors, had before him citations from papers showing how similar calls for raising men in the colonies had been issued on earlier occasions — by Robinson and Fox in 1754, 1755 and 1756, and for the expedition of Vetch in 1709.

[1] C. O. 5/48. Loudon to Pitt, Nov. 22, 1756. Corbett, I, 166 *et seq.*

Sailing vessels were largely at the mercy of the winds and waves, in addition to the delays which inevitably attended their outfit. On both sides, British and French, the result must be largely attributed to good fortune if a concentration of forces such as was planned on this occasion should succeed, necessitating, as it did, the crossing by some half-dozen squadrons of thousands of miles of ocean from various points of departure and by widely differing routes and their meeting at a remote point at approximately the same time. But this was the essence of the game involved in the manipulation of sea power, or, according to Pitt's system, of sea power and land power combined, and the zest of it came from the magnificent distances covered in the process and the éclat which followed a successful hit. In the large majority of cases, on the one side or the other, such plans must fail; but when they succeeded, the praise awarded to the planning which brought the result about is unlimited. This appealed to the colossal imagination of Pitt. Before his mind the entire empire, even the world itself, viewed from Great Britain as a centre, lay clear and definite in its outlines. A man like that could play billiards with half the surface of the planet as a table. In this game of sea power the British, as the result chiefly of environment and experience, had more self confidence and aggressiveness than the French. So conscious were the latter of their inferiority at sea that they were timid both in their plans and the execution of them. This caused them to lose many a favorable chance in the game and also to fail when the real trials of strength came.

Loudon and Hardy had assembled their force at New York by the end of April. There they waited for news of the arrival in the western Atlantic of the fleet and troops from England with which they were to coöperate. But no news came, the reason for the delay being that the battle fleet had been detained in British ports until the men and transports were ready, in order to convoy them across the Atlantic.[1] Finally, after waiting till the first of June, Loudon and Hardy made ready to start. But, through a privateer which had

---

[1] The letters of Loudon and Hardy at this time are in Corresp. of Pitt with Col. Govs., I. The correspondence which accompanied the resignation by Hardy of the governorship of New York in order that he might rejoin the navy, is in N. Y. Col. Doc., VII.

captured one of the French vessels that De Bauffremont was
escorting from St. Domingo to Louisbourg, it was learned that
one hostile force at least was in the neighborhood. Hence
Loudon waited three weeks longer, while two cruisers were
sent to Halifax and back. They reported that all was clear,
and then the expedition sailed, reaching Halifax in safety
at the close of June. It was a fortunate escape, for during
that month the three French squadrons arrived at Louisbourg,
the largest, under De la Moth, appearing off that coast on
the very day when Loudon sailed. Soon Holburne's squadron appeared and, when all the British forces were joined,
they numbered 15 ships of the line, with 20 smaller vessels,
and 14 battalions of infantry, 500 of artillery and 500 colonial
rangers, a land force of about 15,000 in all.[1] After a deceptive
reconnaissance it was resolved to attack Louisbourg, Holburne
first attempting to draw the French vessels from the harbor
in order, if possible, to get a decision at sea. But at this
juncture it was found that the French fleet was nearly twice
as strong as had previously been represented — 18 ships of
the line, three of which carried 80 guns each. The two British
commanders at once agreed that to attack Louisbourg under
these conditions would be to invite defeat. Therefore Loudon
returned to New York with the major part of his force, and
Holburne, after lying off Louisbourg for a time watching for
the French to come out, was caught by a furious storm which
so shattered his fleet that it was only with the greatest difficulty that he was able to bring it into Halifax for repairs.[2]
Holburne was not disgraced, though he did not receive another
command at sea. Loudon has been severely criticised for the
failure of his so-called " cabbage planting expedition," but
by the highest authority and under the rules of operations
at sea he has been cleared from blame. His conduct was regular, though a genius might have broken through the rules
and snatched victory from the very jaws of defeat.

Pitt, meantime, perplexed by an ambiguous relation into
which he was brought toward the execution of Admiral Byng,
fell a victim to the dislike of the king toward both him and

[1] The best account of Holburne's voyage and of events at Halifax is in the
Historical Journal of Capt. John Knox; best edition by Doughty in Pubs. of
Champlain Society.
[2] Corresp. of Pitt with Col. Govs., I, 114–118, 125.

his relative Temple and to the insistence of the duke of Cumberland that, if he was to take the command of the army in Hanover, the foreign secretary must go. Therefore Pitt and his group of supporters were dismissed from the ministry early in April. Though no victories had been won, the popularity of the minister throughout the country had been established, as was proven by the rain of gold boxes and other demonstrations in Pitt's favor after his dismissal. A decade before, in the midst of the previous war, George II had dismissed the Pelhams because they insisted that the aid of Pitt was needed in their administration. At that time the king would not even receive Pitt into his presence. But after a few days of confusion the king was forced to consent to the return of his ministers, though provision was made for Pitt in a merely routine office. Now, in 1757, the administrative confusion and weakness were equally great. The king carried on futile negotiations until about the middle of June with minor politicians of the time, but failed in all his efforts to form a ministry. The house of commons was at the same time trying to fix the responsibility for the loss of Minorca, but its inquiry revealed no serious fault in the conduct of the ministers and decidedly changed Pitt's view of the abilities of Lord Anson. His brief experience in office, together with other causes, was making Pitt less rabid in his criticism. His position as merely a member of the commons was a comparatively irresponsible one and he realized that in order to accomplish anything worth while he must be in office. He also came to appreciate the value of the kind of support which Newcastle could furnish, though he despised it and to the day of his death continued to attack the system of patronage upon which British politics at that time was based. Newcastle also had long been convinced that government could not be carried on without the support of Pitt. It was in pursuance of these converging tendencies that the Pitt-Newcastle ministry was formed, the most important of all the coalition ministries in English history. The arrangements were perfected and the cabinet took office at the close of July, 1757. Newcastle, as the head of the treasury, contributed his powerful vote getting influence in parliament and outside, and Pitt, in his former office and with the same colleague, contributing his remarkable enthusiasm, his personal popularity and his great administrative powers as a war minister.

The extent of Pitt's power may be realized when it is recalled that, together with Holdernesse, who meekly submitted to his leadership, he was foreign secretary, colonial secretary, home secretary and secretary at war. That was the extent of the functions of a secretary of state in those days. Though Anson, who was an able official, was restored to the leadership of the admiralty, the navy board was filled with Pitt's friends. He therefore had under his control every department of the administration except the treasury. Liberal appropriations were assured by his influence in the commons and by the ascendancy of the war spirit, against which for a period of four years the Newcastle interest neither chose nor dared to interpose any effective obstacle. Thus for the time being all the elements of British power were concentrated in a single hand, an autocracy of great effectiveness for war purposes, though existing under the forms of parliamentary government. At only two earlier periods in English history had such power been wielded by a single individual, under William the Conqueror and Henry VIII. These two monarchs, together with William Pitt, were the supreme egoists of British history. Pitt declared that he could save England and that he was the only man who could do it. What he meant was not that he would save her, for she was not in imminent peril, but that he would carry her to world dominion.

At the very time when the Pitt-Newcastle ministry was assuming office, Montcalm and his force of 7819 men, inclusive of 1599 savages, were embarking on Lake George, bent upon the capture of Fort William Henry.[1] This expedition had been carefully planned and timed. The force of French and Canadian troops was larger by two-thirds than that which had captured Oswego, but its numbers were greatly swelled by the presence of so many Indians. The influence of

[1] A feint against that place had been made by a French force under Rigoud the previous March. They came across the lake on the ice and succeeded in burning two sloops, several bateaux, a sawmill, some warehouses and huts near the fort and then retired. The garrison at that time numbered only 346 effective men. See letter of Major Eyre, the commander, to Loudon, March 25, 1757. C. O. 5/48.

the fall of Oswego upon the imagination of the savages was reflected in the flocking of so many of them on this occasion to the standard of Montcalm. Never before had there been such a marshalling of the Indian allies of the French. Thirty-six tribes were represented. They came from the east, the south, the west. Micmacs, Abenakis, Iroquois, Ottawas, Hurons, Mississagas were there; also Pottowattomies, Miamis, Sacs, Foxes and Iowas and many others. Some came from beyond the Mississippi and their dialect none could understand. The majority had been nominally under the influence of French missionaries, but many were still idolators, and all were untamed savages, ready for any excess of barbarity reaching even to cannibalism. Their presence with the army was a necessity and was at the same time a striking demonstration of the magic of the French name among the tribesmen of the interior of the continent. Montcalm's victory at Oswego had made him something of a hero in their eyes. The Iroquois had been clamoring for years for such a demonstration of power on the part of the English, but it had not been forthcoming. And now that Montcalm had gained one victory, this made it easy for him and his lieutenants to keep up a show of control over the horde with which they found themselves associated on this expedition. But it was, after all, an impossible task and the positive aid which was rendered by the Indians was very slight. As the ambush and forest fighting played no part on this occasion, the result would have been the same had they not been present. Why, then, waste so much time and effort upon Indian diplomacy?

The British in their stolid fashion were following the sure path toward dominion. Though they had long practiced the diplomatic art on a small scale and often in a clumsy fashion, in actual fighting they had very little aid from the Indians. And one almost inevitable disgrace they avoided, that complicity, however remote and undeserved, in any such sordid massacre as that which occurred after the surrender of Fort William Henry. Canadian and other writers do well to defend the fair fame of Montcalm and his lieutenants against the charge that they failed to put forth every effort to stop the horror when once it had begun, or that they did not take reasonable precautions in advance to prevent it.

But that is only a part of a much more serious indictment which lies against the conduct of the French throughout the colonial wars. From the beginning to the end of these conflicts they systematically made use of the Indians, led their expeditions and encouraged them in the perpetration of the horrible massacres, burnings and plunderings by which the British frontier was laid waste. It was such events which largely gave character to that struggle, and their history involves a record of barbarity which has rarely been equalled in the history of any people that claimed to be enlightened and Christian. The part played by the priests in this wretched business was more abominable even that that of the French military and civil officers. So much weaker were the French than the British and so much closer were their relations with the Indians, that they might plead necessity as an excuse. To the priests who were directly involved it seemed a fit treatment to mete out to heretics. But in the end it contributed perhaps more than the rivalry between the parent nations in Europe to the ruin of New France, for it nerved the British colonists to the efforts which finally, after so many delays, brought the desired result. It was the conviction that only the destruction of French power on the continent would bring peace and free them forever from such impending horrors that was either stated or implied in the demands which were made by the colonists for the conquest of Canada, till after 1730. Subsequent to that date the danger along much of the frontier became less imperative and the European rivalry furnished the decisive impulse which brought the struggle. Had there been no French on the continent, the British would doubtless have become involved in a long series of destructive wars with the natives; for the British method of dealing with them could end only in their extermination or their complete subjugation, followed by enslavement or segregation. Such in fact has been the result after prolonged and fierce struggles carried on since the overthrow of French power in North America. But so long as the French held Canada and the Mississippi valley, they incited the Indians by every means in their power to commit the atrocities referred to and therefore must be held largely responsible for the horrors before the tribunal of history. War had long been a gentleman's business in Europe, but it proved far from being wholly that when it was extended to America. The best leaders among the French realized this and deprecated it, but they were too deeply involved in these wretched enterprises to prevent them.

The capture of Fort William Henry itself need not detain us long. It was the result of a clear cut military operation, carried on according to the best traditions of the old world so modified as to adapt them to new conditions. And yet in that case the conditions were not so new or difficult as to make the operation specially dangerous. Between Ticonderoga (Carillon) and the fort which was the French objective water communication was open nearly all the way. The only difficult part of the route was the rapids and portage extending for about a mile and a half along the course of the stream which forms the outlet of Lake George. Across this portage the artillery equipment and supplies of the force had to be transported. This involved much hard labor, continued night and day during much of July. Lévis had immediate charge of this work. The administrative arrangements both for the transportation service and for the protection of the camps were admirable. The task was well advanced when Montcalm arrived and by the end of July the entire force had been removed to the northern end of Lake George. With the ample supply of bateaux which had been provided — how unlike the delays which the English always suffered from lack of means of transportation! — the army was quickly conveyed to the place of its destination, a distance of 36 miles. At the southwest corner of the lake, on the site of the modern village of Caldwell, Montcalm established his lines, planted his batteries and began a formal siege on the fourth of August.

Lieutenant Colonel Monro was in command of the fort, with a force of about 2200 men. The bulk of the British army had been withdrawn for service on the expedition against Louisbourg, and Montcalm was fully aware of this fact and also that Loudon and Holburne would probably not be able to carry through their plan during the present season. His own enterprise had been planned and was now being executed with the knowledge that there was in front of him an inferior force, chiefly of British provincials. Webb lay at Fort Edward — or Fort Lydius as the French called it — sixteen miles away, with the possibility of bringing together some 4500 men. He was sufficiently aware in advance of what the French intended and had added about 1000 men to the garrison in July. He had also sent to New York and Massachusetts for larger reinforcements and now waited in vain for their arrival. Since the previous summer much had been done to improve and strengthen Fort William Henry and the entrenched camp connected with it, but it was still lacking in artillery, and, in consequence of the weakness of the structure itself, it could not long stand against the nearly fifty cannon and mortars of various calibre which Montcalm was rapidly planting against it. Smallpox was also raging within the garrison, and though Monro put on a bold front when first summoned to surrender, he knew that he could not long hold out and sent urgent and repeated appeals for help. But Webb, with the force which he had available, would not risk the danger of an ambush or a battle on the way to Lake George. While he waited a force of Canadians was thrown round to the south of the fort and it was practically surrounded. Webb heard of this and wrote to Monro that he had better make the best terms he could with the French. This letter was intercepted and with it in his possession Montcalm knew that success was certain.

When the lines had been sufficiently advanced and the losses and suffering of the garrison had become severe, Montcalm sent Webb's letter to Monro, in the hope thereby to avert needless bloodshed. It had that effect, for on the ninth of August the British surrendered, with the honors of war. The agreement was that the prisoners should be escorted to Fort Edward and should not serve again in the war for eighteen months. As in the case of Oswego, the total destruction of the fort was begun and promptly completed. Had it not been for the massacres, first of the sick, and later of fifty of the well among the British prisoners as they were being started under convoy on their march southward, the plan of the French would have been executed with the completeness and perfection which they attained at Oswego. But the Indians, roused by prolonged appeals from the French, had come out for scalps and they were not easily to be robbed of their chance. The massacre, of course, was accompanied by many other barbarities and they carried away with them 200 prisoners. These the French did what they could to recover and in a goodly number of cases succeeded. The savage horde at once dispersed and this was the last time that Montcalm and his lieutenants had such a troublesome body of allies to contend with.

So early was it in the season that there was still time for a possible attack on Fort Edward, and Vaudreuil criticised Montcalm for not attempting it. But the army there was superior in numbers to the French, while Montcalm had no horses for the transport of his artillery southward. The Canadians, under earlier orders from the governor himself, had to return immediately in order to gather the harvest at home, while the dearth of provisions from which Canada was already beginning to suffer made the necessity for this doubly imperative. Therefore the regulars were at once taken back to Ticonderoga and in due time were disposed in cantonments for the winter. The militia returned to their homes for the harvest.

The fall of Oswego had awakened the sensibilities of the British, but the destruction of Fort William Henry seemed a veritable calamity. The French had thereby advanced their lines to a point from whence they threatened Albany and all western New England. With the close approach of danger corresponding activity on the part of the British was aroused to meet it. Thomas Pownall, who had just arrived as successor of Shirley in the governorship of Massachusetts, ordered three regiments from the western part of the province to march to the vicinity of Albany.[1] De Lancey went to Albany as soon as he heard that Fort William Henry was in danger and did what he could in forwarding militia to Webb. The legislatures of both Massachusetts and New York were summoned. The former approved the governor's conduct in marching troops beyond the limits of the colony without its consent and provided adequate barracks and supplies for Fraser's Highland regiment in Boston.[2] The fact that these concessions were made proves how serious the peril from the

[1] Corresp. of Pitt, etc., I, 94 et seq.   [2] Ibid., 128.

French at the time seemed to be. On the return of the troops from Halifax and the assurance that the French, after destroying the fort, had returned northward, anxiety abated. Loudon provided for the defence of the frontier with the troops immediately under his command. The militia which had been sent in that direction were recalled and no more levies were ordered. With the exception of a raid by the French in November on German Flats (Burnet's Field)[1] quiet prevailed along the northern frontier until the following summer.

Throughout the campaign which had now closed the heartening effects of Pitt's circular letters to the governors, with their appeals for free and vigorous coöperation against the common enemy, had been felt. He had begun sending them when he was first in office and the brief period of his exclusion from power passed almost unnoticed in America. Upon his return to office the appeals for united action were renewed, always accompanied by assurances of full coöperation on the part of Great Britain. The speeches from the throne, together with the addresses from the two houses, strengthened the impression. Pitt's first letter began with these words: " The King having nothing more at heart than the Preservation of his good Subjects and Colonies of North America, has come to a Resolution of acting with the greatest Vigour in those Parts, the ensuing Campaign, and all necessary Preparations are making for sending a considerable Reinforcement of Troops together with a strong Squadron of Ships, for that Purpose, & in Order to act offensively against the French in Canada. It is his Majesty's Pleasure that you should forthwith call together your Council & Assembly & press them in the strongest Manner to raise with the utmost Expedition as large a number of Provincial Forces as may be for the service of the ensuing Campaign, over and above what they shall judge necessary for the immediate Defence of their own Province. . . . And the King doubts not, but that the several Provinces, truly sensible of His paternal Care, in sending so large a force for their Security, will exert their utmost Endeavors to second and strengthen such offensive Operations . . . , and will not clogg the Enlistments of the Men, or the raising of the Money for their Pay etc., with

[1] *Ibid.*, 183.

such Limitations as have been hitherto found to render their Service difficult & ineffectual; And as a further Encouragement I am to acquaint you that the raising of the Men, their Pay, Arms & cloathing will be all that will be required for this Campaign on the part of the several Provinces, Measures having been already taken for laying up Magazines of Stores and Provisions of all kinds at the Expence of the Crown." This was the refrain which Pitt repeated as long as he was in office.

The most favorable response, of course, came from New England. Governor Fitch, of Connecticut, wrote enthusiastically that his colony, "warmed with Zeal for his Majesty's Service," had cheerfully undertaken to raise and equip 1400 men. Loudon wrote, in March, 1757, that the three colonies of southern New England had agreed to furnish the proportion he desired of them.[1] In the same month Loudon also held a conference at Philadelphia with the governors of Pennsylvania, Maryland, Virginia and North Carolina, to arrange a plan for the defence of the southern provinces.[2] They agreed to use their best endeavors with their assemblies to raise and support 5000 men. Of these, 2000 men, including 500 regulars and the three independent companies in South Carolina, should be employed in the defence of that province and Georgia. These provinces, partly from information contained in certain intercepted letters from Louisiana, were thought to be in danger either by sea from St. Domingo or from the French Fort Alabama in the Creek country. Arrangements were also made concerning the transportation and provisioning of the troops to be sent to South Carolina and that they should be under the command of Lieutenant Colonel Bouquet. This plan, however, was not carried into execution, for Pitt, acting upon information which he received direct from Governor Lyttleton, ordered Montgomery's battalion of Highlanders sent to South Carolina.[3]

Loudon had much difficulty in getting any appropriation from Pennsylvania, because of the refusal of Governor Denny

[1] Corresp. of Pitt, etc., I, 14, 26.
[2] Ibid., I, 40 et seq.; N. C. Recs., V, 750.
[3] Corresp. of Pitt, etc., I, 27–29.

to pass the militia bill.[1] But on representations from Loudon, who had taken the advice of Dinwiddie, the governor of Pennsylvania yielded and the militia bill, imperfect though it was, became a law. New Jersey was asked to contribute 1000 men but its assembly, when the general was on his return from Philadelphia, met him in a body and protested that they lacked the money which was necessary for such a grant. Loudon told them that they were a populous province, that his demand was not unreasonable and that the burden of it might be distributed over two years, or adjusted in some other way as was done in New England under a sense of the need of unanimity at the present crisis. The fact that they had offered a bounty of £12 current money to every man who enlisted until the next November, instead of drafting from the militia as was done in other colonies, seemed to Loudon a sufficient answer to the plea of poverty. The bounty money, he declared, would more than maintain the men, had they been drafted and paid the usual wages. But Loudon found that the prosperous farmers of New Jersey were adverse to a draft, of which they had never had an experience, and also felt that proportionately more was being demanded of them than from New York. But large bodies of the New York militia had been repeatedly called into service and it had furnished transport for the troops, even in harvest time, while New Jersey had done nothing. But, of course, the fundamental obstacles were Quakerism and the knowledge that New Jersey was not specially imperilled by the war. As a military man, so impressed was Loudon with the obstructive tactics of the Quakers that he thought they were unfit to be employed in any civil affairs. Justices of the peace even persuaded recruits, when brought before them, not to attest, and granted warrants against them for fictitious debts, throwing them into jail, but releasing them the moment their regiment or detachment had left for the frontier. Desertions also were frequent and went unpunished. So trifling, also, were the taxes paid in most of the colonies that Loudon was convinced that if parliament did not impose a

[1] Governor Denny gave an account of the doings of Loudon at the time of the conference at Philadelphia, so far as they affected Pennsylvania, in a letter to the proprietors under date of April 10, 1757, Pa. Arch., III, 117.

tax for the support of the war, very little assistance would be obtained in money or men. These complaints illustrate strikingly the difficulties which military men always meet in dealing with non-military peoples. As always had occurred in the past, it now turned out about as Loudon said — very little assistance was given in the war by any of the colonies which were not specially imperilled. The amount that was given was roughly apportioned to the danger to which each colony felt itself exposed. That was the way in which wars must inevitably be carried on under the system of loose confederation which then existed.

"I had a further point to guard against," wrote Loudon,[1] "in the Southern Governments, which was the expence of maintaining their People with Provisions." But he was able to make a more favorable arrangement with the southern provinces than with the northern. With the southern provinces he agreed that the king should support only those detachments which were marched out of their native colonies to go to South Carolina, Pennsylvania and Virginia paying also for the transportation of their quotas; all others should be maintained by their respective provinces. As to the northern colonies, they were so in the habit of being fed with money, wrote Loudon, that he could not set them in motion without maintaining their levies, since, except New York, they were serving outside their own colonies, and those of New York were quite up in the back country. "Every man in this country," he added, "would, if possible, throw the whole Expence on the Publick and save the Province from being at one Shilling Expence for the Common Cause," and who that has studied the situation will deny the substantial truth of this statement?

With the accounts for the previous campaign Loudon also had difficulties, for he had to be on his guard against establishing precedents which would be very unfavorable to the royal exchequer. "Under the Article of Artillery," he wrote, "they have included Tents, Drums, Colours, All Camp Necessaries; Platters, Pans, Keggs and a number of other things they have been in use of furnishing their troops, unknown in a regular Army." According to his advice, the colonies must provide

[1] Corresp. of Pitt, *etc.*, 55 *et seq.*

these things and the cost of them should not be thrown upon the imperial government. Various other charges also, for provisions and other things left over from previous campaigns, Loudon urged should not be allowed, as they should be covered by reimbursements already made by the crown or satisfactory inspection of the goods had not been possible.

Loudon also was much exercised over the lack of suitable quarters in the colonies for the troops. The mutiny act of 1755 required that the assemblies should provide quarters and specified supplies for the regulars when within their respective jurisdictions. Loudon, however, had disputes to settle in arranging winter quarters for 1756–7. The difficulty, in New York and Albany, for instance, was that barracks were inadequate and there were so few public houses that there was not accommodation for the troops unless some of them were lodged in private houses.[1] During the war, in Loudon's opinion, the rule restricting billeting to public houses would have to be modified and later, in times of peace, the regulation in the law should be changed. The magistrates of Boston denied that the mutiny act was in force in the colonies.[2] But the general court compromised by enacting some of its principal provisions and thus made the lodgment of the troops in the town legal. By this means the general was relieved from the awkward necessity of ordering troops at once to Boston to enforce the demand of the military.

Preliminary to the expedition of Loudon and Hardy to Halifax an embargo was laid on the coast from Massachusetts to Virginia on all vessels clearing with provisions, except such as were bound for British colonies. The purpose of this was to enable the general to procure transports sufficient to take his troops to Halifax. As was common in such cases, the measure was unpopular with the colonists. Crops also had been poor in Great Britain and Ireland, and, as soon as the government heard of the measure, an order was issued that the embargo should be taken off and none should thereafter be laid affecting his majesty's European dominions.[3] Loudon

---

[1] Corresp. of Pitt, etc., I, 20.
[2] Ibid., 128.
[3] Ibid., 19, 31, 66, 78; N. J. Arch., VIII, 248

was specially irritated by the fact that Dinwiddie, at the insistence of the Virginia assembly, raised the embargo for that province. " To me personally," wrote Loudon, " this is surely as Cruel an Action as it was possible for one Man to do another; for from my having the honor to be Governor of that Dominion,[1] it will be believed that the Lieutenant Governor would not take it upon himself, without my Concurrence; which is doing all that lay in his Power to give me the Appearance of Partiality, which, whilst they see it in that light, must diminish that Weight the King's Commander in Chief ought to have."

Another perplexing subject, already referred to, was the enlistment of indented servants, especially in Pennsylvania, and the fixing of compensation therefor, a subject which had been prominent in that colony in the previous war. In the recruiting act passed by parliament in May, 1756, which specially applied to the colonies,[2] provision was made for enlisting indented servants, compensation to their masters for the loss of their services being duly secured. Shirley, in 1755, had avoided the practice as likely to hinder more than it would promote the success of recruiting. But when orders under the new act arrived, Shirley countermanded his former instructions and the enlisting of servants began. In Pennsylvania protests were raised against it, taking form first in a letter from the council to Shirley and then in an address from the assembly to Governor Morris. In these they referred to the large number of servants who had been raised in Pennsylvania for the American and British regiments in the present war and for service in the West Indies in the previous war. The defence of the Pennsylvania frontier also called for many men, and so many could not have been furnished, had it not been for the large number of servants imported. The hardship of having servants taken away, especially in harvest time, and the concessions which masters were forced to make to those who remained, in order to prevent them from enlisting, were dwelt on. The right of

[1] Loudon had received that appointment in addition to his office of commander-in-chief.

[2] Corresp. of Pitt, *etc.*, I, 46; Pa. Col. Recs., VII, 37, 39, 179; Corresp. of Shirley, II, 386 *et seq.*

the contracting master as over against the government in this matter was emphasized, and the taking of servants in this way was called a violation of the right of property. Magistrates who had failed to assist masters in the recovery of their servants had sadly failed in their duty. Hence the governor was urged to apply to Shirley to have the enlistment of servants stopped. Morris replied that he would at once write to Shirley and send him a copy of their address, though the right they claimed had been denied in the previous war and the point had not been settled.

Governor Sharpe was also writing to Shirley from Maryland on the same subject, stating that acts of violence had been committed and unless the cause of complaint was removed an insurrection might follow. The result of the correspondence between these governors and Shirley was that he and Morris in particular agreed that the king was entitled to the service of all his subjects and the state of the war made it imperative that this right should be enforced. To this end the recruiting officers should be protected in the performance of their duty, while the masters had the right to sue them for damages, and the sooner a judicial decision upon the issue was reached the better. But no decisive steps in this direction were taken and the question came up again when Loudon was commander. Soon after his arrival a bill was passed appropriating £10,000, which it was understood was intended to compensate the masters whose servants had enlisted. After the governor had refused to accept this bill, the assembly ordered that every one whose servants were enrolled should desire the officer who enlisted them to give a statement of the man's name and of the day when he was enlisted. Franklin told Loudon that Pennsylvania could not afford to pay for the servants and did not intend to do so, and that the reason why they desired the acknowledgments from the recruiting officers was that on these might be based a claim on the British government. Loudon told him that payment for them was already arranged and desired a list of the servants involved. An incomplete list of enlistments since Braddock's death for Shirley's and Pepperell's regiments and the regiments in Nova Scotia, but without dates of enlistment, was presented.

Loudon complained to Franklin that the assembly did not follow the method prescribed by the act of parliament by producing before justices indentures and evidences of enlistment, so that legal proofs of enlistments might be at hand. But in the list which Franklin submitted they were lacking, and Loudon claimed that, if he had been appealed to, he could have redressed the wrongs alleged to have been done by the recruiting officers. Whether or not this was true, it furnishes another instance of the lack of confidence and understanding which existed between the colonists and the commander-in-chief.

Loudon's ability in the actual conduct of a campaign was never put to the test. But he appears to have known well the administrative details of his task and to have striven to check the looseness and dishonesty which inhered in colonial life and methods. The criticism which has been passed on his Halifax expedition has been proved to be unjustified. It was a hazardous adventure at best and, considering the chances of positive disaster which attended it, it was fortunate that the force which he commanded escaped capture. The worst aspect of the affair appears in the fact that it opened the way for the capture by the French of Fort William Henry. Had Loudon been present at the time he, instead of Abercromby, might have been in command when the decisive trial of skill with Montcalm came. It would be interesting to know whether the result would have been different. Loudon's part in the operations of 1745–6 in Scotland afford little basis for belief that it would, though the conditions of the battle might have so differed that the British could have won by superiority of numbers. But, like his predecessor Shirley — whom he treated with such contempt — at the close of 1757, while he was in the midst of his plans for the coming year, he was suddenly recalled and the command was handed over to Abercromby. He had failed to win the confidence of the colonists or his superiors and, under the conditions of the service in which he was engaged, must give way to another. He submitted to the routine without complaint.

Pitt now being fully established in power, formidable preparations were made for the campaign of 1758 in America.

The brilliant and popular Lord Howe was already in the American service. Accompanying the recall of Loudon and appointment of Abercromby, circular letters of exhortation were sent to the governors, north and south, calling upon them to urge their assemblies to the fullest possible coöperation in a general attack on Canada and the French by sea and land.[1] It was announced that a considerable squadron, with large military reinforcements, would be sent the coming spring, and preparations should be hastened so that an early beginning of the campaign might be possible. Not only was the siege of Louisbourg to be undertaken as the central operation of the year, but also a formidable land expedition against Canada, and an attempt was to be made to capture Fort Duquesne. All artificial distinctions of rank between officers of the regulars and provincials were removed, and in all possible ways the spirit of coöperation was encouraged. Arms, ammunition and tents, as well as a sufficient train of artillery, were to be furnished by the home government, while encouragement was given that parliament would appropriate money for least a partial reimbursement of the expenditures of the colonies for levying, clothing and paying their troops. As planned, the force which should besiege Louisbourg was to consist almost wholly of regulars, while more than half of the troops employed on the other two expeditions were to be provincials.[2] It was estimated that about 25,000 soldiers would be raised in the colonies, 5000 of whom, from the southern colonies, would march against Fort Duquesne, and 20,000, raised north of Pennsylvania, would march against Crown Point. Though the response to this general requisition, especially in New England, was liberal, it fell short of the numbers desired. Several of the southern colonies provided no troops and in general their levies were neither large nor of good quality. New York profited largely in her business interests from the campaign, while her contribution of troops was not especially large.

As we are tracing the course of French success, we are concerned in this chapter only with the expedition which resulted in the battle of Ticonderoga. This was under the command of

[1] Corresp. of Pitt, *etc.*, I, 134–153.
[2] Beer, British Colonial Policy, 1754–1765, p. 60 *et seq.*

Abercromby, an officer who had already been in the colonies a year and a half, but who apparently had been employed upon no service worth speaking of. His opportunity had now come. The roads and portages northward from Albany had become sufficiently improved, and the bateaux and other craft used in water transportation were being supplied in adequate numbers, while magazines and fortified posts had been built along the way where adequate provisions and supplies could be stored. Now for the first time it was possible to transport a large and organized army northward to Canada itself or at least to the positions where the French had fortified themselves. By the beginning of July in the camp at Fort William Henry were gathered between 6000 and 7000 British regulars and about 9000 provincials. Lord Howe had been assigned to this force with the idea that, though not technically in command, his would be the guiding mind and inspiring example, and so it was proving to be.

Against this formidable array Montcalm had under his command only about 3000 French regulars, with a small body of Canadian regulars and 250 militia.[1] The plan of Vaudreuil was to divert an attack from this quarter by a demonstration along the Mohawk, to be led by Lévis and having as its objective Schenectady, but this had to be abandoned when it became known that the British were advancing in such large force toward Lake Champlain. The regulars under Montcalm were troops of the best quality, who had served with him, at least in part, during two campaigns, whom he thoroughly trusted and by whom he was adored. After deliberation he chose to await the enemy at Ticonderoga rather than to retire on Crown Point. It was a wise decision for, though the fort itself was scarcely defensible, the position was a strong one and more susceptible of defence from a single point than would have been the more open country further north. As the French were made aware by their scouting parties of the size of the force which was advancing down the lake against them, the prospect seemed desperate. Montcalm delayed as long as possible the choice of the place where he would make his stand and the form of the defensive work he would have constructed there. He finally selected

[1] Chapais, *op. cit.*, 402.

a spot a short distance west of the fort, where from a low ridge the ground sloped off on both sides. The slope on its westward side led down from the plateau on which the fort stood toward the low ground along the stream which forms the outlet of Lake George. On this ridge Montcalm's men built a fortified breastwork, about eight feet high, extending in a zigzag course, so that the entire front could be covered with an enfilading fire. In front of the breastwork a deep abattis of trees was constructed, their branches sharpened and pointing outward. On the left the breastwork abutted on a low bluff, at the foot of which flowed the stream just mentioned. From the right of the breastwork open land extended away toward a low range of hills. Like nearly all the defensive works in the colonies, the breastwork was of logs and would no more stand against artillery than the forts at Oswego or at the head of Lake George had done. As Abercromby was bringing some artillery with him and presumably had within reach a large number of cannon, the gloomy prospect which the French were facing is evident. But their spirit was excellent and they worked with the greatest zest during the few days when the breastwork and abattis were in process of construction.

As the British landed at the foot of the lake and advanced along the left bank of the stream, the French withdrew from the position which they had held at the rapids and concentrated near the fort. On the passage through the thick woods adjoining the rapids, in an encounter with a French scouting party, Lord Howe was killed, a misfortune which had much to do with the event that followed. Both Abercromby and his men were filled with discouragement, almost with consternation, by the loss. Temporarily they fell back toward the lake, lay during the night on their arms, and by the delay of a day gave Montcalm more time for completing his plans for defence.

On the afternoon of July 8 the attack on the abattis and breastwork was made by the British. No attempt was made to use artillery, or to flank the position and penetrate to Lake Champlain in the rear of it, thus cutting off Montcalm's communication with Canada. So superior were the numbers of the British and such the contour of the land that this was quite possible. But neither of these things was done or attempted. Instead, the British regulars were hurled in a series of direct frontal attacks against the abattis. They never reached the breastworks, but as they became entangled and frantically tried to force their way through the maze of branches, they were mowed down by the French. With reckless bravery charge after charge was made, the French meeting them all with a murderous fire, till at the close of the afternoon the British withdrew. Their casualties numbered about 2000 and those of the French less than 400. This was the bloodiest conflict of the entire war in America and again, as on Braddock's field, the loss fell on the British. For the result at Ticonderoga there was infinitely less excuse than for the defeat of Braddock. The plainest common sense, enforced by the experiences of the last two campaigns, should have recalled ways in which to avoid it. The stupidity of generals respecting the essentials of war itself never received clearer illustration than on that July afternoon at Ticonderoga.

The British still had ample force with which to defeat Montcalm, but they neglected to use it. Indeed under such leadership as had just been exhibited it would have been risky to attempt anything further against a force so expert as the French under Montcalm had shown itself to be. They at once retired up the lake and the campaign on that front was over. Vaudreuil criticised Montcalm for not advancing southward, but with his inferior force the move was too hazardous and promised too little. At Ticonderoga the French by brilliant fighting had held their position. But it was due to the blundering of the British that they had not been overwhelmed. The battle, therefore, was not a victory for the French in the sense illustrated at Oswego and Fort William Henry, but by means of it they had been saved from a great peril and were in no worse position than before for meeting such superior forces as the British would doubtless again be able to bring against them.

CHAPTER XVII

THE CLOSE OF THE WAR; THE TRIUMPH OF THE BRITISH

WITH the beginning of 1758 the policy of Pitt as war minister came fully into operation in America. He was a civilian in office, as Shirley had been, and so far as America was concerned his plans were scarcely more comprehensive than those of the Massachusetts governor. Such plans in fact had found lodgment in many brains at different times since 1690, varying in scope according to the exigencies as felt at the time and the resources that were available. Now for the first time a minister whose mind was filled with such schemes and ambitions was temporarily in possession of sufficient power to carry them into effect and devoted himself with fiery energy to the task while the means of achieving a complete triumph were within his grasp. With this in view the resources of the navy were brought into full play, aided by a land force from Great Britain of moderate strength, all of which was adequately equipped and provisioned. The earlier failures of the war had to an extent weeded out incompetent officers and, guided by the remarkable insight of the chief minister, their places were being filled with younger men and men of superior ability. Abercromby [1] was the latest survival of commanders of the old type and his repulse at Ticonderoga was almost the only exception to the series of victories which were won by the British from the beginning of 1758 to the close of the war. On the more important parts of the frontier British regulars were more largely employed and less dependence was placed on colonial militia. The extension of frontier posts, the building of roads and the improvement of means of transportation generally during the earlier years of the war had made access easier to the fortified positions of the enemy and thereby had facilitated the employment of organized bodies of troops, whether regulars or provincials.

---

[1] Wolfe agreed with certain American observers in calling him a "heavy man."

Henceforth, on both sides in the north, Indians were not employed in large numbers and conditions approximated more to those of European warfare.

As the struggle progressed conflicts between assemblies and executives in most of the provinces were suspended and they responded better to appeals for joint action and liberal appropriations. The presence everywhere of regulars and their officers; the active coöperation of the British fleet; the sharing of expense by the imperial government, combined with the hope that liberal reimbursements would also be made to the colonists; the stimulating exhortations of Pitt; all these combined, as months passed, to attune the colonists more to war and to the continuance of such efforts as would bring a decision which should be conclusive. For a few years, therefore, nearly all the colonies ceased to have any internal history of importance which was distinct from the war, and, taken as a whole, there followed a genuine imperial effort, the realm and the colonies coöperating on a scale which had never been seen before. Great Britain contributed a succession of armaments, each stronger, especially in naval equipment, than its predecessors, or sent earlier in the season and under orders better suited to attain results of superior importance. Her superiority at sea also enabled her so to restrict the operations of the French fleet in European waters as to prevent its giving decisive aid in America. In the end, therefore, the victory was won chiefly through sea power, and it was conclusively proved that the navy was the main support of the British empire.

Although Pitt's plan of campaign in America for 1758 included an expedition against Fort Duquesne and the attack upon Ticonderoga in which the British so needlessly failed, the operation of chief importance was the one which resulted in the capture of Louisbourg. It was that for which the minister made his earliest preparations, so that the failure of the previous year, due to the late arrival of Holburne off the American coast, might not be repeated. Pitt now had the valuable assistance of Lord Anson, at the head of the admiralty, and it was by the two jointly that the naval operations of the rest of the war were planned. It was their hope that both Louisbourg and Quebec could be captured in a single campaign, these two events being essentially parts of one movement the result of which would be to give Great Britain possession of the Gulf of St. Lawrence and the lower course of the river. An incident of that, as viewed from the purely naval standpoint, would be the conquest of Canada.

Preparations were begun immediately after New Year's. Boscawen was selected as admiral, with Hardy second in command.[1] Amherst was recalled from Germany to command the land force. Sixteen ships of the line, together with seven which had wintered at Halifax, and an abundant supply of frigates, transports and other smaller craft, were to constitute the fleet. But in order to reach the coast off Louisbourg at the earliest possible moment and thus anticipate the French, Boscawen started before the end of February with enough of his largest and fleetest ships to constitute a strong battle squadron. With these, after a long and trying voyage, he entered the harbor of Halifax, May 9. Hardy had been on the coast some weeks ahead of him, but with a force too weak to prevent seven French ships of the line and several smaller vessels, which had run out of Brest, from entering Louisbourg harbor. The Channel fleet, under Hawke, had been instructed, if possible, to prevent any succor from French ports reaching Louisbourg, but this part of the plan had not proved wholly successful. The British fleet, however, including a land force of about 12,000 men,[2] made up of regulars and contingents from the colonies, was successfully gathered at Halifax and proceeded thence, near the close of May, for the siege of Louisbourg. The French garrison numbered only about half of the British land force. The squadron which was shut up in the harbor and which was not allowed by Drucour, the commander, even to attempt to escape, was of practically no use to the besieged, and in the end all the ships were destroyed or fell into the hands of the victors.

---

[1] For the technicalities of naval strategy illustrated by this expedition, see Corbett, *op. cit.*, I, 308. For many details both of this and the expedition of the next year against Quebec, see Wood, The Log of the Conquest of Canada, and William Knox, Journal of the Campaigns in North America, I (ed. by Doughty). The two last mentioned works are published by the Champlain Society.

[2] Seamen and marines in the fleet amounted to as many more.

Because of the disparity of the forces the result of the siege could never for a moment be in doubt, the only question being how quickly the garrison could be forced to surrender. Among the brigade commanders who came with the troops from England was James Wolfe. He was one of the new and younger men whom Pitt was bringing to the front. His promotion to service in America was now due to the insight and resourcefulness which he had shown at Rochefort the previous year, it being certain that, had his advice been followed on that occasion, the raid which was then attempted on the French coast would not have proved the complete fiasco which it certainly was. Now that the method of attack on Louisbourg was under consideration, Wolfe proposed that landings be made and the town be approached from the north and east as well as from the sea. But Amherst feared that this would involve too great a dispersion of forces, and decided to concentrate off Gabarus Bay, the landing place of the New England troops in 1745. Bad weather delayed the beginning of operations and a rough sea made the landing difficult in the face of the French who had intrenched themselves along the shore. But a dash from the boats of the men led by Wolfe on the left effected a landing. Before their onset the French began to retire and with the landing of the detachments under Lawrence and Whitmore the rout of the French was completed and they were pursued back to the fortress. The landing of the men, guns and supplies of all kinds proceeded apace, as the weather permitted.

The siege followed much the same course as the one conducted by Pepperell and Warren thirteen years before, but with much greater precision and certainty of success at the end. The first move of the French was to dismantle the Royal Battery at the back of the harbor. This furnished the occasion for Wolfe to move around with a force and seize Lighthouse Point on the east side of the harbor, opposite the town. From that point and others near it a bombardment of the town and the vessels was begun, and the battery on Great Island at the entrance of the harbor was silenced. Amherst, meantime, from the west, pushed forward toward the walled defences of the place, all of which had been greatly strengthened since its restoration to the French, so that Louisbourg was now the strongest fortress in America. It was hoped that Boscawen would now end the siege quickly by a dash into the harbor and the destruction of the French vessels which were there. Des Gouttes, their commander, felt that in any case they were doomed if they remained, and begged to be allowed to break out. But this was refused by Drucour and his council of war, and the vessels which had been drawn close under the walls, to escape the bombs thrown by the British from across the harbor, were finally disarmed and their crews used to aid in the land defence. Later three of the ships were destroyed by an explosion and fire caused by bombs. Then Boscawen, on the night of August 28, sent in a force which destroyed another of the French ships and seized another, the flagship, and towed her across and moored her under the protection of the British batteries. This left the harbor exposed to entrance by Boscawen and his fleet and, as the approaches from the land side were so far advanced that capture by assault was possible, the only course for the French was to surrender. This they did at once and ultimately Louisbourg, as a defensible position, was entirely wiped out, the French inhabitants being so far as possible removed from Cape Breton Island. But it was decided that the season was now too far advanced for an attack on Quebec. Boscawen hesitated to venture up the St. Lawrence so late in the summer, while the news of Abercromby's defeat revealed the necessity of sending reinforcements to New York to check a possible advance of the French in that quarter. Therefore, with the exception of the destruction of a number of the settlements about the mouth of the gulf, no attack upon Canada was attempted. The main body of the fleet returned to Europe and the troops which remained, with such vessels as were left, were stationed at Halifax and elsewhere, as the need seemed to indicate, to await the opening of another spring.[1] The French, by sacrificing as they did the squadron in the harbor of Louisbourg, had saved Canada for another year.

Abercromby was now recalled and Amherst was appointed commander-in-chief in America, the governors as usual being

[1] Corresp. of Pitt, etc., I, 350 et seq., 377, 379–382, 399. The troops destined for New York were landed at Boston and marched overland to Albany.

notified of the change. But before this transfer was made, the gloom which had followed the repulse at Ticonderoga was to an extent relieved by the capture of Fort Frontenac.[1] As a military achievement this was of very slight importance, for Colonel Bradstreet, the commander of the expedition, took with him 3000 provincials — the force including a few regulars — with which to reduce a garrison [2] of a little over 100 men. The fort also was a weak structure, "dominated by neighboring heights," and intended for little more than defence against Indians. Though for a long period this historic fort had been built of logs, at some time before the outbreak of the last colonial war its walls and a tower had been constructed of stone. But Pouchot, the French engineer, regarded it with contempt, its walls not two feet thick, without glacis, ditch or covered ways; it might stand against Indians but by no means against artillery, which was now being used on both sides somewhat after the European fashion.

Bradstreet, while serving under Shirley, had become familiar with the route to Oswego and with the importance to the British of gaining control over the lower lakes as the means of breaking the line of communication between Canada and the Mississippi valley, cutting them off from the fur trade and diverting the Indians from the French to an alliance with the British. He had previously proposed to Loudon that Fort Frontenac be attacked and by that general, as well as by Lord Howe, the plan had been approved. But Abercromby discouraged it until, under the pressure of a council of war, it was undertaken. With great secrecy as to its destination — whether it should be Niagara, Oswegatchie or Fort Frontenac — the expedition followed the usual route to Oswego. Only a few of the Six Nations joined it, for they had been again discouraged by the repulse of the British at Ticonderoga. At Oswego the force was put on board whale boats and bateaux and in three days, not allowing themselves to venture so far into the lake that it would be impossible to find protection in a cove against a threatened gale, they reached the vicinity of Fort Frontenac. A landing was effected without opposition. On the advance of a force so superior, the garrison

---

[1] See in particular Severance, An Old Frontier of France, II, 210 *et seq*.

[2] Kingsford, Hist. of Canada, IV, 183.

abandoned some entrenchments which had been thrown up outside and took refuge within the walls of the fort. After about one day during which shots were exchanged between the besiegers and the besieged, the former suffering very little, the French surrendered, August 27th. Nine armed vessels, the entire naval force of the French on Lake Ontario, fell into the hands of the English, though the crews escaped. A large amount of plunder was taken — provisions, arms, goods for the Indian trade, furs, 60 cannon and 16 mortars. The latter were used by the English in demolishing the walls of the fort and then, with the exception of a few which they took with them, their trunnions were knocked off. All the barracks or buildings in or near the fort were burned and also a large quantity of provisions. Seven vessels were sunk. Much which might later have been of service to the British was destroyed, but the idea seems to have been to make even a cleaner sweep than Montcalm did at Oswego two years before. Some effort was made under the orders of Vaudreuil to restore the fort, but it resulted in nothing and the line of communication between Canada and the west remained seriously weakened through its loss.

The expedition against Fort Duquesne, the command of which was intrusted to Brigadier General John Forbes, brings us back to conditions as they were in Pennsylvania after the defeat of Braddock. William Denny had succeeded Morris in the governorship. He and the Quakers in the assembly were at loggerheads over coöperation in the war in general, the passage of a militia law, and the conduct of Indian relations. Though the sufferings of the western settlements from Indian attacks had somewhat abated, they had by no means ceased, the western frontier having been contracted in general to the Susquehanna, and active measures of defence along the line of forts which had been constructed in that region being an imperative necessity. But negotiations with the Indians with a view to the restoration of peace between the English and the Delawares and Shawnees were being actively prosecuted. These, of course, had to be carried on somewhat in connection with Sir William Johnson who, with Edmund Atkins, had been appointed in 1756 royal commissioner for the administration of Indian affairs. Even Atkins, whose district included the colonies from Virginia southward,[1] was brought slightly into connection with Pennsylvania affairs, through the Cherokees and Catawbas, whose coöperation against the French and their allies on the Ohio was solicited.

As Pennsylvania was one of the colonies the care of whose Indian relations had been intrusted to Johnson, its dealings were chiefly with him. This connection also was made the closer by the relations of superiority and dependence which had existed between the Six Nations and the Indians of Pennsylvania and the Ohio region. That, however, had been broken by the removal of the Delawares and Shawnees westward and by their revolt and transfer of their active support to the French. Though the allegiance, so to speak, of the Iroquois was divided and numbers of them, especially from the western cantons, were always serving with the French, they were generally counted as allies of the British. For the purpose of Johnson's office they were always so treated, to say nothing of the more extreme claim that since 1701 they had been British subjects. We have seen that for the purpose of warding off interference by Shirley, Lydius and a New England interest, Johnson had shown great sensitiveness concerning his rights as Indian commissioner. Atkins also expressed himself to similar effect, for it was the purpose of the crown in creating the office and appointing them to it, to establish a general and uniform Indian policy, in harmony with the military needs of the time, and to subordinate to this the measures of the separate colonies. In this way the frontier, under the control of the commander-in-chief and the Indian commissioners, would be treated as a unit and no longer in sections as suited the immediate interests of the various colonies which lay adjacent to it.

Though Johnson's assertion of control to the southward was not so imperative, he sought to make it effective as far as the interests of the Six Nations extended, and that was throughout the middle colonies and the Ohio region. His agent, George Croghan, was regularly sent on journeys and to attend conferences in that section, while Johnson sought to bring tribesmen from the south to meet him and the Iroquois at his own residence or at Onondaga. His efforts to raise contingents

---

[1] Pa. Arch., III, 155, 175, 183, 268; N. Y. Col. Docs., VII, 208 *et seq.*

of Indian allies for the expeditions of 1756 and later to the northward involved continuous negotiations of this character.[1] With this end in view he also interested himself directly in measures for restoring peace between the Delawares and Shawnees and the British. Through his influence with the Iroquois he helped to restore them ceremonially to the condition of men and to remove the stigma of feminine cowardice which their proud overlords had sought to affix to them.[2]

But a more serious obstacle to the restoration of peace was the conviction in the minds of the Delawares in particular that they had been defrauded of large tracts of land and that by force and deceit combined they were being driven from their hunting grounds. It was the same feeling which the Mohawk, Hendrick, had expressed so forcibly as to lead to the calling of the Albany Congress. And at that congress, as we have seen, the commissioners from Pennsylvania had secured from the Six Nations a grant of the entire Ohio country, the western hunting grounds of the Delawares and Shawnees. This, with the earlier Walking Purchase, and the transfer of land in the Wyoming region, where the Delawares expected to settle, to purchasers from Connecticut, rankled in their minds and had led them to listen to the appeals of the French and take up the hatchet against the English. In September, 1756, and again a year later, Johnson wrote to the board of trade concerning the jealousy caused both among the Indians of New York and those of Pennsylvania by the large purchases of land which had been made by the British, and mentioned particularly in this connection the grant of the Ohio country which had been negotiated at Albany in 1754.[3] The hostilities in Pennsylvania, as well as the general indifference of the Indians to British interests in the war, he attributed largely, and perhaps with undue emphasis, to this cause. Braddock's defeat and the loss of Oswego had precipitated the trouble, but the land grants had furnished contributory griev-

[1] The records of these are in N. Y. Col. Docs., VI and VII. Much or all of this material is reprinted in 2 Pa. Arch., VI.

[2] The Delawares and Shawnees are said to have declared that they would no longer be treated as women, but as men would take up the hatchet against the English, at a council held at Otseningo, now Binghamton, New York. Pa. Col. Recs., VII, 521.

[3] N. Y. Col. Docs., VII, 129, 169 et seq., 276, 329; Doc. Hist. of N. Y., II, 773; Watson, Life of Conrad Weiser.

ances. Johnson even went so far as to suggest that it might be for the common interest if Pennsylvania would give up those lands for the present, instead of building forts on the Susquehanna and raising troops to defend them. "By presents and management we may be able to keep some little interest yet alive," he wrote to the board, "and perhaps some nations to act a neutral part, yet I am apprehensive meer expence, Speeches and Promises (so often repeated and so little regarded) will never be able to effect a favourable Revolution of our Indian interest . . ." These were Johnson's thoughts in the light of the successes which the French had been winning, though of course it was evident that if the British would unite in a vigorous prosecution of the war the Indians might be overawed and restrained from attempting further hostilities. But pending such an event, he urged that relief should be sought by concessions to the Indians in the matter of their lands.

Such also was the opinion of many in Pennsylvania and it was voiced on behalf of the assembly by Pemberton, Galloway, Hughes and by the Quakers generally in connection with the series of conferences with the Indians which were held at Easton and Lancaster during the years 1756 to 1758. In fact Johnson's opinion, though originating in part from evidence which came to him direct from the Iroquois and from other sources,[1] was also a reflection of what Croghan heard expressed in Pennsylvania and reported to Johnson on his return from attendance on the conferences being held there. On the other hand, the proprietors denied these charges and were supported in so doing by their mouthpieces, the governor and councillors, and by the evidence of earlier deeds produced from the archives and interpreted by Weiser, Peters and others. But the government of Pennsylvania, being unable, with such military force as she could organize, to stop the raids of hostile Indians through her western districts, and following the course of action to which she had been accustomed in the past, had called these conferences and sought relief through negotiation. This procedure did not suit Johnson or Atkins, because it was a survival of the former particularistic method of managing Indian relations

---

[1] N. Y. Col. Docs., VII, 329.

and ignored to a large extent the authority of the newly appointed Indian commissioners. Such a course, however, was to be expected, as it agreed with colonial conditions and precedents, which the mere appointment of two commissioners by the crown, unfurnished with resources of any kind for enforcing their regulations, must be powerless to change. Moreover, the need of Pennsylvania for relief was too imperative to admit of her waiting for it from any source so insubstantial as that of the new commissioners. Therefore the well known conferences at Easton and Lancaster were held.

At these meetings, after the first, Governor Denny presided, attended as was usual by members of the council, Richard Peters the secretary, certain commissioners representing the assembly, Croghan as agent of Sir William Johnson, clerks and interpreters, among whom Weiser, now advanced in years, occupied a position of declining importance.[1] In the later conferences Charles Thomson, master of the Friend's School in Philadelphia, was designated by Teedyuscung as his clerk and Thomson's presence in that capacity, after some protest, was tolerated by the governor.[2] During the more public sessions audiences of interested citizens, soldiers and Indians were in attendance. Denny presided with dignity and in the speeches — doubtless prepared for him by Peters or others — the rhetorical flourishes which were always addressed to the Indians were used with effect. The rights and the point of view of the proprietors were also defended, especially in correspondence which was carried on with Galloway and his fellow commissioners from the assembly. But the central figure of dramatic interest in these conferences was Teedyuscung, the Delaware chieftain who,

[1] Pa. Col. Recs., VII, 203–220, 223, 313–338, 505–549, 638–727; *ibid.*, VIII, 32 *et seq.*, 175–223; Doc. Hist. of N. Y., II, 773 *et seq.*; Watson, Life of Weiser.

[2] Croghan wrote to Johnson concerning this, "Those People, by his having a Clerk, they had a Counsellor for themselves, to put Tedyuscung in mind what they wanted him to say, and it appeared very clearly one day when he had got his speech drawn up in writing and desired the Clerk to read it off as a lawyer would put in a plea at the bar, which I think your honor will think very extraordinary and the most unprecedented procedure ever known at an Indian treaty before this. I was obliged to object and obliged Tedyuscung to deliver his speech himself. . . ."

on most occasions, conducted the negotiations in behalf of the Indians. In spite of the fact that occasionally, during the intervals during the daily sessions, he imbibed too freely of fire-water, his flow of oratory continued on the whole to be abundant, as was also his resourcefulness as a diplomatist. Some of his speeches, whatever their origin, furnished admirable examples of Indian rhetoric, while the successive exhibitions of humility, pride, covert or open defiance, misleading statements, exaggerated claims and diplomatic finesse in general which he made before these conferences, entitle him to recognition as an adept in these arts. He was first employed by the Pennsylvanians as an agent to conciliate his fellow tribesmen to the north and west and to bring them into conference for the discussion of terms of peace. He came back with the statement that he was king of ten nations and their sole accredited spokesman in the conferences. This claim the Six Nations in particular denied and it was a wild exaggeration. Throughout the conferences Teedyuscung rested his plea on the claim that the Delawares and Shawnees had been wrongfully and fraudulently deprived of their lands by the Walking Purchase and by the cession of the territory west of the mountains in 1754. This fell in with the view of the Quakers and the assembly and they doubtless helped to furnish him with this line of argument, he and the interpreters dressing it up in appropriate Indian rhetoric.

The board of trade, on being informed by Johnson concerning the feelings of the Indians in reference to the land grants, notified the Penns and they proposed that commissioners be appointed to treat and bring about an agreement. Johnson was informed of this and therefore sent Croghan as his agent to the important conference held in the summer of 1757. When, however, it appeared that Croghan had no definitive powers and that the questions must be referred directly to Johnson, Teedyuscung refused, because the Six Nations who had been concerned in making the grants would be present and probably influence the decision. Though the governor and the proprietary interest were opposed to the interference of the Quakers and the commissioners of the assembly, the latter, together with the Indians, so far prevailed that at the conference in October, 1758, that part of the purchase of 1754 which lay west of the Alleghanies was relinquished by Pennsylvania. This was the first step toward fixing the mountains as the limit of western settlement, beyond which the country should be reserved to the Indians, which was fully set forth in the famous order in council of October, 1763.[1] As to the alleged fraud connected with the so-called Walking Purchase, near the Forks of the Delaware, the deeds were exhibited at Easton, but no decision could be reached. An attempt was then made to induce the board of trade and privy council to take the matter up, Franklin as agent presenting such a petition in 1759. But the impossibility of settling such a question in England was so obvious that it was referred back to Johnson to make the inquiry and transmit his findings to England for final action.[2] But by that time the danger had passed and it does not appear that further action was taken.

The arrival of a band of Cherokees in Pennsylvania in 1758, because they were the hereditary enemies of the northern Indians, threatened to provoke assaults upon the frontier settlements anew and to confirm the alliance between the tribesmen and the French. Though the friendly intentions of the visiting Cherokees was proven, certain Indian outrages in Berks county, together with the dangerous situation of affairs in general, convinced the governor and General Forbes that a further step must be taken to placate the Indians. This was to send peace envoys across the mountains to carry to the hostile tribesmen the message of Teedyuscung and of the conferences at Easton. It was realized that without an effort of this kind the Delawares and Shawnees would never know how earnest was the desire of the English for peace. The plan also agreed fully with the desires of the Quakers, though political jealousies made it impossible that one of their faith should be selected to head the mission. Christian Frederic Post, a Moravian who spoke the language of the Delawares and had previously been employed on minor errands of this nature, was chosen for this specially dangerous task. Accompanied by a few Indians, he made two journeys, one in July and the other in October and November, 1758, to

[1] Alvord, The Miss. Valley in British Politics, I, 121.
[2] Doc. Hist. of N. Y., II, 769–790.

the region of Fort Duquesne and the Ohio country.[1] The first
journey was specially dangerous, because the Indians were
still loyal to the French and the French garrison would have
been glad to receive the scalp of the missionary. Post was
taken so near Fort Duquesne, holding some of his conferences
just across the river and in the presence of savages the majority of whom were still intensely hostile, that his escape from
capture or death was almost miraculous. But he was sincere and straightforward in speech and bearing and absolutely
fearless of death. Meeting a small number of Indians who
were in sympathy with his effort, interest in his visit spread
to others.

" The Indians, with a great many of the French officers,"
writes Post, " came over to hear what I had to say. The
officers brought with them a table, pens, ink and paper. I
spoke in the middle of them with a free conscience, and per-
ceived by the look of the French they were not pleased
with what I said." On behalf of the people of Pennsylvania
he told them of the desire of the English for peace, how
twelve months before at Easton they had resolved to send
a large peace belt to them and by means of it had already
opened the road from Alleghany to the council fire where
their ancestors had met of old; and now he had come to clear
away the mist from their eyes and show them that the road
was clear and open so that peaceful intercourse might be
resumed. In order to quiet the fear which ever oppressed
the mind of the Indian that the British and French would
unite for his destruction, Post assured his hearers that the
army which was approaching was intended to attack the
French, in order to avenge the blood that had been shed.
" We do not come to hurt you. . . . We look upon you as
our countrymen, that sprung out of the same ground with us.
We think therefore that it is our duty to take care of you,
and we in brotherly love advise you to come away with
your whole nation and as many of your friends as you can
get to follow you." But the fear and suspicion which sprang
from the Indian's earlier experiences and from his consciousness of weakness kept asserting themselves, and Post was

[1] Pa. Col. Recs., VIII, 110, 132, 147, 148, 212, 223. The two journals of
Post are printed in Craig's Olden Time, I.

forced repeatedly to meet the challenge that the British intended to seize all their land and to join with the French for
their total destruction. Had the Indians been wise, as a race
and from the beginning, they would have thrown in their cause
wholly with the French, for in such an alliance lay the only
chance for survival even in a hybrid form. But it was now too
late, for French rule in America was doomed and the red
man was already facing the grim prospect of annihilation before the resistless advance of the British, who as a people
had neither understanding of his characteristics nor sympathy
with his claims. When Post was on his second visit and the
army of Forbes was already near Fort Duquesne, the Indian
spokesman revealed his intuition of the fate that was in
store but their powerlessness to avert it, by the pleading
cry,[1] " Brother, now you told me you have heard of that
good agreement, that has been agreed to at the treaty at
Easton; . . . Brother, you have told me, that after you have
come to hear it, you have taken it to heart, and then you
sent it to me and let me know it. Brothers, I would desire
you would be pleased to hear me, and I would tell you in a
most soft, loving and friendly manner, to go back over the
mountains and to stay there; for, if you will do that, I will
use it for an argument to argue with other nations of Indians."

Such is the record in brief of the negotiations which had
as their object the checking of ravages along the western
frontier and the detachment of the Delawares and Shawnees,
with the Mingoes, or western Iroquois, from the French alliance. This result, as a temporary measure of relief, was
attained and it contributed to the collapse of French authority in the Ohio region. But the decisive blow was a military
one, and it remains briefly to describe the difficulties which
Forbes and his men had to overcome in reaching Fort Duquesne.

Since Braddock's defeat the defence of the middle section
of the frontier, despite the earnest efforts of Loudon to administer the war from one centre, had been chiefly under the
charge of Virginia. For military purposes Maryland and
Pennsylvania signified little. During 1757 Washington was
stationed in the valley of Virginia in command of a few

[1] Olden Time, I, 167.

hundred militia, vainly attempting to defend a vast stretch of mountainous and densely wooded country against the attacks of the savages. As had been found during three wars in New England, the securing of protection by such means was impossible. As Washington kept urging, an offensive movement with an adequate force against Fort Duquesne, the centre and origin of the trouble, was the only effective policy. But Loudon had decided that throughout the southern colonies the defensive alone should be maintained during 1757, so that forces could be concentrated in the north. Dinwiddie continued in office until January, 1758, when he sailed for England, unregretted by the people of his province and certainly by Washington. Jealousy of the young officer on the part of the governor, and an irritating exercise of authority over him, met with proud and even angry protests in return, made official dealings between the two anything but pleasant. Dinwiddie was both fussy and inefficient, always magnifying his official position and asserting the rights of the prerogative, though doing it all in a most unimpressive manner. His style of writing makes one think that he was a sort of improved edition of John Usher, who afflicted New Hampshire so long. However that may be, the tragedies of the frontier which he was compelled month after month to witness without the power to prevent or very much to relieve them, combined with the irritation caused by his relations with the government at Williamsburg, threw Washington into a serious illness which compelled him to abandon his command in November and he did not return again to active service until Forbes' expedition was under way.

Forbes, one of Pitt's appointees, was a good officer, though trained in the old school and afflicted with a disease during most of his campaign of which he died a few months after its close. For the purpose of capturing Fort Duquesne he was furnished with a force of about 6000 men.[1] It included one regiment of Highlanders of nearly 1300 men and a battalion of 360 Royal Americans while the rest were militia from Pennsylvania and the Lower Counties, Maryland, Virginia and North Carolina. Lieutenant Colonel Henry Bouquet, an experienced officer of Swiss descent, was the second in com-

[1] Kingsford, IV, 193.

mand, and was sent in advance to Raystown, now Bedford, among the slopes of the Alleghanies in western Pennsylvania. Sir John Sinclair was quartermaster general. Forbes, while firm, was ready to adapt himself to American conditions and found no difficulty in securing the necessary coöperation of the provinces concerned. The French force, under De Ligneris, which he might expect to meet at the end of his march, numbered probably not more than 1000, though their Indian allies were numerous and alert, as the frontiersmen had known to their cost during the past three years. The fact was that so hard pressed were the French for men to serve in Canada, that all available strength was being concentrated there and the garrisons of far distant outposts, like Fort Duquesne, must depend chiefly upon their remoteness and the Indians for protection.[1] Therefore, as was so generally the case, the problem ahead of Forbes and his men was chiefly one of opening communication with the fort and reaching their objective, rather than defeating the enemy and capturing his position when once it was reached.

The choice of a route to Fort Duquesne was not made without much discussion, and this had its origin largely in the rivalry between Virginia and Pennsylvania, which appeared with increasing prominence as military operations and the advance of settlement brought their frontiers into closer proximity near the upper Ohio. Braddock's route, though narrow and somewhat obstructed through neglect, was available for use and much expense and hard labor would be saved by following that route. As in Braddock's time, the influence of Virginia was cast in favor of Braddock's road, and on this occasion Washington supported that view with much vigor, especially in his letters to Bouquet and in conversations with that officer.[2] Both were engaged in road building and in pushing men and supplies westward. Not only did Washington dwell on the advantage of using the road already built, but on the prospect — it being already August — that there would not be time to cut a new road through the moun-

---

[1] Daniel de Joncaire, however, brought a reinforcement of 216 French and Indians, mostly Indians, to Fort Duquesne at the beginning of August. Severance, *op. cit.*, II, 214.

[2] Washington's Writings (Ford), II, 56, 62.

tains and complete the campaign that season. The continuance of the war longer in that section he could not look forward to with patience. The rival route, which had been selected by Forbes and which was advocated by Sinclair, led through Pennsylvania, from Carlisle to Fort Duquesne by the way of Shippensburg and Raystown, the distance being 193 miles. The distance from Carlisle by way of Fort Frederic, Cumberland and the Braddock road was 212 miles, a difference, as Washington figured it out, of only 19 miles.[1] This, he contended, would be more than offset by the advantages of the Braddock route. For a time also Washington thought that the force was to be divided, part going by one route and part by the other, with the intention of effecting a junction among the mountains before they reached Fort Duquesne. This he thought very bad policy. The Virginians in general were much disturbed over the prospect of superior advantages in trade which the Pennsylvanians would secure by means of the new road, the result, they claimed, of favoritism. So aroused were they that the burgesses threatened to recall the first Virginia regiment at the beginning of December.

But the advantage of the Pennsylvania route in point of distance, the more abundant forage which was procurable there, and the avoidance of specially hard and dangerous parts of the old road among the mountains, determined the choice of Forbes in favor of the new road and to this he adhered. The labor of building it was great, especially as it was made wide enough for the passage of teams and artillery. But the number of men available for the work was large and supplies were abundant. Fortified stations were also built at intervals for the protection of men and storing of supplies, a great improvement on the procedure of Braddock. Scouting parties were kept out as a protection against the Indians who infested the woods. The larger and more effective scale on which the work was prosecuted gave evidence of the experience in such matters which had been gained since the beginning of the war. About the end of August, Bouquet was able to establish a post on Loyalhannon creek, west of the main heights of the Alleghany range and scarcely fifty miles from Fort Du-

[1] The difference, however, was some ten miles more than that.

quesne. Forbes, meantime, suffering intensely from disease, was slowly advancing with the main body of the troops from Carlisle.

About the middle of September Major James Grant of the Highlanders persuaded Bouquet to permit him to reconnoitre the French position in force, with a view even of bringing on a conflict. Grant underestimated both the number of French in the garrison and the dangers of fighting in that densely wooded country of which the British knew nothing but with which the enemy were well acquainted. About 800 men were detailed for this enterprise and Grant divided his force in order better to provoke a sortie and then to draw the enemy into an ambuscade. But the men who were sent toward the fort to draw the enemy out, lost their way in the darkness and fell into confusion. This led to a change of plan and to still further divisions of the British. An opportunity was thus given for the French to make a sortie in much larger numbers than were expected, the Indians giving effective aid as on Braddock's field. The result was a humiliating defeat for the British, in which they lost 273 men and the French only about twenty. Grant, Lewis and several other officers were captured. The usual atrocities were committed by the Indians, according to one story the heads of the slaughtered Highlanders being stuck on poles and their kilts hung around them. The captives were conducted by Joncaire under guard to Niagara and thence sent to Montreal.

This was a costly reverse, the result of over confidence. It encouraged the Indians during the remaining weeks of the advance to greater activity in cutting off British stragglers, seizing cattle and the like. But the final victory was scarcely delayed by Grant's defeat. The western Indians soon went home; so did the French militia from Louisiana and the Illinois country. De Ligneris' garrison, even when thus reduced, saw itself facing starvation as winter approached, and no prospect of relief. Though impeded by heavy rains, Forbes and his army steadily advanced and early in November it was gathered at Loyalhannon. On the strength of reports of the weakness of the French, it was then decided, leaving baggage and nearly all the artillery behind, to push a body of 2500 picked men rapidly toward the fort. A road was opened by men under Washington and Colonel Armstrong of Pennsylvania. As the force thus selected approached the fort, the garrison blew up its magazine and evacuated the works, retiring to Venango. The British took possession. As soon as the news of this reached England orders were issued that the fort should be rebuilt and all necessary steps taken to confirm the hold of the British on the Ohio country and to break in that quarter the French communications between the region of the lakes and the lower Mississippi. But on account of the illness and death of Forbes, Stanwix was appointed to the southern command with this as his special task.[1] The southern colonies naturally fell far short of raising the levies which were expected for this service in 1759, and Stanwix had the usual difficulty in inducing the Pennsylvania assembly to provide the funds desired. Debts due for wagons and cartage and the obstacles put in the way of the issue of bills of credit by proprietary instructions played a prominent part. But these were so far overcome that the fort was rebuilt and named after Pitt himself, and the French were unable to take any effective steps to recover it.

With the occupation of Acadia and the capture of Louisbourg and Fort Duquesne the strategic outposts of the French on the east and west had been taken. Their frontier for military purposes had been greatly contracted and this would enable the British by so much to concentrate their forces and operations during the coming year. Niagara was the only remote outpost of importance for defensive purposes which now remained in the hands of the French. With the exception of the force which must be detached for the occupation of Niagara, the British attack could now be concentrated on the centre of the French position, Canada itself. With the practical certainty that this course would be pursued, the French, and especially Montcalm, had to compare their resources with those of the British in order to forecast the result. In population, according to a census which was now taken, Canada had about 82,000, while the white population of the British continental colonies was about 1,300,000.[2] The disparity in economic resources was even greater. But only a

---

[1] Corresp. of Pitt, *etc.*, II, 17, 125, 130.

[2] N. Y. Col. Docs., X, 962; Dexter, Transactions of Am. Ant. Soc., 1887; Bancroft, Hist. of United States (Latest Rev.), II, 390.

small fraction of the population and capital of the British colonies could be mobilized for an attack on Canada. However, so far as the northern colonies were concerned, they were more available now than they ever had been in the past. The colonies were coöperating now with reasonable efficiency and, what was of equal importance, roads and means of approach by water were now open to all the French positions. The British had to such an extent the command of the ocean that the French government, if it had had the troops to spare, would not have dared to send them in large numbers across the Atlantic for 1759 lest they, with their supplies, should be captured by the British. The British, however, with lines of communication open and not hard pressed by the European war, could send to America both land and naval forces ample for the purpose of conquering Canada. Though estimates of the forces which the British would bring into the field could be only conjectured — anywhere from 30,000 to 50,000 — Montcalm knew with exactness the numbers which were available for withstanding them. They were about 3200 troops of the line, and perhaps 7000 Canadians who could serve outside of the harvest season. As Amherst had 23 battalions of regulars with him on the continent and Wolfe brought about 7000 to operate directly against Quebec, the odds against the French were to be sufficiently great.[1]

Anticipating this as the general situation, Montcalm, Doreil, the commissary of war, and the other leading officers of the king's troops were fully aware of the gloomy prospect which lay ahead. Montcalm and Doreil clearly expressed it in their letters home. At the close of July, Montcalm wrote that, if peace should not be concluded, the situation of the colony would be most critical.[2] Doreil was writing at the same time on the necessity for peace if the colony was to be saved. In September, Montcalm observed to Vaudreuil that the time for petty councils and measures had passed and all private interests should be made to give way before the most vigorous employment of men and time for the salvation of Canada. The character of the war had changed, the trunk of the tree was now attacked and it was a matter of compara-

---

[1] N. Y. Col. Docs., X, 874, 960, 962, April, 1759; Montcalm thought the British would bring 60,000 men against his 10,000 or 11,000.

[2] Ibid., 761, 769, 874.

tive indifference what happened to the branches. Therefore it was his policy to concentrate the small available force on the lower and middle St. Lawrence and try to survive there till peace came. At one time, like Washington during the War for Independence, he contemplated the possibility, if Canada should be lost, of gathering the troops and those of the colonists who would go and retiring to the Mississippi in the hope at least of saving Louisiana.

Vaudreuil, however, planned as usual an extensive campaign for the coming year, including the recovery of control on Lake Ontario. He was complacent, confident and occupied, as ever, with petty details, and the satisfied contemplation of what he and the Canadians had done and he thought would accomplish. After the success at Ticonderoga the hostile feeling between him and Montcalm reached its highest intensity. The exchanges between them were sharp and the situation was fully reported to the authorities in Paris. Vaudreuil's anger was also increased by the sarcastic comments of the officers of the line, who fully supported their commander, and in the interest of peace Montcalm cautioned them to observe greater restraint. Though official intercourse between the governor general and the commander continued and outward civilities were kept up, mutual confidence was totally lacking. So irritated was Montcalm that after the battle at Ticonderoga he insisted on resigning. But as the season advanced and the sombre facts of Canada's situation and prospects were forced on his attention, he resolved, as the military servant of the king, to remain and meet such fate as should befall the colony. This was a disappointment to Vaudreuil, who would have much preferred that Lévis should succeed to the command.

Doreil returned to France in the fall of 1758 and, at the instance of Vaudreuil and Montcalm, Bougainville was sent as a special agent to lay before the French ministers the needs of Canada and secure such aid as was possible. The spirit of Vaudreuil was shown by the fact that while he gave Bougainville a letter of commendation introducing him to Berryer, the colonial minister, he privately informed this official that both Bougainville and Doreil were creatures of Montcalm and did not understand the colony. They reached

France in safety and Bougainville in a series of memoirs showed how great the need of Canada was for troops, arms and munitions, food and a squadron of warships, because now the British colonies were for the first time united against her. They were given a supply of arms, powder and other munitions, 60 engineers, sappers and artillerymen and less than 400 recruits for the regulars. Because of the need of troops in Europe, none could be spared for Canada, the plea being that when the house was on fire one need not be concerned about the stable. The officers were complimented for their valiant service in the past, Montcalm being raised to the rank of lieutenant general and Lévis to that of major general. Vaudreuil was decorated with the grand cross of the order of St. Louis. Other lesser honors were bestowed.[1] They were thus politely left to defend Canada as best they could, contracting their lines so at least to retain for France a foothold there, being assured that the king trusted to their courage and endurance so that at the end they might efface the disgraceful memory of the surrender of Louisbourg. To Vaudreuil, however, the order was repeated to defer to the commander in all affairs relating to war and not to take command in person unless all the militia was called out and after he had consulted Montcalm. This order the governor did not violate.

In April, 1759, at about the time when spring brought the return of Bougainville with his meagre aid and discouraging news, Montcalm wrote in cipher to Belleisle, the minister of war,[2] a scathing exposé of the financial condition of Canada and of the system of gross corruption and robbery which for years had been practiced by François Bigot, the intendant, and the crew by whom he was surrounded. It was a fit reflection of the degenerate court and government of France under Louis XV and Madame de Pompadour, and by means of them both the kingdom and the province were being ruined. Months before, during the enforced leisure of the winter, as he observed the orgy of waste, frivolity and corruption of which Bigot and his fellow officials and contractors were guilty, Montcalm had confided to his journal a comparison between what he saw and suffered at Montreal and Quebec with the do-

[1] N. Y. Col. Docs., X, 940, 943; Parkman, Montcalm and Wolfe, II.
[2] N. Y. Col. Docs., X, 960.

ings of Roman proconsuls of whom Juvenal wrote.[1] Returning
to the subject in his letter to the minister of war, he declared
that, unless saved by sheer good luck, Canada would fall
during the approaching campaign. The government was good
for nothing. Of late harvests had been poor or, because of the
war, the land had been imperfectly cultivated. The number
of cattle was falling off. Provisions were lacking, prices were
high. The people were dispirited and well they might lack
confidence, for Vaudreuil, though himself not specially corrupt, trusted Bigot and his confederates and closed his eyes to
the schemes of plunder by which they were accumulating
large fortunes at the expense of the king and the colony.
"Everybody appears to be in a hurry to make his fortune
before the colony is lost; which event many perhaps desire
as an impenetrable veil over their conduct."

In this strain the general indicated in outline the plan of
operations which Bigot and his friends were pursuing. As
brought out years afterward by criminal inquiry in France,
the plan of operation of Bigot and his friends was substantially the following. The intendant, who controlled trade,
finance, justice, all departments of civil administration, was
the centre of the clique. As the intendant and governor general were now on good terms, no one was interested to expose
the knavery which for several years had been going on. Bigot
also by his skill in business and his social attractiveness won
friends and bound them to him, Montcalm himself even acknowledging his power, while Lévis to a degree yielded to
it. By virtue of his office Bigot had charge of purchasing
supplies on behalf of the crown for the royal troops, militia
and Indians in Canada. A corps of subordinate officials, the
commissary of marine, the commissary general, the naval
controller, the king's storekeeper and others were associated
with him in the ring, and the supervision exercised by the
colonial office in Paris was not efficient. A contract was
formed with a firm in Bordeaux for shipping supplies to Canada where, on the plea that they belonged to the king, they
were admitted free of duty. There, by the use of various
fictitious devices, they were sold to the king, always at enormous profits which went into the pockets of Bigot and his

[1] Journal de Montcalm, Dec. 10, 1758.

friends. They monopolized this traffic and Bigot, using the name of a private trader, set up a warehouse, popularly known as La Friponne, or the Cheat, where the business was done. Heavy profits also were made on transporting the king's troops, artillery and stores, while the furs which belonged to the king were sold at low prices to the confederates instead of being disposed of at auction to the highest bidder. On the plea that the peasants were hoarding their grain, an order forcing them to sell at a low fixed price was procured from Bigot, and when famine was threatened this grain was sold, in part to the king and in part to its former owners, at a large advance.

By such methods as these, further description of which is not necessary in this place, the government and the province were systematically robbed on a scale which throws the peculations of early New York governors into the shade. Large numbers of officials shared in the gains and the poison extended through the entire body politic. It reached even to the remote posts adjacent to Acadia and to those on the Ohio and the upper lakes. Péan, Varin, Bréard, Penisseault, Corpron and many others shared heavily in the gains. But Cadet, a butcher who was put into the office of commissary general, by trading and the falsification of accounts accumulated perhaps the largest fortune of any in the ring. The confederates. with the women of their families, and those of the civil and military officials who made up the gay society of Montreal and Quebec, gambled recklessly. The dances, costly suppers and excursions with which they relieved the monotony of the long Canadian winter, all set off by the liaisons of Bigot, Péan and others with their friends' wives, furnished a sprightly imitation of Parisian society. The scanty resources of the colony were being wasted, famine threatened the country, and yet this group of harpies continued to devour its substance until the British army was at its very gates. Whether willful or not, so blind was Vaudreuil that he recommended Cadet for a title of nobility and, on Péan visiting France, wrote the minister that he might trust all he said for he fully knew the condition of the colony and had the governor's full confidence.

To make the confusion worse, in order to supply a needed circulating medium, Bigot issued legal tender promissory notes, called *ordonnances,* subject to annual redemption in bills of exchange on the royal treasury in Paris. But as delays occurred in redeeming them, they depreciated and in 1759 the amount outstanding had become so large that the ministry stopped payment. Then came a complete financial collapse. Only the severest measures of rationing and saving could avert famine. The service of every able bodied man was needed for defence, though some must be excused to help the aged, the women and the children cultivate the fields. What little trade Canada had enjoyed was now cut off by the control which the British held of almost all routes by sea and land. From the close of 1758 Canada was approaching the condition of a beleaguered fortress and its defenders realized that at best they could not hold out beyond the spring or summer of 1760.

With the beginning of 1759 the eyes of Berryer, the colonial minister, were partially opened. He began to call Bigot sternly to task and in his letters described to him, citing various illustrative cases, the system of robbery which he had practiced by purchases and resales to the government at vastly enhanced prices. " With conduct like this," he continued, " it is no wonder that the expenses of the colony become insupportable. The amount of your drafts on the treasury is frightful. The fortunes of your subordinates throw suspicion on your administration. . . . I am no longer astounded that immense fortunes are seen in Canada." Having dwelt at length on the system of robbery by individuals which has been described, he passed to criticism of the depreciated currency.[1] He condemned its issue without the king's permission as illegal, and declared that the plan of its issue and redemption was " not free from the apprehension of fraud." He then proposed several restrictive measures. But the confidence of the minister in the essential honesty of Bigot, which still continued, was shaken by the enormous drafts on the treasury, which showed unlimited extravagance in the colony and by startling revelations contained in Montcalm's letter, above referred to, to Belleisle. An investigation was then ordered and an agent was sent to Canada for the purpose. Bigot now saw ruin facing him, into which he was being drawn by the very momentum of the system of fraud which he had

---

[1] Parkman, *op. cit.*; N. Y. Col. Docs., X, 938.

devised. As a last resort, Cadet was thrown over and made
to disgorge heavily from his ill gotten gains. But it was too
late, and after the province fell criminal prosecution and
prison faced the conspirators in France. It was a province,
weak at best, but now economically and financially undermined and practically abandoned by France, which Wolfe
and Saunders came to occupy in the summer of 1759.

Pitt's exhortation to the governors of the northern and
southern colonies respectively concerning the next campaign
was issued early in December, 1758.[1] Like his circular letters
of previous years, it promised generous aid on the part of the
home government and called for vigorous coöperation, though
without specification as to details, on the part of the colonies,
they being encouraged by the prospect that the efforts of
another year would bring peace. Toward the close of the
month the minister was able to instruct Amherst, the commander-in-chief, concerning the general plan of campaign. In
addition to the main operation, which was to be directed
against Quebec, and about which very particular instructions
were given, Amherst was ordered with as large a body of
regulars and provincials as possible to invade Canada by way
of Crown Point or La Galette, reëstablishing also the post at
Oswego and, if possible, capturing Niagara. Forts and defensible posts were to be built at points along these routes;
bateaux, wagons and other means of transport were to be
provided by building anew and carefully preserving those
which were available from the previous campaign. The same
course was to be pursued with reference to muskets and other
supplies. Amherst was a good man to conduct this part of the
campaign, slow, methodical, firm, but not overbearing in his
dealings with the colonists and in the discipline of his army.
He did not attempt to hold a conference with the governors,
but soon, in pursuance of orders, began strengthening Fort
Edward and the building of a fort at the head of Lake George
and another at the Oneida Carrying Place, which was later
known as Fort Stanwix. When the time came for his northward advance Amherst had available for that purpose upwards of 11,000 men.

But provision also had to be made for the expedition which

[1] Corresp. of Pitt, etc., I, 414, 417, 422, 426.

was to pursue the well known route to Oswego and thence be transported by water to Niagara. Upon this expedition, as well as on Amherst's northward march after he had passed the French frontier, precautions had constantly to be taken against scalping parties of Indians. Now that the tide was so decisively turning against the French, the Six Nations in particular began to veer toward the British and efforts were made to attract some of the Canadian Indians in the same direction. The results which followed the conferences at Easton also had their effect, and the spectre so often raised by Onontio of imminent destruction of the red man by the British for a time lost its power. During the winter and spring of 1759, Johnson redoubled his efforts to rally a large contingent of Iroquois for the expedition against Niagara. A large assembly from the nations of Indians gathered at Canajoharie.[1] It was harangued at successive sessions by Johnson, presents were bestowed, belts were exchanged, oxen were boiled and eaten, generous draughts of liquor drunk, the war hatchet drawn, and the war dance with which the conference reached its climax lasted an entire night. Johnson was now swimming with the tide and as the result of his conference a horde numbering from 600 to 900 Indians followed him to Niagara. Though discouraged, the French as usual summoned the Indian allies from the west and north. The response was large enough to make life very unsafe through all the lake region for Englishmen who ventured away from the ranks or fortified posts, but the time had come when Johnson was to prevail over de Joncaire.

Early in May John Prideaux received a commission as brigadier general and was put in command of the expedition against Niagara.[2] Soon after the twentieth he assumed command at Schenectady of the force detailed for the purpose. It consisted of two regiments of regulars, together with two companies of the Royal Americans and a detachment of Royal Artillery which was poorly supplied with guns and engineers. Out of the total colonial levies for the year, which were raised after somewhat less than the customary delay, 2560 men from New York and 500 from Rhode Island were

---

[1] N. Y. Col. Docs., VII, 375-394.
[2] Corresp. of Pitt, etc., II, 122; Severance, op. cit., II, 250 et seq.

assigned for service against Niagara. As it had been planned that this expedition should include also the reduction of the French posts between Fort Pitt and Lake Erie, Stanwix was ordered to contribute such aid as he could from the south. To Colonel Frederick Haldimand, later of Revolutionary fame, was committed the task of restoring and holding defensive works at Oswego. Slowly the army of Prideaux pushed its way up the Mohawk, over the carries and through Oneida lake, reaching Oswego in the latter part of June. After four days of hard labor spent at that place in making the boats ready and loading them for the voyage westward, the force started. During the first six days of July, in favorable weather, they rowed laboriously, landing at some cove each night and cooking fresh provisions. On the sixth day the final landing was made at an inlet about four miles east of Niagara.

In the previous March Captain François Pouchot,[1] the engineer who in 1756 had largely rebuilt and strengthened the fort, was sent back to command its garrison and, with such aid as the Indians collected by de Joncaire might give, to defend it against the British. When the siege began the force under his command numbered only 486 soldiers, all of whom except 149 were Canadian regulars and militia. Though a considerable number of Indians had been collected from many tribes and two armed vessels were cruising on the lake, so poor was the scouting service that no information was obtained of the approach of the British. Troops, much needed at Niagara, were also sent to strengthen the posts to the southward in the vain hope of recovering Fort Pitt. This was directly opposed to the strategy of Montcalm and had its origin in the idle and boastful suggestions of Vaudreuil that the French were still able to hold their claims on the Ohio. The hope also that relief might come from Detroit or some other weak and distant posts to the westward was equally futile and deceptive. Though all through the winter and spring the French, and Indians who were consuming their substance at Niagara, were filled with anticipations of coming disaster, they were able to

[1] See Pouchot's Memoir upon the Late War in America, 1755-1760, translated and edited by Hough, for many details concerning the siege of Niagara and of earlier events in the campaigns and conditions in Canada.

find no means of averting it and in the end had little to rely on except such protection as their cannon and the stone, wood and earth walls of the fort afforded.

Niagara was captured as the result of a formal siege operation, similar to those by which the British had twice reduced Louisbourg and the French had taken Fort William Henry, though the siege of Niagara was conducted on a smaller scale than those which had preceded. Unlike the sieges of Louisbourg, it was a purely land operation, and though British regulars and engineers were present, it was not conducted with conspicuous ability on the part of the assailants. In the midst of the siege Prideaux, the British commander, was accidentally killed by a fragment of a shell fired from one of his own trenches. Johnson, though without serious military experience and sharing in the expedition simply as leader of the Indian allies, was now forced to take command. On the 9th of July the British had begun opening trenches, but the first ones were so located that the French could enfilade them and this had to be rectified. " The 11th," writes Walter Rutherford, " we made a great stretch, and the 12th began to raise a battery, when Mr. Williams was wounded. Next morning found it on a wrong direction. The 13th began another, which was also given up, but still pushed on the trenches. . . ." [1] This process, owing to their large superiority in numbers, the British could continue, though with much useless labor and some unnecessary losses, until the French garrison was forced to surrender. Such was the general course of the siege, a bombardment increasing in intensity as the trenches were pushed nearer the fort, till breaches were made, cannon silenced and losses and exhaustion among the garrison became serious. A relief force under Aubry and de Ligneris and gathered from among the Indians, the French settlers and *coureurs de bois* of the Illinois country and the Ohio region, came down Lake Erie and across the Niagara portage to the relief of the fort. But it was poorly led and, like a disorderly rabble, fell into an ambuscade set by Johnson below Lewiston Heights and was cut to pieces. De Ligneris was mortally wounded and many other French officers were slain. The force which was there slain, captured or dispersed numbered some 400 French and perhaps 1000 Indians.

[1] Severance, *op. cit.*, II, 289.

Pouchot and his men were unable to coöperate with their friends by a sortie. Since hope of relief was now gone and the British kept up their fire night and day, the result could not be doubtful or long delayed. It came on the night of July 24th, only a few hours after the relief force had been dispersed. The garrison surrendered and were taken as prisoners of war to New York. A considerable quantity of guns and ammunition thus fell into the hands of the British. Haldimand meantime had been able to repel a French attack at Oswego and the process of rebuilding that post was not again interrupted. Fort Rouillé (Toronto) was also destroyed by the French when the news reached them of the surrender of Niagara. Thus the French completely lost their hold upon Lakes Ontario and Erie, and the result for which Shirley had so persistently labored was attained.

While the events just related were occurring Amherst was advancing, with a force of about 11,500 men, over the accustomed route toward Ticonderoga. The reports which he sent to Pitt, cast in the form of a diary,[1] show that the contingents from New England were slow in coming in, so that the march to Lake George and the embarkation of the troops on the lake were not completed until the twentieth of July. With the provincials — who came from Massachusetts, Connecticut and New Jersey — were associated about 6000 regulars, a battalion of Royal Americans being among them. Without opposition except from a few French skirmishers and Indians, the army passed the abandoned intrenchment where Abercromby had been defeated and reached the fort. Bourlamaque had been left in its command with a force of about 2500, of whom 1200 were colonial troops. He had been instructed by Montcalm to retire slowly before the advancing British and had begun preparing for a retreat to Crown Point, and thence to Isle aux Noix, when Amherst arrived. Only a show of opposition was kept up until the French were ready to abandon the fort. Then, on the night of the 26th of July, the magazine was blown up and part of the works destroyed. This occurred only two days after the surrender of Niagara. Amherst re-

[1] Amherst's Journals are printed in Doughty's edition of Knox's Journal, Vol. III, app.; Corresp. of Pitt., etc., II, 120 et seq., 143. Kingsford, op. cit., IV, 331. For an accurate and mildly eulogistic account of Amherst's career, see Jeffery Amherst, a Biography, by Lawrence Shaw Mayo.

mained at Ticonderoga until the beginning of August, examining the fort with a view to its restoration and beginning the preparation of craft with which to descend Lake Champlain.

Having been informed by a force which he had sent in advance that the French had destroyed the fort at Crown Point and retired further northward, Amherst took possession of that post. There he remained till the approach of winter, keeping a large body of men at work building an elaborate fortress. On such a scale was this work planned that Amherst was able only to begin it. Before it was completed several years had passed and large sums of money had been expended. As it was practically certain from the start that this would not be a frontier position, the unwisdom of this proceeding should have been manifest. But Amherst was nothing if not thorough and systematic. His system was shown not only in this work, but in the discipline which he maintained, in the care which was taken for the order of the camp and the health of the troops. The general also opened a road across the Green Mountains to Number Four, on the upper Connecticut, thus providing a much shorter and easier route over which to transport troops and supplies to and from New England. Some inquiries were made looking toward the construction of a road westward from the lake toward the upper St. Lawrence, but the penetration of the mountain wilderness from which the Sable river descended was too difficult a task for the engineering abilities of those days.

In August Amherst dispatched a message to Wolfe at Quebec, but the messengers who carried it were kept as prisoners by the Indians of St. Francis and sent to Montcalm. It was from the French general, in connection with correspondence over an exchange, that Amherst was informed of this. The Abenaki Indians of St. Francis, urged on by French officials and priests, had long been a scourge to the settlements on the New England frontier, and now, taking advantage of the seizure of his messengers, Amherst resolved to make an end of the evil. Robert Rogers and a body of his rangers were selected for the purpose, and they accomplished successfully the surprise of the village and the destruction of both it and its male inhabitants. But the capture by the French of the boats with which they had crossed Lake Champlain cut off their hope of return in that direction. They were also immediately pursued by a relief party of French and Indians and, divided into small parties, had to make the best of their way through the wilderness southward to the upper course of the Connecticut. After great suffering and the loss of several of their number the band reached the New Hampshire settlements in an utterly exhausted and almost starved condition.

The French had established themselves in force about Isle aux Noix. In October, after finishing two armed vessels, Amherst advanced toward the position of the enemy. But apart from the destruction of one or two of their sloops, nothing was accomplished. After a very rainy season, wintry weather came on and operations were suspended. Except what were needed for the garrisons of Crown Point and Ticonderoga the troops were withdrawn, the provincials to their homes and the regulars into camps to the southward. Had the campaign been vigorously pushed, as was contemplated in Amherst's instructions, Montreal must certainly have been in the hands of the British before winter, and it might have been possible for them to have advanced a certain distance down the river. Whether this could have been accomplished in time essentially to change the situation which Wolfe and Saunders had to face, is doubtful. The deliberation with which Amherst conducted his campaign did not bring down upon him the disapproval of his superiors, because the brilliant success of Wolfe made the conquest of Canada in the coming summer a certainty. In certain respects Amherst was an improvement upon Loudon, but had Wolfe failed, as he might very well have done, Amherst advanced toward the position of the enemy. But, apart predecessors.

We have now reached the crowning event not only of this campaign and the war but of the colonial wars as a whole — the capture of Quebec. This was the goal for which the British had striven so long and so often had failed to reach or had seen their preparations even go for nought. In the seventeenth century Kirke and Phips, with insignificant forces, had reached the town, and Walker had ignominiously failed when the prize was within his grasp. Nearly half a century passed before another opportunity presented itself. And now the circumstances favorable to the British were many and powerful. As the problem was essentially one of opening communication with the objective point at a sufficiently early date in the season, the reduction of Louisbourg and the establishment of a secure naval base at Halifax made the accomplishment much easier than it had been in earlier times. Walker had to start from Boston and after his arrival there had to wait many weeks for his reinforcements and supplies from the colonies. Now, under the administration of Pitt, a body of troops, a naval contingent and a commander-in-chief were left in America over winter. This insured the making of all necessary preparations in America at an early date, so that unnecessary delay upon the arrival of the squadron and troops from Europe would be avoided. The superiority of the British fleet over the French had also by this time been so fully established that operations in European waters were not specially difficult. In this case, however, these were not needed except as a means of preventing attacks on the British squadron and transports, for France had no intention of sending a naval force to the north Atlantic. A few ships were sent with the meagre help which Bougainville was able to procure, and these Commodore Durell might have intercepted, had he acted as promptly as Pitt and the admiralty in England expected he would do.[1] These ships, when they reached Canada, were practically useless, for they were forced up the St. Lawrence far beyond Quebec and would have been unable to prevent the advance of Amherst down the river, had he reached a point where such an undertaking was possible. As we have seen, Canada had been practically abandoned by France before the beginning of this campaign and its fall was expected. All the British had to do was to step in and take it and, so far as the operations of Amherst indicated, there was to be no departure from their usual leisurely procedure.

Had the man put in command of the operations against Quebec been of the type of Amherst or of the earlier commanders who were the product of the Newcastle régime, Montcalm and his men would probably have spent another winter in Canada. Even as it was their escape from such a fortune, with its combination of good and evil elements, was a rather narrow one. But the combination of Pitt and Wolfe, with

[1] Corbett, *op. cit.*, I, 397 *et seq.*

Saunders as the efficient coöperator on the naval side, was an unusual one, so unusual in fact as to be almost accidental. Pitt's tenure of power was unusual in its origin and precarious in duration. Unless he won victories he could not expect to hold his position any length of time, while on the other hand, if his victories became so sweeping as to threaten the balance of power and promote his own aggrandizement to a dangerous extent, he was certain to be forced out of office. His colleagues of the Newcastle group tolerated him most unwillingly and were ever looking for an opportunity to trip him up.[1]

The rise of Wolfe to fame was even more sudden and spectacular. He was only thirty-two when he died. Like Pitt, he was physically weak and predisposed to disease, though his health was fortified by an abstemious life and the outdoor exercise of a military man. In the case of both of them a nervous excitability, one manifestation of which was a sensitive and vivid imagination, gave the touch of what we call genius to their careers. Both were severe critics of contemporary conditions, but neither carried his criticism far enough to lead a revolt against the aristocratic and imperialistic régime of which they formed a part. They wanted to purify that system from some of its glaring faults in order to stimulate it to greater efficiency. The dawn of the French revolution would have been intensely distasteful to them. Wolfe possessed the ambition and the intolerance of abuses which is characteristic of young men. He was a severe critic of his fellow officers and of the rank and file of the British army,[2] as was Pitt of conditions in civil life. Both were Puritans in their respective spheres, and Wolfe was a very effective disciplinarian.

The drunkenness and vice in their coarser forms which prevailed among the British soldiery and their officers were visited with Wolfe's severest denunciation. Never were the disastrous results of promotion by purchase more clearly exposed than in his letters. To his mother he wrote, " The officers of the Army in general are of so little application to

---

[1] See Torrens, History of Cabinets.

[2] See Wolfe's Letters as printed in Beckles Wilson's Life and Letters of Wolfe, and in Doughty, Siege of Quebec, Vol. VI.

business and have been so ill educated, that it must not surprise you to hear that a man of common industry should be in repute amongst them." The spirited advice which Wolfe, then a lieutenant-colonel, gave respecting the attack on Rochefort, attracted Pitt's attention to him and led to his appointment as a brigadier and his designation to the American service. Respecting the expedition against Rochefort, when he was about setting out upon it, Wolfe wrote, " I can't flatter you with a lively picture of my hopes as to the success of it; the reasons are so strong against us in whatever we take in hand, that I never expect any great matter; the chiefs, the engineers, and our wretched discipline, are the great and insurmountable obstructions." After the failure of that expedition, he wrote at length and in more sarcastic terms of its causes and what he had learned by the experience. His conclusions were, " that there never was people [meaning the officers] collected together so unfit for the business they were set upon — dilatory, ignorant, irresolute and some grains of a very unmanly quality and very unsoldier-like or unsailor-like." " Little practice in war, ease and convenience at home, great incomes and no wants, with no ambition to stir to action, are not the instruments to work a successful war withal; I see no prospect of better deeds; I know not where to look for them." But for Lord Howe, who fell at Ticonderoga, Wolfe's admiration was unbounded.

The young and bookish, though intensely practical, enthusiast had clearly shown his mettle at Louisbourg. Bradstreet's stroke at Fort Frontenac had greatly impressed him and he recognized the value of Rogers as a leader of scouts and rangers. But of the colonials in general he expressed to Lord George Sackville such exaggerated contempt that it may have worked disastrously upon British fortunes years afterwards during the war of the Revolution.[1] As to the operations at Louisbourg, he considered them needlessly slow,[2] and that the

[1] Wilson, op. cit., 392. In emphasizing so strongly the defects of the rascally colonists Wolfe forgot that they showed the same faults which he found among the British soldiery, though exaggerated by frontier conditions.

[2] This undoubtedly would have been his criticism of the conduct of Amherst throughout his career as a general. Of the siege of Louisbourg he said, "Our measures have been cautious and slow from the beginning to the end, except in landing, where there was an appearance of temerity." Wilson, 390.

only thing which saved the landing at Gabarus bay from ending in disaster was the poor quality of the French troops who were posted on the shore to oppose the British. He felt that Pitt's original plan was practicable and that Louisbourg could have been captured in time to admit of the expedition against Quebec that season. As to the soldiers themselves, he found them being ruined by rum and salt meat, and became an advocate of much larger rations of fresh meat and, like Amherst, of the use of spruce beer as preventative against scurvy. Like Pitt, Wolfe was a devotee of unlimited war against the French, to the extent at least of expelling them wholly from their colonies and destroying their naval and commercial power. To that end he wished that an additional French squadron had taken refuge in the harbor of Louisbourg, so that it might have been destroyed and French sea power at one stroke hopelessly crippled. Wolfe viewed the American Indians with intense contempt and hatred, regarding them as simply fit for extermination. The atrocities which they and the French had long been committing on British colonists he viewed with abhorrence and his belief that the massacre at Fort William Henry had been instigated or condoned by the French helped to nerve his arm for the final blow at Quebec. As is always true of the thorough-going militarist, men of the type of Wolfe, he on occasion could be ruthless and was so to a marked degree in his destruction of French settlements on the lower St. Lawrence and in his orders for the widespread devastation of the country during the siege of Quebec. These acts were in the nature of reprisals and, had the investment of the town continued longer, might have helped to starve out the French.

In comparison with the veteran Montcalm the experience of Wolfe was brief and slight. His appointment to lead the expedition against Quebec gave him his first and only command. He was made major general " for that expedition only," [1] the position of commander-in-chief in America thus being left in the hands of Amherst. It was the expectation of the government that the two officers and their commands would coöperate, closing the campaign with a joint triumph at Montreal and Quebec. But, as events turned out, they did

[1] Corresp. of Pitt, *etc.*, I, 433; Wilson, *op. cit.*, 401; Corbett, I, 398.

not coöperate at all, in the sense intended, and therefore
Wolfe's command proved to be an independent one and the
glory at its end was all his own and that of the men who
served with him. Wolfe was given a free hand in selecting
his three brigadiers and chose Monckton, George Townshend
and Murray, Townshend, a high-blooded aristocrat, proving
rather supercilious and critical as the enterprise progressed.
With the exception of Wolfe and Townshend, all the general
officers were under thirty. "It was a boy's campaign." [1]
Nearly 9000 men were assigned for the land force of this expedition, all regulars except a small body of American rangers
employed for scouting purposes.

The selection by Anson of Charles Saunders to command the
naval force was of the same nature as Wolfe's own appointment. Saunders had accompanied Anson around the world
and had since rendered faithful service in Spanish and Mediterranean waters. Though he was a silent man and his fame
was never so great as that of several other admirals of his
time, his services now and later were of the greatest value.
With him went Jervis, Palliser and Cook, all of whom bore
names to be famous in the later annals of the British navy.
The coöperation of the fleet with the land force on this expedition was perfect, with one exception, and to that cooperation its final success was due. The exception was
Durell's delay in going up the St. Lawrence early enough in
the spring to intercept the French supply ships, thus allowing
them to get through to Quebec with such relief as they
brought to the Canadians. Saunders' fleet consisted of 22
ships of the line, 5 frigates, 18 sloops and a large number of
transports, storeships, victuallers and other smaller craft.
Durell also had 8 ships of the line and about half-a-dozen
frigates. The entire armament consisted of little less than
170 sail, carrying about 18,000 seamen. The large force of
marines and seamen which it carried could easily be used to
supplement the strength of the land force. So lavish was the
supply of artillery and ammunition for the fleet that a bombardment of Quebec was kept up at intervals for weeks,
resulting in the destruction of a large part of the city. Against
this great display of force the French had no vessels of war

[1] Corbett, I, 409.

which were available or of any account. A garrison numbering about 2000 was stationed in Quebec, and the defences of the city were made as strong as was possible during the few weeks which intervened between the arrival of the relief ships and the appearance of the British. It was decided that the main army, about 14,000 strong, should be stationed behind intrenchments along the Beauport shore, with their right resting on the St. Charles river and their left on the Montmorency. The larger part of this force consisted of Canadian regulars and militia, but the centre was held by five battalions of the regulars from France. A thousand Indians, more or less, were present, coming and going much as they chose, but serving some purpose as scouts and in picking off stragglers among the British.[1] This force, under able and experienced leadership, was required to act on the defensive in a position which nature had made exceedingly strong.

The first difficulties which the British had to overcome were those involved in the ascent of the St. Lawrence. The French had long been familiar with the route, their merchant ships, transports and men-of-war having regularly traversed it year after year though not in battle fleets. But it was a new experience for the British, especially with a fleet so large as that which Saunders now commanded and including so many large vessels of deep draught.[2] Fog was the most dangerous foe, as Walker had found to his cost. To sailing vessels the current and strong ebb tides, as well as head winds, presented serious obstacles to navigation. In the river itself the most dangerous points were in the north channel opposite Isle aux Coudres and the Traverse, the latter being a narrow and intricate passage extending somewhat diagonally along the river just below the Island of Orleans. There were no lights, charts were imperfect and the pilots were not experienced or very trustworthy. Canadian seamen had been so confident that a fleet could not pass the Traverse, that such means of obstructing it as might have been resorted to were neglected. Like Phips in 1690, the British in 1759

[1] N. Y. Col. Docs., X, 1017.

[2] The ascent of the St. Lawrence is best studied in Wood's Log of the Conquest of Canada, published by the Champlain Society. See also the Journal of William Knox.

met with very little unfavorable weather. During their ascent of the river the sky was clear most of the time and the winds on the whole were from the east. Their seamanship also proved quite equal to the difficulties of the Traverse — previously sounded by Cook — and to the other intricacies of the channel. Therefore the voyage from Louisbourg to the upper end of the Island of Orleans was made without accident during the three weeks between the 4th and the 26th of June. So important and so fortunate was this part of the achievement that it virtually insured the capture of Quebec. The transporting of so powerful a British armament so early in the season to the basin below Cape Diamond could hardly fail, in the nature of human events, to decide the issue.

But, so difficult were the approaches to the Upper Town and so strong was the defensive position of the French on the Beauport shore,[1] that the siege might be prolonged until the early approach of winter should compel the British to withdraw and leave the task unfinished. As it was, the siege lasted nearly three months and, as the weeks passed and he found himself no nearer a decision, the possibility of failure certainly weighed upon the mind of the young commander. All of July and August were spent chiefly in occupying Point Lévis, which the French had become so careless as to leave poorly defended; in battering the town,[2] and in experimenting on the line of the Montmorency and amid the shallow waters which lie in front of the Beauport shore, with a view to a possible frontal attack on Montcalm's position. But, as the British men-of-war, because of the shallow water, could not approach near enough to bombard the French position, these feints proved fruitless and left the besiegers as far from the object they were seeking as they were the day they landed on Orleans.[3] Some attention also had been paid to the possibility of throwing troops across the river above the town, but, because of its difficulty and the risk attending it, Wolfe had

[1] Knox, Journal, Champlain Soc. ed., II, 161.

[2] A contemporary account of the destruction wrought in the town is in N.Y. Col. Docs., X, 1058.

[3] As the prime authority for these and other points of strategy see Wolfe's letter to Pitt, of Sept. 2, 1759, and his letter to the brigadiers with their reply near the close of August. Doughty, II, 143, 237; Knox's Journal, Champlain Soc. Ed., II, 60.

abandoned the idea for the present. Some ships and troops, however, under Holmes and Murray, were sent up toward Three Rivers to seize magazines, prevent the French from getting supplies from the country south of the river, and possibly to get into touch with Amherst if he should descend the Richelieu. This move caused some anxiety to the French, but all efforts failed as yet to draw Montcalm from his position.

Though Wolfe's officers and men admired him and were responsive to all his commands, criticism now began to be heard here and there and the admiral realized that the time was drawing near when the large ships would have to be sent home. The pressure was telling on Wolfe and toward the end of August he fell sick. Then he consulted the brigadiers, submitting to them three plans of attack, all centering about the Montmorency and Beauport region. Because of the difficulty of crossing the St. Charles, supposing the French had been driven from their intrenchments to the east of it, the brigadiers rejected all of Wolfe's plans and advised that the troops be withdrawn to the south shore and that operations be begun above the town. In this proposal, though earlier he had put it one side, Wolfe now acquiesced. At the close of August the camp on the Montmorency was abandoned as quietly as possible, enough troops were left on the northern end of the Island of Orleans to hold it securely, and the rest were transported to the south shore. As soon as Wolfe had recovered sufficiently from his illness to assume active command, his attention was wholly devoted to the new plan. He first loaded nearly all of his troops upon the squadron and took them up the river, where, by moving back and forth and threatening a landing at various points he compelled Montcalm to send reinforcements above the town. Bougainville, who was in command there, was also forced to march his troops rapidly for long distances up and down the river in order to be ready to oppose a landing at any point. In this way the attention of the French was distracted and their plans confused. When by this manœuvre the attention of the French had been fixed upon points several miles above Quebec, Wolfe perfected his plan for a landing at the Anse du Foulan (Wolfe's Cove), about two miles above the city. This involved careful reconnoitring of the north shore, the selection of the troops, the seamen, the ships and the barges which must be detailed for the purpose, arranging the time, the signals and all the minutiæ which were necessary to the success of a surprise attack to be made just at dawn and under such perilous conditions as existed, both on water and land, at that time and place. Admiral Holmes was selected to support Wolfe in the transport of the troops across the river. At the same time Saunders, with the main squadron and the troops on board it, was to make a demonstration in front of the Beauport lines, as if an attack was intended there, its purpose being to hold the French in their intrenchments until Wolfe and his force of 3500 men were on the plains back of Quebec and ready to give battle.

For weeks, since the silencing of the guns of the town, the British fleet had had complete command of the passage up and down the river. To this fact and to the careful planning of Wolfe, followed by the perfect coöperation of all the forces involved, the success of this complicated plan was due. Montcalm was taken by surprise. The bad relations between him and Vaudreuil prevented him from drawing promptly to his support the full strength of the force which lay in the trenches beyond the St. Charles. There was no time to summon aid from Bougainville up the river, for every hour of delay would have enabled the British to bring up more men and cannon from the fleet. Therefore, with such troops as could hastily be brought to the Plains of Abraham — approximately equal in number to that of the British — he resolved to meet the attack in the open. In duration it was only a skirmish, for the decisive encounter was over in ten minutes, though much more firing and more casualties occurred before Quebec surrendered. And yet, though much time had been wasted in the early part of the siege, though the time had fully come when a decision must be reached or failure would have been the result, this must be regarded as a brilliant achievement, for by means of it the citadel of French power in America was captured. But the dramatic interest in the event was heightened a hundredfold by the double tragedy which accompanied it. The deaths of the two commanders lifted the event out of the realm of mere military success and defeat or of political change into that of sentiment. Wolfe in particular has been taken out of the category of ordinary men and raised to the rank of a hero. Writers, at the mention of his name and deeds, become lyric. But what really happened was that, backed by superior force and aided by fortunate circumstances, to which he contributed by good management, Wolfe made connections; that is, after much delay and futile experiment, he hit upon a plan which led to success, and it was crowned with a timely death, a consummation for which Wolfe helped, perhaps consciously, to prepare the stage.

But the victory at Quebec did not complete the conquest of Canada. Though the British had won successes and the French had been forced to retire at all points, there had been no more actual coöperation between the forces employed than had been the case in previous campaigns, and Pitt's plan for the year had not been carried through to complete success. Vaudreuil and his troops were able to retire up the river from Beauport and join Bougainville. The French continued to hold the central part of the province through the next summer, which was the most they had expected to do. At the battle of Sainte Foy, the next spring, Lévis repulsed the British under Murray, who had been greatly weakened by disease and deaths during the winter, and he might have recovered Quebec, had it not been for the timely arrival of relief from England.[1] Haviland in the summer forced the French back from Isle aux Noix, while Amherst advanced from Oswego across the lake and down the St. Lawrence, and Murray, after the retirement of Lévis, advanced from the east. The three forces converged on Montreal. There, on September 8, almost a year after Wolfe fell at Quebec, Vaudreuil capitulated and all Canada passed into the possession of the British.

[1] Knox, Journal, *op. cit.*, II, 415.

INDEX

NOTE: In Professor Osgood's text many persons are mentioned by their surnames only an attempt has been made, successful in nearly all instances, to identify these individuals by bracketed inserts so that there will be no confusion. Several errors in the spelling of proper names have been found in the text, and these have been pointed out under appropriate entries. The editor desires to thank Miss Alice McKinnon Holt, of Yonkers, N. Y., who is largely responsible for this index. — D. R. F.

of Louisbourg, 418; reference to appointment of, as Commander-in-chief in America, succeeding Abercromby, 419; instructed by Pitt in plan for campaign against Canada, 441; advance of, toward Ticonderoga, 445; examines fort at Ticonderoga and takes possession of Crown Point, sends rangers to destroy the Abenaki settlement of St. Francis, 446; advances down the St. Lawrence toward Montreal, 457.

Anderson, [John], member of New Jersey council, **II.** 122; **IV.** 3.

Anglicanism, *see also* Churches, Ecclesiastical relations, Pietism, Religion, Society for the Propagation of the Gospel; a governmental body, establishment in the colonies, **I.** 33; Fletcher clashes with house on affairs of, 253; the clergy one of important questions of Virginia, 328–329; low price of tobacco reduces support of Virginia clergy, 341; act passed in Virginia increasing allowance to clergy, 344, 347; Blair testifies in London in behalf of clergy, 349, 351–352; Maryland capital moved from Catholic St. Mary's to Protestant Annapolis, 366–377; hostile sects in New Jersey, 383; sends a missionary to Fort Hunter, 482; early extension (*see* table of contents for Part I, chap. xvii); Jersey, **II.** 86–87; naturalization act of New York affects Protestants, 113–114; churchmen support Nicholson, bitter against Governor Hunter of New York, 118; high churchmen oppose Governor Hunter's reappointment, 124; ecclesiastical ambitions and jealousies interwoven with struggle in New Jersey, 125; policies of Virginia assembly, 163–164; French Protestant refugees granted land at Manakin Town, 165; Virginia organized as King William's parish, 168; support of clergy receives attention of Virginia council, 182; final change in act for establishment of, 199; claims of Calvert family closely associated with church affairs, 202; act passed forbidding Catholic priests to baptize or celebrate mass, 203–204; parish system confirmed in North Carolina, 387; the famous "Hallesche Nachrichten" compared with the bishopric of London and the Society, 502;

partaking of the Lord's Supper a requirement for naturalization, 524; conversion of Calvert Family to Protestantism of importance to Maryland, **III.** 5; measures taken against Catholic influence in Maryland, 9; anti-Catholic laws of Hart's administration, 11; law of 1702, for establishment of, 13; bill of, 1728, reduces remuneration of clergy, 13; clergy protest against bill of 1730, 14; appropriations to Georgia to maintain a missionary at Savannah, and minister among Scotch at Darien, 46; Georgia established as refuge for persecuted Protestants and others, 62; includes Puritan sympathizers, 77; under early Hanoverians, (*see* table of contents for Part II, chaps. x–xi); growth of denominations under voluntary system in Rhode Island, 241–242; causes of weakening hold of the Saybrook Platform and consociations in Connecticut, 447; controversy over relative merits of episcopacy and presbyterianism, 453; Episcopalians emphasize Act of Union, 455; advent of Anglicanism, challenge to Calvinism, 460; colonists regard colonial episcopate as an infringement of liberties, 462; low level of authority shown by bishop and commissary, 465–466; conditions in Virginia described, 468–469; interests of, as patron of higher education advanced by founding of colleges and schools, 482.

Anglicans, Anglicanism (other than in chapters on subject: Part I, chap. xvii; Part II, chaps. x–xi; Part III, chap ii), *see also* Church, English hand in hand with royal powers, **I.** 353; intrigues between Basse and, 386; Livingston urges Anglican missionaries for the Iroquois country, 476; Anglican clergy oppose Governor Hunter's demand for removal of anti-proprietary members of the council, **II.** 122–123; extreme faction of, defeated in New Jersey, 125; growth of, in Pennsylvania, 259; in Maryland, **III.** 5, 11, 12; exploited in controversial pamphlets by John Checkly, 150–151; in the Narragansett country, 257 *note;* presence of, felt in all the colonies, 407; united opposition of, to revivals, 427; Governor Dobbs tries

Carter, Landon, a local magnate of Virginia, III. 475, 478; IV. 354.

Carter, Col. Robert, member of Va. council, II, 166; as agent for the Northern Neck grant, makes extravagant boundary claims, and displays personal greed for land, IV. 94; popularly known as " King Carter," as senior member of the council administers the government until the arrival of Gooch, 95; protests against encroachment of new grants, 96; letters and papers of, submitted to the board of trade, 97.

Carteret, John, Lord (afterward Earl Granville), receives from Spotswood statement concerning his conduct of piracy affair, I. 549; becomes palatine of Carolina and rises to large influence as statesman in England, aids in smothering bill for regulation of charter and proprietary governments, II. 294; spokesman for proprietors of South Carolina, 350; in reply to board of trade, opposes South Carolina's complaints and petition for royal government, 353; receives correspondence from Nicholson, 383; declines to surrender his share in Carolinas, 398; rights in Ga., III. 47; N. C. holdings, IV. 164.

Carthagena expedition, III. 222, 497–501.

Cartlidge, Edmund, Indian trader, III. 379.

Cary, John, economic writer, I. 128–129; II. 301 note.

Cary's Rebellion, in North Carolina, II. 227, 404.

Cary, Robert, a London merchant, II. 234.

Casco, Dudley at, I. 405–406, 407.

Casgrain, Abbé, Canadian historian, III. 512 note, 515 note.

Castle Island, Nicholson at, I. 436–437.

Castle William, rumors of false muster rolls at, III. 157.

Caswell, Richard, of North Carolina, IV. 214.

Cataraqui, Iroquois opposed to rebuilding of fort by the French at, I. 252.

Cathcart, Lord, commands land force in Admiral Vernon's expedition against the Spanish in South America and Cuba, III. 497.

Causton, Thomas, storekeeper for the trust, in Georgia, III. 52; suspended from office, but not proven guilty, 53; orders Watson confined as a lunatic, 71; leading magistrate in Georgia, III. 110; brings suit against John Wesley, 111.

Catholics, Roman, Revolution checks tendency in Virginia to appoint Catholics to office, I. 329; overthrow of Calverts in Maryland severe blow to, 353; Governor Seymour aggressive toward, 199; seriously affected by requirement of Anglican faith for proprietors, II. 204; oppression of, 516–517; Charles Carroll insists upon rights of, to hold office in Maryland, III. 8; Maryland anti-Catholic laws of Hart's administration, 11.

Cavalier, a French half-breed, active among the Shawnee Indians, III. 391.

Chabert, reference to as brother of Captain Joncaire, IV. 333. See Joncaire.

Chafours, Vaudreuil's brother-in-law, I. 418.

Chamberlain, John, II. 127.

Chambers, John, counsel for Zenger, II. 460.

Champante, John, his continuance as agent desired, II. 49; associated with Cornbury in board of trade matters, 62; involved in financial matters, 65–66; writes that the ministry knows of Cornbury's maladministration in New York, 81; appropriation for his salary as agent, 114.

Charles II, knights William Clarke, I. 31; reactionary legislation during reign of, II. 5.

Charles V, of Burgundy, revives imperialistic ideal, I. 44.

Charles, Robert, agent for New York, IV. 38, 193.

Charleston, South Carolina, regarded as central point of defence, III. 510; fortifications of, destroyed by a hurricane, IV. 260–266; garrisoned by a Highland regiment, 272.

Charter, charters, of 1632, again in force in Maryland, III. 4; original petition for Georgia, 36; of 1637; issued to Gorges for Maine, 55; comparison of first and second, in Massachusetts, 127; of 1691 unites Maine and Massachusetts in one province, 148; situation peculiar to provinces having royal charter, 158; explanatory charter of 1725 for Massachusetts, 178; of incorpora-

against Canada, 429, 430, 432; participation in expedition against Acadia, 436, 438; cooperates in combined effort for conquest of Canada, 441, 443; accused by Larkin of evading law in manufacture of woolens, 546; mission started at Stratford, **II.** 42; Muirson in charge of Stratford mission which becomes important, reaction of New York, 43; policy of, regarding taxes for Presbyterian and Congregational churches, 44; Cornbury has command over militia of, 62; Dudley's complaint against, 138–139; warned by Ashurst of activity against charters, 141; customs officials arbitrary, 297; Pigot appointed missionary of the Venerable Society, to Stratford, **III.** 121; power of selectmen employed against churchmen, 124; income from lands allowed to revert to schools, 125; churches of, under Saybrook Platform, 128; Narragansett controversy, 234; commissioners sent to Albany Conference with Six Nations in 1744, 391; assembly passes a law against itinerant preachers and Separatists, toleration act of 1708, repealed, 442; protest of ministers against civil interference in ecclesiastical affairs, 443; act passed requiring civil sanction for religious body of learning, 444; ancient persecuting statutes dropped in 1750, but Saybrook Platform and taxes on Separates still continued, 446; calls special session of general court to prepare for expedition against Louisbourg, 521; reference to claim of to the Wyoming Country, **IV.** 309; proposes a limited and temporary support in Indian relations, 310.

" Considerations requiring greater care for Trade," anonymous pamphlet, **I.** 131–132.

Contrecœur, [Pierre C. P. de], French commander, overtakes Trent, and forces his surrender, **IV.** 338.

Converse, Major [Isaac], put in command of Massachusetts forces, **I.** 47; accompanies defensive troops, 93; returns to service in defence of Wells and is promoted to rank of major in command of eastern settlements, 97; scours frontier, Indians agree to cease hostilities, 112.

Convicts, transportation of, to colonies

not favored by board of trade, **I.** 158.

Convoys, necessitated by colonial wars, **I.** 59; arranged by agreement between privy council, its committee and the admiralty, 119–120; for Virginia and Maryland, **II.** 168–169.

Coode, John, makes treasonable charges against certain Virginians, **I.** 333; his prosecution ordered by Nicholson and council, 377, *and note*, 381; complaint of, against Nicholson, **II.** 162; allowed to return to Maryland, 186.

Cook, [Capt. James], in Saunders naval expedition against Quebec, **IV.** 452.

Cooke, Elisha, appointed commissioner of special council of war, **I.** 74; associated with Mather in negotiating for Massachusetts charter, 123; sent to welcome Bellomont on his arrival from England, 287; an extremist, opposed to Mather, 294; included in list of councillors named in charter, 300; opponent of new charter, election to council therefore vetoed by Phips, 317; rejected three times by Dudley as councillor, opponent of his policy, **II.** 135; finally accepted under stress of circumstances, 136.

Cooke, Elisha, (the younger) Massachusetts; attacks Governor Shute, **III.** 146; is removed as clerk of superior court, has dispute with Bridger, Shute vetoes election of, to the council, 147; claims Maine is proprietary province of Massachusetts, 148; pamphlet on, " Vindication etc.," 152 *note;* described, 155–156; influence of, shown in opposition to Shute, 159–160; leader of committee appoints to vindicate previous assembly, 161; agent to London, 177; is elected to council 178; heeds committee which replies to Burnet concerning appropriation for his salary, 179; rejects council's proposal, drafts " The Advice," 181; demands letters of administration on Allen estate, 207; loses popularity in Boston and fails of election to assembly, 326; interested in Muscongus Patent and other ventures, 328–329; attacked by Dunbar, 330; replies to Dunbar's claim, 331; influence of apparent in boundary dispute, 342.

Cooper, Thomas, of S. C., **IV.** 121, 123.

plans for recall of charters, 139–141;
characteristics of his administration,
142–143; reference to address sent
to the queen asking for removal of,
146; sponsors Blackwell's plan for a
private bank, reference to his presidency over the Dominion of New
England, 150–151; opposes land
bank project whose supporters make
unsuccessful attempt to remove him
from office, 158; reports falling off
of woolen trade in New England,
328; is requested to investigate
Usher's affairs, **III.** 201; relations
harmonious with New Hampshire,
204; retirement of, 206; member
of royal commission in Narragansett
controversy, 234; receives royal
commission to determine question
of Mohegan lands, 287; opposed by
Fitz-John Winthrop, **III.** 310 *and
note.*

Dudley, Sir Matthew, applies for charter to work mines in New England,
but colonies protest against it as a
monopoly, **I.** 497–498; his renewed
efforts to secure charter are opposed
by Ashurst and the Massachusetts
interests, 504.

Dudley, Paul, attorney general, son of
Governor Dudley, discloses in letter
his father's viewpoint on charter
and other matters, **II.** 138; is involved in criticism of Governor
Dudley, 146; presents memorial to
Massachusetts council attacking private land bank scheme, 156–157;
effort of (Massachusetts) house to
exclude from council, **III.** 162.

Dudley, William, member of commission from Massachusetts to Canada,
III. 215.

Dulany, Daniel, attorney general of
Maryland in bitter contest with
Henderson over renumeration to
clergy, **III.** 14, 101; member of
committee to prepare bill on fees, 25;
defends views of lower house on
judge's oath, 29; publishes pamphlet on " The Right of the Inhabitants of Maryland to the
Benefit of the English Laws," 30.

Dumas, Captain, an able associate of
Contrecœur at Fort Duquesne, **IV.**
349

Dummer, Dr. Jeremiah, agent for
Connecticut, **I.** 202; secures information about Tories, 227; as agent
for Massachusetts, takes up opposition to Bridger, 516; prominent in

advocating New England naval
stores, 518; accused of insulting a
merchant at the Royal exchange,
519; is instructed by Dudley regarding land bank application, **II.**
158; represents both Massachusetts
and Connecticut as agent to England, 294 *and note,* publishes " Defence of New England Charters,"
295–298; supports authority of
admiralty officials over common
courts, 302; books collected by,
added to Yale College library, **III.**
120; writes Judge Sewall concerning prosecution of Quakers and
Baptists, 130; opposes bank party,
144; opposes Bridger, 148; agent
in London, 176; agent for Connecticut in Narragansett controversy,
235, 236 *note;* procures gift of books
for Yale College, 298–299; officially
but not actively connected with
Winthrop-Lechmere case, 312; succeeded as agent by Wilks, 315; removed from governor's office, 321.

Dummer, William, lieutenant governor of Massachusetts, asked to call
synod of New England churches,
III. 136; reproved by lords justices,
137; assumes control in Shute's
absence, 173; administration of,
ends with Burnet's arrival, 178;
questions Dunbar's authority in
attempting to establish " settlement of Georgia," 328 *and note.*

Dunbar, David, surveyor general, *etc.,*
plans large tracts for royal navy supplies, hostile relations with Massachusetts, **I.** 521; personal qualities,
is made lieutenant governor of New
Hampshire, hostility of Governor
Belcher, 522; mentioned, **III.** 211;
John Wentworth's successor, has
bitter controversy with Belcher,
220; colonel, surveyor general of the
woods, receives correspondence from
Governor Belcher, 320; is accused
of intriguing with Cooke against
Belcher, 326 *and note;* effect of
English plans upon career of, 327;
takes steps to establish province of
" Georgia " under his governorship, 328 *and note;* relations of,
with Belcher and Cooke, 330; proceedings of, denounced by committee, 331; succeeds Wentworth
as lieutenant governor, 332; is
opposed by Belcher, 333; returns
to England and is temporarily imprisoned for debt, 334.

Dunbar, Col. [Thomas], comes with Braddock to America, **IV.** 341; reference to regiment commanded by, 342; left in command of camp at Little Meadows, 349; reports upon destitute condition of his troops, 352; conduct of, is condemned by Dinwiddie, 352; receives orders from Shirley, 362.

Dunkers, develop complete monastic system, **II.** 500.

Dupplin, [Thomas] (Viscount), signs report of the board of trade on New Jersey rioters, **IV.** 35.

Duquesne [de Meuneville], Marquis, governor general of Canada, expedition to Ohio region fitted out by, his connections with the disreputable Bigot, **IV.** 332.

Durell, Commodore [Philip], fails to intercept French fleet, **IV.** 448; delay of, 452.

Dutch West India Company, against pirates, **I.** 526.

Duvivier, Major [Charles], leads French from Louisbourg, **III.** 515.

Dwight, Joseph, of Massachusetts, **IV.** 304 *note.*

Dyer, William, surveyor general of customs in America, **I.** 162.

East Boston, *see* Noddles Island.

East India Company, **I.** 50, 532, 542; **II.** 318.

East Indian Trade, **I.** 138, 140.

East Indies, trade in, **I.** 128, 530.

Eastland merchants, **I.** 517.

Easton, John, governor of R. I., **III.** 246.

Eden, Charles, governor of North Carolina, accused of protecting pirates, **I.** 549; a leader in revising the laws, **II.** 388; Gale complains of, to England, his connection with pirate Teach, 391; date of his death, 392; receives instructions concerning land grants, 403.

Edmundson, John, of Maryland, **I.** 360.

Education, project of free public school brought before assembly of Maryland, **I.** 366; John Wesley's school in Georgia, **III.** 110; negligence of North Carolina respecting, 116; no book of learning to be had less than a century or more old, 119; income from lands allowed to revert to schools in Connecticut, 125; maintenance of common schools in Connecticut, 270; receives impulse through founding of College of New

Jersey and beginnings of Dartmouth College, 448; William Livingston advocates transfer of, from clergy to laity and criticises existing conditions, 486.

Edwards, Rev. Jonathan, **III.** 141; a leading personality in the Great Awakening, 409; his education influenced by reading, his marriage, his mental powers, 412; significance of his " Work of Redemption," 413 *and note;* famous treatise on " Freedom of the Will," 414; his Calvinism, 415; death at Princeton, 422; publishes " Thoughts on the Revival of Religion in New England," 433 *and note;* his viewpoint, 435–438 *and note;* treatise on the " Religious Affections," prompt influence of his writings, 448; his " Humble Inquiry concerning the qualifications requisite to a full communion in the visible Christian Church," published during two year controversy over his principles, 449; his " The Freedom of the Will," final dismissal from his parish at Northampton and retirement to Stockbridge; a summary of his powerful influence as an exponent of Calvinism, 450.

Effingham, Lord Howard of, his policy to transfer leadership from council to governor, checked by the revolution, **I.** 329.

Egg Island, *see* Isle aux Œufs.

Egmont, John, first Earl of, first president of Georgia trustees, forced to admit failure of restricted land tenure in Georgia, **III.** 58; considers importation of negroes unfavorable to small landholder, 64; resigns seat in the common council, 65; softens terms of letter to Oglethorpe, 66; opinion of, regarding Indian trade relations in Georgia and South Carolina, 399.

Egremont, Lord, secretary of state sends urgent call for colonial troops, **IV.** 220.

Elections, annual in Connecticut, consistent with steadiness of policy and permanence of official tenure, **III.** 277.

Eliot, Rev. John, of New England, **II.** 30.

Ellis, Henry, governor of Georgia, recommended, **IV.** 252; promotion to full rank of governor, 254; assists in final adjustment of Bosomworth case, 255; ordered by Pitt to remove

York petitions queen for power to appoint New York agent, 108–109; letters and memorials to board of trade, 142–143; administration of proprietary colonies, 153–154; chartered colonies claim admiralty jurisdiction and proprietors petition for vice admiral commission for governors, 194; appoin'ment of governors and proprietors, 201; proprietors oppose establishment of admiralty courts, corporate colonies claim admiralty powers, rival judicial bodies are established, 206; opposition of justices to admiralty court, 208; protests against admiralty courts made to secretary of state and board of trade by Penn, 209; Baltimore and Carolina proprietors make languid defence of colonies bill, 217–218; William and Mary fully acknowledged in law passed by new provincial assembly of New York, penalties for rebels and traitors, 229; Fletcher indicates to lords of trade quotas which colonies should contribute for defence of New York, 235; New York assembly passes act for quieting disorders in province, 229; legislature established by Sloughter, 236–237; council of New York sends address to crown complaining of Phips and asserting claim to Martha's Vineyard, 246–247; appropriation act passed by New York assembly for defensive measures, 260; New York reports to king in favor of one governor for New York, New Hampshire and Massachusetts, William Penn suggests outline of colonial federation, 268–269; acts of New York assembly to remove disabilities of Leislerians, 280; territorial affairs chiefly within sphere of, 282; Bellomont's proposed act to vacate large estates, 285; vigorous protests against bill to secure rights of Massachusetts house of commons, 317–318; Virginia executive, 337–339; committee on revision of laws appointed periodically in some of the colonies, 343; part taken by, in initiating legislation and government action in Maryland, 368–369; formal surrender of New Jersey proprietors to the crown, 396; members of council involved in piracy bribery, 532; commissioners designated to constitute a special court of admiralty for piracy trials, 544; address to queen asking for removal of Cornbury, II. 93; Governor Hunter of New York authorized by his commission to open court of chancery, 106; system of finance provides uncertain support, 107–108; elective tenure of members of council and assemblymen, 140–141; passes law authorizing naturalization, 168; proclamation to county commissioners of Virginia to render account of available arms and ammunition, 170; receiver or treasurer accounts regularly to governor and council and his report is passed to British treasury, 181; Virginia council affirms its right to appoint county clerks, 182; president and council of Maryland implore consideration of board of trade for "poor province," 193; letter to board of trade and queen on need of coinage in Maryland, 195–196; act passed forbidding Catholics to baptize or celebrate mass, 203; judicial system of Maryland under discussion, court fees too heavy, 204; further effort to improve courts during Seymour's administration, 206; governor and council of Maryland inform burgesses that crown orders Quakers to contribute to cost of militia and defence, 210–211; receiver general and treasurer the two leading finance officials of Virginia, 241; burgesses draft letter to king telling of discontent at being governed by a lieutenant govenor, 240; address sent to king urging building of forts for Virginia, 252; chartered colonies make effort to strengthen defence of their rights, 294; legislatures encourage manufactures, 325–326; South Carolina petitions king for royal protection, 350; South Carolina reports on delinquency of proprietors and appeals for royal government, 351; the powder receiver, 354; South Carolina assembly denies proprietors right of veto, 358; assembly passes resolutions to establish right to petition, 379; complaint to home government against Governor Everard of North Carolina, 399; governor's right to appoint clerk, 400; under Georgia charter, III. 38; provincial government in Georgia, 48; office of store keeper for the trust,

of the continent, 331; purpose of expedition of 1753, 332; force surrender of English under Trent and build Fort Duquesne on site captured, 338; become masters of the Ohio country, 339; defeat of Braddock, 350; offensive activities of, in New England, alarm the English, 359; surrender Beauséjour to the English, 360; occupation of Ticonderoga by, 365; military strength of, in Canada, 373 *and note;* contend with the English for control of the lakes, their force inferior but more experienced in navigation of the lakes, 380; inferiority of, to the English at sea, 394; responsibility of, for Indian atrocities, 399; advance of, threaten Albany and all Western New England, 402; loss of Fort Frontenac weakens line of communication between Canada and the west, 421; rule of, in America, doomed, 429; strategic outposts of, on east and west, now taken by the British, 434; lose hold upon Lakes Ontario and Erie, 445.

Friends, migration of, into Virginia, II. 523; make Pennsylvania haven of refuge, IV. 41.

Frisby, [James], as member of Maryland council, I. 355, 359.

Frontenac, Count, governor of Canada, destroys Schenectady, is recalled for second term, I. 77-78; confers with Indians, 88, 90-91; ready to pay for peace with Iroquois if English would not, 457; finds combination of Iroquois, English and Dutch a menace to French expansion and the fur trade, his influence exerted to maintain friendship with Indians of the interior, 459-460; returns for second term and begins attack on Iroquois, followed by proposals for peace treaty, 461-465.

Fry, Joshua, prepares map of Virginia, *etc.* IV. 223; holds conference with Indians at Logstown, 289; as commissioner carries presents to the Miamis; map sent in confirmation of Virginia's claim to western territory, 290 *note;* commander of Virginia troops, 337; follows after Trent, 338; death of, 339.

Fundamental Orders, last traces of, disappear, II. 398.

Fur trade; rivalry in, between British and French, III. 363; significance of in expansion by the French, IV. 281;

shared in various degrees by all the colonies, and closely connected with Indian relations, 283.

Fury, [Peregrine], agent for South Carolina, III. 508 *note;* IV. 123 *note,* 146, 273-274.

Furzer, Benjamin, on naval store commission, I. 498.

Gale, Christopher, chief justice of North Carolina, proprietors' deputy and member of North Carolina council, a leader in work of revising laws, II. 388; goes to England with complaint against Governor Eden, 391; continues in office after Eden's death, 392; complaint to England against Burrington, leads to governor's removal, 394; becomes Everard's adviser, and later his bitter enemy, 395; his court records furnish only account of dispatch between Everard and Burrington, 396.

Galloway, [Joseph], of Pa. assembly, IV. 424.

Garden, Rev. Alexander, commissary in S. C., II. 23; commissary of South Carolina, replies to inquiry of Bishop Gibson, III. 87 *note;* leading official representative of the Bishop of London in the continental colonies, 92; holds annual visitations of the clergy, 108; writes Bishop of London concerning charges against John Wesley, 111 *note;* finds Whitefield's methods offensive, 113; demands his trial, 114; suspends him from office but without effect, 115 *and note;* denounced Whitefield and the revival, 427.

Garth, Charles, agent for S. C., IV. 275.

Gee, Joshua, of board of trade, I. 518; supports measures covering white pine trees, 520; subscribes to fund on Penn's behalf, II. 258; literary sponsor of the " British Merchant," 306; on naval stores, 312-313; publishes " Trade and Navigation of Great Britain Considered," on Whig spirit and policy, 314; views on industrial and social dependence of the colonies, 314-315; his colonial legislation policy, 315-316; urges checking of linen manufacture in the colonies, 331-332; sends warning to Keith, 539.

George Tavern, beyond Boston Neck, III. 163.

Georgia, (other than in Part II, chap. ix, and Part III, chap. xiii; *see* table

whites, 347–348; final defeat, Governor Hunter tries to induce Senecas to attack the Yemassees, 349; South Carolina passes law for regulation of trade with, 352; South Carolina act opening Yemassee lands for settlement, Indian trade act, 355; proprietors claim Yemassee lands for baronies, 359; board of Indian commissioners in South Carolina, 369; new South Carolina appointees, Virginia disputes new trade regulations of South Carolina, 370 *and note;* crown takes over administration of Indian affairs, (1756), 371; Yemassees attack southern frontier 379; French become active among Creeks and Cherokees, Captain Fitch and Colonel Chicken sent to counteract this influence, 380; North Carolina protests measure against Core Indians, 390; relations with, considered by Burnet, 418; French trade with, 419–420; land titles of extinguished, 434; Mohawk tribe gives Cosby a large tract of land for king, 456; Clarke has conference with, at Albany, 471; duty affecting trade with, 476; massacre brought on by Tuscarora war, 494; said to have promised Palatines a grant in Schoharie, 496; successfully established by Oglethorpe of Georgia, III. 49; chief object of his attention, 51; is appointed commissioner of, 52; governing board of Georgia has supervision over, 69; affair of Bosomworths and Lower Creeks in Georgia, 70; war with Abenakis becoming imminent, 156; Râle's War, 166; encroachments on Abenaki territory, 167; conferences and relations with, 168–169; treaties of 1713, 1716 and 1717, with the eastern tribes, 169; Pigwackets, a band of Sokokis, 170; Narragansett territory open for settlement, 233; ownership of disputes by Connecticut and Rhode Island, 234; Mohegan controversy, 281; in New England succumb before advance of alien white people, 284 *and note;* education of Samson Occom and Indian school which developed into Dartmouth College, prominence of Mohegans in Connecticut annals, 284; cause of Mohegan controversy, 286; commission of review, contest over succession to the dignity of Sachem, 288; personnel of new commission of review, 289; a third commission appointed, 290; conclusion of third commission, 291; active cooperation, of Six Nations against the French sought by Governor Shirley, 566–568; aid of Creeks and Cherokees sought by Oglethorpe in attack on St. Augustine, 503; become disgusted and desert, 507; Quakers attention to relations with, IV. 65; encroachments of British and French settlers disturbs relations with, 79; famous treaty of 1744, at Lancaster, Pennsylvania, insures temporary quiet in Virginia, 102; urged to aid new colony in Georgia, 137; trade with, should be free, board of trade decides, 139; discontent of Six Nations declared by Clinton to be due to ill usuage by traders, 180; conference of Clinton and Shirley with the Six Nations, 193; Johnson seeks protection for tribes allied to the English cause, 222; Virginia sees necessity for alliance with, 224; conference with, at Augusta, Georgia, 250; attitude of Georgia and South Carolina, 256; beginning of the Cherokee War, 257; Creek's territory invaded by South Carolina grants, 258; expenditures for presents to, 262–263; beginning of hostilities between the Creeks and Cherokees, 263; conferences at Albany, in 1751 secures truce between the Six Nations, and the Catawbas, 265; peace is concluded between the Creeks and Cherokees 266; Glen's conference with the Cherokees at Saluda Old Town, 268; Lyttleton's conference at Fort St. George, 270–271; Cherokees capture Fort Loudon, but are in turn subdued by troops from Fort Prince George, 272; the Miamis abandon their English allies upon approach of the French, 333; Dinwiddie invited cooperation of against the French in the Ohio Valley, 335; Shirley holds important conference with, at Falmouth, 359; Maine Indians satisfy Dummer's treaties, 360; tribes flock to Montcalm as hero of Oswego's capture, 398; atrocities committed by, incited largely by the French, 399; attempt by the British to establish a general and uniform Indian policy, 422; Walking Purchase and other large land grants, a cause of jealousy among the Indians, 423; conference at Easton and Lancaster, 424–425; Walking Purchase and the cession of Western territory deplored by Teedyuscung, 426; Pennsylvania sends envoys to placate the Delawares, 427–429; the Six Nations veer toward the British, Johnson rallies Iroquois at Canajoharie for expedition against Niagara, 442.

Indies, (the), John Law's Company of, I. 491.

Ingoldsby, Richard, lieutenant governor of New York and New Jersey, praised by Randolph for maintaining peace in New York, I. 170; is made commander-in-chief on death of Sloughter, his troops suppress Leisler movement, 230; pleads for annexation of neighboring territory, 235; shares intrigue against Quakers for opposing expedition against Canada, 435; his brief administration after death of Lovelace, II. 95; in spite of order for his recall, assumes office until Hunter's arrival, his commission finally revoked, Nicholson-Vetch expedition the important event of his administration, 120.

Innes, Col. [James], in command at Fort Cumberland, IV. 351.

Instructions, to governors, I. 34–35; binding power of, questioned by assemblies, 37; to Phips and Fletcher, 106–107, 110–111; to Allen of Massachusetts, Andros of Virginia, and Fletcher of New York, 126; concerning examination by board of trade, 134; prohibit receiving of presents, 156; regarding prosecution of councillors of Virginia and Maryland for payment of just debts, 157; regularly issued, covering provisions of acts of trade, 160; to procure passage of Maryland port act, 164; to Nicholson, empowering him to waylay direct trade of colonies, 172; circular letter on strict obedience to orders of commissioners of customs, 177; regarding admiralty courts, 189; circular letter on enforcement of acts of trade, 197–198; to William Penn, 202; require them to send complete body of their laws with opinions as to action which ought to be taken, 343; to Copley of Maryland, 354, 361, 373; to Nicholson of Maryland, 374; to Fletcher of New York, 375; to Bellomont of

New York, 388; to Cornbury of New York and New Jersey, 397–398; regarding continuation of trade with Spanish, despite war, 400; to Dudley of Massachusetts, 404; regarding projected expedition against Canada, 430, 441; for capture of Henry Avery and crew, 535; to Rogers of island of Providence, 547; concerning church affairs, II. 7–8, 9–10; concerning finance, 69; to Cornbury, 87; to Hunter of New York, 106; concerning appropriations for adequate and fixed salaries, 133; to Nicholson of Virginia, 181; to Hart of Maryland, 195; concerning appointment of four itinerant justices, 206; concerning amount of land to be cultivated, 219; to Spotswood of Virginia, 226–227; on trade relations, 321; to Johnson of South Carolina, 365, 358–359; to Nicholson of South Carolina, 376; to Burrington of North Carolina, 399–400; to Hart of Maryland, III. 4; to Ogle of Maryland, 20; Lord Baltimore disallows any land affecting right of clergy under act of establishing the church, 101; to Belcher of Massachusetts, 140; to Shute of Massachusetts, 145; to Burnet, concerning assembly provision for his salary, 179; to Benning Wentworth of New Hampshire, 224; to Jonathan Belcher, 321 and note; 323; to Belcher regarding bills of credit, 260; to Philips of Nova Scotia, 327; later revoked, 330; to Dunbar revoked, 330; to Belcher, limiting issues of bills of credit, 346; to Oglethorpe in war with Spain, 503; to Thomas of Pennsylvania regarding measures of defence, IV. 64; to Johnson of South Carolina, concerning exciting crisis, 115; payment of quit rents, 116; to Arthur Dobbs of North Carolina, 203, 205, 207, 218; to Fauquier of Virginia, 233; to John Reynolds of Georgia, 245.

Intestacy law, discussion in Connecticut, III. 312–313, 314; proposal for new law, 315; cases of Phillips vs. Savage and Clark vs. Tousey, 316; Connecticut law of intestacy allowed to stand by implication, 317 and note.

Ireland, trade of, with colonies stopped by England, I. 120; Cary draws parallel between position of New England and, in British trade system, Sir William Petty's views re-

333; brings reinforcements to French at Ft. Duquesne, 431 *note;* conducts captives from Ft. Duquesne to Niagara, 433; collects Indians to defend Niagara, 443.

Joncaire, Louis Thomas, Sieur de Chabert (d. 1739), helps to increase French influence among Indians, **I.** 470; adopted by the Senecas, accused of advocating Ft. Niagara for personal gain, 478–479; helps build stock-house in Seneca country, 481; strengthens influence among the Iroquois, **III.** 365; negotiates with Senecas regarding magazines near Lake Ontario, 366; builds and commands " Magazine Royal " at Niagara, 367; Burnet alleges his presence in Seneca country a violation of Treaty of Utrecht, 368; sent to conciliate Iroquois, 371.

Joncaire, Philippe Thomas, Sieur de Joncaire et Chabert (elder son of L. T. de Joncaire. Known as Captain Joncaire), activity of, among western Iroquois, **III.** 376; attends conference at Logstown, **IV.** 297; reported to be advance agent for France in Ohio country, 303; takes possession of Fraser's trading post in Pa., 433.

Jones, David, speaker of the New York assembly, **IV.** 192, 308.

Jones, [Frederick], chief justice, of North Carolina, pleads in Moseley's favor, **II.** 392.

Jones, Rev. Hugh, doubts validity of Blair's ordination, **III.** 98.

Jones, Robert, committee member of Pennsylvania assembly, **IV.** 54.

Jonquière, [Jacques Pierre de Taffenel], Marquis de la, in command of remnant of French expedition returning to France, (1746), **III.** 536; corresponds with British over exchange of prisoners, **IV.** 297; letter of, indicates impression upon the French of English activity in the Indian country, 299–300.

Journal, a Boston paper, **III.** 530 *note.*

Journal of the board of trade, one of the monuments of the board's labors, **I.** 145.

Journal of the committee of trade; records of meagre until 1691, **I.** 125.

Jouvencel, [Couchet], presents memorial to the board of trade, **IV.** 215 *note;* appointment of as agent for North Carolina, 219 *note.*

Jowles, Col. [Henry], appointed to Maryland council because favorable to crown, **I.** 355; Copley's alleged arbitrary methods against, 365.

Justice, *see* Courts, *also* Executive, British.

Kalm, [Peter], the Swedish traveller reports to Peters on Indian affairs, **IV.** 80.

Kay, [Nathaniel], the collector (of R. I.), attack upon, **III.** 255; opposed to prevailing financial policy, 260.

Kay, Rev. William, minister of Lunenburg parish in Virginia, supported by bishop of London in the case of Landon Carter, **III.** 475.

Keith, George, a Quaker, accepts Anglicanism, **II.** 30; member of Society for the Propagation of the Gospel in Foreign Parts, is sent on preaching tour through colonies, 32–33; officiates at Dudley's inauguration, issues report to Society on church prospects in colonies, 36–37; is backed by Nicholson and Cornbury, 39, attention of, directed more to Quakers than Independents, 40; recommends missionary for Rhode Island, 41; influences plan for mission among the Iroquois, 41.

Keith, Sir William, governor of Pennsylvania, his qualifications inquired into by board of trade, **I.** 203; drawn into hostile relations with Five Nations, insists that each colony must treat directly with its own Indians, 485–486; attends conference at Albany with Five Nations, 488, 490; discriminates against Quakers, **II.** 263; succeeds Gookin as governor of Pennsylvania, 289; presents memorial to board of trade on colonial manufactures, 331; presents "Discourse" to the king on colonial settlement and trade, 333 *and note;* encourages Palatines to settle in Pennsylvania, 498; is made governor of Pennsylvania, 530; his official utterances favorable to proprietary interests, 531; receives new commission and instructions from Penn, issues proclamation, 533–534; assumes independent rôle, 535; skilful in dealing with people, 536; suspected of sharing in Governor Spotswood's plan for imperial control, 537; his ignoring of council offensive to proprietary interests, 538; receives instructions and re-

from Nova Scotia, 538; impressment of seamen for convoy of, met by mob violence, 562; contempt of, for colonists, 563; sues Douglass for libel, loses, but case is dropped upon his appointment as governor of Jamaica, 564; is consulted by governor Clinton regarding rate of pay for soldiers, **IV.** 191.

Kocherthal, Rev. Joshua, an evangelical clergyman and a leader of the Palatines, **II.** 492.

Labor, *see also* Slaves, wage in New Hampshire, **I.** 290; scarcity of, and wages high, 500; high cost of, an effective check on manufacturing in the colonies, **II.** 331.

La Chine, Iroquois massacre of 1668 at, **I.** 77.

La Corne, [Pierre de Chapt], Chevalier de, a French trader, stationed at Niagara, **III.** 367.

La Demoiselle, name given by the French to Old Britain, head of the Miami confederacy, **IV.** 286.

Laer, Col. John, not considered by Randolph to be qualified for collector in Accomac, **I.** 166.

La Galissonière, [Michel Rolland Barrin], Count de, corresponds with British over exchange of prisoners, **IV.** 279; his notable memorial of 1750 emphasizes strategic value of Canada, 291.

Lake George, (Lake St. Sacrament) rechristened by Johnson, **IV.** 364; battle of, 365.

Lake, Sir Bibys, one of the assigns of the Muscongus Patent, **III.** 328.

Lake Winnepesaukee, blockhouse ordered built at, **III.** 214.

Lamb, [Sir Mathew], counsel for board of trade criticises detail of Massachusetts bill for a return to specie basis, **III.** 557–558; on measure requiring sheriffs to take oath or affirmation in N. J., **IV.** 17 *note;* supports Gooch's objections to certain Virginia laws in revision of 1748, 110; endorses objections to act of 1747, regulating the duties of justices of the peace in minor causes, **IV.** 145.

Lamb, Robert, appointed by agents of Massachusetts as member of naval stores commission, **I.** 499.

Lancaster, (the), one of Commodore Warren's ships, **III.** 524.

Land bank, *see* banks, banking.

Land grants, effect of, on Indian relations, **I.** 468; all ungranted land in the colonies counted royal domain, 499; act for vacating Fletcher's grants, 513; given to French Protestants at Manakin Town, Virginia, **II.** 167–168; regulation of, in Virginia, 182; acts affecting, 221–222; concession for, obtained from crown, 253; application for, from Sir Robert Montgomery, 365; in North Carolina, 388; blank patents for, in North Carolina, 389–390; Governor Everard issues fraudulent, 398; instructions to Burrington concerning, 400–401; conditions of settlement concerning, 403; recording of deeds and titles for, 438–439; in danger on Long Island, 456; given by governor and council to Vrooman and seven partners, in territory already occupied by Palatines, 496; limited in Georgia, **III.** 36; in Georgia, 47; protest against inheritance laws, 48; demand for removal of restrictions, 55; concessions made in Georgia, 56; but principle of tail male not yet abandoned, 57; restrictions on landholding continued in Georgia until 1750, 58; new provision for in Georgia, 68; power of Georgia board over, 70; obtained from Mohegan Indians, 284; the leading controversy in South Carolina during Johnston's administration, **IV.** 116; Act of 1731, prejudicial to the crown, 117, speculators in attacked by St. John of South Carolina, 119; Whitaker expresses legal opinion concerning, 120; grantees attempt to assert legislative absolutism, 122; restriction of head rights in South Carolina, 132; North Carolina appoints a committee to inquire into abuses connected with issue of blank patents, 152; a marked feature of Johnston's administration, 152; blank patents as determined by law offices in England, 159; irregularities of, in North Carolina, 204; governor urges restriction of, in North Carolina, 209; requirements of patents in, 210 *note; (see also* quit rents), controversy in Virginia over fee of pistole, 226 *and note;* the board of trade makes concessions regarding fees, 228; the board of trade places limitation upon, in Virginia, 229; uncertainty concerning

the Indians for Pennsylvania, **IV.** 288; attends conference at Logstown in 1753, 289.

Montreal, joint advance of Haviland, Amherst and Murray converge on, **IV.** 457; capture of, gives the British possession of all Canada, 457.

Moodie (or Moody), Capt, [James], of guardship "Southampton," in controversy with Governor Nicholson and council of Virginia, **II.** 177.

Moody, Rev. Joshua, attacked by Keith, **II.** 37; again comes to the front, **III.** 198.

Moody, Major Samuel, accusations against, **III.** 171; removal of, 173.

Moore, Arthur, Tory member of board of trade and able adviser of Bolingbroke, **I.** 139 *and note;* leading spirit in promoting freedom of trade, **II.** 305.

Moore, Colonel James, proclaimed revolutionary governor of South Carolina, **II.** 361; North Carolina refuses to recognize, 364; under royal régime becomes speaker of assembly and lieutenant general in command of militia, 365; named special Indian commissioner, 371.

Moore, George, member of the N. C. assembly, **IV.** 214.

Moore, John, asked by Quary to serve as advocate, **I.** 207; created sole Indian trade commissioner of South Carolina, 493; appointed by the Fords to receive rents and sell land, supposed to be Penn's enemy, **II.** 258; collector of royal customs at Philadelphia, in dispute with Keith, prosecutes Lawrence, 541–542.

Moore, Maurice, a leader of opposition in North Carolina, **II.** 391–392; is elected speaker of assembly, 395.

Moore, Maurice, member of the N. C. assembly, **IV.** 214.

Moore (or Moor), [Rev. Thoroughgood], agent for New York with Chidley Brooke, lost on voyage to England, **II.** 43; writes clergy are unanimous in desire for suffragan, 45.

Moore, Roger, of N. C., opposed to Johnston and Smith faction in the council, **IV.** 169.

Moores, (the), of South Carolina, settlement of, with their friends, **IV.** 149; reported, with Moseley to be "the principal proprietors of the blank patents," 154; oppose in-

corporation of Wilmington as a rival town of Brunswick, 163–164.

Moravians, *see also* Pietism; settlement of, at Bethlehem, **II.** 501; arrival of David Nitschmann in Georgia, **III.** 109; settle in Berks County and begin missionary work among Indians, 382; exempt from bearing arms and therefore opposed by Peters as settlers for the frontier, **IV.** 77.

Mordaunt, [Charles], Viscount, head of the treasury, **I.** 117.

Moreton, prominent in behalf of Quakers, **III.** 131.

Morgan, Thomas, petitions governor concerning anti-Leislerians, **I.** 277.

Morris, Anthony, is removed by **Penn** after Quary's official complaint, **I.** 208; his removal from commission of peace urged, 538.

Morris, Capt., [Charles], in command of a New England Company at Annapolis, prepares map of the Bay of Fundy, at Shirley's request, **III.** 571.

Morris, Capt. Roger, conveys Shirley's military dispatches to England, **IV.** 372.

Morris, Lewis, chief justice, denies right of Basse faction to hold court and is imprisoned, **I.** 391–392; is made a justice and member of Hamilton's council, threatens bloodshed, 395; supports conduct of Hunter, **II.** 20; presides in church trials, his views on church matters, 22; member of the Society for the Propagation of the Gospel in Foreign Parts, 32; returns from mission to England, 33; supplies information on religious matters; urges need of bishop for colonis, 45; ancestry of, as East Jersey proprietor, 86–87; quarrels with Cornbury, 91–92; his account of Cornbury's administration, 94; upholds Hunter in salary complaint and is expelled from assembly, 100; leader of the country party in advocating taxation measures, 109; chairman of committee of the whole on Hunter's speech resulting in appropriation act, 112–113; is appointed chief justice, 114; helps Hunter to write farce called "Androborus, the Man Eater," 118; arraigned by assembly for conduct of the late house, 119; consulted by Burnet in dispute with De Lancey, 425; salary

stimulated importance of shipping and carrying trade in, 520 *and note;* aggressive campaign among dissenters of, in opposition to Anglicans, led by Mathers, **II.** 36–39; bears brunt of conflict on the frontier, 99; remains separated by jealousies of colonies, 142; the classic land of the chartered colony, 295; Dummer controls conditions in, with those in New York, 296–297; not attractive to immigrants from the continent of Europe, German settlement in, 510; arrival of immigrants in, 518; churches of, rebuffed in attempt to call a synod, **III.** 137; attitude of churches in, toward Anglican invasion, 141–142; becomes deeply involved in paper money régime, 153; ship building a leading industry, 154; Râle's War, 166; a distinct section geographically and economically, 186; tendencies toward union of, 187; leadership of Massachusetts in, 189; no one in, authorized to administer oath to governor, 198; statute of 1751 prohibiting issue of bills of credit in, 263; campaign against proprieties and corporate liberties in, 268; consociation of churches defined, 302; diverges from principle of primogeniture in the inheritance of land, 307; claims of council of New England, revived, 327; the Muscongus Patent, 328; seeks cooperation of the Six Nations and New York against the French, 391; under lead of Massachusetts, prepares for major operation against Louisbourg, 520; colonies cooperating, 521–523; plan to reimburse from British Exchequer the expenditures of, in expedition against Louisbourg, 552; expansion of, outlined, 564; Massachusetts under Shirley takes leading part, 565; spirit of cooperation in, strong under Shirley, **IV.** 363; extent of forces of, in campaign against Crown Point and Niagara, 364.

New England Courant, see *Courant.*

Newfoundland, board of trade complains of illegal trade with, **II.** 320.

New Hampshire (other than in Part II chap. xiii; *see* table of contents), attack on Dover, town left without governor or general court, **I.** 71–72; formally taken under protection of Massachusetts, 80; province of, organized under Samuel Allen as proprietor and governor, his son-in-law Usher lieutenant governor, relation of N. H. to Massachusetts, Rhode Island and Connecticut, 99–100; not included within large province [of Massachusetts, 126; relied on for masts since frontier warfare destroyed Maine forestry, saw mills running at Exeter, 169; admiralty court established by, 189; 700 families in, Allen's nominal governorship of, terminated on appointment of Bellomont, Partridge succeeds Usher as lieutenant governor of, 290; Allen's land claim comes before superior court, 291; united with Massachusetts under provisions of new charter, its official independence delayed a half century, 293–294; names of towns attacked in French and Indian raid, 406; imitates defensive measures of Massachusetts, unpreparedness of province, bounty offered as inducement to men, 407–408; asked for aid in raid against Acadia, 413; participation of, in Acadian expedition, 436–438; general assembly of, urges inhabitants to sow hemp, lumber exported by, to south of Europe, 500; Bridger fails to secure convictions in court of, act for presentation of mast trees in, 510–511; issue of township grants is stimulated in, 520 *and note;* supply of naval stores in, less than that of Maine; riot at Exeter, 521; Dunbar succeeds Wentworth as lieutenant governor, 522; industries of, **II.** 330; settlement of seventy families in; a center of the linen industry, 518; affairs of, administered by Shute as governor of Massachusetts, **III.** 145; the English plan for a new province to be called, "Georgia," 327; plan terminated by official order, 333; conditions in, at time of Governor Belcher's appointment, 335; financial conditions described by Atkinson, 336; bills of credit a subject of dispute, 337; boundary question, 339; effort of, to settle dispute, 340; special board of commissioners appointed, 341; assembly appoints John Rindge as agent, 342; royal commission renders decision in boundary dispute, 343–344; origin of dispute over New Hampshire grants, 345; issue of merchants notes in, 248; denounced by Bel-

for Frederica county but fails to do so, 68; famous journey of, in 1739 into Creeks' country, 396 *and note;* is made sole Indian commissioner for Georgia, 397; returns from England with appointment as commander-in-chief of the forces of South Carolina and Georgia, 502; plan of defence against the Spanish, 503; seeks aid from South Carolina, in attack on St. Augustine, 504–505; complete failure of expedition causes controversy, 506; mismanagement of evidenced by assembly report, 508 *note;* acquits himself bravely in defence of Frederica, 509; final return of, to England, 510.

Ohio Company, obtains a grant in Virginia, Pennsylvania traders are accused of, misrepresenting motives of, **IV.** 79; Virginia recommends bringing settlers to grant held by, 224; origin and personnel of, 287 *and note;* employs Christopher Gist to make a tour of exploration, 288.

Old Britain (La Demoiselle), head of the Miami confederacy, devoted to the British interest, **IV.** 286; killed by the French and Indians under Langlade, 290.

Oliver, Andrew, connected with the " Silver Scheme," **III.** 354.

Oliver, Nathaniel, supporter of private bank project, **II.** 155–156.

Oliver, family of, in New England, prominence of, **III.** 316.

Orford, Earl of, on pirates, **I.** 533.

Orkney, Earl of, first titular governor of Virginia, **II.** 161.

Osborne, Sir Danvers, appointed to succeed Governor Clinton in New York, **IV.** 307; suicide of, 308; letters to, regarding treaty with Six Nations is read at Albany Congress, 312.

Oswego, founding of, **II.** 443; **III.** 371; its geographical relations, 372; both a trading house and garrison, 374; discussion over funds for support of, 374; burden of support is imposed on Indian trade, 375; New York assembly makes provision for garrison at, **IV.** 193; establishment of 1744, act passed for support of garrison and trading house at, 196–197; Father Piquet reports upon the advantage of, to the English, 293; especially valuable for observation of the French, 303; a weak and neglected military post prior to

1755, 367; campaign of the French against 376–377; sufferings of the garrison and state of defences at, 378–379; difficulty of protecting, against the French, 381; surrender of, 383; reference to massacre following surrender of, 398.

" Otter " (the), a guardship, sent to protect Delaware Bay, **IV.** 69.

Oxford [Robert Harley, Earl of], patron with Bolingbroke of the " Mercator," **II.** 306.

Page, John, member of Virginia council, **I.** 330.

Paine, Elisha, of Canterbury, Ct., becomes Separatist minister, is imprisoned, **III.** 445.

Paine, Solomon, of Canterbury, Ct., becomes Separatist minister, **III.** 445, 446.

Palatines, quota of, for later expedition against Canada, **I.** 443; flock to England in 1709, parties of, arrive in New York and De Graffenried's group in North Carolina; payment and land grants to, 512–513; treatment of, 514–515; missionary maintained among, **II.** 35; minister for, 44; settlement of, in New York connected with Hunter's arrival, 98; Hunter recommends naturalization of, 101 *and note;* located on the Rapidan, in Virginia, by Spotswood to revive iron and other ores, 224–225; arrive in England under Joshua Kocherthal, later come to New York, 492; dismayed over conditions they must face, secure grant of law and friendly reception from Indians; in conflict with Hunter and law speculation at Albany, 495–497; Burnet gives permission to, for purchase of land on the Mohawk, 498; Conrad Weiser, characteristics and achievements, **III.** 378.

Palliser, [Captain, afterward Sir Hugh], in Saunders' naval expedition against Quebec, **IV.** 452.

Palmer, Anthony, president of Pennsylvania council, **IV.** 67; his authority limited, 68.

Palmer, Colonel William, leads expedition against Spanish settlements, **II.** 380; **III.** 507.

Palmer, Eliakim, agent for Connecticut, correspondence of Governor Law, with, **III.** 281 *note;* appointed, with Bollan and Warren to give dis-

Piscataqua, Massachusetts declines to contribute to support of, **I.** 419; contribution needed for support of fort at, **II.** 137.

Pitcher, James, commissary of musters, is sent to America in advance of Braddock, **IV.** 342.

Pitkin, William, appointed commissioner to general court, **I.** 74; delegate to congress from Connecticut, 81; calls on Governor Fletcher on his arrival at Hartford, 104; petitions general court on church matters, **III.** 292; is refused commission at Hartford Church, 293; a commissioner to Clinton's last Indian conference, **IV.** 304 *note;* a commissioner from Connecticut to the Albany Conference, 312; a member of the committee appointed to formulate and report upon a plan for colonial union, 316.

Pitt, William, appeals to colonies for an appropriation for war, **IV.** 213, 216; orders removal of Gray's settlement in Georgia, 256; appeals for cooperation against the French, 257; paymaster of the American forces, advice of, regarding defensive measures, 341; appointed secretary of state for the southern department, 389; personality and qualifications, 390–391; falls a victim to the dislike of the king, 395; is dismissed from the ministry, but returns to power in cooperation with Newcastle, 396; is practically an autocrat, 397; in circular letter to the governors appeals for cooperation against the French, 403; policy of, fully operative in America in 1758, 415; his tenure of power unusual and precarious, 449.

Plaisted, John, one of Brenton's deputies, **I.** 507; a member of New Hampshire council, **III.** 206.

Plant, [Rev. Matthias], urges repeal of Massachusetts system of legislation on church affairs, **III.** 138.

Plater, George, attorney general of Maryland collector at Patuxent, **I.** 167; writes Blathwayt in his own defence against Randolph's criticism, 169; accused by Randolph of encouraging illegal trade, his removal is recommended, 192.

Plowman, [Matthew], collector at New York receives instructions from the king regarding Perth Amboy, **I.** 384.

Plumstead, Clement, receives correspondence from Thomas Penn on conditions in his province, **IV.** 39 *note.*

Plymouth, asked to contribute aid for defence, **I.** 72–74; joins in attack on Quebec, 88–93.

Pollexfen, John, member of board of trade and author of " Discourse of Trade, Coyn and Paper Credit," **I.** 135, 137 *and note,* 138; influence of, upon failure of projected treaty of commerce with France, 139; territory assigned in preparing of extracts, 140; presents to board of trade memorial on administration of justice in the colonies, 156; dropped from board of trade, 223; attends meeting of board of trade, 259.

Pollock, Thomas, questions Spotswood's authority in pirate Teach affair, **II.** 391; president of North Carolina council after Governor Eden's death, 392.

Pomeroy, [Rev. Benjamin], a revivalist preacher associate of James Davenport is arrested with him, **III.** 423; released without punishment, 424.

Pontchartrain, [Louis Phelypeaux, Count de], French minister, receives letter from Subercase concerning unpreparedness of Port Royal, **I.** 438; approves suggestion to inform Massachusetts governor and council of England's design to impose yoke of parliament upon northern colonies, 440; sends d'Aigremont to report on Detroit, 479.

Popple, William, secretary of board of trade, **I.** 139; reads papers at colonies bill hearing, 217; requests in writing charges against Fletcher and Nicholson, 271; receives correspondence from Basse, 386; receives letter from John Nelson in support of Dudley, **II.** 143; writes Spotswood about manufacture of iron in Virginia, 224; presents bill for regulation of colonial government, 294; receives letter from Governor Hunter concerning churchmen at Burlington, **III.** 90; writes Burrington regarding repeal of North Carolina election law of 1715, **IV.** 166.

Porter, Edmund, a prominent North Carolina colonist, a bitter enemy of Governor Everard, **II.** 395; friendly to Burrington, 395; agent to England, 396; judge of admiralty court and chosen member of council by Burrington, 399; is charged with use of admiralty court as personal instrument, 400; becomes an opponent of Burrington, 407, 409; becomes a member of the council under Johnston, **IV.** 149.

Portneuf, [Sieur de], lays siege to Fort Loyal, **I.** 78; leads French and Indians in attack on Wells, 97.

Port Royal, not adequately equipped to combat the French, its abandonment considered, **I.** 113; employed as point for exchange of prisoners with Canada, merchants forbid Church to recapture because of their trade interests, 419–421; Dudley sends two successive expeditions against, but both are conspicuous failures, 423–428; capture of, name changed to Annapolis, French *habitants* free to annoy English garrison at, 436–439.

Portsmouth (New Hampshire), representation of, in assembly, **III.** 207; dispute over number of councillors from, 208–209.

Postal service, Nicholson petitions for post route between Virginia and New England, **I.** 335; post office established, 384; Virginia council recommends provisions for speedy conveyance of public letters, **II.** 171; bill affecting colonial postmaster; first attempt to establish mail route between Williamsburg and Philadelphia, 247.

Post Boy, a Boston paper, **III.** 540 *note;* publishes letter from Governor Shirley to Secretary Willard, 563.

Post, Christian Frederic, a Moravian, chosen to head mission to placate the Delawares, **IV.** 427; sincere, and fearless, 428; second visit of, 429.

Potter, Cuthbert, sent as agent by Nicholson to ascertain conditions of Northern colonies, **I.** 332–333.

Potter, William, of London, publishes " The Key of Wealth " advocating bank founded upon personal credit, **II.** 149–150.

Pouchot, Captain François, engineer, strengthens the fortifications at Niagara, **IV.** 367; regards Fort Frontenac with contempt, 430; in command of French forces at Niagara, 443 *and note;* unable to effect a sortie, 445.

Povey, George, receiver general of plantation revenues, **I.** 24.

Povey, Thomas, lieutenant governor of Massachusetts and New Hampshire ordered to Piscataqua and to improve defensive forces at Wells, Berwick and other places, **I.** 406–407; attends Queens Chapel, **II.** 36; paid by council for his services as commander of the castle, house protests as arbitrary act, 136; is appointed lieutenant governor of Massachusetts and New Hampshire under Dudley, 128; a royal commissioner in Mohegan controversy, **III.** 287.

Powle, Sir Henry, distinguished lawyer and parliamentarian, **I.** 117.

Powlett, Earl, repaid by the Penns for sum expended in boundary dispute, **IV.** 44.

Pownall, John, his paper on French and Indian relations accepted with thanks by the Albany Congress, **IV.** 317; general agent and inspector in the colonies offers to bear Johnson's charges against Shirley to England, 368–369.

Pownal (or Pownall), Thomas, governor of Massachusetts, publishes his " Administration of the Colonies," **I.** 17; is appointed to succeed Lyttleton as governor of South Carolina, **IV.** 271; arrival of as governor of Massachusetts, 402.

Poyer, Rev. Thomas, sent to the colonies as a missionary, **II.** 19; writes of contentions with Independents, 22.

Poyning's act in Ireland, Gee would apply system of, to colonies. **II.** 316.

Presque Isle, the French build a log fort at, **IV.** 332.

Press, *see also* Newspapers; periodicals, public opinion finds voice through, **I.** 57; strict censorship of, 302; active in trade controversy, **II.** 305; well developed in England by 1730, **III.** 37; newspapers furnish avenue for expression of public opinion, 354; becoming active in Massachusetts, 150; an influence in politics, censorship of, 151; " factious pamphlets," 152; censorship of, demanded by Shute and council, 158; " News from Robinson Crusoe's Island," 159; of New York, a medium of appeal to natural rights of white men and Indians to use of the soil, **IV.** 29.

Prevoost, David, member of New York assembly, **II.** 413.

Price, Roger, champion of extreme

a colony of Swiss under Jean Pierre Purry, **IV.** 118.

Pynchon, Col. John, of Springfield, an envoy to the Iroquois, **I.** 75; commander of Hampshire County regiment and a central figure in military affairs, 109–110; commissioner to Albany conference with the Five Nations, 251.

Quakers, shown favoritism by Hamilton, **I.** 202; trials of compared with witchcraft cases, 311; numerous and active in Maryland, 353; more numerous in Maryland than in Va., object to taking oath and are ordered dismissed from office in both provinces, 359–360; preponderance of in New Jersey largely unfits province for defence in war time, 383; of New Jersey not friendly to Gov. Basse, 386; regard Basse as an adventurer, 391; Cornbury instructed regarding act to secure right of solemn declaration in place of taking oath by, 398; of Rhode Island oppose Dudley's claim of authority over military forces, 403; of N. J. and Penn. oppose expedition to Canada, Ingoldsby intrigues to throw blame on, 435; compared to Puritans and Anglicans, **II.** 5; included in majority against the English Church, 11; attack Dr. Bray's act affecting service books, to have benefit of Act 7 and 8, William III, 13–14; Keith preaches to, 33; objects of Keith's attention more than Independents, 40; Cornbury refuses to receive the affirmations of certain, 90; Ingoldsby makes charges against and urges their exclusion from office, 120; bill passed allowing Quakers to affirm and to serve as jurors, 121, 125; Dudley shared attitude of colonial aristocrats toward, 140; regarded by Seymour with aversion, 203; in Maryland, district Seymour, ordered by crown to contribute to cost of militia and defence, 210–211; oppose Spotswood in defence plans, 227; tendency of to seclusion opposed by Germans, 267; largely in majority in population of Pennsylvania, but not a unit in its support, 267; refuse to be concerned with war, 277; frown upon Evans' proclamation for enlistment, their disgust with Evans culminates, 278;

attitude on war adds to general dissatisfaction, 285; act to provide for affirmation by is disallowed by England, 287; passage of act relating to affirmation by, 288; discrimination against, in North Carolina, 387; interests strengthened by appearance of James Logan, 432; both English and Scotch arrive in colonies, 523; Mrs. Hannah Penn's note to Keith on Quaker membership in council, 539; with Baptists give Rhode Island its chief characteristics, 81; maintain an organization to help colonial members, 84; gain steadily in North Carolina, **III.** 115; Burrington comments favorably upon, 116; undisturbed in Massachusetts under second charter, 126; make little headway in Connecticut but become numerous in Massachusetts, 128; combine for general assault on religious restrictions in Massachusetts, 129; secure disallowance of act of 1722, 130; first law passed in Massachusetts to give relief to, 130; act for exemption of, from taxation, 131; first concession of Massachusetts to, 138; important element of, in Rhode Island helps to paralyze efforts in time of war, 232; their ideal superior to that of the Calvinist, principles of, as to War become a significant question in colonial politics, **IV.** 49; stoutly maintain their right to " liberty of conscience," 54–55; point out futility of colonial militarism, 56; justification of, by outcome of expeditions to Canada and Crown Point, 57; protest enlistment of servants as infringement of property rights, 58; attention to Indian relations, 65.

Quebec, attacked by Mass. and Plymouth, **I.** 88–93; fortifications of, extended, **III.** 536; campaign of British against in 1758, **IV.** 441; capture of, the crowning event of the colonial wars, 447; the French prepare to defend, the British find difficulty in ascent of the St. Lawrence, to, 453; besieged for three months, 454; decisive encounter on Plains of Abraham, gives to the British the citadel of French power in America, 456.

Quit rents, provisions of, **I.** 235; Fletcher's excessive land grants would deprive king of, 282; needed

England with appointment as commissary for New York and New Jersey, 21, 23; active in securing six missionaries for New York, 41; recommends Muirson for Stratford, Connecticut, 43; greets Lord Cornbury on his return to New York, 61; is given prominent place in force written by Hunter and Morris, 118; influence of, in New York, III. 92; opposed to the revival movement, 427.

Venerable Society, *see also* Society for the Propagation of the Gospel in Foreign Parts, purchases house and estate for bishop of Burlington, 89; records relating to house at Burlington, and bequest of Frankfort Land Company in Pennsylvania, 91 *and note;* effort of to raise funds for settlement of bishops in America, 92; chief functions of, 93.

Verelst, Harmon, accountant for the corporation of Georgia, III. 39.

Vernon, Admiral Edward, James Vernon's brother, III. 39; an opponent of Robert Walpole, commands English expedition against Spanish in South America and Cuba, 497.

Vernon, James, a trustee of Georgia, son of James Vernon, secretary of state, his achievements, III. 39–40; proposes two presidents for Georgia, instead of a governor, 41; proposes new form of civil government for Georgia, 67.

Vernon, James, secretary of state, receives letter from Penn about assembly, I. 539; receives recommendation from board of trade that a squadron of three vessels be sent to the East, 542; writes of king's order to admiralty, 543; asks that Champante remain agent for province, II. 49; receives complaint from Gerard Sly against Nicholson, 162; his letter referred to Virginia committee on revision of the laws, 171.

Vetch, Col. Samuel, his memorial to the board of trade, I. 152; cargo dispute, 213; gets into serious difficulty through trading with the enemy, 420–423; visits England and Scotland, proposes revival of plan for joint attack upon Canada, crown approves preparations of, described, 429, 435; appointed governor of Nova Scotia, is left in command of forces at Port Royal, now Annapolis, 439; summoned from Port Royal to accompany sea expedition against Canada, 441–442, 445; precedes fleet to Gulf of St. Lawrence, 449; tries to persuade Walker to keep on to Quebec, 450; accompanies expedition against Canada, II. 95; his illegal treaty with French in Acadia made occasion of attack upon Dudley, 143–146; in command of expedition for conquest of Canada, 280–281; expedition finally abandoned, 283; sees in Acadian peasants possible defenders of British interests, III. 513.

Vicars (or Vickers), [John], a captain of Shirley's regiment describes suffering of the garrison at Oswego, IV. 378.

Viele, Arnold, interpreter to Mohawk Indians, I. 462.

"Vigilant" (the), a French sloop captured by Warren, III. 530.

Villebon, [Robineau, Chevalier de], sends privateers from St. John to prey on English shipping, is attacked by forces under Church and Hathorne, I. 113–114.

Villiers, Coulon de, the French under, attack Bradstreet's force, IV. 377.

Virginia (other than in Part I, vol. I, chap. x, vol. II, chaps. xxi and xxiii, and Part III, vol. IV, chaps. vii and xii; *see* Table of Contents), customs officers of, I. 22; treasurer and escheator of, responsible for quit rents, office of auditor created by assembly of, 24; permanent revenues established in, 25; salary of governor of, 155; law for encouragement of manufactures and act for establishment of ports, 163–164; Randolph considers it only province which has peace and good government, 171; accused of piracy and illegal trade, 205; makes discouraging reply to Sloughter's circular letter, 234–235; protests payment of revenue to New York, 250; Quakers and others forced either to take oath or resign office, 359–360; affected by Tuscarora War, 484–487; Governor Spotswood attends conference with Five Nations at Albany, 488–490; has proper climate and soil for hemp culture but favorable legislation brings no results, 509; Spotswood prepares for production of naval stores, 517; uses

DATE DUE

NOV 9 '69			
DEC 1 '69			
GAYLORD			PRINTED IN U.S.A.